LETTERS OF
GERALD FINZI and HOWARD FERGUSON

LETTERS OF

GERALD FINZI AND HOWARD FERGUSON

EDITED BY

Howard Ferguson and Michael Hurd

THE BOYDELL PRESS

First published 2001
The Boydell Press, Woodbridge

ISBN 0 85115 823 4

The Boydell Press is an imprint of Boydell & Brewer Ltd
PO Box 9, Woodbridge, Suffolk IP12 3DF, UK
and of Boydell & Brewer Inc.
PO Box 41026, Rochester, NY 14604–4126, USA
website: http://www.boydell.co.uk

A catalogue record for this book is available
from the British Library

Library of Congress Cataloging-in-Publication Data
Finzi, Gerald, 1901–1956.
  [Correspondence. Selections]
  Letters of Gerald Finzi and Howard Ferguson / edited by Howard Ferguson and
Michael Hurd.
    p. cm.
Includes bibliographical references and index.
ISBN 0–85115–823–4 (hardback: alk. paper)
  1. Finzi, Gerald, 1901–1956 – Correspondence.   2. Ferguson, Howard, 1908–
– Correspondence.   3. Composers – England – Correspondence.   I. Ferguson,
Howard, 1908–   II. Hurd, Michael, 1928–   III. Title.
ML410.F4565 A4 2001
780′.92–dc21
[B]   00–140123

This publication is printed on acid-free paper

Typeset by Joshua Associates Ltd, Oxford
Printed in Great Britain by
St Edmundsbury Press Ltd, Bury St Edmunds, Suffolk

Contents

To
Stephen Banfield

Foreword

When Howard Ferguson died on 1 November 1999 he had only a few days before finished finally checking the typescript of his and Michael Hurd's edition of his correspondence with Gerald Finzi. I had first heard of his plans for the edition shortly after he had asked me to act as his musical executor in 1988. Thereafter the book regularly cropped up in letters and conversation: Gerald had been the friend closest to him in his composing years and their friendship had had much the same artistic and personal significance for each other as that which, in an earlier generation, had been shared by Vaughan Williams and Holst. Thus at the end of a long and extraordinarily productive life as composer, performer and musicologist, Howard wanted very much to share this correspondence with the public as an illumination of his and Gerald's lives and music. Firm plans for publication had not been completed by the time of his death and thus it has fallen to me to bring Howard's last project to fruition.

In the Preface Howard himself acknowledges all those who helped and supported the project in his lifetime, notably Christopher and Nigel Finzi and Stephen Banfield, but the actual publication of the correspondence has only been made possible with support from further sources. It was clear from a reading of Howard's first draft that a certain amount of further explanatory text and footnotes would be required for the contemporary reader, a point which Howard readily accepted. Michael Hurd very kindly undertook to revise the whole edition in collaboration with Howard, and provide the necessary extra material, nearly all of which was seen and approved by Howard before his death. Howard's estate stands very much in Michael's debt for the care, attention and enthusiasm which he has brought to the project.

Throughout his life Howard had had a warm relationship with the RVW Trust, which had regularly given financial support for the recording of much of his and Gerald's music. The Trustees, encouraged by Ursula Vaughan Williams, kindly agreed to support this publication too as a fitting memorial to the two composers it had helped so often in the past. Howard's family and executors would like to acknowledge the generous grant which has made this book possible.

We should also like to thank Bruce Phillips, who read an early version of the typescript, made many useful suggestions and finally brought book and publisher together, for on his advice Boydell & Brewer accepted the work for publication. We are warmly grateful to the Managing Director, Richard Barber, and his colleagues for that.

Howard's memoir published in 1997, *Music, Friends and Places*, was felt by many of his friends to lack the sparkle of his impish sense of humour. The correspondence in the present volume is not at all deficient in that respect and will give a lively impression of the personalities and interactions of two remarkable musicians and their views on the world in which they lived.

Hugh Cobbe
30 October 2000

Preface

The following correspondence between Gerald Finzi (1901–1956) and Howard Ferguson (1908–1999) was transcribed under the guidance of Professor Stephen Banfield from the originals, now in the Bodleian Library, Oxford. It was used as an aid to his biography, *Gerald Finzi, an English Composer* (Faber, 1997). Since then it has been suggested that the letters themselves might be of interest on two counts: (i) it is comparatively rare that so much of the two sides of a correspondence has survived; and (ii) the letters give a picture of musical life in England during the years 1926–1956 as seen through the eyes of two musicians.

Thanks for permission to print the letters are due to Professor Banfield; to the Bodleian Library, Oxford; and to Christopher and Nigel Finzi, the sons of Gerald.

The poems by A.E. Housman on pages 186 and 203 of *More Poems* (Jonathan Cape, 1936), and also the nonsense-poem on page 172, are reprinted by kind permission of the Society of Authors.

The Letters have been printed as they stand in the autographs, except that printed letter-headings have been normalized, and spelling mistakes have been silently corrected. All other editorial matter is enclosed within square brackets.

I am most grateful to Hugh Cobbe for reading through the typescript and making some invaluable suggestions, and to Catherine Walters for her expert typing.

Howard Ferguson
Cambridge, 1997

Abbreviations

B.B.C.	British Broadcasting Corporation
B.M.	British Museum
B.N.O.C.	British National Opera Company
G.F.	Gerald Finzi
H.F.	Howard Ferguson
H.S.	Harold Samuel
L.P.O.	London Philharmonic Orchestra
M.M.	Mainly Musicians Club, London
N.G.	National Gallery
O.U.P.	Oxford University Press
Q.A.L.	Quia Amore Langueo
R.A.F.	Royal Air Force
R.A.M.	Royal Academy of Music
R.C.M.	Royal College of Music
R.O./R.O.M.	R.O. (Reginald Owen) Morris
R.V.W.	Ralph Vaughan Williams
V.W.	Vaughan Williams

Prices:

These, naturally, are given in the British currency of the time: pounds (£) shillings (s) and pence (d). In the letters, shillings and pence often are expressed by the convention of placing an oblique stroke between them, so that, for example, 6/9 means 6 shillings and 9 pence. By the same convention a dash after the oblique indicates no pence, so that 3/− means 3 shillings.

Introduction

Gerald Finzi and I first met in the autumn of 1926 at the house of R.O. Morris and his wife Jane. At that time Gerald was studying Sixteenth-Century Counterpoint (not composition) privately with R.O. (always so called because he disliked his names Reginald Owen), while I was R.O.'s pupil for harmony, counterpoint and composition at the Royal College of Music. A more significant meeting took place some weeks later (as recounted in my memoir, *Music, Friends and Places* (Thames Publishing, 1997), when we collided outside the Albert Hall after a concert conducted by Richard Strauss. From that moment we remained close friends until Gerald's death in 1956.

Gerald lived in a small house in Caroline Street, just behind Sloane Square station, while I lived with the pianist Harold Samuel, at first in Clarendon Road, Holland Park, and later in East Heath Road and Willoughby Road, Hampstead.

In 1928 Gerald told me the alarming news that he had tuberculosis, and would have to go into a sanatorium for some time. In fact, he entered the King Edward VII Sanatorium at Midhurst in Sussex in 1928, and remained there for four months.

I did not start to keep G.F.'s letters consistently until just before he went to the Sanatorium.

Howard Ferguson
Cambridge, 1997

LETTERS

Though seven years younger than Gerald Finzi, Howard Ferguson was, in terms of musical experience and personal maturity, very much his senior. Nor was this surprising, for the pattern of his early years had been such as to arm him with a self-confidence and sense of purpose much greater than that which Finzi's experience of life had provided.

Born in Belfast on 21 October 1908, Howard Ferguson was the youngest of the five children of Stanley and Frances Ferguson. His father was the Managing Director of the Ulster Bank and, though his mother played the piano, the family was not particularly musical. His sisters, however, endured piano lessons as a necessary 'accomplishment', and it was this that awoke his interest and led him to demand lessons of his own.

He was lucky in his second teacher, Frederick Sawyer, and later even luckier in an encounter with the distinguished pianist Harold Samuel (1879–1937), who not only awarded him a prize in the 1922 Belfast Musical Competitions but, recognizing in him an exceptional talent, suggested that he should accompany him to London where he would prepare him for entry into the Royal College of Music after a period of general study as a day boy at Westminster School.

Most parents would have found the idea alarming, but the Fergusons recognized Harold Samuel's utter probity and agreed to entrust their son to his care. A suitable family was found for him to lodge with, but when this arrangement came to an end he joined Harold Samuel's own bachelor household. With him, however, went his beloved Nanny, May Cunningham – affectionately known as Pu (short for Pussycat) – who would not only vouch for his welfare, but could also help care for Samuel's elderly mother. From this moment Howard Ferguson became, to all intents and purposes, the son and heir that Harold Samuel never had; and it says much for the strength of his musical purpose that, however loving and supportive his blood family had been, he was content to exchange their artistic limitations for a life in which music was paramount and every day brought fresh insights into its mysteries.

Ferguson enrolled as a student of the Royal College of Music in 1924, studying harmony and counterpoint with R.O. Morris (1886–1948) and conducting with Dr Malcolm Sargent (1895–1967). Piano lessons continued, privately, with Harold Samuel. He also began to find his way not only as a composer but also as a potential executant.

Howard Ferguson met Gerald Finzi in 1926: first through R.O. Morris, and then, more significantly, at a concert in the Albert Hall when an accident with the thunder machine during a performance of Richard Strauss's Alpine Symphony *revealed a mutual sense of humour and thus cemented a lifelong friendship. Their correspondence began to blossom in 1927 while Ferguson was in America. Harold Samuel had been booked for a four-month tour, and as R.O. Morris had recently been appointed to the staff of the Curtis Institute in Philadelphia it seemed sensible that Ferguson's lessons with both men should continue uninterrupted. Once again his parents raised no objection, for Pu was to accompany them as their housekeeper. They set sail for New York on 18 December 1926 and in the following year Gerald Finzi received the first of two ebullient accounts of life and music in America.*

Gerald Finzi's experience of life and music had run on rather different lines. Born in London on 14 July 1901, he was also the youngest of five children. His parents were Jewish: John Abraham Finzi of Italian descent, and Eliza his wife of German stock. Both could lay claim to a long line of prosperous, intellectually sophisticated ancestors to whom music was important. Eliza was an accomplished pianist, and even composed a little, but Gerald was the only member of the family to whom music was a way of life.

It was also a solace, for his childhood was soon to be clouded by a series of cruelly premature deaths. First his father, from cancer in 1909; then three brothers: Douglas, from pneumonia in 1912, then Felix, who committed suicide in 1913, and finally Edgar, killed in France in 1918. By that time, however, Gerald and his mother had moved to Harrogate where, for one happy year, he was the pupil of a rising young composer, Ernest Farrar. Yet even this relationship was not to last. Farrar enlisted in 1916 and was killed on 18 September 1918 – just three weeks before the war came to an end. He was thirty-two.

Finzi's studies now continued under the strict, academic eye of Edward Bairstow (1874–1946), organist of York Minster, until 1922 when he moved, again with his mother, to Painswick in Gloucestershire, there to begin that transformation into the quintessential English pastoral composer.

Untroubled by the need to earn a living, Finzi gradually began to find his musical voice. His first cycle of Hardy songs, By Footpath and Stile, *belongs to 1921–1922 and marks the beginning of a lifelong identification with a poet whose pessimism mirrored his own evaluation of life's little ironies. In 1924 his orchestral* Severn Rhapsody *was selected for publication as part of the Carnegie Collection of British Music, but two years later, conscious of certain limitations in his technique, he moved back to London in order to study once more with R.O. Morris. It meant that he would begin to mix with a wider range of young musicians. One of them was Howard Ferguson.*

1926–1927

12 Clarendon Road, London W.11; 3 October

Dear Mr Finzi,

Please forgive my delay in answering your letter. I received it while away from London, and have only just returned this week. I enclose the Sonata [G.F. had asked for the loan of a Sonata for Violin & Piano, written by H.F. c.1925 at the R.C.M. It was later destroyed.] but fear it won't be the least good to you – try Beethoven!!

Best wishes, Howard Ferguson.
I sail for U.S. in December.

[Harold Samuel had been booked for a four-month tour in the U.S.A. early in 1927. As he was going to be away for so long he decided to rent an apartment in New York, and take along Pu (H.F.'s ex-nanny) as housekeeper. As R.O. Morris (H.F.'s composition teacher) had just become Head of the Theory Department at the Curtis Institute in Philadelphia, H.F.'s ever-helpful parents agreed that he too should go to America, so that lessons with Samuel and Morris should be uninterrupted. Thus it came about that Harold, Pu and H.F.

4

sailed for New York on the Cunarder *Celtic* on 18 December 1926. Their apartment in New York was at 410 West End Avenue.]

[21 Caroline Street, London S.W.1; late December 1926.] G.F.'s ink drawing of H.F.'s arrival in Philadelphia, Pa., where (in spite of all the luggage) he was *not* staying.]

The arrival of Ferguson in Pa.

410 West End Avenue, New York, U.S.A.; 9 February

Dear Finzi,

Greetings from the land of the unfree; greetings from this the dirtiest city in the world [compared] to your poor dear despised only second dirtiest London. You say it is dirty, but you don't know what dirt is until you come here; I always had the impression that this was a clean place, now that I am here I know better. You can't leave a book on the piano overnight without its becoming covered with dust; I spend all day washing my hands, and by the evening I am – dirty. Everything you touch is dirty, in fact the whole place is *dirty*.

Having got that off my chest, I will go on to say really how very much I am enjoying myself here, in spite of all the dirt, dust and what not. New York is a mad city, an odd mixture of the most blatant vulgarity and the most surprising beauty in the buildings, and in the people of extraordinary callousness and great kindness. There seems to be a feeling in the air generally of 'Make as many dollars as you can, and don't mind the other person', and yet all the people one knows are overwhelmingly kind and generous. It is a strange mixup and truly a mad place. To live here long would drive me cracked, and only the thought of England in two months keeps me from loathing the place; as it is, it is wildly exciting and rather like an overdose of champagne.

I have been twice to Philadelphia to see ROM. He and Mrs Morris both seem very well and have a very nice place in Spruce Street. I believe she likes it better than he does, but both say that without the annual visit to England it would be an unthinkable business. They greatly admired your picture of my arrival in Pa. with the docile 'Enery [the Morris's beloved cat, left behind in London] and were quite touched by your interpretation of his beautiful character as shown by him lying in company with the 'leetle birds' all untouched in the cage – a lovely thought!!

The journey from here to Phila. takes only two hours, and the country from the carriage (coach in American) window looks as though it had been so frequently subjected to hurricanes that the inhabitants had not thought it worth while to erect anything more permanent than wooden houses. This, and the fact that the whole country looks desolate and untidy makes the journey a none too thrilling one.

I have not yet been anywhere else, so can only hope that the other places are not so terrible.

I have been to a concert every third day since my arrival here on average, and have paid to get into exactly none of them, which shows the great kindness of people in asking one out in this country.

As you asked me to, I have got you a full score of the Bloch 'Concerto Grosso'; it was the only kind they had and as you (foolishly) told me not to mind the price, I cheerfully handed out 10 dollars for it. This price (£2 in English money) seemed rather a lot to me, but I did as I was told and got it. I hope this is all right? Will I keep it until I return or send it on to you? Whichever you wish.

Having displayed my virtues – such as they are – I am going to ask you to do me a great kindness. Will you go to the exhibition of Flemish Art at Burlington House now in progress, and buy, beg, borrow or steal a catalogue of the works exhibited – preferably an illustrated one (if such there be), and costing anything up to 30/– or £2. If you would be so kind as to keep this until I return to the lovely land, when I can pay and relieve you of it. Also, when you write me to say whether you want the Bloch to be forwarded to you, could you please let me know when this exhibition closes, as I am wondering whether I will arrive in London for the tail end of it. I apologise for bothering you about this, and pray forgiveness!

We arrived here on a very foggy day. I arrived in Phila. in a blizzard.

Very best wishes to you for everything, from Howard Ferguson, and please excuse my filthy writing – my hand seems in a particularly bad mood tonight.

We return on the Alaunia sailing from Montreal on 29 April.

P.S. Sorry to bother you again. It has suddenly struck me that there may be various catalogues for the different periods of Flemish painting; if this is so, it is the early artists I am interested in, more particularly those that flourished any time before 1550. If there is a general catalogue it would of course be interesting to have that, but if there are more specialized ones, it would be the one dealing with the painters that worked before the middle of the 16th century that I want.

I am really most penitent about bothering you with all this, and beg humbly to be dealt-with lightly when I come back!

P.P.S. Are you interested in Michelangelo? [In case G.F. would like a reproduction of the Michelangelo drawing in the Metropolitan Museum]

410 West End Avenue, New York City; 5 March

Dear Finzi,

To begin with, my most humble apologies for using this machine [a typewriter]. The beauty and elegance of your writing frightens me into so doing, for decorative though I know my hand to be, I am afraid it might cause you some sleepless nights trying to read yet another of my screeds.

Then, oh Maestro, how, oh how can I express my profoundest reverence for those truly great and noble creations (that sounds like the latest ladies' gowns, modom) which you so graciously sent to your humble follower? I never have known what chiaroscuro was until I saw those works, and now I have no more idea than before. I have arrived at such a point that to do anything so concrete as drawing on paper is anathema to me: I now confine myself to making pictures in my mind, and transferring them to the retina of the spectator by pure will-power. This I find altogether more absolute.

But enough of things artistic, and to return to mundane worldliness. It was most kind of you to go to the exhibition to get the catalogues I enquired about, those that you describe are just the sort of things I wanted. I hope they won't be in your way if I ask you to keep them until I come back; most certainly the care of the Bloch *Concerto* will not lie too heavily on my head, so I will hold onto it in case it would get messed about in the post.

When I see the date at the head of this letter I want to shed a tear, for is it not the closing day of the exhibition? It must have been a wonderful collection; too wonderful to last so short a time, it ought undoubtedly to have been kept open until my return! I have carefully gathered all the reproductions of any pictures that I have seen over here and stuck them in a book, so what with that and the Souvenir you so kindly got for me I won't be so badly off.

Yes, I fear I have been composing. I have just finished a Mass [unpublished, destroyed and unperformed] for six-part chorus with a sprinkling of soloists thrown in, to be served without accompaniment. Its great virtue is its brevity; perhaps you wouldn't even admit that! The Oxford people are going to publish those two songs [they didn't] that I showed you last term, Hubert Foss was over here and got them rammed down his throat, poor man. How is the Concerto [G.F.'s Violin Concerto]? Well I hope, and grown since I last saw him.

(I must go to bed now, as I have been to Philadelphia today and am rather wearied therefrom. Good night until tomorrow.)

A few weeks ago I heard Honegger's opera *Judith* [with Mary Garden in the

7

title role!]]¹ in Boston; it seemed to me to be a long way better than any other French music that I have heard. I have since been looking at the score, and have come to the conclusion that it is a good but not a great work: it reminds me oddly of acidulated *Samson and Delilah*. Other new works I have heard are de Falla's Concerto for harpsichord and seven solo instruments [Landowska and the Boston Symphony Orchestra, 3 Feb. Carnegie Hall] which was in so large a hall that you could scarcely hear the wretched instrument: what small part of it did manage to float across the intervening space seemed to me both arid and acrid; on closer acquaintance however, it might become more pleasing. At the same concert I heard the *Sacre* for the first time. He [Stravinsky] certainly seems to have something to say, and to say it with no uncertain voice, although I'm not quite sure that I always like what he is talking about. Of other things, a Concerto for piano by one Aaron Copland, half of a Symphony by Mr St Ives,² an opera *Les Malheurs d'Orphée* by Milhaud, and a Symphony by Prokofiev all seemed to be of varying degrees of ghastliness. The last [the 'Classical'] was a very little milk of Mozart with a large amount of good (or bad) water. As yet I have heard nothing of Bloch's, and fear I will not, as I can't see his name on any forthcoming programmes.

The date of our departure gets pleasantly nearer, for I have begun to long for the sight of green country. As far as anything can be definite with us, we sail from Montreal on 29 April on the Alaunia. How lovely it will be going up the St Lawrence for, I believe, two days, and in Spring too. With again many thanks for all the trouble you have taken over getting catalogues, and all best wishes and luck until I return. Yours, Howard Ferguson

P.S. I think the Anglo-Belgian Union can do without an application from me, which shows my Scotch descent!

[12 Clarendon Road, W.11; 13 May]

Dear Finzi,

Many thanks for your letter which I received on my return to England's green and pleasant land last Monday morning. As I am off to Ireland this afternoon I am afraid I won't be able to meet you just yet. I will only be away for ten days, so it will not be long before we can foregather and exchange (as you put it) spoils and debts.

I will be back here in London on the 24th of this month, so if you could give me an idea of when you would be coming up [from the country] we could probably arrange a trysting place and a time; almost any evening (or afternoon, at a pinch) would do for me, except the weekend after Whitsun.

¹ Mary Garden (1874–1967). Lyric soprano. Debussy's first, and definitive, 'Mélisande' – a role which might seem an unlikely preparation for tackling the intrepid assassin of Holofernes!

² Charles Ives (1874–1954). The concert, conducted by Eugène Goossens, included the first public performance of any of Ives' orchestral works – two movements of the Fourth Symphony (1916). A performance of the complete work had to wait until 1965.

By the way, and in case you don't know, there is an exhibition of the works of William Blake at the Burlington Fine Arts Club, 17 Saville Row: it goes on until the end of July, so you have plenty of time to see it.

Your Bloch *Concerto* is safe and sound and will I hope remain so until you receive it; I am sorry its delivery has been so long delayed. How is your Concerto?[3] It is glorious to be back in England: we were almost drunk with excitement when we got back, seeing green fields, green trees and green everything was too much for us.

I must turn off the flow now, as I haven't even packed [for Ireland]. Good luck and good wishes until I see you in about a fortnight. Howard Ferguson.

It was a lovely crossing; I wasn't sick!

14 Deramore Park South, Malone Road, Belfast; 21 May

Dear Finzi,

Many thanks for your letter which I have just received. I am afraid that at present I am not very certain of what I will be doing in London on the 24th and 25th; the one thing I do know is that I have to go out to dinner somewhere on Tuesday evening. Would it do if I called round at 21 Caroline St during Tuesday to tell you when I could come to visit you? I would leave a note if you were out. This is the only plan I can think of, and as you wouldn't have time to send me another one, I will follow it.

I am sorry your hearing of the Concerto [G.F.'s Violin Concerto, played by Sybil Eaton with the British Women's Symphony Orchestra under Malcolm Sargent] didn't turn out as it should – still, hearing it even badly played is helpful, if not very pleasant.

I must cease now. Best wishes until I see you, Howard Ferguson.

14 Deramore Park South, Belfast; 26 May

Dear Finzi,

I am almost certain I shall be able to come and hear Rubbra's thing on Friday.[4] Unless anything unexpected turns up, I shall be with you at 5.45.

Best wishes, Howard Ferguson.

12 Clarendon Road, W.11; 30 May

[Dear Finzi]

I received your postcard about ROM's tea this afternoon [a tea we gave to ROM on 24 June] and have noted its contents in my diary.

The poem I was talking about when I last saw you is called 'Echo's Lament for Narcissus', by Ben Jonson and begins 'Slow, slow, fresh fount, keep time

---

[3] G.F.'s Violin Concerto.
[4] Probably the *Phantasy* for two violins and piano, Op.16. His first large-scale work (1927). Dedicated to Finzi.

with my salt tears'. You will find it on page 242 of Walter de la Mare's *Come Hither*. I cannot bear to deprive you of your one copy of that great and glorious poem 'You' by G. Hubi-Newcombe,[5] so have made two typewritten copies of it, and am enclosing it in this letter: it is almost too good to be true. I also enclose Algie's[6] letter to the *Musical Mirror*. The other enclosure is a notice I picked up in Augeners [music shop] today which I thought might interest you.

I was very sorry I couldn't come down to the country next weekend to see you, everything must be looking lovely. I returned yesterday from Blakeney: it was my first visit to Norfolk, and I enjoyed it greatly. The country was much hillier than I had expected to find it, and very beautiful: the churches are so many and so splendid.

I must cease now, with many thanks for taking me to hear Rubbra's work and for the pleasant time we had afterwards. Yours, Howard Ferguson.

I am leaving you to write to ROM about the tea in case I don't see him.

12 Clarendon Road, W.11; 7 June

Dear Finzi,

I am going to the Folk Song and Dance thing at the New Scala on Saturday afternoon, 18 June (at 2.30), and wondered if you wanted a seat too. I don't know whether you saw the Holst ballet [*The Morning of the Year*] when it was done at College, but if not, I think I remember you saying that you wanted to go. As I have yet to get my seat, I thought I might as well get yours too, if you want one. Where do you want to sit?

If you have nothing better to do afterwards, come home here for some food and we can examine music after that. (I offer *Der Rosenkavalier* as bait!) If you are busy Saturday evening, how about Sunday?

I want to show you a new song I have written. Could you bring that one about the comet ['The Comet at Yell'ham'] which you showed me when I saw you last, as I would like to see it again very much.

I hope you had better weather than we had over Whitsun. I am keeping those three dates for ROM's tea.

I think that is all, and really this is beginning to look like a poem by Walt Whitman, so I had better stop. With best wishes, Howard Ferguson.

12 Clarendon Road, W.11; 29 June

Dear Finzi,

You will remember you are coming here for dinner on Monday night. In the afternoon I am going to pay a second visit to the Blake exhibition at the

[5] Georgeanne Hubi-Newcombe (1843–1936). Soprano, lyricist, and song composer whose sentimental verses evidently delighted Finzi and Ferguson as much as they appalled them.

[6] Algernon Ashton (1859–1937). Prolific English composer and pianist whose works were published mainly in Germany. Professor of Piano at the Royal College (1885–1910). His music, fluent and Brahmsian, deserves reassessment.

Burlington Fine Arts Club; if you have not yet braved the doorkeeper with the book, perhaps you would like to join me? If you would like to come. I shall be in Piccadilly outside the entrance to the R.A. at 3.30. I will wait until 3.40, and should you not be there by that time, I will conclude that you are too busy, or do not want to come, and go on by myself. By this ingenious plan you are saved the trouble of writing an answer! Yours, Howard Ferguson.

I will pay my share of ROM's tea when we meet.

Langham Hotel [where H.F.'s father stayed while in London on Bank business]
W.1; 2 July.

Dear Finzi,

Of course, if you will have it, here it is [in handwriting]; I warn you, though, you won't be able to decipher it by the simple means of reading it from a looking-glass, it is a much more complicated matter than that.

Perhaps it is the habit of being someone else's secretary on the typewriter that induces a somewhat stilted style when I perform on that instrument; again, perhaps it is that my natural style is that of a secretary's! Whichever the case may be, you seem to prefer muddling over this scrawl to having it in clear black and white, so on your own head be it! We shall meet in Piccadilly in front of the R.A. at 3.30 on Monday afternoon.

Best wishes, H.F.

[14 Deramore Park South, Belfast]; 15 August

Dear Finzi,

It has occurred to me that I have never paid my half of the bill for RO's tea! This is very serious, and must be remedied at once; please send in the A/c complete with tips and anything else there may have been.

I hope you had a good time in the country. I have just returned from Switzerland, where H.S. and I have been staying for a fortnight; I had never been there before, and enjoyed it immensely. I am departing on Thursday with some of the family for a fortnight's motoring in Scotland, which I do not know very well. Let us pray for the weather!

In case you want to see it, but do not want to buy it: I have got the Ravel fiddle sonata. The first movement is lovely, but the other two seem to be rather like an epileptic cat in a bad mood — someone I know said it sounded like people picking their teeth after a heavy dinner — however, when I get to know it better, perhaps it won't sound so painful. I hope not.

I think this is all. Please remember the 'tea bill'. Yours, H.F.

Crianlarich Hotel, Perthshire; 22 August

Dear Finzi,

I have purchased a new fountain pen (having lost my old one) and am not yet on amicable terms with it, so goodness help you.

Although you may scarcely credit it, I am too conscientious to let the bill pass unsettled: I shall pay next year!

We are having a glorious time here, motoring all day and returning at dinner-time to the hotel. We are due to move on to a new base in a few days, from where we will repeat the same performance; the roads are so rough that they seem to have left me with scarcely any inside — but that is one of the joys of motoring. Really I am enjoying it immensely. I have, of course, assumed the Ferguson tartan, and execute a Highland fling every two hours on top of the car to unstiffen my legs.

I arrive in London on 17 September so will miss the Bloch Concerto by a short head: what a bother. If you want to hear the Brahms D minor Concerto finely played, go to hear H.S. do it on Wed. 31 August [at the Proms]. I will be able to hear the London Symphony [Vaughan Williams] on 22 September.

I have brought away with me to while away the evenings, Blake's complete works in the new Nonesuch edition. It is the same as your beautiful 3 vol. edition except that all the alternative readings have been left out, so enabling it to be issued in one pocketable volume. The editor is Keynes. It is beautifully printed, and considering that it contains 1152 pages, is very handy. To me, who have never known much of Blake's writings, it is wonderfully interesting.

The more I play the Ravel fiddle Sonata, the more intelligible it becomes; when I return to Ireland I will try to get a fiddler to play it with me, when, no doubt, it will reveal still more of itself.

I hope you are enjoying Dolmetsch père et fils [the Festival] never to mention wyf and daughters. All best wishes, H.F.

14 Deramore Park South, Belfast; 4 September

Dear Finzi,

I am horrified at your taking my drawings seriously: they were, of course, caricatures, and meant to be taken as a joke. I am even more horrified at the manner in which you correct them — it is most reprehensible; motors with flinging Highlanders should be drawn thus: [missing; probably together with the following page].

Good for March Church roof; I am so glad it has revealed the Botticelli [the Mystic Nativity in the National Gallery, of which I gave G.F. a photo] — it is something worth revealing.

I have had the misfortune to hear examples of Miss Pain-Dung's[7] music: as far as it is concerned she is well-named.

---

[7] Susan Spain-Dunk (1880–1962), English composer and viola player. Her *Idyll* for strings had been premiered at the 1925 Promenade Concerts, her overture *Kentish Downs* and tone poem *Elaine* following in successive seasons.

The first movement of the Ravel still seems to me to be beautiful, and I think I agree with you about the second! As for the third, I don't think I will probe its depths (or, more likely, shallows) until I hear a respectable fiddler play it.

Strangely, I too had singled out those two letters of Blake to Dr T.[8] as being a clear exposition of his aims.

The D minor Bach [Concerto] must have been a very exhilarating performance. I cannot imagine a finer conception of the cadenza of the Brandenberg [No. 5] than that of H.S. To hear those two works in one evening would have been a great joy.

I saw Dryburgh Abbey near Melrose for the second time a few days ago; there is a great peace about these ruins, with grass growing where the floors were, and fruit trees climbing on what used to be inside walls. It is a lovely place.

Would you be so good as to buy me a 3/– ticket for the London Symphony [Vaughan Williams] at the Proms on 22 September, as I don't want to miss hearing it by not being able to get in. Apologies for bothering you with this. Best wishes, H.F.

12 Clarendon Road, W.11; 30 September

[Dear Finzi]

If I may, I shall be with you at 5.30 tomorrow afternoon: if I may not, ring up and I shall postpone my arrival until 7. The College library doesn't run to Scarlatti or Rameau operas; the Parry Room is full of them but we cannot borrow from it, alas. H.F.

[12 Clarendon Road, W.11]; 12 October

[Dear Finzi]

Thank you very much for the Chelsea Music Club's address; they have sent me a ticket, so I shall be there. What an objectionable person you are: I have changed all the things you suggested in the song! Many thanks. H.F.

12 Clarendon Road, W.11; 11 November

[Dear Finzi]

A.B.C.D.? – M.R.N.O. – S.D.R. – R.D.R.D.?

[Solution: Abie see de goldfish?
            'Em are no goldfish.
            'Es day are goldfish!
            Are day, are day goldfish?]

---

[8] In 1799 the Revd. Dr John Trusler, on commissioning paintings of 'Malevolence' and 'Benevolence' from William Blake, thought fit to dictate their style and manner, thus provoking a declaration of the artist's credo.

13

What is to be done? This Saturday is 5 November [Guy Fawkes Day] and I am coming to you. How about going for a walk in the country this Sunday if it's fine? H.F.

12 Clarendon Road, W.11; 5 December

[Dear Finzi]

Oh misery me! That wretched cold *did* come on, despite all our whiskeys and lemon and aspirin, and I have been in the house with it ever since I saw you, in a complete state of liquidation. I had to put off going to our Emily[9] yesterday, and fear I must put off tonight, though I am much better and it breaks my heart to do so. I seem to be fated not to hear Casals conduct again.

If you are at the Phil. on Thursday, come down to the street-level entrance hall in the interval, and I will return your copy of *Nan* [John Masefield's play]. I have read it and think it is very fine indeed. Would you set it complete? It certainly seems to want music, but I can't quite make out how or where.

If you are not there on Thursday, let me know by postcard if you are coming or not on Saturday: and if not, where to meet you the next day. How about the same indicator board as last time in Baker Street Station, but at 9.45?

If you know of anyone who would like the enclosed ticket, please give it them, for it is, alas, no use to me. I think that is all. Howard Ferguson.

12 Clarendon Road, W.11 [; after 5 December]

[Dear Finzi]

Many thanks for the postcard; I am almost free of my 'vapours' and am going out today. By all means come on Saturday at 7.15 if you can manage it. If you cannot, I should like to see you some other time before I go on about the *Requiem* [G.F.'s *Requiem da Camera*]; half an hour will do. H.F.

14 Deramore Park South, Belfast; 21 December

[Dear Finzi]

Herewith a little Christmas present [H.F.'s piano-duet arrangement of the Prelude to G.F.'s *Requiem*] for your copyist. When you give it to him, you might say that the position of the notes on the staves and the way their tails turn is important, and the staves should be copied exactly; also, the indication of the instrumentation should, in my opinion, be put in as I have them, as I think they are a great help when playing the work — they draw your attention to where the various phrases begin, etc. I have written the 'key' to the abbreviations on the page after the end of the work. I have left one note in pencil in the left hand of

9 Dr Emily Daymond (c.1885–1949) was the first woman Doctor of Music in England. She became Director of Music at Holloway College, Egham, and was a devoted admirer of, and unofficial secretary to, Sir Hubert Parry.

the bass player at letter E, as you weren't certain what you wanted there. I have done my best with the marks of expression [G.F. was apt to omit them]; if you don't like any of them change whatever you want.

When looking over the work I found that four bars before D I had written out a Bass Clarinet part as an ordinary clarinet. I regret to say you didn't notice this! It is now corrected. I think everything else in it is O.K.

How is the Concerto [G.F.'s unfinished Piano Concerto] getting on? Well, I hope, and strong and hearty. Just to show you that 'I too have not been idle', I enclose a little piece for the piano [later destroyed] that I have written: it being the first serious thing I have done for that instrument, I have dedicated it, appropriately enough, to you.

I was going to send you back the full-score of the *Requiem*, but on second thoughts I shall keep it and bring it over with me, as it would make too big a parcel.

I am very grateful for your suggestion about my M.S. writing. You will see I have adopted your method: it is much quicker and looks a great deal neater than the old way. Blessings on you!

Tea is going in, so I must stop. A merry Christmas, and all the best wishes. H.F.

14 Deramore Park South, Belfast; 23 December

[Dear Finzi]

Many thanks for the first movement [of G.F.s Violin Concerto] which has arrived safely. Will I not have to play the last movement, or is there not an extra copy of it yet? If you have one, could you let me have it if you want me to do it with Sybil [Eaton], as I am hopeless at reading your 'fast' music. May I say one thing? Certainly. Well then, in the fifth bar after M, does the bass want to come down slap on the tonic, as it is at present written? It seems to pull things up rather, though of course you may want this. I feel that it would give a greater sense of forward motion, if, for the first half of the bar the left hand wandered about the mediant, continuing as written from the second half of the bar onwards. I don't know why I feel this, and am probably blathering. On looking at it once more I think the reason is, that as the tutti entry of the subject just before M is in B flat, when you have had the little 4-bar episode after M and find that it only lands you back into the tonic of B-flat again, you feel that it has all been a waste of time; whereas, if you don't actually touch the tonic, you wouldn't get that feeling of going round in a circle. The 'Savoy sequence' after R doesn't strike one at all.[10] I had to look for it before I found where it was!

I hope the *Requiem* arrived, and wasn't mucked about in the Christmas rush.

Some time ago you asked me whether I knew of any book on Rowlandson; [the rest of this letter is missing]

[10] G.F. evidently feared that a touch of Gilbert and Sullivan had crept into his music!

Howard Ferguson left the Royal College in 1928 having spent his final year under the guidance of Ralph Vaughan Williams (1872–1958) – a kindly, encouraging, yet ultimately less helpful composition teacher than the more acerbic R.O. Morris had been. Although the Oxford University Press had already accepted his Five Irish Folk Tunes *for publication and he had begun work on the* Two Ballads *for baritone and orchestra, he realized that he would never be prolific. He therefore decided to work also as a performer of chamber music. To this end he formed a piano trio with Eda Kersey (violin) and Helen Just (cello) which was later expanded into The Ensemble Players. It was the experience of working with The Ensemble Players that led him in 1933 to compose the work that, together with his Violin Sonata No 1, made him famous: the Octet for two violins, viola, cello, double bass, clarinet, bassoon and horn.*

Through this time he lived with Harold Samuel – Pu and her niece Betty running the household and thus making possible their busy professional lives. The year 1936, however, proved to be particularly strenuous for Samuel. An adjudication tour of Canada, plus recitals in America, was followed by a South African tour. During the voyage home he suffered a heart attack, and though he seemed to rally his condition began to deteriorate and on 15 January he died.

Ferguson, now Harold Samuel's principal heir, gave up their London home and for a while lived in the gardener's cottage at the site in North Hampshire where Finzi and his newly-married wife were planning to build a house. But this proved not entirely practical, and early in 1939 he took the lease on a property in the Hampstead Garden Suburb: 106 Wildwood Road. It was to be his home for the next 24 years.

Finzi's progress, meanwhile, was relatively uncertain during this period. Struggles with a Violin Concerto for Sybil Eaton (with whom he was briefly infatuated) proved as exhausting as its first performance (4 May 1927) proved unsatisfactory, and the work joined the long list of pieces which he would tinker with over the years. Indeed, the strain of wrestling with it affected his health, and in the Spring of 1928 he was ordered to spend several months in the King Edward VII Sanatorium, near Midhurst in Sussex, on the grounds of suspected tuberculosis. Though the Sanatorium turned out to be an architectural oddity (and was immediately dubbed 'The Caliphate' by Finzi and his friends), the stay itself proved tedious and the diagnosis unfounded.

He returned to London to wrestle with a Piano Concerto that quickly assumed such a Goliath of a challenge that Ferguson felt it only proper to address him thereafter as 'Dave'. When it came to songs, however, his efforts, though just as protracted, bore more satisfactory fruit, and it is to this period (1929) that his second Hardy set, A Young Man's Exhortation, *belongs.*

The year 1930 found him teaching composition at the Royal Academy of Music – an experience that undoubtedly taught him more than he was able to teach the procession of not very promising pupils that came his way. The drudgery ended, however, in 1933 when, on 16 September, he married a young and singularly beautiful artist, Joyce (Joy) Black.

It was the best thing that ever happened to him. Joy gave him the sense of purpose and stability that had been missing from his life. Her encouragement and discrimination proved vital both to his development as an artist and to his happiness as a man. It was a perfect marriage.

Still pursuing the pastoral dream, they went to live at Aldbourne in Wiltshire, money on Joy's side now supplementing his to ensure a lifestyle of modest comfort. They began to raise a family: two boys, Christopher born in July 1934, and Nigel in August two years later. On 8 March 1939 they moved into Church Farm, the house they had caused to be built at Ashmanworth — the house that would be an artistic centre and cultural haven for the rest of their lives. There Finzi and his wife would amass one of the most comprehensive private collections of English poetry (which, after his death, would form the Finzi Book Room at Reading University), and an equally fascinating collection of neglected eighteenth-century music (which is now to be found in the library of St Andrews University). There they would plot the further publication of Ivor Gurney's songs and poetry, which they had begun when he languished in the City of London Mental Hospital. And there in the gardens they would investigate the propagation of ancient types of English apples, helping to save them from oblivion with as much enthusiasm as they devoted to championing the music of neglected British composers. There, in short, they lived lives that admirably combined idealism with hard-working practicality and creativity.

On 3 September 1939, however, a harsher reality intruded when England was forced to declare war on Nazi Germany. Finzi promptly joined the local Defence Volunteers and, complete in forage cap and battle dress, stood ready to defend Newbury from enemy invasion. In 1941 he found more important work on the staff of the Ministry of War Transport, his uncertain health absolving him from active service.

Ferguson, on the other hand, found himself at Uxbridge serving as a musician in the Royal Air Force — a duty which left him free to organize and take part in the lunch-time concerts which Myra Hess had instigated at the National Gallery. Beginning on 10 October 1939, these ran without break for six and a half years: 1,698 concerts providing an invaluable daily boost to morale — not to mention 'the best sandwiches in London'. The experience incidentally brought him into close contact with an exceptionally wide variety of talented young musicians, with two of whom (the pianist Denis Matthews and the violinist Yfrah Neaman) he would later form distinguished performing partnerships.

Finzi also realized that music had a part to play in time of war. In December 1940 he founded the Newbury String Players which, as its conductor, provided him with the invaluable experience of practical music-making and stimulated his research into neglected areas of British music. In the meantime, he staked out his own claim to immortality.

The work that changed the world's perception of him as a composer of importance and originality was a setting of poems by Thomas Traherne for voice and string orchestra: Dies natalis. *Typical of his method of composition, the music had been quietly simmering since 1925. In 1938 he submitted what he had so far achieved to the organizers of the Three Choirs Festival who immediately accepted it for performance at Hereford in September the following year.*

That performance never took place. War brought the Festivals to an end and they were not resumed until 1946. Dies natalis *therefore received its first performance in London's Wigmore Hall on 26 January 1940. Though well received, it was slow to achieve the classic status it now enjoys, but its gradual success was sufficient to mark him out as a*

17

composer of consequence. Together with the cycle of Shakespeare settings for baritone and string orchestra, Let Us Garlands Bring *(composed over an equally protracted period, 1929–1942), it remains the work by which he is best known.*

1928

14 Deramore Park South, Belfast; 3 January

[Dear Finzi]

I don't know whether I have already acknowledged the receipt of your two letters, the first from Glos. and the second from Lunnen; if not, I do so now.

If the last movement of the [Violin] Concerto is to be played, you can do it. I always did contend that you were a much faster pianist than I was. The first movement is coming along nicely, thank you.

I'm sorry to hear of the decease of the song in the *Requiem*,[1] though I didn't know it well enough to say that I am deeply grieved.

If it interests you, there is a small exhibition of Rowlandson's work in the catacombs of the Tate; I am not sure for how long it is on, or when it started. Also, what would probably be more accessible to you at present, some of the pictures forming the exhibition are reproduced in either the December or January number (I think the latter) of *The Connoisseur*, a monthly magazine devoted to art.

Would you be in if I came round to Caroline Street at about 8.30 on Sunday evening? If you were, we could arrange when the Concerto [Violin Concerto with Sybil Eaton] is to be run over. If this isn't any good for you, would you drop me a postcard to Clarendon Road, were I arrive on Saturday.

All best wishes for 1928, H.F.

---

[1] A setting of Thomas Hardy's 'In Time of "The Breaking of Nations"'. Rewritten later and restored to the *Requiem*.

21 Caroline Street, S.W.1 [January]

[12 Clarendon Road, W.11; mid-January]

[Dear Finzi]

I have been sick and abed with the vapours ('flu) ever since Friday, and am at present somewhat wobbly about the pins and the middle of the back. In spite of this I think I will be able to struggle to the Phil. on Thursday, when I will be in the vulgar 3/– seats in the Gallery, as H.S. will be in the downstairs seat.

I send the enclosed notice for a variety of reasons: one of them is that I think you might like a little musical relaxation on the 1st February. The beauties of the poems [by G. Hubi-Newcombe] speak for themselves. H.F. [Also a handbill for Beatrice Harrison's Wigmore Hall recital, on which H.F. has written:] I can see the angels, mother!

> There once was a player called Harrison
> Whose costume, of glorious caparison,
> Was the means of inviting wails
> From neighbourly nightingales.
> And the Princesses said 'sans comparison'.

[Added by G.F.:]
> There once was a Harrison daughter
> Whose playing was limpid as water.
> The nightingales thrilled
> As she bowed and she trilled,
> And the Princesses flocked as they oughter.

19

12 Clarendon Road, W.11; 1 February

[Dear Finzi]

Just to say that I thought it [G.F.'s Violin Concerto at Queens Hall; 1.2.28, Bach Choir Concert conducted by R.V.W.] went splendidly, and that I enjoyed it very much.

I see what you mean about altering the structure of the 1st movement, and I believe I agree with you. Apart from that I thought it went very well – orchestration and everything coming off excellently. The slight smudge in the orchestra just before her short cadenza was not, I think, due to you but to the bad playing of the band, as were several other places in that movement that might have been clearer. (Not that the 1st movement sounded monotonous, it didn't.) But, bless his heart, V.W. is not a born conductor!

The 2nd movement is, of course, lovely; and the 3rd comes off as well as you could wish. One could certainly hear Sybil [Eaton, soloist] all the time – even on her 'low-powered' instrument.

I think you can be pleased with the performance it got, which is not to say it couldn't have gone better. All the best, H.F.

Turville Court, Henley-on-Thames [house of H.S.'s friend C.J. Conway]; 4 Feb

[Dear Finzi]

Can you come to Clarendon Road to do *The Bartered Bride* on Wednesday? If not, either Thursday or Friday. Let me know to No. 12.

I walked for six miles yesterday – not too bad for 'fluey legs! I hope you have had a rest after last Wednesday. Those performances take it out of one horribly. Yours, H.F.

[Turville Court]; 7 Feb

[Dear Finzi]

So glad you can manage tomorrow: come along at 6.0, or earlier if you feel inclined. If anything turns up that I cannot have you I'll wire, though I think all will be well. How about a walk on Sunday?

The enclosed came out of the 'Radio Times': I'm sorry to say I can't get SGB[2] [Birmingham BBC broadcast of Schönberg's 3rd String Quartet and Berg's Lyric Suite], so you had better get hold of someone who can, or else get van Dieren or some other kind heart to take you to the studio, where you would hear it 'in the flesh'. Hope you had a good rest while away. Yours, H.F.

---

[2] The call sign for the Birmingham radio station – the equivalent of London's 2LO.

'Nest-o'-Rest', 12 Clarendon Road, W.11; 11 Feb

[Dear Finzi]

Blast and damn. I won't be able to manage next Sunday for a walk and the Bloch Quartet, as Emily D[aymond] wants me to go down to Holloway College and play that day. I tried to get it postponed to the following Sunday, but couldn't. Will you go for a walk on the 26th instead? Just off to Shere (in Surrey) for another restful weekend. See you Saturday, H.F.

[12 Clarendon Road, W.11]; 15 Feb

[Dear Finzi]

This is not so bad as it seems: they are not going to do the Bloch Quartet on Sunday after all; it is postponed until sometime in March. And anyway it isn't the Bloch Quartet at all, it's the Piano Quintet. If you are still free on Sunday I may be able to walk, that is, if Emily D. continues in the cold she has. I had a splendid time in Surrey, and am now fully recovered. 5.30 Saturday? H.F.

[12 Clarendon Road, W.11]; 22 Feb

[Dear Finzi]

In case I don't see you in the interval tomorrow night, this is just to say that I don't expect I will stay for the Dvórak Symphony (you will remember we heard it last term, and were bored). If you feel the same as I do about it, let's meet in the usual place and have a walk. I believe it is the last thing on the programme.

Bring your book, and we can arrange some time to finish 'The Bartered Bride'.

My address is: c/o C.J. Conway [H.S.'s friend] 2 Orme Square, Bayswater. Best wishes, H.F.

2 Orme Square, Bayswater; 29 Feb

[Dear Finzi]

I was very sorry to see, from your non-arrival at the concert tonight, that you weren't feeling up to it; but I was also glad, from the same fact, that you have the sense to stay at home when you aren't feeling well. I would have called in to see how you are feeling tomorrow, but I am off to York on the 10 a.m. train, so cannot. You didn't miss anything by not going to the concert: the whole thing was a wilderness, and I wouldn't have given tuppence for any of the items, except perhaps the first of the Bartok pieces. It was interesting to hear them, nevertheless.

Do take care of yourself. A stitch in time *does* save quite a number of extra ones sometimes, and it is better worth while going a little easy now, than having to stop for a comparatively long time later. I hope you will be feeling better when you receive this. I shall be back from York on Friday – afternoon, I think, All the best, H.F.

[12 Clarendon Road, W.11]; 7 March

[Dear Finzi]

The letter [to an importunate lady who thought she was in love with G.F.] seems all that could be desired. You don't send me a copy of the notes you gave her, though from your letter you sound as though you thought you had – still, I expect they were O.K. I think you are quite right to dispel the illusion.

Better get 9/– seats for Saturday, as it looks as though it might be the last Sat. evening I could go before the holidays. I think Sunday will be all right for me too. Yours, H.F.

12 Clarendon Road, W.11; 19 March

[Dear Finzi]

Will be with you 4.30 tomorrow cum *Fennimore and Gerda* [Delius] and a little more brightness than when I last saw you – I hope so anyway, for such a funereal mien does no one no good! If this doesn't suit, give me a ring during the morning. [H.F.]

[12 Clarendon Road, W.11; undated]

[Dear Finzi]

Unfortunately I cannot manage tomorrow afternoon, so will hope to see you on Tuesday, if it's all right for you. I am terribly sorry to hear of your having to go away [to a sanatorium], and I hope that it will at least make you completely well. H.F.

12 Clarendonstrasse, Flamändepark [the point being that G.F. didn't know German]; 15 March [wrongly dated?]

[Dear Finzi]

Ich habe die billeten für 'Das jünger Waldley' fur nexten Wodenstag, in das erster rower dem Uppercerklen. Das ist 6/9, als ich die gegotten al Herren Keith Prowse Ltd.

Allas, ich kann nicht manager ni Saturtag ni Sontag, fur meiner Parenten will be hier gestillen Tuestag nexten mite be possiblen fur die musick; iffitis, kom als Clarendonstrasse 12, under wil woll geplai ausdrücksvol. Sie ü soon. Mit respeckts, Howard Ferguson, E.T. [nickname 'Equal Temperament']

12 Clarendon Road, W.11; 23 March

[Dear Finzi]

I'm so sorry I cut you off in such haste yesterday: I was in the midst of playing the 2nd piano part of a concerto for H.S. at the time, and had to get my dinner in after that, before sallying forth to join the King and Queen! Solomon [at the Royal Philharmonic Society] was like unto the curate's egg: but the many dull patches were well worth enduring for the some really beautiful things it contained. About the Children's Concert tomorrow – I believe it starts at 11. Anyway, will you meet us in the street-level entrance hall 10 minutes before it is due to begin, and H.S. will take us each by the hand and lead us in as his somewhat illegitimate children. If you don't feel like coming, get Edith[3] to give me a ring before 10 o'clock.

As I told you, I got your Stanley Spencer book. I liked it so much that I got one for myself too. See you tomorrow! H.F.

12 Clarendon Road, W.11; 26 March

[Dear Finzi]

Das ist ein poem von T. Hardy [Hardy's 'Winter Words' were appearing one by one in the *Daily Telegraph*] – but no, I will show you what a fine linguist I am, by writing to you in English this night. I do not think it to be so fine a poem as those that have already appeared to date; but nevertheless, not to be wholly unworthy of so great a master. I will continue to send them to you as they come out. I would be obliged indeed if you would keep them as I continue to send them, for, should I ever desire to refer again to them for any reason or other I would then be able to do it simply ad lib. and without bother to your honoured self or myself. This being so, thank you.

Professor Samuel is to Holland on Wednesday morning, and I to Ireland on Thursday afternoon, till and after when Deo Volente. How are you and your digestion? Well I am hoping. Please to let me know your address that I may forward my epistles thereto with accuracy. If there is anything I can assist you before I leave to Ireland on Thursday, please to let me know. With honoured sir my complimentaries, Howard Ferguson, E.T.

(One would almost think I was a Welshman from the above.)

[14 Deramore Park South, Belfast]; 6 April

[Dear Finzi]

Well, as they say in fairy stories, here I am again. Through the abject deceitfulness of the Daily Telegraph I am only able to send you three Hardy poems, this is of the third one arrives today in time for me to enclose it. Otherwise there will only be two. They actually have the audacity to only print one every third day now!

I had a 'calm sea and a prosperous voyage' coming over here. At least, the sea was hardly calm, but the voyage was prosperous enough, for I slept the whole time, and so avoided the unhappy symptoms.

I don't think I told you before I left that Pu [my housekeeper, and former nanny] has to go into Middlesex Hospital sometime this month. As yet, it isn't for anything serious, but they want to X-ray her and find out just what is the

---

[3] Edith Pyke. Gerald Finzi's housekeeper.

matter. They don't seem to think that it is the most serious thing [cancer], so we can only hope that it isn't.

I am being fairly lazy at present, but have found time to finish off my Fugue à la Haydn's *Creation* (for chorus) — a work which I believe you aren't acquainted with, nor need you be — and to re-score my cheerful little song [Blake's 'Never seek to tell thy love'; later destroyed] for flute and string quartet instead of fl. and trio. In its new form I think it is altogether more satisfactory.

I brought over my Purcell Harpsichord and Organ volume [Purcell Society vol. VI] with which to while away the time. Do you know the Suite in G minor? It is very beautiful; and have you ever noticed the extraordinary resemblance between the 'Ground in Gamut' and the Goldberg Variations of Jon. Seb? I suppose the bass progression is a very natural one, which they both might quite easily arrive at separately — in the same way as the Crucifixus and Dido's Lament — but even some of the variations (one, at least, of them) bear quite a family resemblance. I only refer to the first half of the Aria of the Goldbergs, for the second part goes, of course, further than Purcell thought of. I have not got a copy of the Goldbergs with me, so can't verifie this; nevertheless, I feel fairly sure of what I say.

I have taken to the pastime of your childhood — the writing of fairy stories! I enclose my first effort for your criticism, and I hope approval.

I hope you are feeling all right. Try to take things fairly easily — which I suppose is about as much use as telling an avalanche to stop avalanching! My blessings on you. H.F.

The Tale of Two Minstrels

[Enclosure.] Once upon a time there lived a Princess who owned vast wealth and was very beautiful. She was called the Princess Mona and she dwelt in the pleasant land of Har, and altogether she had numerous suitors for her hand. Amongst these suitors were two minstrels: one came from warm Southern lands and the other from the cold North, and they continually sought to please her with sweet music. One day he who came from the South — he was called Iznif Gredla[4] — composed a song which he meant to sing to her, and he sang it to his friends that he might accustom himself to the performing of it. Now, the suitor from the North (who was called Ethelred Tempester) was also composing a song which he meant to sing to the fair Princess, but far from being ready to try it over to himself or his friends, he was unable to get any further than the forty-first barline, which was very awkward as he had already drawn forty-six barlines and they had to be filled-in somehow or other.

Well, one day Ethelred was walking disconsolately round the castle walls, trying to think what he would do about it, when suddenly he heard a voice singing from within the castle walls. He stopped with one foot poised in the air and listened . . . It was the large, rich voice of his comrade from the South. He listened again. His large rich comrade from the South was singing the song he

[4] Though 'Inznif Gredla' is an anagram for Finzi, 'Ethelred Tempester' (for Ferguson) is not so derived. It may, however, be an elaboration of E.T. (Equal Temperament), Finzi's acknowledgement of his friend's equable nature.

had composed for the Princess Mona. He listened yet again, and listened longer . . . What a fair song it was, and how fairest fair were the interludes he played upon his lute between the strophes. Why were they so fair and beautiful? He did not know; but that, if anything, made them even fairer and more beautiful. The song ceased, and he brushed away a silent tear with the corner of his lace pocket-handkerchief and walked on, quietly humming to himself. He was thinking of his own song and wishing he could finish it . . . If only he could think of something as fitting as the interludes to Iznif Gredla's song . . . Why couldn't he? he wondered, but that didn't make him finish it any the quicker. He had stopped humming his own song, and was trying to recollect one of the interludes he had liked so much, but he could only think of the beginning of it: however he hummed this to himself once or twice. How did it compare with his song, he wondered? and he hummed his own and then the other. He did this several times, and was beginning to think his own wasn't too bad after all, when suddenly – heavens! – the interlude made the perfect finish that he had been looking for so long! But what was to be done? Was he to use the other's song by finishing his own with part of it, or was he to leave his own unfinished and the other's untouched? He pondered this for many days and oftimes into the night, and after he had received quite a few grey hairs over the whole business he decided that he *would* finish his own song with the part of Iznif's.

Well, that was that, but it isn't the end of the story, for some time after, the beautiful Princess Mona decided that she would give a party. And to this party she invited all her suitors, acquaintances, friends and relations, for she intended to entertain them all by getting the singers among them to sing, the Minstrels among them to play, and the Bishops among them to preach. In this way she saved quite a lot of money.

In the natural order of things, the two minstrels, Iznif Gredla and Ethelred Tempester, were asked to perform. They blushingly said they would, and each asked if he might perform a little piece of his own composing, to which request the lovely Princess Mona raised no objection. As it happened, Iznif was the first to play, and, as if you haven't already guessed, he sang the song he had composed for the Princess. There was much applause at the end, and Iznif was even allowed to kiss the lily-white hand of the Princess Mona for having composed such a song in her honour. Then Ethelred arose from his seat, and, as you probably have also guessed, sang the song that *he* had composed for the Princess. Well, when he reached the forty-second barline of his song, there was a sudden commotion from the part of the banqueting hall in which the minstrels were, and on looking round he saw Iznif drawing himself up to his full six foot four. He stopped short, and Iznif said in a voice that could be heard by all; – Well, I really can't make up my mind as to what he *did* say. And as you are the true, original and only writer of fairy stories, I am going to ask you to help me by giving me some idea of what you think he would have said under the circumstances. What did he say?

[Finzi's reply:] 'Thou hast stolen my interlude'. Well, that was a great surprise to all the people present; but before the two minstrels could come to blows the Princess stepped down from her dais and said 'Ladies and Gentlemen, commoners and minstrels, I will marry Ethelred Tempester, for he has stolen to finish his song, and anyone who could do such a base thing must be very much in love. So they were married and Iznif Gredla composed a song which he sang at their nuptial celebrations, and it was a very sad song and he had tears in his eyes as he sang it. The End.

[This refers to a quotation H.F. used (consciously) in a small piano piece, long afterwards turned into No. 2 of *Three Sketches* for Flute and Piano.]

Hilles House [the home of Detmar Blow], Stroud, Glos.; 10 April

Dear Fergie,

Thanks – thanks. I thought 'I am the one' [Hardy poem] beautiful; the others less so, but they are all much appreciated. Alas for the deceit of the Daily Telegraph.

You will see that I have come away to the country 'till my time comes' [to go to the Sanatorium], or, in the words of the Psalmist, 'before I am no more'; but I don't expect to be here for more than another few days, as I must put things in order at 21 Caroline Street the moment my summons comes. No work, of course, is possible in a happy open household, but I play with the children and look over twenty or thirty miles of country and see the shining Severn winding below. As far as being a composer is concerned, the next 4 to 6 months will be a complete wash out, and I curse almost as vehemently as Job. Perhaps I shall just manage to do a two-part invention in the Caliphate [G.F.'s name for the Sanatorium], for as V.W. said the other day, we can all compose away from the piano, but it sounds quite different when we play it! I am told, by the way, that he asked rather significantly if I should be allowed visitors. But that is too much to hope for. At Morley College the other day I heard extracts from 'The Fat Knight' [V.W.'s opera *Sir John in Love*] and the whole of the new ballet 'Job' – on two pianos of course, played by Norah Day and Valley Lasker. What I heard of 'The Fat Knight' contained the worst music V.W. has ever written, though it goes with great pace and has certain new rhythmical developments (as far as he is concerned). 'Job' is quite another matter. It lasts 50 minutes and embraces all things. The beginning and end are as lovely as the loveliest parts of 'Flos Campi', the violent parts are equally satisfactory. There is a curious grave and ceremonial quality about it, but V.W. may turn it into something else, as it's so unpractical and needs a double stage for dances in Heaven and dances on earth. I do hope he doesn't, for it's a lovely work.

Most sorry to hear about Pu, and hope all will be well. I shall be very glad to hear that it is really nothing serious.

I haven't noticed the Purcell resemblance, but when I get back I'll look it up. I think the G minor Suite contains that lovely lovely Sarabande; the first part is very Elgarian. Bliss [Arthur] I'm glad to say, is not going to live in Paris after all, but is going to get a house in London. I hear that Sumsion [John][5] has got Gloucester Cathedral, and if so three cheers.

---

[5] Herbert Sumsion (1899–1995), known as 'John', succeeded Sir Herbert Brewer as organist of Gloucester Cathedral.

That's all the scandal I can supply you with. For further instalments apply to Gordon Bryan [pianist scandalmonger].

As for the Fairy story . . . .

Blessings from yours ever, G.F.

                                        14 Deramore Park South, Belfast; 13 April

[Dear Finzi],

Many thanks for the letter, and the truly touching end to my Fairy Tale, but more of that later − or perhaps not more of it later. Through the incredible deceit of the D.T. [*Daily Telegraph*] you are only having two poems this week. I have not seen the second one yet, as it is only due to arrive today, but even if there was no other, the first one is well worth sending you alone. I think it is very lovely. To make up the deficit I am sending you a touching cutting that RO sent me from America: it's a picture with the caption 'WINS DIVORCE AND ALIMONY: Former Lilian Talbot told New York judge her musician husband, Felix Salmond [English cellist, dedicatee of Elgar's Cello Concerto], made hideous faces at her.' Have you ever seen Felix Salmond?

I envy you having heard 'Job' and 'the Fat Knight' [*Sir John in Love*]: what you say about the latter seems to fit in very well with what I have been thinking about comic operas of late. I brought 'Master Peter's Puppet Show' over with me to have a look at. It is, as you know, a delightful work, and you yourself told me that it comes off wonderfully. When you get to the bottom of it there are only about eight pages of music in the whole work − if there is as much as that − and yet as a work of art in the comic opera style it couldn't be bettered, as far as I can see. 'Gianni Schicchi'[6] is almost the same, the only difference being that it contains no music, and from what you say of 'The Fat Knight', it seems to be in the same boat too. Another example is 'The Barber of Seville'. Now, is all this to say that a comic opera should not be burdened with much music? It certainly does say that it needn't be, but should it actually be? Take 'The Boar's Head' [Holst]. It is more or less music from beginning to end, and looks as though it should be a splendid little work, and yet in performance it falls as flat as a pancake (so you and everyone else who has seen it tell me). Serious opera is, of course, another thing altogether. 'The Shepherds of the Delectable Mountains' [RVW] is music from beginning to end, and is also one of the most moving things that ever happened. Is it possible that on the whole music moves too slowly to be attached to the whole of a comedy? It can certainly be attached to parts − when the action begins to ease up and take breath, and by all means join those parts with notes, only do let them move along quickly. Do you think that is a possible solution of the comic opera difficulty? I am very sorry to let all this off on you, but I must say it to someone; if it is too much for you, place it gently on the fire!

I have just read a most interesting and provoking book. It has the fairly

---

[6] H.F. revised his opinion in later years.

comprehensive title of 'Art' and is by Clive Bell, who is a well known art-critic I believe. It might interest you. If you want to read it, it is one of the Phoenix Library and costs the large sum of 3/6. Much of it possessed some strange quality which simply made me laugh with rage: a great deal of it was very illuminating. I enjoyed reading it very much.

I have been delving into the Jarnach works that I have.[7] I am now used to his idiom, and can get at what is underneath better than before. I like the Sonatina a good deal better than the three pieces you lent me, but am not yet sure that I completely like it.

I'm very glad to hear you were staying in the country, it must have been very lovely in the fine weather. I'm learning to drive the car, heaven help me! I think that is all there is to tell you, for further scandal apply to . . . but then, I don't know him yet: perhaps some day I will be able to refer you to him!

Blessings on you, H.F.

Let's have a competition to see who can write the worst two-part invention away from the piano.

Hilles House, Stroud, Glos.; 22 April

Dear Fergie,

Thanks for the Hardy. As before, one is beautiful, the other less so. I *have* seen Felix Salmond, so fully understand. I'm keeping those gems from the New Yorker for consolation in moments of depression. For you must know I've had my marching orders. Tomorrow I return to 21 Caroline Street, and on Wednesday to King Edward VII Sanatorium, Midhurst, Sussex. Shakespeare's whining schoolboy, in his first term, never had a greater sinking-feeling in his vitals than I. But enough of that. I've just seen the Gloucester Festival list, and that Sumsion is conductor. Three cheers. Dame Ethel [Smyth] was here to lunch again the other day, and I must say I quite enjoyed her brilliant conversation. Of course she walked all over the place, hat on one side, coffee-cup in hand, singing (?) the 'Two Interlinked Folk-songs'. (You were quite right about the resemblance to 'Flos'.) If you interlink two English folksongs – 'The Outlandish Knight' and 'The Female Highwayman' you get a wonderful new name for Dame Ethel – 'The Female Knight'. All my own invention. When I put on the wireless to hear Walton's 'Sinfonia Concertante' (she had never heard of Walton!) The Female Knight said that all wireless sounded out of tune to her, but that we must be sure to listen-in to a concert of her own works on such and such a date! The Walton sounded less good on the wireless, but that was the fault of the wireless, I'm sure. The first movement is still a bit scrappy, but on the whole it's a fine work. I also heard Ireland's new piano Sonatina on the wireless, and liked bits of it.

Bloch's 'Israel Symphony' sounded a very fine work – not as a piece of

[7] Philipp Jarnach (1892–1982). French-born Catalan composer, pupil of Busoni.

composition, qua composition, but in a noble, impassioned and violent way. I shall really look forward to hearing it properly.

Do you know Holbein's portraits at Windsor? I've just been looking at some wonderful reproductions, and one day we must certainly call at Windsor when the King is out for a walk: they are in the Library there. Have you read André Maurois' 'Disraeli'? It's quite as good in its way as 'Ariel' though, of course, we can never love Dizzy as we love Shelley. It certainly shows how posterity lays the lion and the lamb together; that there is no ultimate truth about anything (except as we see it), and that everything we hate most in the world, even to baseness of motive, may triumph equally with what we admire more – and bring equally good results!

I've read the Clive Bell, and hope to take on your challenge (two-part invention), but it's difficult to say what I'll be allowed to do, so don't be surprised if I can only write half a dozen lines for a letter – (Probably you'll be very glad after all this rigmarole.) (I ought to explain that I'm writing in a crowded room, in between the intervals of painting three savage-looking red-indians, and being killed (and eaten) by them as a bear – thus any incoherencies.)

I think you're almost right about light opera. If you flirt with another art – the stage – it must be a compromise. Holst in 'The Boar's Head' certainly does not compromise, and makes a musical work only. Comedy moves quickly and the music moves as music i.e. only relatively quickly. In other words, Holst makes music win – at a loss. From the musical point of view this is quite right, as the art of a composer is to compose – and compose as finely as he can, but it's fatal from the operatic point of view. There is a lot more I want to say about it, now that you've started me, but I can't face the noise going on, or keep my thoughts collected.

What of the Carnegie list![8] They turned down my poor old Cinderella-of-a-Requiem a second time. I should really begin to think it a bad work and destroy it, if the recipients had not been Rootham and Stanley Wilson – neither of whom is worth tuppence. I've not heard the David Evans *Concerto*, but should say it's a good work. Bless you & forgive all this. G.F.

14 Deramore Park South, Belfast; 23 April

[Dear Finzi]

Another couple of poems, not so satisfying this time – at any rate, not to me. Another one should appear tomorrow, and if it does, I will enclose it in this letter, which will not reach you any the later for having been kept over. But I have a feeling you have gone to the Caliphate [the Sanatorium]. I hope you had

---

[8] Between 1916 and 1929 the Carnegie United Kingdom Trust published fifty-six new works by contemporary British composers (full scores and vocal scores) in handsome editions. The publications that irritated Finzi were *Brown Earth*, a choral work by Cyril B. Rootham (1875–1938), and the *Skye Symphony* by Stanley Wilson (1899–1953). The promising work was the Concerto for String Orchestra by David Moule-Evans (1905–1988).

a comfortable journey thither, and found everything in order on your arrival. If the food, drains, beds, concubines, hookahs or anything else are not as you wish, let me know, and I will have the Lord Chamberlain Extraordinary see to them at once. Speaking of writing away from the piano, I too have found that it is apt to sound a little different from what you expected! But that is, after all, as the poet has it – 'Honi soit qui Dieu et mon droit non exspectare in omnibus', but then, I needn't remind you of that, remembering the good old days of the Classical Tripos at the 'Varsity. And speaking of the 'Varsity, do you remember how our crew bumped Brasenose in the Tepids of '63? Ah! those were the days, my boy: men were men then, and not the idle skallywagging effeminate young whippersnappers in divided skirts that they are now. Ah no! it was a very different matter then. You remember that affair I had with that pretty younger Miss Custen – Alice was her name I believe; Gad, she was a charmer; that day we went on the river together in a punt – she knew how to lead me a pretty caper! And by Jove, we caped even faster than the tune she played. We could teach'em a thing or two today.

Speaking of capers, I see that Hearty Hamilton is going to conduct that naughty caper 'Heldenleben' at the next Phil. I also notice it is the last item on the programme. Good! I shan't have to miss anything else by leaving before its upward striding theme strides up. Had you the good fortune to hear Bloch's 'Israel Symphony'? I didn't even listen to it by wireless, though I would very much like to have. I have finally conquered the Jarnach *Sonatina*, but regret to say that I very much doubt whether it was worth all the energy I expended on it. The only sort of pleasure I seem to get out of it is the rather doubtful one of feeling 'What a good boy am I' to have got to the end of such a heavy pudding!

This letter is rather short; as you have perhaps noticed, I have not very much important news to communicate. Bless you and be good. H.F.

12 Clarendon Road, W.11; 26 April

[Dear Finzi]

'Home to our mountains' once more – that is to say, to the Heights of Clarendon, and to real work again. Actually, 'real work' will not start for a week, as only someone who hadn't tried it would suggest working in this house when the Bach Week [H.S. at Aeolian Hall 30 Apr.–5 May 1928] was on: however, we can't butter our jam on both sides, and I feel very sorry you are missing the May Week, as H.S. calls it. I see from your letter that I was almost right about your arrival at the Caliphate, only, like all true Prophets and Seers (whether of Caroline Street or Clarendon Road) I was a day or two out in my feelings. A-weel! and I can only hope that you aren't *too* uncomfortable in body and soul, and that things aren't as bad as that cheering prospectus you showed me.

I just arrived here yesterday, and today have been to see Pu in hospital, where she has been for a little over a week. Though we don't know definitely yet, it seems that her stomach has slipped a little to the left and downwards, de-arranging her digestive organs so that she is unable to digest food properly. I hope it is nothing more than this: I believe she will only have to wear some belt or other to keep her internal arrangements straight, and that will be as nothing. She asked after you.

Have I told you that we definitely have a cottage in Surrey [at Capel] for May, June and July? It is somewhere near Leith Hill, though exactly where I am not quite sure; I think we are going to move-in tomorrow week. When we get there I will let you have the address, though letters sent here will always reach us. You might let me know if there is any hope of visiting you, and if so, when and where, and then I might be able to let you know when it would suit me to go. Also have I told you that I cut some more bars out of the end of the *Sonatina* [for piano, later destroyed], making it less long-drawn-out than before? I think it is more satisfactory now. I have started a Fugue for piano: how far it will go I don't know. *And*, one of the truly great happenings of the world, I have learnt to drive a motor car while on holiday! I actually drove 50 miles the day before I left Ireland, and 30 miles the day before that – through towns, villages and cows: well, perhaps not *through* the latter, I hope not anyway.

I am very glad to hear from you about Sumsion; he should be a good person there [at Gloucester Cathedral], and a pleasant change from an older man. I am indeed sorry to hear about the Requiem – what bloody fools they are; if you ever again feel like tearing it up, refrain, for there is always a willing repository for it in the Dutch Hills [Clarendon Road].[9]

I certainly agree that the duty of a composer is to compose music as finely as he can, but a comic opera composer must keep his eye on the feelings of the audience and the speed of the plot, otherwise the opera will be comic in a sense not intended by the composer, and he will have wasted his time and energy in writing a work that is useless for the object for which it was written. (That sounds rather involved, but you know what I mean.)

The Female Knight is a truly great person: how well I know the way she stands, with cup in hand, haranguing the multitude. I do not know the Holbeins, but will hope to make their acquaintance at some favourable date in the future. Do read the Clive Bell book, it is most interesting. I will get hold of 'Disraeli'.

All best wishes, and be good! H.F.

The Caliphate, Pinnacle of the Golden Dome; 30 April

Dear Fergie,

It's difficult to know where to start! I can tell you details of the routine when we meet. I could not write before as I was in bed until Sunday and no writing (except a few pencilled notes) was allowed until the temperature was down, which meant a perfectly deadly doing nothing. Now the temp is down and I've begun the slowly graded exercises – starting with $\frac{1}{2}$ a mile morning and afternoon. What energy. On the credit side, the discipline is not so severe as it

---

[9] Clarendon Road is in Holland Park.

sounded in the book of rules: the building is fine of its sort, the birds, situation, grounds all lovely. The medical side too – dentistry excepted – they got a local dentist up from Midhurst, who did the most disgraceful piece of tooth extracting I've ever had, on the supposition of an abscess which wasn't there. He hurt like the devil and has left a bit of the root in. I hope I shan't have any bad after-effects! But no more local anaesthetics for me, other than temperature charts, sweepstakes or the like. I can see that a composer is a great rarity – (somehow it got about, though I don't know how) – and the padre on his rounds asked me if I knew Madame Guy D'Hardelot[10] (or however you spell the good lady's name). But there is a general feeling of good will and helpfulness, and, thank God, a certain amount of ragging, and I'm doing my best to become a temporary Bank clerk – (I only hope I shan't develop Cockney) – though I was afraid at first that I should never be able to speak a word to anyone.

No work, I'm afraid, is going to be possible, and I must just get into the lazy state of mind, so that I shall get better all the sooner. One begins to accept it, as old age is accepted by those who, in their prime, would swear to commit suicide first: I feel like Samson in bondage – it's all amusingly like school, except that boys are not friendly towards newcomers and here they are. Otherwise I'm stuck all around with the lack of difference between grown ups and children.

Visiting is allowed every Saturday and Sunday 2.0–6.0, only one must know a day or two beforehand if poss: I'm afraid the walks we hoped for would not be possible yet, but we could wander around the grounds, or sit in my room if raining; you can also have tea here, but if you don't want it, bring a couple of apples and we'll eat them in the woods. You would see no distressing sights – (such as there are they are all in bed) and I need hardly say that there is no danger! Your E.T. is welcome everywhere, but thrice thrice welcome here. If you do come, can you bring some interesting min. score or suchlike as I've no music here. Just a single work to keep me going till I see you again. Could we get a copy of the Schütz work we heard at Cooper's concert – I can't remember the name of the fellow who sang it [Keith Falkner], but you know him well.

I do hope Pu will be all right. I often think of her and of you in the midst of the 'Bach Week'. But forgive this scrawl; now that I'm allowed up, time for writing is strictly limited and I can only repeat in one letter what I've said in another. God bless you. G.F.

You'll find me horribly gross and fat. Give my love to Pu when you see her or write. Thanks for the Hardy – not so good this time. Can you bring the *Sonatina*? The gong is ringing for bed and I must fly.

---

[10] Guy d'Hardelot (Mrs Helen Rhodes, 1848–1936), French pianist, and composer of sentimental songs.

12 Clarendon Road, W.11; 6 May

[Dear Finzi],

Very glad to receive your letter and to hear all the 'crack'. I hope to goodness the rock of ages that the dentist left in your jaw won't get obstreperous – I don't think they very often do unless the tooth itself is decayed, which doesn't seem to be so in your case. The visiting hours are much more reasonable than I expected, and I will let you know when I'll be able to come down later, that is, when we get settled in Surrey. You don't say what the nearest station is, but you can tell me sometime else. The address of the ancestral country seat is: 2 Wigmore Cottages (some would call it 'Wigmore Hall'), Misbrooks Green, Capel, Surrey. I will certainly bring a miniature score when I come; what kind would you like, ancient or modern? Bach or Bartok? Hard or Bright?[11] All are at your service, and you shall have any you like. In the meantime, here are some very beautiful postcards[12] [comic cards], which I hope will pass away some of your time pleasantly. Also *one* Hardy poem – they get less and less and fewer as the weeks go on, though I think this one is better than the last two I sent you. There is one other enclosure. We take up residence tomorrow at the family residence (Wigmore hall). Pu is out of hospital, and I am very pleased to say she has nothing worse the matter with her than what I told you last week, so all she has to do is wear a belt. She sends you her love, and thanks for your enquiries. I'm in an awful hurry what with the moving and all, so forgive inconsistencies. The Bach Week went off splendidly, and the audiences seemed to enjoy it all. I asked Keith Falkner about the Schütz Sinfonia Sacra that he sang: alas, it is only published in the complete works of that gentleman, which I see from Grove are issued in 8 or 10 volumes. I shall make further enquiries. The Philharmonic was bloody. H.H. [Hamilton Harty] conducted the Schubert like a pig, and like a fool I stayed to hear 'Heldenleben', as I thought it would be interesting to hear it again: I left in the middle. The Berlioz was the only half-light (and a rather grubby one at that) on a very murky programme. Do read Clive Bell's 'Art'. The Fugue promises to turn into the last movement of the *Sonatina*: wot a lark.

Have just been down to see the ancestral seat for the first time. It is semidetached, but astonishingly private and delightful, and not nearly so bad as it sounds. It is very quiet otherwise. I wonder what the other inhabitants will think of two pianos??! I'll continue this some other time as it is late, and all the packing has to be done tomorrow morning.

Bless you, and be good. H.F.

---

[11] 'Vif et gai', a performing direction typical of French composers of the time.
[12] Saucy, seaside postcards by Donald McGill (1875–1962).

The Caliphate [; May 1928]

Dear Fergie,

Of course I know the quotation now! Standing alone it lost all its majesty, but as Parry was a harmonic thinker, this can be forgiven. Did you send it as a tribute or an admonition?! The nearest stations are Midhurst 4 miles and Haslemere 7 miles. Although we are such neighbours, both stations look very difficult to get at from Capel. A bicycle might help you out in some way. I know Capel. (Gross and Fleshy Benjamin[13] had a house at Beare Green, by the way). Any miniature score you think fit. (Parry's 'Job' too, if you like!)

I may go and see your friend Mr [Warwick] James about my teeth when I get out, if I can manage it. I'm delighted to hear about Pu, and hope she will be down with you in Capel.

See how fine my constitution is, for the med. superintendent, who found TB of some years standing on my first examination in London, can now find very little the matter at all, and told me I *might* be out in 2 months. (But no swimming or running for two years.) It is interesting to find that most of the cases one finds here are not the puny types of fictional TB, but athletic people who have done too much, or even energetic people.

The country is wonderful here and I'll never say another word against Sussex. Would that there was a single intellect here, but it's all Bank and Insurance clerks, etc. Two of your countrymen, Patrick Brennen and Michael Mulherne – a railway clerk and jockey respectively – are worth most of the rest put together, as they are so funny and 'Irish'. Bless you, G.F.

Thanks for the Gill (sic) cards. I love them very much. The Hardy is not so bad.

Capel, Surrey; 13 May

[Dear Finzi]

You will see from the above that the Wigmore Cottages part of the address can be left out; this saves quite a lot of ink and time. I don't think you can have a very good railway Guide at the Caliphate, for I can get to Midhurst from here with only one change, and what's more, there's quite a good service of trains! This, by going from Ockley or Holmwood (which are both quite near us) and changing at Pulborough. However, I have a deep-laid plan. Will it be all right if I come down for the weekend of June 2nd and 3rd? (I would have arranged sooner, but things here won't fit, so I couldn't.) If so, I intend to cycle from here to Midhurst on the Saturday morning, stay Saturday and perhaps Sunday nights, and cycle back on Monday morning. Would that be all right? There aren't any inns or cottages near the Caliphate that I could stay in, are there? If not, I could stay in Midhurst, and either cycle or bus up from there. I will

---

[13] Arthur Benjamin (1893–1969), Australian-born composer and pianist. A fluent, engaging (if rather lightweight) composer. An excellent cook and *bon viveur*, he became somewhat portly. Best known for his *Jamaican Rumba*.

certainly bring the family orange in my pocket, and we will suck it for tea. I enclose a Hardy poem, which I'm afraid will be the last, as newspapers seem rather difficult to get hold of here. I like it better than most that have appeared lately. Also, a beautiful notice that I received from Ba-ba[14]. It's a gem. I am sending some music under separate cover [H.F.'s manuscript of Schütz's 'Fili mi, Absolom'] I am making a piano arrangement of it and am going to try and get it published. It is far too good to remain in the obscurity of a museum.

I'm awfully glad to hear you are getting on so well. I hope to goodness you will only be there for 2 months; if you are, do come here for a weekend, a week or whatever you like; it is very pleasant; and peaceful withal, though semi-detached. I had already realized that parts of Sussex were very lovely: I have walked in the country around Storrington and Amberley, and on the Downs.

Going back a little: from the point of view of her music, I think I would call the lady Guy d'Harlot.[15] I have just finished 'Disraeli'. It is a fascinating book. Good and bad are truly man-made inventions: there is no such thing as good or bad. They are both words, and words seem to have a strange quality of taking on whatever meaning their creator wishes. I may call you a bloody fool, but I certainly do not mean that same thing as when I called Poulenc a bloody fool. When people dub a man great, they forget that he may be the very opposite of this in some things.

Bless you. H.F.

The Caliphate, Pinnacle of the Golden Dome; 14 May

Dear Fergie,

If you let me know at once, and for certain, wet or fine (for one has to book ahead) I could most probably get you a room at 'the cottage' which is in the grounds and exists for the purpose of putting up friends and relatives. June 2nd and 3rd would be splendid: I could walk 3 miles morning and afternoon and the rest of the time (12–1 and 6–7 excepted) we could spend in talking and fighting. You know what the people here are like, so that if other people's friends and relatives are also putting up, do not expect paragons of intellect! A postcard to let me know will do. The Blisses are coming next Saturday, which will also be very pleasant. I heard a terrible transmission on the wireless of 'Oedipus Rex' [Stravinsky], but thought some of it very fine. Thanks for the Hardy poem, which I like. I'm afraid it has been a bit of a bother to you and if so, please forgive me. Beatrice Harrison as a circus manager must be very entertaining. What a gang. No need to bring the family orange as I'm now getting extra fruit on my own. The 'music under separate cover' has not yet come, so I will wait until 4 o'clock before posting this. Yrs, G.F.

[14] Beatrice Harrison (1893–1965), English cellist, sister of the violinist May Harrison (1891–1959).
[15] See G.F.'s letter of 30 April 1928.

Do you know Harold Scott (of Harold Scott and Elsa Lanchester fame)? His brother, also an actor (musical comedy) is here – the only person who isn't a half-wit.

P.S. The music hasn't come, so I'll post this.

Capel, Surrey; 15 May

[Dear Finzi]

I meant to imply definitely in my letter that I was coming June 2nd and 3rd, wet or fine, hail or snow, rain or blow; so please do book me a room in 'the cottage' right now (as our American friends say). Bless you. H.F.

The Caliphate, Pinnacle of the Golden Dome; 18 May

Dear Fergie,

I have got you a room where I think you will find everything all right – Mrs Gausden, Sanatorium Drive: she has a dear little boy of about 2 years old called Peter. If you can, get there for lunch, and then come on to the Caliphate at 2.0. Pray for fine weather.

Now about Schütz: it was a complete surprise as I thought 'music under separate cover' would be a joke – something 'vif et gai'. I'm really most grateful. I think there can be no doubt about the change of tempo: besides I think I remember it as minim equals semibreve; but this may be only my imagination. Probably you would find the explanation in RO [*Contrapuntal Technique in the 16th Century*] section 'time and proportion'. I suppose the quaver Sinfonia is the key to the tempo (unless an entirely new tempo is adopted there) – and I hope and pray that it was never played in the tempo of the opening Sinfonia – however fine a feeling of agitation it produced. If you publish it, you'll find a piano duet version quite unnecessary. I'm doing a rough piano version for my own use (and yours if you can use it) and halving the time and the bars, i.e. 3/1 becomes 3/2. (I think that is adopted in the miniature score of Palestrina's 'Missa P[apa Marcelli]'), and at the change of tempo I'm leaving it as written. One or two other points which you needn't bother to answer, as long as you can remember them when you are here.

1. I'm doubtful about the last chord in bar 16, particularly as there is no 7th in the continuo part.

2. B.31. Can it be possible? I hope so! I forget whether they used to allow a diminished 5th to follow a perfect 5th, or a perfect 5th to follow a diminished 5th. In the former case a natural would put it right.

3. B.41. Why tenor clef for the first half-dozen notes, and is it really a unison passage or a passage in 3rds. Which brings one to

4. Is the organ continuo part sufficient as a bass by itself? In performance did they double the first few bars with the Bass trombone?

5. B.49. E. flat or natural in trombone II and continuo?

6. B.51. As you say, E flat in II.

7. B.56. F sharp in continuo?

8. What does a vertical line in a bar mean? Is it a comma? Bar 8, for example.

9. The figured-bass doesn't seem all there; a good many accidentals to 3rds are left out, or else I don't understand it, which is more probable. For instance, the continuo player (if he were a gentleman) in b.49 would play the 3rd and 6th: thus the marking should be 6/3 and the 3rd flattened?

10. Did they play detached as written, or sostenuto (as far as trombones can play sostenuto)?

11. B.60. The unison passage is undoubtedly wrong. How else account for the semibreve with a sharp underneath?

12. B.61. Either B, as you suggest, or D.

13. Bless you, G.F.

Capel, Surrey; 19 May

[Dear Finzi]

Good for Mrs Gausden. Tell her I will be there for lunch Saturday, and if not I'll pay for it. I'll be at the Caliphate at 2.

Have you ever read Rabelais? Urquart's translation is glorious; it might cheer you up. Also it might not, but I think it would. Many thanks for your interesting letter re the Schütz. I was speaking to Emily Daymond about it on Wednesday, when I found that she too had made an arrangement for Keith Falkner. However, she had not thought of publishing hers, so we are going to talk it over next Wednesday. By the way, are they meat-eaters at the Caliphate, or do they allow you to 'vegetate'? If they don't, I have written a beautiful rhyme about you: Said young Finzi in horror, 'How now? I'm growing as broad as a sow: And not only that, But I'm doing it on fat and on lean of the mortified cow'. (Mortified: French, mort = dead). Now, to try and dispose of your questions.

Curiously enough, I have halved the time, but not the bars of the first section too, and left the section after the change of time as in the original. At first I thought that the quaver of the Sinfonia equalled that of the preceding section, but now I'm inclined to think it is a new tempo altogether, a little quicker than the preceding. I have corrected my score at the B.M., and now it is absolutely right.[16] [A lot of emendations follow.] H.F.

Capel, Surrey; 27 May

[Dear Finzi]

I see next Saturday is Ember Day: please have all your embers burnt or cleared away before I arrive. And remember them not – oh horrible! By the way, what are Embers? The real fact of the matter is that I have nothing very

[16] The manuscript of Schütz's *Fili mi, Absolom*, checked at the British Library collection.

much to tell you this week. One thing I have never had the courage to speak about: However, as you aren't present now I will tell you of it, and so prepare myself for next week! About six months ago, someone who should have known better (in fact, I am to become a moth – hush, silence) asked me if I would write a school song for my preparatory school in Ireland. I, who should have known better, said I would do my best. Almost immediately after that I got an idea for it, but after some time rejected it as being too like a certain English composer dead about 10 years [Parry], so I left it for some time, and tried again, only to find that the only thing I could think of was my blasted original idea. Well that was that, so I left it again. Comparatively recently I returned to the attack, and found to my surprise that my first idea was still the only thing I could think of. It began to look omnibus, [sic] so I thought I would try developing, changing and pruning it and see what would happen then. I have done this, and to my amazement have turned out something that I like: in fact, the blooming thing is finished! I will bring it on Saturday, when you can tear it limb from limb. All hymn-tunes have names, and as school songs are more or less in the nature of hymn-tunes, I am going to call mine 'The New Jerusalem'.

We are having wonderful weather now, and the walks are glorious. We now grow strawberries and raspberries!

For a long time I have been horrified to think that I had lost the pleasure in the anticipation of things: thank God this is not so. Blessings on you. H.F.

2 Park Crescent, Portland Place, W.1 [house of Warwick James, friend and dentist of H.S. and H.F. Undated.]

[Dear Finzi]

I am in rather a hurry, so will write you later on. I will be back in Capel on Wednesday, but till then will be running about more or less.

I heard the 4th Mahler Symphony at College on Friday: most interesting. It is very long indeed, but seems to have great beauty, of the kind of 'The Songs of a Wayfaring Man'. It has a strange simplicity and very great sincerity.

Bless you. H.F.

Capel, Surrey; 14 June

[Dear Finzi]

So sorry for the delay this week: as I said in my note to you, things have been rather hurried. I got home from Midhurst without mishap and with only a few drops of rain to help me on my way. I bade farewell to Mrs Gausden at about 8 a.m. and arrived here at 11. She was very reasonable, and only charged me £1 for the whole business, meals and all, so I'm not broke! Since then quite a lot has happened, but nothing of great import.

On Tuesday I heard my Cello Trio [2 Irish Folktunes arr. for three Cellos; Wigmore Hall 5 June 1928; since destroyed]. It was the most bloody performance that ever happened (you will say the most bloody but one!). But bless their poor hearts, it was too difficult for them to play, so they can't be blamed. It sounded like a herd of cows in pain. That evening I cheered myself by hearing that opera 'about a Tea Cosy' [*Cosi fan tutti*]. It was delightful. The one blot being, as it was the last time I heard it, that Steuart Wilson[17] *would* sing out of tune. After College the next day I went home to collect some music, and found a parcel from the O.U.P. awaiting me, containing the Irish Cello Tunes [5 Irish Folktunes, arr. for Cello and Piano]. In fact they're out: at long last, and after waiting over a year! Jimmy [Ivor James] was playing at the Oriana Concert at the Aeolian Hall on Monday evening, and did three of them. He said it would be their christening [No! He did all five at Wigmore Hall on 25 Oct. 1927]; I suggested that perhaps the lavatory would be a more suitable place in which to perform the ceremony.

V.W. showed me the new 'Boris' [O.U.P. edition]: as far as I can see it is more or less the same as the Chester one. Mrs V.W. went to 'Cosi' on the Saturday I was with you. On Saturday I went to Cheyne Walk to see if ROM and Mrs were back [from America]. Sure enough they were, having arrived at 1 o'clock the night before. Very pleased to get back, naturally, and he says he is going to get Bliss to drive him down to see you. They are afraid 'Enery [the cat] has become kitchin-ified in their absence, but hope to gently return his ways towards the drawing room. Who do you think gave me a lesson yesterday? ROM, as V.W. had to go away examining somewhere. He had only time to look at the *Sonatina*, liked the 1st movement, but not so much the 3rd. [Vaughan Williams took H.F. for composition at the R.C.M. while R.O. was in America.]

Do you remember that sort of Courante I began for 4 hands about 3 months ago? I have suddenly finished it, and like it. Neither ROM or V.W. have seen it, Gawd 'elp me, but I do like it.

Heard 'Shepherds' [V.W.] yesterday. 'Shepherds' wonderful; but they applauded and raised the curtain after it, which was bloody. I think it should be done without scenery, and by people looking like those [Eric] Gill bas-reliefs [in Westminster Cathedral] – remote and somewhat cold. The de Falla [*Master Peter's Puppet Show*] was rather a disappointment and didn't come off as well as I thought it would. Perhaps I had thought too much about it, and got too fixed a preconceived idea about how it should be done. The Schubert ['The Forgotten Sentry', D.190] was charming, but nothing more. Good performances, though the puppets themselves were disappointing. Herewith shirt-buttons ferreted out for you by Pu. Bless you. H.F.

---

[17] (Sir) Steuart Wilson (1889–1966), English tenor and administrator. Became the Arts Council's first Music Director, and in 1948 Director of Music for the B.B.C. Principal of the Birmingham School of Music (1957–1960).

The Caliphate, Pinnacle of the Golden Dome; 15 June

Dear Fergie,

Firstly, all honour and glory to Pu: thank her very much. I'm glad Mrs Gausden was all right and reasonable; perhaps you'll see her again on the 31st. My sympathy over the Cello Trio, but (as you say) the bloodiest of all performances is copyright: there was only one such, and never will be again, world without end, a-men.

Yes, I had a characteristic letter from Mrs RO. She and RO are motoring down with the Blisses tomorrow (Saturday) and you can imagine I'm looking forward to it. Mrs RO wrote that 'Henery' was delighted to have them back again, but of course didn't show it!

Yes. I remember that 'sort of a courante', but only saw the first half-dozen bars. Good. Right about the curtain and 'The Shepherds'. I don't object to the idea of the scenery, so long as there is no attempt at Realism. When I saw it at Bristol,[18] they had a mild suggestive and symbolic setting that was quite all right. But no doubt a plain backcloth would be just as satisfactory. After seeing the de Falla two or three times, I think it is spoilt by one thing, and that's the very thing that's intended to be the climax — Don Q's final soliloquy. The climax is really the destruction of the puppets and the attempted noble ending is an anti-climax. As to the score and the music, qua music, I think it's a perfect delight, and nearly approaches what I'm always wanting — except for that most detestable and bloody habit of repeating nearly every bar and every phrase. It isn't even varied in the scoring. But what scoring! It makes me really jealous.

It was interesting to hear about the Mahler. I wish I could hear some of his big stuff or see some of the scores. Hearsay holds him in contempt, but I never feel like that as I know he went through Hell in his lifetime, and I've a sympathy for the metaphysicians — although I know how absurd it is, and know that all thoughts have been thought (the rest is splitting of hairs) and that the minds' range is as a stone tied to a string and whirled round — now this side, now that side, but never beyond a limited radius unless it flies off altogether and becomes a Will Blake. So the best thing, in theory, is to get back to musical patterns and designs which *appear* to have (but probably have not) more variety than when guided by external ideas. But as for practice — that's best explained by Drummond in 'I know that all beneath the moon decays'.[19]

Oh how I wish I could get away from this Caliphate where the gates are locked at six o'clock and one can never be quiet or alone. And I'm librarian now! G.F.

---

[18] *The Shepherds of the Delectable Mountains* had been performed by a semi-amateur group run by the composer Philip Napier Miles (1865–1935) at the Victoria Rooms, Bristol, in 1924. Manuel de Falla's *Master Peter's Puppet Show* received its first public staged performance during the same week (13–18 October), together with Napier Miles' one-act operas, *Markheim* and *Fire Flies*, and Purcell's *Dido and Aeneas*.

[19] William Drummond of Hawthornden (1553–1649), Scottish poet. The reference is to Sonnet II: *Poems*, Edinburgh 1616.

Capel, Surrey; 17 June

[Dear Finzi]

Many thanks for the letter. I hope you have sewn the buttons on the right side of the cuff, and not where the buttonholes ought to be. Please ask Mrs Gausden if she can put me up on the 30th and 31st, as I want to come down then – that is, assuming you are still there. I leave it to your discretion as to when you ask her. I'm so glad ROM went down to see you this weekend. I'm inclined to agree with you about the de Falla, except that I can't think much of the music is good apart from its dramatic significance. Frankly, it didn't come off when I saw it – so it seemed to me – but I can well imagine how delightful it would be if performed impeccably and with perfect timing between the puppets and the music. I am wondering whether it is intending to be anything more than a rather precious but amusing entertainment. Personally, I think the score is fascinating, but it doesn't seem to give very much more than that.

We must certainly hear some Mahler if we get the opportunity. I don't know if I remarked on it before, but the Symphony I heard was very like 'The Songs of a Wayfaring Man' extended to great length. I should like to know more of him.

If we say that all thoughts have been thought we say that all music and all poetry has been written, and we shall cease to think or try to write music or poetry. Thank God we are incapable of this. Cheer up, old lump, it is bloody, but things are only aggravated by worrying over them. With the blessings of His Excellency, H.F.

Capel, Surrey; 24 June

[Dear Finzi]

I have to shoot up to Scotland tonight somewhat suddenly [to play at a private house], and will not be back until Wednesday. I shall keep my letter over till then, when I shall be able to tell you all about it. It's probably going to be rather a lark. H.F.

[G.F. left the Sanatorium at the beginning of July.]

Capel, Surrey; 5 July

[Dear Finzi]

I couldn't get the Mahler 4th. Expecting the three of you for lunch at one o'clock on Saturday. We are going to see 'The Fat Knight'[20] on Sunday morning probably. I got to Pulborough 40 minutes before the train left last Sunday, even though it was about twice as far as I had thought! I ate my ham sandwiches with the greatest relish. See you Saturday. H.F.

---

[20] Vaughan Williams' opera *Sir John in Love*.

Capel, Surrey; 13 July

[Dear Finzi]

If this gets to you in time, it is to wish you many happy returns and what-not [for birthday]. I can see you looking like this [sketch of miserable face] at the thought of it.

I'm going over to see ROM [on holiday at nearby Holmbury St Mary] this afternoon. William-George [our cat] is taking me, though I don't know if he'll come.

I went to hear 'Les Noces' [Stravinsky] on Wednesday night. All I can say of it is that it was the one thing on the programme that seemed to have anything to it, though what that 'anything' is I wasn't able to find out. A second hearing might clear it up — preferably without the attendant dancing.

I am rewriting the Mass. Someone has expressed a mild interest in it, and even if it doesn't get as far as a performance [it didn't], I will at least have the comfortable feeling that I have made it singable (which it is not at present). I believe I like the work as a whole now. Practically none of the music is being altered.

I find that our Scotch motor tour will begin about 1st Sept., thus walking before that would be out of the question, what with Haslemere [Festival]. That leaves us with 15–23 Sept as the only possible time. How about it? If you think it's too late, say so, and we will leave it for the present. Personally, I want to do it. No other time is possible for the present. So far, every paragraph in this letter has commenced with a capital I. Let's have a change.

Be good (if possible), and blessings on you. H.F.

Hundon, near Clare, Suffolk; 14 July

Dear Fergie,

I had a busy two or three days in London after Capel, and before settling down to what hope will be a busy time here, there are just a few things I want to tell you.

See Stravinsky's 'Noces' if you get the chance; I liked it — not as European art, but rather in the same way as we should like some curious oriental or asiatic music. 'Barabou' and 'Ode' were utter muck. The performances of all were bad and the Stravinsky shocking. A tribute to the work that one could tell when the pianos were out! It sounds very much better than one would imagine from a paper performance.

'Cosi fan Tutti' was as charming as ever: fairly empty house, and I thought you were quite wrong about Steuart Wilson's singing. I found nothing out of tune.

Rubbra has now abandoned stockings or socks, so it is sandals and five toes; — But he has written a magnificent Fugue for Piano — (in 6/8 or 9/8, like the one you are doing). As you value your life write and ask him to show it you, or, better still, get him to play it, as it is very difficult. I'm not suggesting that you couldn't play it, but you would get a much better idea from his playing of it. It's one of the best 'running fugues' I've ever seen. The Prelude is not so good; I think he'll scrap it and do another.

I had tea with the Blisses on Tuesday. They were in good form. Arthur is now on the Philharmonic committee and livening things up considerably – though the programmes will still be dull as they were chosen by the outgoing committee. He is also going to teach one day a week at the Academy.

The Howells' came along Monday evening – which was very nice of them and should show you that H.H. really has modesty in him. Alas, I played him a Hardy song and he said 'A lovely poem', which of course is quite right! Anyhow, I'll forgive him. Your Gordon Craig ['The Art of the Theatre'] is still at 21 Caroline Street. I'll finish it when I get back. Thank you all for my weekend at Capel. It was splendid. G.F.

Hundon, near Clare, Suffolk; 14 July

[Dear Fergie]
1) Many thanks
2) Mass: do you still feel adamant about that dominant 7th [of which G.F. disapproved]?
3) I can't say about the 15th–23 September, though I should also like to do it. Let's leave it open and fix it up early in September. Give me a Poste Restante in Scotland. [G.F.]

14 Deramore Park South, Belfast; 30 July

[Dear Dave. Ever since Sanatorium days I called G.F. 'Dave'; partly because of his constant struggle there with his Piano Concerto, which reminded me of David and Goliath, and partly because of his former nickname, David Livingstone.]

Herewith your 'piece'. From what I can see, I far prefer it as it is written. To put it into B flat would make it sound too like a continuation of the preceding movement; which would hardly be appropriate, as they are so vastly different in character. The end of the slow movement looks most beautiful, though of course one can't say from such a small bit.

I'm afraid the walk's hit on the head, as I have received a notice from College this morning to say that next term begins a week earlier than previously arranged. This is a blasted nuisance. You see, if I came to England any earlier than that (15 September), it would completely muck up the Scotch business [a motor-trip with my Mother and Father]. Another time, I hope. I hope it hasn't made a mess of your arrangements.

I'm trying to orchestrate that 'Andantino varié' of Schubert's (D.823 for Piano Duet) that you and I played with such expression when in Surrey. As I know nothing whatever about orchestration, the result should be rather odd; still, it is good practice! I'm also trying to write some easy Variations for Piano, and a song for bass and (probably) orchestra ['A Lyke-Wake Dirge', Op.1].

Well, that's that, and it is about all there is to tell you. I drove the car 60 miles yesterday, and through town today. Oo-er!

H.S. has decided to remain in London; nevertheless we are going to move to a somewhat healthier part of it: St John's Wood or 'Amstead, probably. I am sorry about the walk. Give your Mother and Dave [G.F.] my best wishes and love. H.F.

14 Deramore Park South, Belfast; 17 August

[Dear Dave]

Many thanks for postcard received some time ago. There has been nothing very much happening of late, and so, nothing to write about. We leave for Scotland on Monday week, but letters sent here will be forwarded. Handel's Organ Concerto No.1 from Paris by wireless was very fine indeed: did you hear it? How's Dave [Piano Concerto]?

My childish Variations [since destroyed] (8 of 'em) are finished, and I have but to write a Grand Finale to match your Grand Fantasia! Bless you. H.F.

Invergarry (for the night); 30 September

[Dear Dave]

Have you ever considered Hardy's 'Three Strangers', the first of the 'Wessex Tales', as an opera plot? Of course you would have to write it yourself, or get someone else to write it, but it seems possible. The only part that seems doubtful is the end.

Hope you're well. We flourish (as the bay tree), and enjoy moving about sipping the froth off the scenery. It's a pleasant change. Yours H.F.

21 Caroline Street, S.W.1; 3 September

Dear Fergie,

I don't know whether this will reach you in the wilds of Scotland, but thanks for the card. Yes, I have thought of 'The Three Strangers', but (as usual) the trouble is with the librettist who won't materialise. That's why I shall have to fall back on a ready-made libretto by means of adapting a play − I'm not capable of writing my own libretto. V.W. likes the Robert Bridges better than the 'Merry Devil' but of course I've decided on nothing yet.

I had a fine weekend with the ROs. He likes my new Morceau de Salon [Fantasia of Piano Concerto], but says it can't be in a Piano Concerto, but must be the Fantasia for a Fugue. Have also done a couple of songs, but nothing more. Kodaly's suite from 'Hary Janos' (I don't know where the accents fall) is a first-rate piece of work. Benjy's [Arthur Benjamin] *Concerto* was quite a good shape, effective and slick, but as usual he has nothing to learn as he has nothing to say. Lambert's 'Pomona' is a hundred-fold improvement on his 'Romeo &

Juliet'.[21] Drinkwater's 'Bird in Hand' is a delightful comedy and now I'm off to see the Ur exhibition at the BM. Yours G.F.

12 Clarendon Road, W.11; 18 September

[Dear Dave]

Edith [his housekeeper] tells me you get home tomorrow. Will it be all right if I come round for few minutes early Thursday morning? I will be away from that afternoon until (probably) Tuesday, and it will be the best time for me. Saw ROM today: he's flourishing. Bless you. H.F.

12 Clarendon Road, W.11; 25 September

We, Howard Molyneux Ferguson, having heard the New Amphion Speaker Chassis (price £6) are of the opinion that it is probably the best loudspeaker we have heard; and are also of the opinion that it would be a better thing to buy than Burndept's Magnavox. Wind and harp come out with particular fidelity on the new instrument.

Signed by the grace of God and the good King. Ferguson of Clarendon.

12 Clarendon Road, W.11; 27 September

[Dear Dave]

I remember what I wanted to ask you: is 'An Experiment with Time' [by J.W. Dunne] worth looking for? and if so, what is its proper name. A postcard will do. H.F.

12 Clarendon Road, W.11; 9 October

[Dear Dave]

Back again. If you have time, ring up tomorrow before 10 (or at lunch time) that we may arrange something. How about something on Saturday and a walk on the Sawbath? I was sorry to have to put you off last weekend, but it could na be helpt. Have written a new 'stirring toon', i.e. a school song! Why does one ever say one will do these things? (Or ring up before dinner) H.F.

21 Caroline Street, S.W.1; 20 October

Dear Mister Ferguson,

I'm just off to Hundon [his Mother's house in Suffolk] for the weekend. Here are two tickets for the German singers on Wednesday afternoon. I shall be going to the St Martins lunch-hour show [25 Oct. 1928], but find I can't

---

[21] Ballets by Constant Lambert (1905–1951). *Romeo and Juliet* was first performed in 1926, *Pomona* in the following year.

manage this one; so would you do your best to use the spare ticket. I'm sorry when foreigners can teach us anything, but they certainly can.

With regard to the other enclosure, it's now or never. [This refers to a spoof chamber work we thought of submitting to the International Society of Contemporary Music.] What about a seven or eight part chamber work? 'Tis only a matter of deciding what to use and fixing up an equal length of bars. And we need not use only contemporary works: a little Bach upsidedown would not be amiss.

The Ravel Concert went very well – except for the repetition of complete works, like the Harp 7tet – which made it terribly long. I still find the latest works, like the fiddle sonata and the 'Chansons Madécasses' a bit bloodless and dull (No. 2 of the Chansons excepted). But I won't back my opinion against Ravel, who knows perfectly well what he is about and is a brave little composer, courageous and looking forward, and in his way as many-sided as V.W. – only with the Devil's technique. The first movement of the fiddle sonata he took much faster than I've heard it. The 'Blues' [2nd movement] were terribly sad – not at all gay as the newspaper suggests. I think we shall find the explanation is 'Dance Little Lady' in 'This Year of Grace'.[22] Bless you. G.F.

Scandal-monger Bryan [Gordon Bryan, pianist] announced in his Eunuchy voice that an exact repetition of this concert (with Ravel) would be given in January (16th I think). So you may be able to hear for yourself.

12 Clarendon Road, W.11; 26 October

[Dear Dave]

So sorry I haven't been able to go to either yesterday or this evening's concerts: yesterday I wanted to do some copying, and tonight I thought I had better stay in, as I had rather a strenuous time coming over, and want to be as 'peaceful' as possible now. Am in the middle of a Gesange [see below] (very 'ernst' but not 'vier':[23] I don't think it will be finished for some time. How about foregathering on either Monday or Tuesday for some music? I'm so fond of music: I don't know why. H.F.

[12 Clarendon Road, W.11]; 30 October

[Dear Dave]

You're right. I have to play in Sutton on Thursday night. On the contrary, I was *not* a fool! I would rather feel well and not hear the concert than hear it and be ill!! Sometime next week, but not this Saturday or Sunday. Am now O.K. H.F.

---

[22] Noel Coward's 1928 Revue, featuring Jessie Matthews and Sonnie Hale.
[23] Brahms' *Vier Ernste Gesänge*, Op. 121, 1896.

12 Clarendon Road, W.11; 1 November

[Dear Dave]

Splendid. I am very keen to hear the Ravel, and Gieseking is a fine musician as well as being a fine pianist who doesn't play too fast. Will you feed here first? Nor Wednesday nor Thursday any good, but we will arrange when we meet on Monday. Am playing in Sutton tonight, so won't hear 'Falstaff' [Elgar]. Blast. I have the new Bartok Piano Sonata. H.F. Can you ring up any time tomorrow?

[12 Clarendon Road, W.11]; 3 November

[Dear Dave]

H.S. is going to the B.B.C. thing on Monday evening and wants us to have something to eat with him first. Therefore do meet us at Oxford Circus tube (in the street) at 6.15. He knows you are veg. so do come. H.F.

I'll bring the Ravel.

[12 Clarendon Road, W.11]; 22 November

[Dear Dave]

It's quite all right about tonight – I think you were very wise not to come up: travelling is such a bore, and takes up so much time. I don't think I can manage the 3rd, but let me know if and when you are coming to town – some time ahead, if possible. The Dirge [H.F.'s 'A Lyke Wake Dirge', Op.1, No.2] is finished. Schubert Mass at Phil very dull. 'Don Q' [Strauss] bloody. H.F.

12 Clarendon Road, W.11; 30 November

[Dear Dave]

How about a Swoiry Musicale on Saturday (tomorrow), or if you can't do that any time on Sunday but the evening. If I don't hear from you, may I come Saturday about teatime? Greetings, dark sir. H.F.

Hundon, Clare, Suffolk; December [before Christmas]

Dear Fergie,

Nostalgia trembles before
Mr Constant Lambert.
Gerald Finzi Pinxit.

This isn't a very cheerful Christmas present! [The proofs of G.F.'s 'New Year Music'.] All I hope is that you won't bother about it if there is any work of your own that you want to do. Like Pharaoh, you must occasionally 'arden your 'art. But if you do it (or if you don't) please could I have my 3 sheets back by the first week in January. The last day for sending-in is the 7th. Whether they do the silly piece or not, I shall be glad to have it finished. Any remarks you care to make will be gratefully received. The scoring of the first bit seems a bit thick, but [Gordon] Jacob swore it would be all right. Do you think so? I wonder does one put all the stage directions into the parts? I can't imagine a Double Bassoon playing low D *fff* Appassionata. In this Piano Duet version, I'm not putting in the scoring.

I hope Mr Samuel was duly impressed by the portrait [of Constant Lambert].[24] If the outlandish city of Belfast, Ireland, has a bookshop, try and get Minor Elizabethan Drama (ii), pre-Shakespearean Comedies. I think 'Ralph Roister Doister' has possibilities of a libretto. By much condensation I've got a good First Act. The difficulty would be in the Second Act, of which

[24] A cartoon that G.F. had drawn.

the battle would be the culmination. How one would end after that, the other Ralph only knows.[25]

Rubbra has written a great big Triple Fugue for orchestra [the only full-score was left in a taxi by Sargent, and never recovered]: full of fine things.

About Lion [a kitten]. I don't want to appear like the house-agent with the inevitable client after the same property, but my old nurse has asked for a kitten for her sister. So I told her that I would ask you (not that she knows, ignorant woman, who you are). So could you let me know? But I am anxious that any kitten you have should come from 21 [Caroline Street]. It would cement the two nations, like a royal marriage. I can't swear that Lion would be another William-George, but Edith thinks he is the best kitten we have had so far. And now a happy Christmas, and all good luck in 1929. Plenty of work, a good performance [of 'A Lyke Wake Dirge'] at Birmingham, and everything else you want. Bless you. G.F.

Also, one doesn't give approx. metronome marks in the parts – except perhaps at the beginning?

12 Clarendon Road, W.11; 23 December

[Dear Dave]

Herewith a little Christmas present [H.F.'s piano duet arrangement of G.F.'s 'New Year Music'] – but don't let your hopes arise: it isn't anything unexpected. It will probably be late for Christmas, so you can consider it a New Year's present – and a Christmas one too, says my early Scotch self – beside, it will be so appropriate to the New Year. Anyway, it is a present, and you can take it for whatever you like. I hope it is all right, and that I haven't left any notes out: you had better go over it to make certain, as I am by no means sure that everything is there. Forgive pencil; I didn't think it was worth doing it out in ink, as I knew you would have to copy it again in any case. There seem to be quite a few instruments playing away at the beginning, but if Jacob says it's O.K., I expect it will be. I have marked what appear to be two misprints in the margins. About the stage directions in the various parts, I don't know myself. I think the best thing to do would compare any score with a bassoon or horn part, and see what's left out and what in. I've bought Mr Roister Doister, but have not yet read him.

About Lion. I think it would be best for us not to have him, as we will be changing house so often in the near future, and will be, for some time at least, without a home of any sort (August and September), that it would be very awkward for any cat – and for us too. I consulted Pu, and we came to this conclusion, reluctantly, Mr Finzi, in view of your kind offer; but no doubt, should the occasion arise in the future, you and Rufty[26] will rise to the occasion

---

[25] *Ralph Roister Doister* (1553) by Nicholas Udall (1505–1558) is the earliest extant English comedy. The 'other Ralph' is Ralph Vaughan Williams.
[26] The 'mother' cat.

– you by repeating your kind offer, and Rufty in her usual careless way. Every best wish for the New Year, and be good. Mit mein Zalutasons, et tous mes compliments. H.F.

I'm going to send the song ['A Lyke Wake Dirge', Op.1, No.2] into the Patron's Fund, as Adrian Boult is going to America and I don't want it done by the deputy. He may do it in October, but I'll try the Patron's Fund anyway.

Metronome marks: only at the beginning of parts, I think. Now you know where I learnt my piano playing.

Hundon, Clare, Suffolk; 28 December

Dear Fergie,

That was somewhat quick work and skilfully done, too: and gratefully received. The two misprints *were* misprints, and though there are one or two things left out (apart from the Harp gliss.) I think they are probably omissions deliberate: all except one point, where I have great hopes you were caught napping! However, we can try it over when we foregather or when they return the score, as I'm sure they will. I'm most obliged to you, and am so glad there was no question of interfering with your work. I've not been able to do any, though I've been trying to. So it's been neither rest nor work.

> There once was a city called Belfast
> Which succeeded in holding Hell fast.
> > God from the skies
> > Looked down in surprise
> At the tents of the Devil so well cast.

A halfpenny if you can improve it. I went up to London for the Bach Choir Concert. After our disappointment with the Kodaly ['Psalmus Hungaricus'] from the Piano version, I'm glad to say that it again sounded noble. Going through the score and the Piano version together, I see there is little connection between the two. I suppose it was originally an orchestral conception. Boult conducted splendidly and Falkner sang the 82nd Cantata as it deserved.[27] Was there ever a longer aria than the 2nd? In one mood throughout and perfectly justified. The whole concert was too long and the Bach Magnificat didn't begin till about 10.20.

You sent your love to Dave, but he's asleep. V.W. by the way seemed to dislike the Fantasia. All right about Lion, as long as I know. If you ever do have another cat, have it from our nursery.

About Roister Doister: it's rather difficult at first, or even second reading, to see it as a libretto; but if you have it well in your head, it will all be clearer when you come to my cut version of Act I (p. 4–p. 5). Individual lines are cut out all

[27] *Ich habe genug* by J.S. Bach, 1727. (Sir) Keith Falkner, baritone. Director of the Royal College of Music (1960–1974).

over the place; 5-ft lines reduced to 4-ft wherever convenient, as well as all pp. 11, 12 & 20 and part of 13. Act 2 would start at present Act 3 and the fight would be the climax. What then? The letter-scene would have to be cut, I'm afraid. And is it all worth while?

A happy New Year, also from my Mother. Bless you. G.F.

14 Deramore Park South, Belfast; 30 December

[Dear Dave]

The first thing I have to tell you is, buy Mary Webb's 'Poems', and read them and 'The Spring of Joy' at the end of the book. Many of the poems are very beautiful, and I feel sure you will love 'The Spring of Joy'. The only thing I have read of hers is 'Precious Bane', which I thought fine, but now I feel I must read some of the others too. What a strange thing it is that our having a complete edition of Mary Webb's works is due to one of them having been mentioned by a Prime Minister in a speech.[28]

The other thing I wanted to speak about was Delius' 'Sea Drift'. I have been browsing on your piano score of it. It seems to me that only parts of it are great. This was rather a disappointment, as I had expected it to be on the top level the whole way through; but now that I have got over the first 'let down', I bask in the exquisite beauty of the really fine parts. I have heard people say that it is his finest work; if that is so, I don't think it says too much for him, for somehow one feels that a man's greatest work should show a more consistent level of beauty than this one does. I admit that it contains moments of very great beauty indeed, but also others which seem to be by no means up to this standard. Perhaps it is that Delius cannot sustain himself the whole way through a long work. For me, 'The Cuckoo' is still his finest work. (By 'beauty' in the above I mean, not moments of beauty – there are plenty of those – but consistency of inspiration, lack of 'padding'.)

My admiration of the Bartok Piano Sonata grows the more I know it. I cannot yet say whether my admiration extends to love or no: probably I will be able to tell when I hear someone else play it. I certainly feel he has a fine mind.

I will be in London again on Monday, tomorrow week. There is a very interesting B.B.C. Symphony Concert on Jan 18th. Will you be going? Best wishes for the New Year. H.F.

---

[28] Mary Webb (1881–1927), novelist and poet. Her bodice-bursting novels of pastoral life were wickedly parodied in Stella Gibbons's *Cold Comfort Farm*, 1932.

1929

Hundon, Clare, Suffolk; 2 January

Dear Fergie,

As you will be in London on the 7th, perhaps you will be able to use this ticket. If not, I don't want it back: you could leave after the Schönberg. 'Sea Drift' sounded beautiful in performance, but I don't for a moment think it's the best Delius. Apart from 'The Cuckoo' there is the 'Song of the High Hills', as well as at least two orchestral works — 'Brigg Fair' and 'In a Summer Garden' — which I love better and are consistently beautiful. Mrs RO showed me Mary Webb's poems. She, like you, very enthusiastic about them — but I only just glanced over them and so probably got quite a wrong idea when I thought them a bit wishy-washy. I shall certainly get them.

I hope to go to Gloucester for a few days, but expect to get back to London fairly soon, as I must get my mouth X-rayed. Certainly I shall be back in time for the B.B.C. Concert, and if you get a ticket you might get one for me at the same time (a 3/— upstairs). G.F.

12 Clarendon Road, W.11; 11 January

[Dear Dave]

Herewith ticket for Friday. Do let me know when you'll be up, and we will arrange a 'soirée musicale'. The B.N.O.C. [British National Opera Co.] will be at Golder's Green from the 28th January, when I expect they will do 'Falstaff' [Verdi]. I will get notices and tell you all about it, and we can arrange when you want to go. I can't go to the Phil, alas. I'm sorry for V.W. that he doesn't like the Grand Fantasia. H.F.

I can now get through the Bartok with some right notes.

12 Clarendon Road, W.11; 14 January

[Dear Dave]

May I come to tea on Friday before the B.B.C. Concert? I shall come straight on from College and will be with you around 4.30. Love to go to the C.M.C. [Contemporary Music Centre]. You come here for dinner first — about 6 or so. (That's Wednesday.) Salaams. H.F.

Second thoughts: it would be much simpler if you came here on Friday at 4.15, and stayed on to dinner. Why not then come and see 'The Mock Emperor'? [Pirandello's 'Enrico Quarto', with Ernest Milton, for which H.F. was playing in the theatre band.][1]

---

[1] The Queen's Theatre.

12 Clarendon Road, W.11; 4 February

[Dear Dave]

Three of the Mahler 'Kindertotenlieder' at the Patrons' Fund on Friday morning. I will go. May I come and see you after my lesson on Friday (about 4.30), and stay for dinner, please, if it isn't putting you out, only I'll have to dress at No. 21. Salaams. H.F.

14 Deramore Park South, Belfast; 21 April

My dear Dr Livingstone,

I have been meaning to write to you for some time but have been delayed in doing so by the thought that I might have been able to make some suggestions about 'Roister Doister' if I waited a little and thought about it. Alas and alack this delay has been pointless, for I haven't had one sensible idea about the whole thing. Having read, marked, learned and inwardly digested it I have come to the conclusion that it might make a very good opera libretto. BUT it seems to me it will want complete rearrangement, with additions and subtractions (lots of both). I shall be very interested to see what you have done with it in the way of arrangement, but until I do see that I can only suggest what I myself feel about it. The main thing is that I think the central idea of it is excellent: that is Roister Doister in love with Custance (mostly for her money), and Merygreeke and she in a plot to make a fool of him. I imagined it in 2 Acts (Act 1 to the end of Act 3 in the play; Act 2, from the beginning of Act 4 to the end, but not by any means in the same order as in the play); and so far as I can see it wouldn't need any change of scene. The one thing that troubles me is whether there is enough in the play to fill 2 Acts of an opera? Naturally if you set it as it stands there'd be more than enough, but as I said, I think the arrangement of it is all wrong from a libretto point of view. It has just struck me, would it be possible to introduce a secondary (and successful) love affair between one of Custance's young ladies and one of Roister's young men? This means a certain amount of rewriting, but I don't see how that can possibly be avoided whether you put it in or no. Another trouble is Goodluck: can one bring him in at the end of the opera as is done in the play? I believe it would be quite possible to leave him out altogether; but if you did not want to do this, I feel very strongly that the unnecessary complication of Custance's supposed infidelity to him should be left out. Such a diversion is all very well in the play, where it can be got over with the requisite speed, but with music attached it would drag and unwind itself with intolerable slowness. The same applies to the episode with the Scrivener. As a coda I will say that unless you are ready to rewrite the play you shouldn't embark on setting it. If you are willing to do this, I think it has the bones of an excellent libretto, though you'd have to put the flesh on them! One good point is that I believe the 'battle', which is the climax of the work, would be ten times more successful in an opera than in the play.

Having tried some constructive rearrangement myself, I can say that by far the most difficult problem is to make the various episodes develop the plot cumulatively, and to make them run one into the other naturally. By the first, I mean amongst other things, the avoidance of such scenes as one gets in the 'Ring', when one character on the stage laboriously explains to another some situation about which the audience already knows all there is to know. But it is a difficult business, and the more I think on it the less likely do plays seem without alteration to make good opera librettos: the two things are so totally different. For example, explanations are all right in a play, but usually tiresome in an opera; in a play you daren't hold up everything to recite a piece of poetry, but in an opera you can sing a song. And so on. But to stop talking about Opera! I heard 'Israel' [Bloch] over the wireless and found a completely unlooked-for resemblance to Delius in it – so much emotion and so little construction (at least, so it seemed on first hearing). 'Tapiola' [Sibelius] was a great and pleasant surprise. I've been having a good rest, and have done more or less nothing, which is a great relief after moving [to East Heath Road]. By the way, I return to Engelond on Thursday, and the address of the country seat is The Rew Cottage, Abinger Common, Surrey [where H.S. and H.F. stayed May–July]. Hope you're well and behaving nicely, and give my love to the ROMs if you see them. My blessings on you, honoured sir, from yours truly, H.F. Stanley (Esq).[2]

Hundon, Clare, Suffolk; 23 and 24 April

Dear Fergie,

I think you've hit on the same points in Roister Doister as I did. In my version the first two Acts become the 1st Act. The delightful (but unsuitable) letter scene is removed – as well as a great deal else. I haven't done more than my 1st Act for the very same reason that worried you – what to do with Gawyn Goodluck. I didn't think rewriting would be so necessary as cutting and stitching together. However, the best thing would be to show you my copy when we next meet and you can see what you think of it.

I expect to come up to London any day after the 8th or 9th and start my grand walking tour about a week later. I want to be at Bampton on Whit Monday [to see the Morris Dance], but I might pass through Surrey and hand you Roister Doister on the way. Thanks awfully for having read through it and thought about it. I went up to hear 'Israel' [Bloch] and liked it. There was a definite shape about it, even if of a rhapsodic kind. What I disliked was that once he came to a climax he never seemed to come off! And it was so Biblical (in the Old Testament sense) that I can't see where Delius comes in. I agree about 'Tapiola'. RO doesn't. You're right about RO's Toccata. It's fine now. We played it through when I was up. Haydn's Piano Sonata No.3 in E flat is delightful. So is the slow movement of Mozart's Piano Concerto in A. It's in F sharp minor I think, a 6/8

---

[2] Finzi and Ferguson often addressed each other as Dr David Livingstone and Henry M. Stanley, explorers, as it were, in music's jungle.

movement. Among the books you left at 21 Caroline Street I've only managed to get through one (so far): the Blake Pencil Drawings [ed. Geoffrey Keynes, Nonesuch Press 1927]. A ravishing book. I've started the Engraved Designs [ed. Binyon] but don't like the medium so much. Edith knows where the books are put away, if you should want them at any time. And now for the shock. 'Falstaff' [Verdi]. It was deadly. Apart from 'Sir, your servant', a little song about 'when I was young' and the final Fugue, there was not a note worth hearing twice. I went full of enthusiasm after what we had been through on the piano and I rather expected it would show up the faults of 'The Fat Knight' [V.W.], but it was quite the other way round. Verdi only got the better in one way: the libretto was much more lucid than V.W.: two people made into one and general contractions of that sort (so that the pinnacles were more and the details less) were a great advantage. Also, Verdi gives some sort of reason for Falstaff's happy ending, and V.W. only makes him become benign for no reason at all. In V.W.'s favour was Shakespeare's English instead of the rubbish Verdi had to set and the still greater rubbish of the translation we had to listen to. The B.N.O.C. [British National Opera Company] did it finely and if you don't believe what I say, you had better go and see it. Probably you'll do what RO did and leave in the middle. I know this opinion is heretical, as I could see by the pained face of Lloyd Powell and others when I expressed it.

But I hope your face won't be pained when you read this, but that you will remain calm and placid. Yours, Livingstone (Dr).

The Rew Cottage, Abinger Common, Surrey; 5 May
Belieber Herr Livingstone,

Many thanks for your letter. I was indeed surprised to hear about 'Falstaff', but you never can tell. Also, please excuse this paper I'm using.

Strange and happy to relate I will be in London Town next week from Wednesday–Saturday (8th–11th); cannot we meet? Not on Wednesday, but Thursday or Friday perhaps. I'm staying with Mrs O'Sullivan, 7 Lansdowne Road, W.11. I'm at College 3–4 on Friday but otherwise O.K., except perhaps I had better not be out in the evening. Might I come Thursday afternoon early, or would that be upsetting your plans? We could play pretty music. Comment vous portez-vous? Je vais très bien, et ma mère a trois petits chats. Où est le parapluie du jardinier, parce qu'il fait mauvais temps, n'est-ce pas? I'm going to the Bach Choir Concert at College on Wednesday week (15th), and then on to Scotland by the midnight train to play at Newton Stewart for Keith [Falkner]. Are you going? Have you heard anything from the Patrons' Fund? I have had the honour of having 'A Lyke Wake Dirge' [Op.1, No.2] returned to me: 'Not with a definite refusal', but returned all the same. So nice to know it wasn't definitely returned. It's lovely down here: you must come down sometime. Let me know about next week. Stanley (Herr Docktor).

Harold Brook Choir do Bliss's new thing next Wednesday evening, but I can't go.[3]

Dunster, a.m.; 1 June.

Private

Dear Fergie,

Read and inwardly digest. Incidentally, keep till my return (in about 10 days' time). It seems that I'm blocked whichever way I turn. Of course, if the Ox. [O.U.P.] had a high standard of publication I should not mind so much, but as it seems they will publish anything – even Jacob's Piano Concerto or the completest rubbish under the sun – except what I send them, I do almost think there must be some reason outside purely musical ones. However, we'll talk about it when I get back from this most wonderful holiday. Give my love to Pu. Do you know this part of Somerset and Devon? G.F.

[Langham Hotel]; 10 June

Dear Dave (Short for David Livingstone, Lord Burlington),

Welcome back to this charming town of London. You say you're arriving on Tuesday; that being so, might I descend on you for Friday night? If your Mother or anyone else is staying or it is otherwise inconvenient, say so and I will find another pillow for my head that night. Mother and Father, with whom I am staying until then, will probably leave on Friday evening about 7.30, so if you could have me I'd come on to Caroline St. when I had seen them off, having already had my dinner! Let me know to this address, then we can arrange the affairs of the world and talk over all sorts of things.

Yours sedately, H.F.

Rew Cottage, Abinger Common, Surrey; 15 June

Dear Dave,

All tickets for the opera at College next Wednesday and Thursday have gone, so we'll have to make our own music. Will see you at about 4.30 on Thursday, when I shall also expound some suggestions about Ralph Roister Doister. H.F.

Hundon, Clare, Suffolk; 23 July

[Dear Trumpfoot]

I handed on Sir Howard's letter to the master who seemed pleased with it, and no doubt will tell me to reply in a day or two. Now I'm just writing friendly-like, as secretary-gardener to secretary-chauffeur. I don't think Mr Livingstone

---

[3] Pastoral: *Lie Strewn the White Flocks* (chorus, mezzo, flute, timpani and strings: 1928). Harold Brooke was one of the directors of Novello & Company – Bliss's publisher.

really wanted the enclosures, as he usually only keeps such correspondence until the incident it is concerned with is closed. Also, I saw him put 'the foot-sufferer's friend' [silly advertisement] into the waste-paper basket: so I took it out when he wasn't looking, as I think it makes a nice picture.

What fine news about 8 East Heath Road. I begin to regret more and more the house in Well Walk! As soon as you get in the new house you will start and finish all in a week or two movements II & III [of H.F.'s 'Short Symphony']. I heard Ashley Duke's 'The Dumb Wife of Cheapside' (written for the wireless) – it's a version of 'The Man who married a Dumb Wife' – I really think this is what I want.[4] I shall listen-in to it again this evening. Yours truly. G.F.

The Rew; 26 July

Dear Dave,

When I was last in London I left my copy of Blake's 'Heaven and Hell' in the right-hand bottom cupboard in your spare-room, together with your other Blakes. I wrote my initials on my one in case of muddle. I hope this is O.K. 8 East Heath Road seems to be all right. Blessings on you. H.F.

Slieve Donard Hotel, Newcastle, Co. Down: 2 August

Dear Dave,

I shall be at this address until 22nd August.

Thanks so much for letting me know Sir D. Livingstone's attitude in the matter: my mind is now at rest. I, like you, am at the moment writing as under-second-gardener to third-chauffeur's mudguard-wiper. So here goes.

I am overjoyed to hear about 'The Dumb Wife of Cheapside': do let me know when you decide anything further about it and what about it, and what it is, and anything and everything. I know nothing of it, and have not even seen a copy of it. I suppose if you thought of doing it, you'd have to get Ashley Duke's permission; and it is just possible that, as it was written for broadcasting, the rights of it may belong to the B.B.C., in which case you would, I suppose, have to get their permission. But one could always find out all this from A.D. himself. I am still hopefully searching the horizon for one [a libretto], and as far from finding it as when I last saw you. One lives in hope!

I am writing on the sand-hills, and though the sun is not exactly cracking the leaves, I have found a nice sheltered spot and am pleasantly warm. When I have finished writing I have Marcel Proust's 'Swan's Way' to fall back on: from what I have seen of it, it is quite a strong enough couch to hold me. Judging by the English translation I think it is perhaps as well I didn't try to read it in French.

You remember our talk at Hundon about mental 'stays'? I don't know

---

[4] Ashley Dukes (1885–1959), theatre manager, critic and dramatist, best known for *The Man with a Load of Mischief* (1924). Founded the Mercury Theatre (1933) as a base for his wife, the dancer and choreographer (Dame) Marie Rambert (1888–1982).

whether it was the 'arguing' that addled my brain or not, but certainly I can now see plainly which I could wear if I wanted. Blessings on you me boy, and be good. H.F.

21 Caroline Street, S.W.1; 12 August

[Dear Fergie]

I'm up for a long weekend and found the really lovely bottle [G.F. had a collection of pretty bottles], which is king of all, both in shape and colour. Mrs RO came round to see it. And how wonderful Schubert's Piano Trio in E-flat, Op.100, is. I've wrapped your Blake up in paper with the other books you've left – other cupboard, top section.

I've just come back from Noel Coward's 'Bitter-sweet'. Really I don't know whether his tongue is in his cheek or hanging out. It's the music that 'everyone does', only perhaps a little more derivative. Yet how I wish I could do these ordinary things that everyone else seems to be able to do. Dave doing handsomely. G.F.

'The Dumb Wife of Cheapside' is admirable. But alas it does not seem to be published.

Hundon, Clare, Suffolk; between 2 & 15 August

Dear Fergie,

There's no more to tell you about 'The Dumb Wife of Cheapside' beyond that it's a version of 'The Man who married a Dumb Wife'. Meanwhile, I've been trying to find someone who knows Ashley Duke, on account of my poor credentials, and I've just heard from Mrs Bliss that she knows Mrs Ashley Duke – a teacher of ballet-dancing under the name of Madame Rambert (so it looks). When she is back in London I must try and fix up something.

I've never read a word of Proust but from hearsay (and its equivalent see-write) I'm wondering if you will be obstinate enough to finish it to the bitter end.

Are you going to join me in the Delius Festival in October? I'll face 5 out of the 6 days, but can't swear to 'The Mass of Life' again. Did you see that they are going to do 2 scenes from 'Fennimore' What a wonderful season it's going to be, what with the Proms, B.B.C. Symphony Concerts, Courtauld-Sargent ditto, Delius Festival, Philharmonic, Beecham's opera, Stuart's opera, and thousands of smaller concerts.[5] I heard a *Sonata* for Cello & Piano by Debussy – very noticeable for not possessing a single idea. But how are those pizzicato notes in the middle movement done: between middle-C and the B-flat above. They sounded the nearest approach to Segovia and his guitar I've heard. If you

---

[5] In December 1928 Robert Stuart announced the formation of The London Opera Company and a forthcoming season of operas by Monteverdi, Purcell, John Blow, Handel, Gluck, Mozart, and Weber. Stuart figured as one of the producers.

remember, when you next see your friend Jimmy [Ivor James] or Mrs James I wish you'd ask, as they are sure to know the work.

Joyful news about the Sinfonietta [H.F.'s 'A Short Symphony']. I get back to London permanently on 21 August. Yours, G.F.

I've ordered all the Field Concertos, except one which is unobtainable.[6]

Hundon, Clare, Suffolk; [15 August]

[Dear Fergie]

There are two vergers at Eton, and as one of them annoyed us so much you will be rejoiced to hear that they are known by the names of Holy Poker and Holy Tongs; also that three of the Tenors are known as Thunder-guts, Bogus-bass, and Chins. Talk about universality in the particular; these are immortal names.

Yrs, G.F.

[Windsor Park, Belfast; September]

Dear Dave,

It seems a long time since I have 'taken pen to you'; indeed have I written at all this holidays apart from a spasmodic postcard or two? I don't believe I have: shame on me! Though I must confess there have not been many things to tell you about. The one thing that leaps to my mind is that my Trio [with Eda Kersey and Helen Just] has an engagement to broadcast from London on 2 October in the afternoon. I'm very pleased about this, as it is our first thing, and should be quite a good kick-off. I think we are going to play the Mozart E major and the Brahms C minor. You can turn off for the Mozart and listen for the Brahms, or you can turn off for both of them. Am I not kind-hearted? As we had to call ourselves something, and all the names I wanted were already taken, I had to fall back on the one thing I could think of – The Ensemble Players. Is it very dreadful or only moderately so?

I have been 'Proming' once a week by wireless. The first week was unlucky being that somewhat dreadful Mozart-Haydn night, which, though it may have been entertaining to look at, was certainly not entertaining to listen to. One of the items was the Sinfonia Concertante of Haydn for violin, cello, oboe and bassoon, and if you can think of anything more unpleasant than the noise those four instruments make when playing together I can't. I wonder why he did it? The one really lovely thing on the programme – the Mozart A major Piano Concerto – sounded perfectly horrible. This may mean that had I heard the Haydn in the flesh I might have liked it more; I couldn't have liked it less. Next week's programme is the British one (Rule Britannia!), with Arthur Bliss's Two-Piano Concerto. I'm glad for this, but the rest of the programme might

[6] John Field (1782–1847), Irish pianist and composer whose music greatly influenced Chopin.

have been more exciting – Hamilton Harty, John Ireland, Frank Bridge – ugh! I suppose you are going to all of these in person: lucky thing!

I'm looking forward to getting back to London, as I can't work here with any comfort: playing is not so bad in an irregular way, but for writing it is almost hopeless. As I think I told you, 8 East Heath Road is now definitely ours. However it isn't so simple as it looks, as it certainly won't be ready to move into on 14 September, which is when I shall probably arrive in London. I haven't decided what I shall do, but I must do something as we shall have to rehearse the Trio a good deal before 2 October.

How's Dave getting on?[7] I have removed six bars from the 1st movement of the [Short Symphony], but can claim no more in the constructive line, even if you allow that removing six bars may sometimes be constructive. You have, I suppose, no more news of the 'Dumb Wife'; it would be fun if you could get it for a libretto. You remember the 'Dramatic Crook Opera' that we discussed when I was at Hundon?[8] It may possibly come off, though it is impossible to say whether it will or not. Do you remember me speaking of the delightful Miller family of Campden, Glos? They were over here for a holiday in Donegal, and on their way back to England the boy stayed with us for a week. I don't know whether I ever told you that he was by way of writing poetry (whether seriously or not, I think he is too young to tell). In any case he said he would like to try his hand at it, so he is doing so, and from the first short instalment he has sent, I would say doing it admirably. The idea is a short thing with only four characters, but very boisterous – in fact 'An Uproar'! I hope it will come off. Don't tell ROM about it, as supposing it did work out, I'd rather like to burst it on him! Blessings on you, Dave, and be good. H.F.

[Windsor Park, Belfast; September]; 6 September

[Dear Dave]

Glad to hear from you. Many thanks for inviting me while the house is getting ready, but as it will probably be a month, I'm not going to inflict myself upon you! Even so, yours was a kindly thought. I shall arrive in London Town on (I think) 14 Sept, so will be just in time to hear Walton's 'Sinfonia Concertante' that night. Have sent for a 3/– Gallery seat: will you be there? Though Bliss's Two-Piano Concerto came through rather noisily last night, I'd very much like to hear it again. See you Saturday week, I hope. H.F.

21 Caroline Street, S.W.1 (really in Battersea Gardens); September [undated]

Dear Fergie,

Of course I'm delighted about your broadcasting, though I think you might have done a bit better over the title, since every chamber music party consists

---

[7] Finzi's Piano Concerto, the cause of his 'David and Goliath' struggles.

[8] An opera plot invented by H.F. The thought of writing an opera was very much 'in the air' at this period.

(theoretically at least) of ensemble players. However, titles don't much matter and 'The Razor Blades' or 'Cobbett's Glory' would do just as well.[9] You can also get tips from seed, bulb and flower catalogues.

I've done much Proming: Arne's little Piano Concerto was well worth reviving: it can hold its head up in good company. I thought your friend Angus Morrison played it to perfection, though I don't think I'd like to hear him in more lurid music. Lambert's work ['The Rio Grande'] was a brilliant affair and 'all London was there'; not, I think, a lasting work. Personally I liked the 2nd half with its lovely clashes better than the quiet and rather dull introduction. A good conductor, by the way. But the Warlock made a pitiful exhibition of himself.[10] He was rather drunk and completely unable to give a beat of any sort. The baton just trembled and shook! I liked the work.

In a way it's mad to be in London during the wonderful weather, but I couldn't go on any longer [he found his Mother very trying] in Suffolk, as I think you can understand., Let me know then if you want to be put up here whilst moving into No.8.

David (Piano Concerto) is checked I'm afraid, though I really think the last movement is in the jigsaw state, that is, with a little thinking all the odd bits may fall into place. 'The Dumb Wife' seems to have been just published. Reading it, it seems unsatisfactory for setting. O miserable come-down. But I'll see what you think when you get back. Not that I dislike it at all, but the prose seems so unrhythmic (as I suppose Prose really should be), that it would be impossible to set the wife's incessant gabble unless some rhythmic scheme could be devised – preferably dactylic.

I'll not say a word to anyone about your crook affair. I imagined the Millers were quite young – about 30 – with a family of infants! I had no idea there was a grown up boy. Good luck with it. Yours, G.F.

33 Holland Villas Road [the house of our friends, the Craies]; 20 Sept.
Dear Dave,

Herewith Prom. ticket. Alas I will not be there. I have one for Wednesday and Thursday nights, but didn't know whether you wanted one. If you do, the best way to get them is to send a stamped addressed envelope. Do you want one for Wed. and Thurs. week? Brahms and British. I'm going. I may appear rather earlier on Monday than I said. May I come in? You can go on working if you want to. H.F.

[9] A reference to Walter Cobbett (1847–1937) and his efforts on behalf of Chamber Music. In 1905 he established a prize for a 'Phantasy' string quartet, as a modern analogue for the Elizabethan 'Fancie'. His *Cyclopaedia of Chamber Music* was published in two volumes in 1929.
[10] Warlock conducted his *Capriol Suite* as part of the concert (29 August) that included Constant Lambert's *The Rio Grande* (premiered by the B.B.C., 27 February).

33 Holland Villas Road, W.11; 23 September

[Dear Dave]

The Elgar is most lovely [miniature score of 'Falstaff']. Thanks very much indeed for it. The trouble is it's so resplendently bound that I'll have to have all the rest of my music done to match. Will you pay? May I come to dinner before Delius tomorrow – between 6 and 6.30. Only ring up if impossible. [H.F.]

8 East Heath Road, N.W.3; 28 September

[Dear Dave]

I forgot to tell you that the B.B.C. Concert on Monday is impossible for me: I've promised to play for Solde [Isolde Menges], so that's that. Symond's puppets were amazing. Yrs, Howard Molyneux Ferguson. [Typewritten by H.F.]

> Said that funny young fellah G. Finzi,
> (Sometimes called for short Frinzi or Quinsy)
>   'Gastronomical feats
>   Such as eating of meats
> Make my stomach go all of a spin-zy.'

[Handwritten by G.F.]

> That funny young man called Fergie –
> Scorner of Schönberg and Berg, he
>   Swore that his line
>   Was Hubi-Newcome divine
> And with rhythms of that lady did erg* he.

*erg: the unit of work done in moving a body through one centimetre of space against the resistance of one dyne (Cassell's 'New English Dictionary').

1930

Hundon, Clare, Suffolk; 7 January

Dear Fergie,

I expect you will be back soon from The Emerald Isle. Probably the Italian Exhibition has already done the job. I'll be back on the 14th for The Royal Crematorium [teaching at the R.A.M.], when I shall have to instruct Molly Selby, Audrey Thomas, E. Talbot, Joan McTurk, Leila Goulden, G. Robbins and Mary Donnington in the theory of music, harmony, the first species and such things, about which I know nothing and care less. What a lot of tarradiddle and bunkum it all is.

On the 20th the B.B.C. have a 'try-over' 10-1. – a sort of Patrons Fund minus the audience, with a view to finding new works. They are doing my 'New Year

Music'. Looking over the score again I find it to be a dreadful work, but I shall go through with it, if only to hear my trombones. They write that I shall be 'admitted if I care to come'. If you are not playing in Timbuctoo on the 20th would you make an attempt to join me there? I don't know whether they will admit you. You could say that you were my uncle or son. Curwens won't do those songs, though they write a very fulsome letter and Jacobson told (Herbert) Lambert that some of them were 'absolute masterpieces'.[1] Of what use to me: I can't put it on my visiting-cards. Of course there were criticisms but I gather it is really a financial question. So we must go on, and go on, and go on writing 'absolute masterpieces'! However, the world is not too bad when you consider that I met yesterday, for the 2nd time in my life, a woman who said 'I like nature very much.' Ever, G.F.

8 East Heath Road, N.W.3; 13 January

Dear Dave,
You were right about the Italian pictures. I arrived here at 8 on Friday morning and was down at Burlington House by 10! Strange to say, they are quite as wonderful as the papers say.

Can you come here tomorrow (Tuesday) or Wednesday evening for food: any time after 6. Give me a ring during the day if you are home.

Adrian Boult and Keith Falkner are doing my old Dirge ['A Lyke Wake Dirge', Op.1, No.2] at Birmingham on 26 June. I'm delighted, as I want to hear what it sounds like. So glad the B.B.C. are doing the 'New Year Music'. In haste, Horatio Nelson.

8 East Heath Road, N.W.3; 20 March

[Dear Dave]
The Bliss on Tuesday was very beautiful, as was the rest of the concert apart from the Szymanovsky Fiddle Concerto. My movements are uncertain as Mother and Father are coming to London sometime next week. In haste. H.F.

8 East Heath Road, N.W.3; 4 May

Dear Dave,
Thanks so much for the B.B.C. ticket: I shall probably go, if only to hear the Hindemith ['Das Unaufhörliche']. Enclosed is your page of MS: I have done

[1] Herbert Lambert (1881–1936), photographer and maker of harpsichords and clavichords, based in Bath. His researches were crucial in the successful revival of early keyboard instruments and greatly influenced the work of Thomas Goff (1898–1975). His collection of seventeen composer portraits, *Modern British Composers* (F. & B. Goodwin, 1923) is outstanding. His name is charmingly perpetuated in Herbert Howells' book of short keyboard pieces, *Lambert's Clavichord* (1928).

the best I can with it under the circumstances, but this doesn't amount to much.

Am in the hell of a rush: I have to learn five large new works (including 'Nights in the Gardens of Spain') [De Falla] by the end of this month, and I don't know how I am going to do it: quite a lot of other things as well. I think the B.B.C. in Belfast is going to do the Fugue [last movement of 'A Short Symphony'] (which is now scored) on the 31st of this month: it will most likely be dreadful, but I shall hear more or less how it sounds. Clavichord [made by Morley, a 21st birthday present from my Mother & Father] has arrived, and is lovely. See you soon. H.

8 East Heath Road, N.W.3; 14 May

[Dear Dave]

Is Friday lunch possible? That is, may I come? In haste, H.F.

8 East Heath Road, N.W.3; 13 June

Dear Dave,

I was with Helen yesterday, and she told me that all but about half a dozen of the tickets for Tuesday [Helen Just's recital at Leighton House, 17 June] had gone. I thought I had better get one for you while the going was good, so here it is. I think it is quite a nice programme and you can always leave before the Popper, even though it is great fun. See you soon. H.F.

8 East Heath Road, N.W.3; 18 July

Dear Dave,

This is a solemn and serious letter, so please give it due meditation, consideration and thought.

My mind is at the moment running on OPERA, and as I feel that something must be done about it I have been looking round for librettos. The only two things I have seen which appeal to me at all are 'Gammer Gurton's Needle' and 'Ralph Roister Doister'.[2] Now this last is, by all the rules of whatever you like, your property, as you first showed it me, and I most probably would never have known of it but for you. Therefore, if you still have *any* idea of setting it, that's that, and I shall bother no more about it. I can always fall back on 'Gammer Gurton's Needle' (even though it doesn't sound a very comfortable couch.) However, if you are not thinking of doing it ['Roister Doister'], I believe I might be able to make something of it: and so feel it is a pity to miss the chance, if you are not going to use it. Please be

---

[2] *Gammer Gurton's Needle*. With the exception of Nicholas Udall's *Ralph Roister Doister* (see letter December 1928), the earliest surviving British comedy. Performed Cambridge, 1552, probably by William Stevenson.

absolutely sincere about this, and I implore you, don't tell me you are not going to do it if you have any feeling you might. You know me well enough to be able to say exactly what you feel, and it would be a poor compliment to me if you did not do so. Yours, H.F.

I am expecting you on Tuesday evening for dinner: H.S. will be here, so bring [your] Concerto.

Lambourn, Berks.; 8 September

Dear Dave,

Here I am until the 16th. I have been here a week, and it is a delightful place: splendid walks on the Downs, and everything else.

Are you in England, or have you slipped off the 'Grande Corniche'? I hoped to receive a postcard from you of Vesuvius in eruption, but evidently Vesuvius didn't erupt. Where are you? When did you get there? And what did you do?

I will be at the Sibelius Concerto on Tuesday 16th, and the night after, and the night after that. Will you be there?

Have finished the 'Roister Doister' libretto: it is a funny mess! I have got it into one long Act, but as this is the 3rd time I've 'finished' it, it may not be the end yet. I very much want to show it to you to see whether you recognise it or not. If you are home, a postcard to Hampstead will get me, or when I arrive. Just going to have supper so au revoir, a reverdice, nicht rauchen, etc. Yours, H.

[8 East Heath Road], Hampstead; 16 September

[Dear Dave]

What could be nicer? I'll see you between 5.30 and 6 on Thursday. H.

8 East Heath Road, Hampstead, N.W.3; 23 September

Dear Dave,

Herewith notice of No.22 Well Walk. I asked the man at Potters about a reserve, and he said that although there was not one on it yet he was sure there would be – he said 'about £3000'. And as I see it is only a 32-year remainder of a 99-year lease, what the devil is the use of that?

Will you forgive me if I ask you to postpone coming here on Tuesday next? I have had the most delectable invitation to spend the week in the country at a house [home of Michael McKenna at Mells, Somerset] where I can work, and I cannot resist it. You couldn't manage to come up here this Saturday or Sunday evening instead could you? I'm afraid I can't do Saturday afternoon as I have got to rehearse. Come if you can. Yours, H.

65

8 East Heath Road, N.W.3; 24 September

[Dear Dave]

Sorry! I am mistook (the queen's forsook)[3] NOT Saturday, but Sunday if you can, and by all means leave it open until Friday. If you can, come up here after lunch, and we will take an airing on the 'eath, then have tea and supper, and play pretty music. H.

8 East Heath Road, N.W.3; 4 October

[Dear Dave]

So sorry I could neither come this evening or let you know before now. I am only this minute (1.30) back, and have to stay on for dinner at the house at which I am playing this afternoon. Greetings to yourself and the Huttons (Mr and Mrs Graham Hutton]. F.

8 East Heath Road, N.W.3; 9 October

[Dear Dave]

Can you ring me up between 9 and 10 tomorrow morning (Friday) that we may fix a time to go to 'The Tempest'. I have discovered the perfect edition of Shakespeare (also, alas, one of the most expensive!): it is that edited by 'Q'[4] and Dover Wilson for the Cambridge Press, price 6/– per vol. (one play in each). Only a few are out yet. H.F.

8 East Heath Road, N.W.3; 14 October

[Dear Dave]

Have two seats for 'The Tempest' on Friday evening. May I come along to you at about 6 or just before? Better let us eat early as it begins at 7.45. H.F.

8 East Heath Road, N.W.3; 15 November

Dear Dave,

Hope you are feeling all right after the concert [R.O. Morris's works, at Wigmore Hall, 14 Nov. 1930]. Do take things as easily as possible at the moment: that tooth business takes it out of you a lot more than you realize.

Do you want to go to any of the enclosed, and if so which? I rather tend to 'Fledermaus'. Send me back the circular and I will get tickets. I liked as much as I saw of the Huttons. If you want to write about next week, my address until lunch-time Tuesday will be: at Court Farm, Broadway, Worcs.

Last night [the ROM Concert] was splendid. H.F.

[3] Purcell's *Dido and Aeneas* misquoted. The Witches sing: 'Our plot has took, The Queen's forsook!'
[4] Sir Arthur Quiller-Couch (1863–1944), critic and scholar who wrote under the pseudonym 'Q'.

Court Farm, Broadway, Worcs.; 17 November

[Dear Dave]

Can you get tickets for Old Vic Thursday matinee: Pit-Stalls are the thing if there are any left (3/−). Can you come Hampstead Saturday evening − Friday impossible. H.F.

8 East Heath Road N.W.3; 27 November

[Dear Dave]

Is 'Twelfth Night' done in the Cambridge New Shakespeare? I forgot to ask you last night. The shop tells me it is not, but I thought I saw it at your house. H.

[21 Caroline Street, S.W.1; pre-Christmas]
[V. & A. postcard from G.F. of 16th Cent. German stained-glass window, showing Tobias and Sara asleep in bed together.]

> At this holy time I send
> A sacred picture to my friend.
> Lascivious minded, he'll opine
> The sender's thoughts are not divine;
> But no; this couple from the Bible come,
> So let your wanton thoughts be dumb.

A happy Christmas and forgive these ribaldries, but it's not really a beautiful piece of stained glass! G.F.

1931

8 East Heath Road, N.W.3; 8 January

Dear Dave,

Please forgive me typing, but I want to send a copy of this letter to Caroline Street in case the Cornwall one misses you, and it saves time to do both at once.

What I am going to ask you may sound rather Prima-Donnish, but I think you will understand. Could you possibly ask Miss Chamnis if your songs could appear on the programme of the 15th January as being performed by 'John Armstrong and Howard Ferguson', and not by 'John Armstrong, accompanist Howard F' or 'At the piano H.F.'? I wouldn't care a tuppenny cuss if it were any other audience, but as this one consists mostly of Music Club people I do feel it might be better that way (purely from my own point of view) if possible. I should have asked you to do it before, but to tell the truth it didn't occur to me, however, I think there is still time if you would drop the old girl a line as soon as possible. In any case, apologies for clucking over such a seemingly small point.

Anscombe [Bookbinder] has sent up the things he was binding for me and I am delighted with them: also with the price he charged me!

I have purchased some skates and skating-boots and am prepared to sally forth and break some bones: why don't you get some [he didn't]? It might be rather fun.

Do give me a ring when you get back that we may arrange a meeting. Ever, H.F.

Stafford House, Winn Road, Southampton; 6 April

Dear Dave,

When we got off the boat [from a Mediterranean cruise] my Father had to go straight into a nursing-home to undergo an operation [for prostate trouble]. It went off most satisfactorily, but he has to have another one sometime next week – I think on Monday – so for the present plans are rather indefinite. If all goes well I shall probably return to London – for the 'insides' of the weeks anyway – on the 15th and try to get some work done. I may be up for the day (to get the score and parts of the Symphony [H.F.'s 'Short Symphony'] so that I may correct them): if I do so it will most likely be on the 9th, as someone else who is with us is going up to London then too.

I'm so glad to hear that you had a good time at the Scilly Isles; also that you enjoyed the journey back. Give me the heated and rubber-sprung swimming-bath every time.

I seem to remember that you get back on the 10th: if I am wrong, let me know to Hampstead. H.

Southampton; 17 April

[Dear Dave]

I was recalled here at 7.30 on Wednesday morning, as Father had had a haemorrhage during the night and had been very ill indeed. Mercifully he is getting over it slowly, and if he continues as at present all should be well. I would very much like to get to the Milford concert, and if I am in London, which I should be if all continues well, I will certainly go. We might go down to Epsom hand in hand? H.

8 East Heath Road, N.W.3; 7 May.

Dear Dave,

I'm sorry. I could not bear to see 'Lear' again so soon after last night. I think it is the most terrible play I have ever seen. Is it all necessary? The part about Gloucester, I mean. I am not usually squeamish about the theatre, but I felt almost physically sick after that. surely one shouldn't feel like that in the middle of one of the greatest tragedies? Not only did it seem excessively unpleasant in itself, but it seemed to be of so different a sort of horror to the rest of the play as to make it stand out from the rest, so giving it, surely, a much greater significance than it should have had. The Elizabethans may have been able to stomach this sort of thing – they may have revelled in it, as we do in a 'shocker', but I assure you I cannot. Therefore, my dear, strike me off the list of guests for your Sadlers Wells evening, and I will bless you endlessly. H.

8 East Heath Road, N.W.3; 12 May

Dear Dave,
    I explained myself badly. The Gloucester episode was most likely perfectly O.K. in Shakespeare's time, as it would not have affected an Elizabethan audience in the same way as it does us. My feeling is that nausea is not the right emotion to experience in a great tragedy, and that is certainly the main emotion I felt at that moment: no doubt there were others present too, but that was uppermost. I was so different to all I felt about the rest of the play, which is terrible enough in all conscience; that it stood out quite apart from the rest to such an extent as I cannot believe Shakespeare to have intended. My quarrel was really with the production of that particular point, which, I felt, was much too blatant for a present-day audience.
    See you Thursday, when you shall have our copy of the Score Reading ['Exercises in Score-Reading' by ROM and HF, OUP 1931]. H.

8 East Heath Road, N.W.3; 26 May

Dear Dave,
    Herewith all I can discover about that Botticelli. I have not come across any separate reproduction of it, but most likely it has been photographed, and a print could probably be procured from one of those shops in Museum Street. I myself have the 'Klassiker der Kunst' Botticelli, in which it is reproduced.
    Hoping this is what you want. H.F.

St Andrews [at a summer-school]; next address 14 Deramore Park South,
Belfast; 10 August

Dear Dave,
    Thanks for the pretty postcard from Church Stretton: oddly enough I have wanted to go and stay there ever since I once passed through it in the train. Now you will be able to tell me what it is really like, where to stay, and in fact all about it. It looked as though it might be a glorious place for walking.
    I have been having a good time up here: not very much work, and pleasant music in the evenings to cool the fevered brow. The most delightful being string Quartets played by Jimmy[1] and his crew. Have you ever heard the Schubert G

---

[1] Ivor James (1882–1963), cellist. Member of the English String Quartet (1909–1925). Joined the Menges Quartet (Isolde Menges, Beatrice Carrella and John Yewe) in 1931.

major Quartet? It is one of the great things, and if you do not know it already you must hear it as soon as you get a chance. It is a gigantic work, fit to stand by the side of the C major Quintet: indeed, it might be called the Quintet's tragic counterpart – not really tragic perhaps, but terrible.

Have you been able to get any work done? I myself did not expect to, nor will there be much chance in Ireland with all the hurly-burly of my sister's wedding, etc. How I detest weddings: I feel it would be for the best if both they and funerals were held in the strictest privacy – always excepting, of course, those state ones for which you or I might be commissioned to write suitable works of rejoicing or woe.

Have you thought of sending any of your works in to Boosey & Hawkes? They are doing good stuff now, and are rather setting out in that line I believe. It might be worth trying.

Isolde [Menges] has been doing the fiddle Sonata [H.F.'s Violin Sonata No.1, Op.2] with me (at least, as much as there is of it): I like the sound of it, and she seems to also. Oh that it were possible to do the last movement before the autumn, but alas I don't see that there is a hope.

The temperature here is mostly below zero, but today, the sun having deigned to appear, we were able to unroll the top layer of our furs. 'Oh to be in England now that winter's here.' To Ireland on Friday, then Italy (the Lake of Como) on the 7th September, as we think Germany might be a little over-exciting for out frayed nerves.

Blessings on you, and to Hutton greetings, if you are still with him. From H.F.

Belfast; 23 September

Dear Dave,

Thanks so much for your letter and postcard. Yes, I think Brass Bands at the Crystal Palace on the 26th September might be amusing: in fact – Mr Howard Ferguson will have much pleasure in accepting Mr Gerald Finzi's invitation (kind invitation, sorry). That is always supposing that we really have returned by then: I expect to be in London by the 21st Sept, but with H.S. you can never tell for certain. Already we have changed the destination of our trip three times; it is now the Bavarian Highlands, but where it will be next the good gods alone know.

About H.S. and the Brass Bands I cannot say. I think the simplest thing will be for me to write and ask him and then let you know what he says. In any case, many thanks for the invitation.

Having had your fortune told in Wales you are now all square with me, who had mine told by Becky Clarke [viola player] in London. A most embarrassing performance! You may console yourself with this thought on your engineering propensities, that they should at least enable you to construct the most convincing bridge passages. (Joke, ha ha.)

About the opera: I too want to see 'The Bartered Bride' and Miss Smith's work:[2] therefore let us go together, if you will. The only thing is, will I be back in time? If either of these works received their last performance before 20 Sept, you must go without me and not miss it. I think the company is virtually the B.N.O.C.: have you seen that Adrian [Boult] is conducting some of the works?

I have been playing the Brahms Chorale Preludes a good deal, and grow to love them more and more: all except the one on 'Schmücke Dich', which is curiously flat and uninteresting, seem finer each time one plays them. You, I know, are not very keen on most of them, but even so we must go over them again when we meet, as I feel sure there is so much more in them than at first meets the eye. They are less obvious than any of Brahms' work, the only other things at all like them being the 'Four Serious Songs'.

You were right about 'Silver Ley': it is a lovely book. I enjoyed reading it tremendously and am looking forward to 'Corduroy'.[3]

Weddings are bloody. If you have a public one, my boy, I'll put arsenic in your soup. Registrar's Offices may be cheerless, but at least one gets it over quickly. Bless you, H.F.

Varenna, Italy; 12 September

[Dear Dave]

This is a very lovely place. Our inn is just at the point, is clean, and gives us perfect food. And we are having sun! We set off again for home on Friday, and call for the night at Milan and Basel, arriving in London on the evening of Sunday 21st. Hope all goes well. Yours, H.

8 East Heath Road; 13 October

[Dear Dave]

Afraid it is no good about the Courtauld-Sargent Concert at which the Sibelius is being done. My source of tickets has failed me this time, alas! Hope you are sleeping better. H.

8 East Heath Road, N.W.3; 30 October

Dear Dave,

Unfortunately the 10th is no go, but could you have us on Wednesday 11th perchance? That is, to feed with you and introduce H.S. to de Ropp [Robert de Ropp: relative of Mrs R.V.W.]. I have told him all the peculiar things I can recollect of the boy, so he will be prepared and I do not think there is any likelihood of his going up in the air: he will be too interested. Yours, H.

[2] Dame Ethel Smyth's opera *The Wreckers* at Covent Garden.

[3] Novels by Adrian Bell (1901–1980), published by the London firm Cobden-Sanderson in 1930 and 1931 respectively. Other titles include *The Cherry Tree* (1932) and *Folly Field* (1933). They are all gentle romances set against a Suffolk farming background. Bell published a volume of *Poems* in 1935 and was a compiler of Times crossword puzzles.

8 East Heath Road, N.W.3; 23 November

[Dear Dave]

Am expecting you any time you are free tomorrow afternoon: you can work here. H.S. will most likely be back about 6.30, so it might be as well to do what we have to do before that if possible; if not, we can always go up to my room.

Knee quite recovered, thanks. H.

1932

8 East Heath Road, N.W.3; 11 January

Dear Dave,

Have you seen the enclosed table, which appeared in 'The Radio Times'? Perhaps it might be of use to you in deciding just what constitutes a Chamber Orchestra, a Small Orchestra, an Orchestra, a Full Orchestra and a Grand Orchestra.

Let me know when you return as I want to see you. How have you got on in the country, or haven't you? I have finished the Sonata [Violin Sonata No.1], thank God. Blessings on you for 1932. [H.F.]

8 East Heath Road, N.W.3; [undated]

[Dear Dave]

So sorry to bother you again. Is Lambert [Herbert, not Constant] a vegetarian? If he is, could you possibly give me a ring any time today: if not, don't bother. I should hate to produce a mutton cutlet if he happened to be one.

By the way, I have got all muddled up in my dates and am free this weekend: if you are still unattached let's talk about it on Wednesday. H.

8 East Heath Road, N.W.3; 7 February

[Dear Dave]

It would be worth coming to have a look at both the Willoughby Road houses; they might be possible. I think 'To Joy' [G.F.'s setting of Edmund Blunden's poem] is a most moving and beautiful song. H.

8 East Heath Road, N.W.3; 18 February

Dear Dave,

I was most disappointed not to be at Bournemouth on Wednesday afternoon [for G.F.'s 'New Year Music']. The 5.15, on which I had planned to return to London, turned out to be a Summer train only – fortunately I thought of ringing up to enquire – and the one after that would have brought me back too late for what I was doing that evening. As my wireless is still at the works I went over to the ROs and listened there. It did not come through entirely satisfactorily, for they amplified the beginning and end to such an extent that the whole work was *mf* from beginning to end. However, one could imagine that and make allowances for it. Musically it sounded splendid. I like the work very much – it sounded just as I had imagined it – and think it seems absolutely satisfactory. Did you? See you next Monday 11.0 a.m. H.

14 Deramore Park South, Belfast; 21 April

Dear Dave,

Like a goose I have come away without GJ's [Gordon Jacob] address, and wonder whether you would supply the want on the enclosed envelope, which contains a letter asking for a lesson when I get back. He was not able to give me one before I left, and I still want to show him 'The Twa Corbies' [Op.1, No.1] score. Since coming home I have only been able to draw some pretty barlines on innumerable sheets of MS paper for a final decent copy: not daring to put in any notes, as most likely all of them would have to be removed after GJ looked at the rough copy. Still, barlines are a bore and it is a blessing to have them drawn. I have also learnt my pretty Beethoven Sonata; which is perhaps as well, as I have to play it on the 29th.

Back to Hampstead on Wednesday next, the 27th, in time for Bliss's 'Colour Symphony'. Arthur is coming over here on the 30th for 'Morning Heroes'. Isn't it infuriating that I shall not be here?

Heard Bax's 'Overture to a Picaresque Comedy' at a concert last week. Gloriously vulgar and totally unlike Bax, but the greatest fun. Who would have suspected him of it? How did you like Prokofiev's 3rd Piano Concerto? I enjoyed it; but the pieces which he played on Sunday afternoon – oh dear!

Nothing else very interesting. Blessings on you, my boy, and hopes that all goes well with you. H.

8 East Heath Road, N.W.3; 3 May

Dave,

Before I go to you tomorrow (Wednesday), my sister and I are going swimming at the pleasant Marshall Street swimming-baths: will you come too? We should get there between 3.45 and 4, so just turn up if you feel inclined. Bring your own bathing suit if you have one, otherwise they will make you hire one. Plan over [-leaf]: (We needn't wait for each other.) H.

You go down Regent Street as far as Foubert's Place, which is a small entry; turn into it, and walk to the end.

8 East Heath Road, N.W.3; 16 June

[Dear Dave], Bravo! It was splendid. I had to leave before the Delius, but enjoyed the rest tremendously (in spite of Kutcher [violinist]).[1] H.

Crescent Hotel, Morthoe, Devon; 13 July

Dear Dave,

How are you? We are flourishing as bay leaves, and enjoying the sun so much that we are all colours from scarlet to mahogany. It being a wet day today I cannot get any browner for the moment, so am writing to you instead to enquire of you one or two things.

Can you give me the address of that place you stayed at with Graham Hutton near Church Stretton? As I told you, I shall be wandering about there for a while with Mike James before Worcester [the Festival], and should like to know of anywhere pleasant where we might stay. Also if you know of anywhere at Ludlow, or any other pleasant places in that sort of district, do let me know of them. Never having been there myself, all information will be welcome. By the bye, I suppose, one carries 'A Shropshire Lad' in one pocket, with 'Last Poems' in the other to balance it?

Don't bother to answer at once, but when the spirit moves you. I shall be here for the rest of this month, and in Belfast for all of August.

I heard the Sibelius concert by wireless: most impressive. We were vastly struck by 'Tapiola'. I envied you being there. Hope the weather keeps decent for your canoeing trip; have a good holiday. H.

Greetings to Lambert [Herbert] if you happen to be there.

Could you get the Oboe 5tet done by 31 October, for the Daily Telegraph competition?

14 Deramore Park South, Belfast; 17 August

Dear Dave,

I was glad to have your letter and to hear that the canal trip went well: it will be interesting to hear more about it − with maps − when we meet again in September, for these things are best reported (as one might put it) 'colla voce'. I shall reciprocate with a full account of my wanderings.

Are you divorced from wireless, or did you perchance hear the Ravel left-hand Piano Concerto from the Proms last night? I drove 58 miles in an hour and a half in order to be back in time to hear it: this feat may have unbalanced my judgement, but I certainly thought it was much better than the other Piano Concerto. I listened to Bax No.3 last week, and must confess to being a wee bit

---

[1] Finzi had organised a student concert at the Royal Academy of Music on 16 June, including the Bax Oboe Quintet, songs by Vaughan Williams and John Ireland's Cello Sonata. The Griller Quartet had been booked, but had to cancel through illness. The Kutcher Quartet (Samuel Kutcher, 1899−1984) which replaced them, was evidently not in the same class.

disappointed. Are the endless repetitions of short sections in the last movement – admittedly always differently scored – altogether satisfactory? Sometimes one got the feeling that climaxes were reached more by piling on additional instruments than by specially careful building up of the material. Perhaps I am wrong about this, and in any case, I very much want to hear the work again, in the flesh.

Have you ever read H.M. Tomlinson's 'Sea and Jungle'? In spite of its somewhat retired-colonel's-big-game-shooting-reminiscences-sounding title it is a wonderful book, with nothing to do with colonels or big-game-shooting. Also a new, and interesting book called 'The Map of England' by the sometime Director of the Ordnance Survey? This last is fascinating and I will lend it to you if you would like to look at it.

My writing is becoming quite unreadable, so I had better stop. Someone once said there were three kinds of writing: longhand, shorthand and offhand. Mine's the last. Ever, H.F.

8 East Heath Road, N.W.3; 14 October

My dear Dave,

Bless you for your letter! I am very glad indeed that you liked it [H.F.'s Violin Sonata No.1, 1st perf., Wigmore Hall 12 Oct. 1931, Isolde Menges and H.S.] on Wednesday evening, and that you found it satisfactory. I too felt that it really was so, now that the last movement has been hacked and cut into shape. This latter may not be so orderly and tidy as the first two, but at least it now fits into the general scheme. RO (per letter) was not so sure about this; but, as he remarked, he had not seen it since it was in its original form, and so came to it almost for the first time, whereas he knew the first two movements well; and so, I think it is quite likely he will come round to the last if he hears it again. I shall see him tomorrow, and talk it over. His was the only doubtful voice over that point, I think. Wasn't it a magnificent performance? I was tremendously excited by it, and would have willingly thrown my arms round their respective necks on the stage (a la Adela [sic]),[2] had they given me half a chance. But enough of this babble – I saw Rubbra, who was charming about it, both before and after. Shall I get a cloak like that, and take up dancing (and a yph)?[3] Again Bless you. Ever H.

Have a seat for you Tuesday: see you, not much earlier than 6.30 or 6.45, as I shall be rehearsing.

[2] Adila Fachiri (1886–1962), Hungarian-born violinist, sister of Jelly d'Aranyi. Holst wrote his Double Concerto (1930) for them.
[3] 'Yph' = 'Wife'. Rubbra was about to marry the French violinist Antoinette Chaplin.

8 East Heath Road, N.W.3; 3 November

Dear Dave,

How lousy about Hawkes – I'm so sorry. What can one do? I haven't yet heard about the Sonata, but am not exactly filled with hope, more especially after what I hear from you. It seems to be an impossible position. You'll be interested to hear that Mr God Howard-Jones[4] has set the seal of his approval on my Sonata, and is going to do it at the CFMC's concert at the Grotrian [Hall] on 12 January. Isolde has very sportingly said she will play it with me: which is uncommonly nice of her.

Would you like a ticket for Chelsea Music Club Tuesday 15 November, as I have an extra one? Hindemith Wind Quintet, H.S. in solos, and the Beethoven and Mozart quintets for wind and piano: Mozart magnificent. I shall sit with you when not turning pages. H.

8 East Heath Road, N.W.3; 15 November

[Dear Dave]

I had (of course) meant Wednesday the 23rd for Macbeth, as I too hope to go to the Elgar on the 30th: but you, not being a clairvoyant, could hardly have been expected to divine that. I shall see about Old Vic seats. Are you going to the B.B.C. tomorrow evening? If so I may see you, as I shall be there with your friend Sir Thomas Armstrong.[5] I called yesterday in passing, but you were out. H.

Dover [going to Egypt by cargo boat]; 4 December

Dear Fergie,

A last chance of writing, as we are off Dover, the pilot leaves and will take letters. It's all going to be splendid – of course I've already noticed that my Keatings [anti-flea powder] will be necessary! But I like the chaps very much and the Captain's a nice quiet chap, who produced a Yo-yo this evening! No cards TG [thank God] but rather a lot of wireless. Good food, no regulations and I can use the Captain's private room as much as I like (and his lavatory, he says). No letters are being forwarded at all, so I wonder if you would mind looking in at 21 before you leave for Ireland – just to see if there's a letter from the B.B.C. – or those songs I sent 'em. Probably they'll return them, but there's always a faint chance that they might ask some questions – as to who I would like to accompany or sing 'em. In that case you can answer anything you like! But I've really no hopes. Don't bother if it's a fag. Also write on a piece of paper and put with the letters, the date of [the performance of] your fiddle Sonata and

---

[4] Evelyn Howard-Jones (1877–1951), pianist. Founded the Federation of Music Clubs (1923) to promote the performance of chamber music.

[5] Thomas Armstrong (1898–1994), then Organist at Exeter Cathedral, later (1955) Principal of the Royal Academy of Music. He was not, however, knighted until 1957!

how I get tickets. By the way, keep 29 and 30 January free, as I think Iris Lemare will get rehearsals on those dates. Forgive this mess. The Chief Steward's pen. Hope H.S. appreciated my letter. Mrs Black [Joy's Mother] is dead, poor thing. But I'm glad she didn't suffer. G.

[Postcard sent from Cairo; 24 December]

[Dear Fergie]

I thought I should hate Cairo after the wonderful voyage and good company, but it has turned out well worth while, as I've been seeing a good deal quite outside the usual tourist itinerary and have been going round with cotton buyers into the most incredible villages, made of mud and dung – yes, and drinking coffee with Sheiks! 'That's the life, dearie' (vide George Belcher)[6] [G]

1933

14 Deramore Park South, Belfast; 1 January

Dear Dave,

Every good wish to you for 1933, and welcome home [from Egypt]. Though you told me what the date of your arrival would be I have forgotten it, so can only hope that this letter reaches Caroline Street before you do, so that it may be there to greet you. I am longing to hear about your adventures (for adventures you must certainly have had, you being you!): don't try to tell me of them by letter, as that would be a hopeless as well as a lengthy task, but wait until my return to London when we can have a grand re-union and tale-telling. I expect to be back in Hampstead on Sunday next, the 8th, so if you happen to be in town and feel like ringing up any time during the morning I shall be there from 8 o'clock on (the train gets in at 7.20 a.m.); but don't ring in the afternoon as I shall be out from 2.30, though back again (probably) in the evening.

First and foremost, the two final Elgar concerts, at the first of which AB [Adrian Boult] conducted the Introduction & Allegro (a magnificent performance) and the Enigma [Variations], while old Elgar himself conducted the 2nd Symphony. This latter was a great disappointment to me: I don't think it is in the same street as the 1st – in fact, I began to get thoroughly bored toward the end of the last movement, and did not even feel that it was satisfactorily constructed. Having said that, I come to the most important news of all – is it possible you have not yet heard it? A 3rd Symphony is to be performed this year by the B.B.C., to whom it is dedicated![1] This is quite official, as it has been in

---

[6] George Belcher (1875–1947), painter and etcher. Contributed to *Punch* and *The Tatler*, etc. His cartoons often illustrate working-class/ragamuffin sagacity.

---

[1] The copious sketches of Elgar's unfinished Symphony were skilfully woven into a coherent

the Telegraph and all the other papers. Also vague rumours of the final part of the Apostles-Kingdom trilogy, but of this I am sceptical, feeling it to be the usual Elgar-rumour, recurrent as Spring. If it did prove to be true what a great thing it would be, for it seems sad that the complete design of the Apostles-Kingdom should be left unfinished. The performance of The Kingdom, which we had for the grand finale of the Festival, seemed to be a fine one, apart from the two male soloists who should have been strangled at birth. I found much of the work most moving, but must confess that The Lord's Prayer at the end rather did it for me: why such a thing should prove so intensely embarrassing is more than I can imagine, but it certainly did − to me at least. And anyway, it makes the end just that much too long (this seems rather a failing of EE's) so why have it? Elgar alone knows (and he won't split).

Of other concerts, there was the Lemare-Macnaghten one on 12 December, at which there was little of interest besides Britten's perky little 2-part Children's Songs, and his Fantasy Quintet, which I felt showed more ability and promise than actual attainment: however it was so much better than any of the other new things that it stood out. I don't think much of the playing of Ann Macnaughten and her young ladies, though one must admire their enthusiasm and the way they play everything from memory: this latter feat at least signifies that they have rehearsed the works; but how much better, as someone said, if they would do their final rehearsal from memory, and play from music. Herbert Lambert[2] and I were charmed by the appearance of the cellist, and went to speak to her at the party afterwards: but alas, her conversation (and voice) was hardly the equal of her looks, and my interest languished. Herbert was more persevering.

Talking of Herbert reminds me of the charming Lady of French Letters [Ruth Bethel, who taught French at Westfield College], with whom I walked and talked after The Kingdom. We were speaking of you, and wishing we could get a letter off to you by airmail to Cairo, to arrive before Christmas: the difficulty was that no one knew your address. Then I had a brainwave − to send it to Sir Gerald Finzi, The Turf Club, Cairo. However, in the end neither of us had the courage to do it. Wasn't it a shame?

The only other concert I went to was the Courtauld-Sargent. The Kodaly 'Singspiel Overture' with which this opened was bad − not even amusing, and the Bax No.4 with which it finished was sadly disappointing. It is a gay work in contrast with the other three, which are either gloomy or ferocious, but alas it is also (at first hearing anyway) immensely long and seemingly vague in shape. This was all the more disappointing after the fine shapeliness of No.3. I shall be most interested to hear what you think of it when you have heard it, but I cannot imagine you will see much in it.

work by Anthony Payne and first performed by the B.B.C. Symphony Orchestra in October 1997.

[2] Herbert Lambert was an outstanding Bath photographer. His *Modern British Composers* (seventeen marvellous portraits) was published by F. & B. Goodwin in 1923.

And now, having told you all the concert news, I think I had better stop or you will be wishing me further. I am enclosing two tickets and programme for 12th Jan (Thursday week) [my Violin Sonata No.1 at Wigmore Hall], which you may like the use of if you can. Bless you, my boy, and ring me up sometime or other. Ever, H.

8 East Heath Road, N.W.3; 4 January

Dear Dave,

Yes, the dinner was 3/– each, but you have forgotten the beer and the tip, therefore I enclose a P.O. for 5/6, which must be about half of the bill for the three of us.

13 Rosslyn Hill is no good at all: it is the house I expected, and is a barrack of a place on a very trafficy main road.

Hope you had a good day with William Bliss:[3] at the moment it (the weather) does not look too good, but it may be better out of London.

I don't think I will bother you with any more portfolios at the moment, having just got a new supply from Augeners (at their price, damn 'em), many thanks all the same. So glad you slept better on Thursday. Ever, H.

[Postcard from G.F.; Lisbon, 8 January]

[Dear Fergie]

This is the last lap and I should be back about Friday. Why not come along Sunday? And tell RO, if you see him, that I'm not bringing a parrot home this time, but a dozen bottles from here. Ever, Dave.

8 East Heath Road, N.W.3; 18 January

[Dear Dave]

On second thoughts, may I come tomorrow midday instead of late afternoon? Only ring up if this is impossible: otherwise I shall be with you shortly after 12. How about a walk Sunday? H.

8 East Heath Road, N.W.3; 6 February

[Dear Dave]

Should I ask you to change (I can say definitely later in the week), would you be able to have me at Lye Green for the weekend 17–19 March [H.F. went in March, and then met Joy for the first time] instead of 24–26 February, or will you not be there so late in March? Say Yes or No on a postcard, and I will let you know for certain later in the week. Also give me Lye Green address. Sorry to bother. H.

[3] A waterways enthusiast.

8 East Heath Road, N.W.3; 27 February

[Dear Dave]

Damn and blast! If I haven't got to go and play somewhere at 5.30 on Tuesday afternoon: as it was 'bithneth' I felt I couldn't refuse. I'll come on to Caroline Street as soon as it's over, probably about 7, but maybe a little later. What a curse! (C.T.D.'s thing is being done tomorrow.)[4] H.

8 East Heath Road, N.W.3; 8 March

Dear Dave,

This afternoon I am going to go brazenly to Caroline Street and ransack your music cupboard: do you mind? I may be going on Saturday afternoon to hear 'The Mass of Life', and would very much like to have the score as you are not, presumably, using it. Also I want to see if you have a score of the Stravinsky Violin Concerto, which is being broadcast on Sunday. If, by any unforeseen chance, you happen to want either of these works yourself, for goodness sake let me known on a postcard, and I will hastily return them. Ever, H.

8 East Heath Road, N.W.3; 30 March

Dear Dave,

So sorry I was not able to let you know about yesterday: your card only arrived by the midday post, so that gave me no time to send a reply.

As things turned out, I had just time to go and hear Davie's Trio at the R.A.M. before meeting H.S. at Paddington. It sounded a good deal better than I had expected from looking at the score; but whether there is anything behind it or not I would hardly like to say. I don't somehow think there is, though it is difficult to tell with a work such as that, where the lack of 'dexterity' allows so little to come through. It was quite well played. I was attracted by the String 6tet of a man called Tyldesley,[5] which contained some lovely things.

To Ireland on Thursday: back on 19th. Love to Joyce. H.

8 East Heath Road, N.W.3; 1 April

[Dear Dave]

24 Well Walk is for sale: they are asking £2,600 for it. Potters agents. I cannot go over it myself as I'm off at 8 o'clock tomorrow morning to Holland with H.S; (If you look skyward you may even see us!) but you know the house, for it is next door to the Fay Compton one. I did not go to the Hindemith 'Lehrstück' in the end, as I thought the other was as much as I could bear (in fact, we left in the middle of that). The Bliss on Sunday was good, but completely re-written. I'll return score on Thursday. Ever, H.

[4] Cedric Thorpe Davie (1913–1983), Scottish composer. Professor of Music at St Andrews University (1945–1973). The 'thing' was his Piano Trio.
[5] Possibly Richard Tildesley (b.1908) then studying composition at the Royal Academy of Music.

Nangitha, Treath, St Martin SO, Cornwall; 13 April

[Dear Fergie]

This is the cottage where I am till the 30th. All very lovely, so I have no wish to do any work! Also I am not able to get a piano. So for that reason only I'll be glad to be back. Otherwise it's glorious. A tree to dive off, boating and no visitors. Ever, G.

I know you hate having books recommended, so *don't* read Max Beerbohm's 'A Christmas Garland'. I've never read better parodies.

Belfast: as from 8 East Heath Road, N.W.3; 17 April

Dear Dave,

Many thanks for your postcard. The cottage looks delightful, and I envy you your tree, from which you can dive into the river: it all sounds very pleasant, and should be doubly so just now, at this best time of the year. Over here things are looking lovely. The blackthorn better than I ever remember seeing it, and primroses such as one dreams about but rarely sees.

I too am without a piano, having decided not to hire one for the short time that I am over here: sometimes it is a very good plan to get away from them – I was beginning to feel just before I left London that this was one of the times. However, I have done one or two things more or less in the musical way since arriving here. A little copying (does one ever finish copying?), and also correcting Rowe's set of parts of my 'Two Ballads' [Op.1]. Also, I got someone to try through those three songs [Three Mediaeval Carols, Op.3] which I did at the beginning of the year. Oddly enough, they sounded quite nice – much better than I expected.

On the way over I started 'The Way of all Flesh', and have since finished it. It is a splendid book, don't you think? Now I'm in the middle of Goss's 'Father and Son'. (You see, I do improve [by reading recommended books] if slowly.) Though it has greater beauty and gentleness than the Butler, I'm not sure that I find it so interesting.[6] And talking of improving in that direction (if you follow me?) I believe I have already read the Beerbohm 'Christmas Garland': if you showed it to me I could make sure. I am not reading The Life of Constable [by C.R. Leslie] just yet, as somebody [G.F.] has promised it to me for a birthday present. Library binding, I hope.

Tomorrow the family returns to London in a cohort, for my brother's wedding, which takes place on Thursday. What a pity you are not there to throw confetti on my top hat. Blast weddings – that is to say, public ones. As I have to go out with the family that evening, I will not be able to go to the B.B.C. Contemporary Concert on Friday. However, as the programme comes from the direction of Central Europe, I am not as sorry as I might have been. I have sent my tickets on to your friend Boys [Henry Boys, ex R.C.M.] who is the only person I know to be

---

[6] Sir Edmund Gosse (1849–1928), author of *Father and Son* (1907), and Samuel Butler (1835–1902), author of *The Way of All Flesh* (1903).

in London at present that likes that sort of entertainment. He also had my tickets for the last one, and was vastly mystified to know who I was, how I know him, and where I got his address from. The last was quite simply done – from the R.C.M. address files. He enjoyed the Hindemith, poor fellow.

What disappoints me more is that I shall miss the broadcast of Arthur's [Bliss] Clarinet 5tet on the 25th, as one of the H.S. Brahms Concerts is on that evening. I shall be at the Brahms 'Requiem', 'Schicksaleid' and 'Horn and Harp Songs' at Queens Hall, with Beecham, on Sunday: lovely programme. Let me know when you are back. Ever, H.

P.S. It may interest you to know that on 21st of October, 1805, the Battle of Trafalgar was fought and won. (Presumably it was lost too, but that is beside the point.)

Devon; 19 April

Dear Fergie,

How exciting about the Battle of Trafalgar Oct 21 1805 [H.F.'s birthday]. Curiously enough, in France they have what they call 'le quatorze juillet' [G.F.'s birthday]. In case you are not so well up in French as you are in German, I had better explain that it bears no relation to 'Romeo and Juliet' (a play by Shakespeare). Well, birthdays must fall somewhere. Here is a little confetti for your brother's wedding. Rather late, but you can post it on.

Plans have been changed and I'm leaving here on the 24th (next Monday) and may come back the same day or via Bath or by sea. At any rate, I shall be in London by Wednesday or Thursday and will phone up.

I've put in the extra bar you suggested in that thing. Ever, G.

If I get back on Tuesday I'll listen-in to the Clarinet 5tet [Bliss] at RO's. But if he's out or anything, I may come up to your place, even though you'll be at the Brahms. Love to Pu and Nunky [H.S.]. G.

8 East Heath Road, N.W.3 [no date]

Dear Dave,

The best thing will be for you to write to the Box Office, New Scala, on or after 5 January, enclosing a postal order and asking for what seats you want (how about Dress Circle 3/6?): I'm quite willing to pay for 2, so why not get 4 together as you suggest. Tuesday 20th is best for me: I cannot manage the 21st.

So glad Falmouth is warm. I wish I was. Greetings, H.

Helford; 21 April

[Dear Fergie]

Someone I know in Falmouth asks me if I know of anyone who would like a complete Goethe – 20 to 30 vols. Gratis of course. About the size of Tauchnitz vols, but bound. One or two might need re-binding. Green, half cloth. Date

1840 and no illustrations. The print seemed pretty good – if German gothic can ever be good. Personally, I should advise accepting, but RSVP to 21 CS so that I can let her know as soon as I get back. G.

8 East Heath Road, N.W.3; 22 April

Dear Dave,

How nice of the lady with the Goethe. But hark ye! Did you happen to notice whether this set contains the Letters ('Briefe'). If it did, I should love it. But if not, I hardly think it would be fair to take it, as I already possess a complete Goethe (minus letters) Of course, if the good lady is hankering for a 'good, quiet, appreciative home' for the volumes, I have no doubt I could find her one, even if it were not my own. But perhaps I may leave you to decide this point, for you know the circumstances.

Would you like one ticket for the Brahms concert on Saturday afternoon next (3 p.m.) 29: String 4tet No.1, G major 5tet (the magnificent one), and B-flat 6tet. And two tickets for the previous evening, Friday 28th (8.30): Clarinet Trio, Clarinet Sonata No.1 and A major Piano 4tet. Or are you already going to either of these? Let me have a postcard.

By all means come up here on Tuesday 25th to listen to the Bliss Clarinet 5tet. I wish I could hear it. If you happen to be in town tomorrow, Sunday evening, and feel like hearing Mahler No.4, come up then too, as I shall be listening. It begins shortly after 9 o'clock. There is a score here. Welcome home again. H.

8 East Heath Road, N.W.3; 17 May

[Dear Dave]

I should have said 'tomorrow (Wednesday)' on my postcard, but I thought the date at the head of the card would give you what I meant. Thursday is no good for me either, so we meet Friday at about 5.30. H.

Cut in Bax 1st movement from 3 before 40 to 41 evidently authorized, as he was there.

8 East Heath Road, N.W.3; 31 May

Dear Dave,

Will you meet me on Monday at the corner of Bow Street and Flora Street (that is, The Covent Garden Theatre corner) at 6.50. You must either have had a meal or bring sandwiches with you: I will have eaten before getting there. I am going to bring your score of 'Otello' (for which, very many thanks), though there is hardly any likelihood of following with it. Let me know if you cannot get your ticket for 'Hugh the Drover', then we will get H.S. to scrounge one (or two) for you.

Have finished new movement of Octet: only one more to do. In haste, H.

[from Joy, on their engagement; Aran Isles; received 3 May]

Dear Fergie,

I wanted to write and thank you for your awfully nice note before leaving but I didn't have a moment. I appreciated it so much, and am so glad you are happy about it too – it's a great and glorious thing to Gerald and me. We are just off in a drifter to film the harpooning of the 25-ft sun fish sharks which they tackle in small boats. The Gaumont Co have been trying to film the lives of these people for the last 18 months, and this is one of the last episodes – the complete atmosphere of timelessness is very refreshing – one eats and sleeps prodigiously.[7]

My warm greetings to you. From Joyce.

Excuse pencil – the ink has run out, and the boat doesn't come in till tomorrow!

[21 Caroline Street, S.W.3]; 1 June

Dear Fergie,

Right. I'll be here at 6.50. Shall be spending the afternoon with Holst at his nursing-home in Ealing and will come straight on from there. Would you send me a card (to 21, as I shall get back there on Monday morning) telling me the best way, and full time it takes, to get from Ealing Common to the corner of Bow and Floral Streets.

Delighted to hear about the Octet. Any chance of hearing it on Tuesday? It's a good job you're able to do the songs next Tuesday, as I'm seeing Foss [of the O.U.P.] on Thursday and finally deciding. The first talk I had with him was satisfactory.

My Joy sends her love. We're checking estimates for 30 Downshire Hill. G. Housman's 'The Name and Nature of Poetry' worth reading.

[8 East Heath Road, N.W.3]; 4 June

Dear Dave,

You must be wondering why the wire and this wild change of plan? The reason is this: Pu and Betty will probably be well enough to go away this coming week, and this being so, H.S. and I are more or less bound to flit too. I rather think we shall wander about Exmoor if the weather holds. However, I expect to be back in London on Friday 16th, and have written to our Mr Aveling (at the College) to ask if he can let me have three tickets (you, C.T.D. [Cedric Davie] and self) for that evening for 'Hugh the Drover'. Then we can descend on you at Lye Green on Saturday 17th. Of course if the Aveling bird cannot let us have tickets for the Friday we are dished, and heaven knows what we will do. But we can discuss that on Tuesday.

Now about Monday. Take a Piccadilly Line train (the little low ones) from

[7] Hollywood producer Robert Flaherty's film *Man of Aran* was released in 1934.

Ealing Common Station, allowing yourself about ¾ of an hour. Get out at Covent Garden Station (no change), and walk as follows [shown on plan]. The time of meeting is 6.50: the place the corner of Floral and Bow Streets. Ever, H.

Bingles Cottage; 16 June

[Dear Fergie]

Yes, we can have lunch any time you like, 12.30 onwards. Apart from seeing Morley about my old piano at about 10, I've got nothing on until 12.30. So come as early as you like. Perhaps you've already seen the Bumpus exhibition, or think you had better leave it till some other time. It's on the whole of this month. G.

Bingles Cottage; 21 June

Dear Fergie,

About next Monday: if you feel so inclined, what about going on after supper to see Rostand's 'The Fantastics' at the Lyric, Hammersmith. I don't mind one way or the other, though I certainly mean to see it some time or other. Anyway, if you feel like it, try to book beforehand, as I believe there's a run on it. Three tickets, of course. If you haven't already been to Foyles, would you see if they have a 2nd-hand copy of Granville Barker's 'Prefaces to Shakespeare, Series I'.

I went to hear the Duke of Ellington last Monday.[9] Worth it, if only for the attack and precision and to see how all these odd sounds that one hears are made. Slightly aphrodisiacal, and all far too dazzling for my slow mind to be able to follow. Otherwise the whole show is pretty worthless. It, and the audience, made one feel there's something to be said for a Hitler. (There was one attempt at a joke – about 'some people liking chamber music, but personally I think it's all pose'.)

See you Monday, and if possible we'll run through a song or two. Just at first, I didn't quite grasp what you meant when you mentioned it, as I had already seen Foss and left the tenor songs with him. But of course there are all the baritone ones to be gone through. Ever, G.F.

Bingles Cottage; 14 July

[Dear Fergie]

Don't forget to let me know about Wednesday. I rather want to talk about that oboe thing [G.F.'s 'Interlude' for Oboe & String 4tet]; show you 'Death Masks';[8] celebrate my finishing at the R.A.M. Joy will probably be here to lunch too. Could you make it 12? or meet me at Bumpus at 11? I rather want to see that wonderful map (air archaeological survey) exhibition again.

I've finished 'The Life of Frank Harris'. Without exception he seems to have been the most odious man who ever lived. G.

---

[8] A book of photographs.
[9] At the London Palladium, 19 June.

Bingles Cottage; 17 August

Dear Fergie,

It was a sweet act to send 'If Papa were only ready to die'. Edith [Pyke, his housekeeper] heard me reading the words to Joy and said 'Wilf [her husband] knows that song'. So you see, it's not so far from reality as one might imagine.

Plans. I hope to go for a short walk next week and then settle in the country for my 15 days 'probation' before getting married. That'll be in the middle of September – actual date and place unspecified. (And Fergie, no presents by request). Then away to Scotland for about a month. So we'll be back in London mid-October. The house [30 Downshire Hill, N.W.3] is getting on grandly and Edith gets in on Sept 3rd, and from that date it will be our address wherever we may be. Till then, Bingles will always find me. So you must forget all about 21 Caroline Street, and I shan't be sorry to do so myself.

I managed to get the Oboe work off – but don't expect they'll like it or want to do it. There's some decent music in it and a certain amount of rant, which I had to stick in to fill things up when I got rather pushed towards the end. Later on I'll unscrew it and put it together again, and I rather have the feeling it really has the makings of a 1st movement and not a middle movement.

Let me know how things go. Blessings. G.

14 Deramore Park South, Belfast; 19 August

Dear Dave,

Many thanks for your letter. I'm so glad you appreciated 'If Papa were only Ready': I felt that it had the true ring which would appeal to your sense of toujours le mot juste. No doubt the music also moved you – in just what direction had better be left unsaid.

That was great work getting the Oboe thing off in time. Probably when you next see it you will decide that what you now call 'rant, shoved in to fill it up' is the best music of all. Things have a way of turning out thus, have they not? In any case, rant or no rant, it was splendid to get it done.

I am glad to know your movements, and will duly remember to 'send all communications after the 3rd ultimo (is that the right word?) to 30 Downshire Hill'. And here's wishing you every happiness there, and long life to enjoy it. But one thing to which I do most strenuously object, and that is – 'no presents, by request'. Dave dear, it would be a queer thing if you did not allow me to give you and Joyce a wedding-present – or let us say rather, a present when you get married, for that sounds less formal and grim. In fact, I'm bothered if I would stand for such orders. Therefore, put your two large heads together and think out something you would like me to get for you when we all get back to London in the Autumn – if you fail me in this, it is on pain of receiving a silver salver, covered with a touching inscription, on which to place all your visiting-cards. *Now* will you help me?

And, as occasions such as this do not happen every day, there is one other thing I want to tell you, whether you will or no. Ever since I have known you,

you have been a damned good friend to me, you have never changed one whit, and you have always been there: and when one can say all that about anybody it means a good deal. Not long ago, when I told you something of what I felt and had felt about F-C, you were surprised about my feeling so violently about any body: I assure you, it does sometimes occur, even though it may not be very apparent outwardly. Therefore know this, dear Dave: that your friendship has meant a very great deal to me and I consider myself jolly lucky to have it: that sort of thing does not come everybody's way.

The parts of the Octet are now corrected (Rowe did them for me), and now I am in the midst of making a duplicate score – boresome work, but it has got to be done. Eyes have rather given out under the strain, but I am dropping drops into them and lotioning them with lotions, and hoping for the best. Nothing at all serious, as I can still write (as you can see), but rather a bore. Have altered some of the things you suggested, but still cling lovingly to my 'Brahmsian bit' [of which G.F. disapproved], which does not seem to offend me – as yet.

I shall be in London for the day on Thursday 31st Aug, to hear 'The Pastoral' [Symphony] of R.V.W. at the Prom that evening; then back permanently on, probably Monday 11 September.

My love to Joyce, and remember to put your heads together: if you don't there may be an avalanche of salvers (silver and otherwise) on No.30. Ever, H.

Norfolk [; 19 August]

[Dear Fergie]

This is really not a very exciting postcard, but it'll show you whereabouts we have got to. It has been lovely rambling through Suffolk and Norfolk, and we got to Norwich just in time for a first night at the Maddermarket Theatre – an extraordinarily good production of 'Romeo & Juliet'. Love from Joy and myself. [G]

As from 30 Downshire Hill, N.W.3; 28 August

Dear Fergie,

You've won, and blackmail carries the day. The threat of a silver salver is quite enough. So, though I don't like the idea of your spending, we'll put our heads together and make it one of the more necessary and permanent things which we should otherwise have had to get.

Curious what you write about your eyes. When I was finishing that Oboe piece, I was so rushed in getting it scored and copied that for several days and nights I had to sit at a stretch, with an occasional break of an hour to two's sleep. At the end I could see nothing that was nearer than arm's length, and I really began to think I should have to come down to spectacles! My hearing also went and felt exactly as though I had a very bad cold and was in the Hampstead tube at the same time. But both got all right after a few days' rest.

I listened-in to V.W.'s Piano Concerto and still felt the same about it. The middle of the slow movement is as lovely as ever and the chromatic Fugue magnificent, though much too short (however, he says he is going to lengthen it), but the shape of the last movement and the material of the first, most unsatisfactory. The chief thing about it is in a lot of 'Job' and the [4th] Symphony (which he's now scoring).

Dan Godfrey's doing that 'Introit' [G.F.'s, for Violin and Orchestra] on 8 Nov. So will you listen-in.[10]

Auld Fergie, I very nearly wrote in my last letter pretty well word for word what you wrote in yours, only t'other way round. But then I left it out, as I thought it would sound too like a valediction, coming from me, when really things will be very little different, except that I shall be a nearer neighbour and a more complete and happier person married to my Joyce. She, by the way, has just shouted down 'Love to Fergie when you're writing'. Till October. G.F.

P.S. Young Davie [Cedric Davie] once asked me if I wanted to sell my typewriter. At the time I didn't. Now it seems that as Joyce has one, there's really no need for me to keep mine. I should feel rather uncomfortable selling it to him and would much rather give it. But I don't want him to feel under an obligation and also don't know that it would be good for him − do you know what I mean? Bear it in mind and let me know sometime or other. Anyhow, I don't expect that 3rd-hand it's worth more than £1 or so.

I'm going through the songs with John Coates tomorrow.

Edinburgh; Wednesday [no date]

Dear Fergie,

So you see, we've got as far as this. Edinburgh gave us rather a shock, after all we had read about Prince's Street. And the War Memorial was considerably worse than we had expected. They could have done something so splendid with a situation like that, instead of plastering it up with all those incompetent reliefs. However, everything else has been splendid − except Newcastle − and I'll give you the itinerary when we get back.

Sylvia [Sylvia Spencer, the oboeist] and the Macnaghten 4tet aren't doing the Oboe work. Anne writes that they don't think it up to my level!! I'll be very interested to hear what you feel about it. I'm sure the form is unsatisfactory at the moment, but feel that the stuff is not so bad. Executive artists are usually foul judges, but at least they've heard it and I haven't. So I've asked them if they would mind just running through it, so that I can get an idea. I wonder who this Augustus Lowe is, who is accompanying John Coates on 5 Dec?

---

[10] Sir Dan Godfrey (1868–1939), conductor of the Bournemouth Municipal Orchestra (later Symphony Orchestra), was an indefatigable champion of new British music.

30 Downshire Hill, N.W.3; November [no date]

Dear Fergie,

Here's the score [of Octet] and also a few minor suggestions. I thought they played it with a bit more spirit at the show [1st performance of Octet, Stratton 4tet etc., Grotrian Hall 21 November], though you may have trembled once or twice. Everyone seemed really enthusiastic about it. I should be most amused if you'd show me any cuttings you may happen to see, particularly Mr Darnton in 'The Music Lover'![11] Movements 1 & 3 were most lovely and 2 was absolutely satisfactory. 4 I personally don't like so much, though I should have been very grateful to have done half so well myself. The whole length was good and in that respect Schubert showed up badly – the concert didn't end until quarter to 11!

Jessie Snow's 4tet and Butterworth [Trust] have fixed up 5 December for that Oboe movement. The dears are meeting specially for it, which quite humiliates me, as I really only meant them just to stick it in at the end of a rehearsal. 5.30 to 6.30. Could you turn up at 6 sharp as they want to run through before anyone comes? 22 Acacia Road. Do. Same night as the songs, but that's always the way. G

1st mvt, p.15, bars 2 & 3 [of the Octet]. Did you really want the horn to bellow on those high notes, like a cow in need of a bull? That was the main thing one heard, instead of part of a whole.

2nd mvt, p.5 bottom line & p6 top line. The accompaniment felt as though it was meant to be light, but didn't quite achieve lightness. It seemed to need staccato semiquavers.

p.18, last 4 bars. Both at rehearsal and performance these seemed to belong nowhere and come from nowhere; I mean the bassoon.

3rd mvt, p.7 top line and first 2 bars of 2nd line. Couldn't you manage the woodwind accompaniment a bit differently? It's a foul noise and sounds like a shop-ballad on the word 'love'.

4th mvt, p.56. Wouldn't that tune be better on all the strings (except DB) in unison? The accompaniment would stand it and it wouldn't anticipate things (when it turns up in octaves later on).

p.9 and on. The violins seemed ineffective: all right for 'The Planets' but inadequate in a chamber work.

p.26 bar 1 and p.27 bar 9. I was struck on all occasions by the cello playing the bass-note twice. Can't explain it, but it sounded unsatisfactory.

p.31. Instead of that bang at the end, can't you possibly have a run-up: you know the sort of thing I mean.

Forgive me. G.

[11] Christian Darnton (1905–1981), British avant-garde composer. Assistant editor of the *Music Lover* (1930–1932).

1934

Beech Knoll, Aldbourne [Gerald & Joyce rented this house]; 14 January
Dear Fergie,

For the life of me I can't find anything worth finding [in the proofs of H.F.'s Octet], though it's a very difficult job without anything to check it with. There are a good many places where a missing or additional accidental might exist, for all I can tell, without making much difference – no reflection on the Octet, but I mean that a thing seems final in print and so would seem equally final if it were different. Oh dear me, this is expressed so badly – if you know what I mean.

p.4, bar 7, 1st beat strings. Are the triplets all bowed as in Violins 1 & w or first two notes only, as in viola and cello? See this point also on p.4, bar 8, Viola and p.12, bars 6–9 p.37, bar 2, 1st Violin C-sharp.

That's all. I've loved going through it and have admired it even more, workmanship too. The three points I've always complained about still seem the same to me: viz the wretched little bassoon squirt on p.28; the faked-emotion feeling of the climax (and the woodwind repeated notes) of the slow movement, and the un-chamber-music-like feeling of those 8 of 9 bars of repeated B-flats in the fiddles in the last movement. As for the 1st movement, I think it's absolutely perfect, and without flattery, I think it's more likely that the Schubert 8tet will be stuck-in to be played with yours than the other way round, as you originally intended.

We listened-in to the V.W. concert on a very bad wireless. The 'Quodlibet' sounded really brilliant,[1] which is hardly a term one would use for V.W. We also listened-in on Saturday to H.J.W. [Sir Henry Wood] 'Fantasia on British Sea Songs'. Now have you ever heard this? I could hardly believe my ears.

Don't go to all the theatres: we'll be back about the 18th. If you're getting tickets for the Phil on that day for yourself, you might get three for us and drop 'em in at Downshire Hill 'to await arrival'. I'm so afraid all the 3/– ones may be sold if we only arrive on the day itself. But don't worry if it's at all an inconvenience, or if you think we shall be able to get tickets at the door. (I say three because Margaret [Joy's sister, Mags] will be coming too.)

Bless you, and the Octet. Our love, G.

---

[1] *The Running Set*. Based on traditional dance tunes. First performed on 6 January at the Albert Hall as part of the National Folk Dance Festival and presumably relayed by the B.B.C.

Beech Knoll, Aldbourne; 18 January

[Dear Fergie]

You do wisely not to go to the blithering concert on Monday. I should like to avoid it myself. Lucky you're in the country over the weekend. Expect me fairly early next Tuesday — a little before 6, as there are several things to talk over. Blessings. G.F.

14 Deramore Park South, Belfast; 2 April

Dear Dave,

Something most peculiar has happened (no, I have not fallen in love!). Indeed it all seemed so improbable and so unlikely to lead anywhere that I did not think there was any point in telling you before. Which sounds mysterious, but isn't meant to be. A couple of days after the Phil performance of the Octet [with the Griller Quartet], Ralph Hawkes of Boosey & Hawkes wrote saying that he was sorry he had been unable to hear the work, but would I care to bring the score in one day? 'Ah-ha', said I to myself, 'That's 'The Times' notice, that is'. So I left the score in when I was passing, and arranged for Nunky [H.S.] and self to play over the duet-version to him and to Charles Woodhouse, whom he wanted to hear it — though Lord knows why. That seance took place the day Nunky and I left London.

What was my amazement this morning when I received a letter from Hawkes to say they would be pleased to publish the work! Can you beat it? — and this from people who were not even asked to do it. I told you I did not think it was worth while trying anybody with it, particularly those who turned down my innocent little Three Songs [3 Mediaeval Carols, Op.3]. Publishers are quite beyond me! They are going to bring out a miniature score and the set of parts. Naturally I am all up in the air about it.

Forgive this scrawl: I had to let you know about it. Love to Joyce & yourself.
Ever, H.

30 Downshire Hill, N.W.3; 22 April

Dear Fergie,

I must admit that I expected your first sentence (publication of the Octet) to be followed by an announcement of your engagement, difficult as it would have been to believe! But what followed was really equally surprising & delightful. All my congrats. The 8tet is only getting what it deserves, so though I'm surprised I'm also not surprised; if you know what I mean. It's all rather remarkable and cheering, and perhaps they'll take the Three Choir songs now [Two Ballads, Op.1].

We're just off to Aldbourne and shan't be back until July. Bank Holiday has passed off without anything particular to tell you about, and no one used our front garden as a lavatory. Aunt Jane planted out some bulbs which previously had flowered indoors as hyacinths and they have come up this year as daffodils. Otherwise the world's just the same, except for the news about the 8tet.

Love to Nunky and you from us both. G.F.

8 East Heath Road, N.W.3; 28 April

Dear Dave,

I should have answered your letter sooner and written to thank you for the most charming (and improving) gift, but things have been very rushed – not only when I was over in Ireland, but also during this last week since I have been back. The Octet parts were in such an unholy mess, and that fool of a copyist had left so little room for corrections etc. (none, to be precise), that I decided the only thing to do would be to write them out again, and this I have been doing with infinite labour. It would have been possible to send them to a copyist, but I did not do so, a) because I am too ikey to pay for one; and b) because had I done so I should probably have had to spend as much time correcting them as it takes to write them out myself. All very tiresome, but it's worth it to get them just as one wants. The thought of the awful unalterableness of print has made me make a few minor corrections here and there, but nothing serious.

Curwens are going to do those Three Songs [3 Mediaeval Carols, Op.3; 1st perf. B.B.C. 4.1.34, Dora Labette and H.F.] which were broadcast at the beginning of the year. Oddly enough, I wish Boosey were going to do them; but as you know, they wouldn't.

On coming back to that fiddle work I played you [scrapped], I now find myself almost entirely agreeing with you about it. However, I am not just so kind as you were, and simply say it's not good enough. As it stands, that is, for I still like a lot of the stuff in it – even unto the opening, which you did not take to greatly. My proposed remedy is to put it on a back shelf for a time, write another thing or two (if possible), then take it out again and entirely recast it. Still for violin and orchestra I should imagine.

So far, most of this letter seems to be taken up with the 1st person singular. You must excuse this please. Just to show that there is no ill feeling, we'll return to it once more and say that I'm afraid I have already fixed up with [Thorpe] Davie to go to the Sibelius concerts – that is, for the 1st and 3rd, for I don't think I'll be here for the 2nd. May we, however, come and breathe down your necks from the row behind, when you bring along your grand score of No.7: that is, if no one else has already engaged that position.

No.8 (East Heath Road, not Sibelius) transports itself down to Birchington [to a bungalow belonging to H.S.'s sister, Ethel Judge] – near Margate, my dear: you wouldn't know it – about 17 May, for a month before H.S. sails for S. Africa. It sounds frightful, but may not be so bad. Pu, Betty and H.S. will all be the better for a month by the sea: perhaps even I may be. Up to town once a week to give lessons to the harem.

Is the dust flying from the manuscript-paper? I hope so, and that things are going well with you. You wouldn't like to add to the dust, would you, by writing a nice easy piece (or several nice easy pieces) for B-flat Clarinet and Piano [H.F. had begun to have clarinet lessons with Frederick Thurston]. Must be in the keys of F, B-flat or E-flat or their relative minors, and must not modulate further than those keys. Slow and thoughtful pieces preferred.[2]

I hope J. keeps well. Give her my love. And let me know when you come up to town, that we may meet.

The Sibelius Concerto and the 'Enigma' the other night at the Phil. were wonderful. Beecham deserves several laurel wreaths.

The efforts of the Cinema Stars moved me greatly: in just what direction need not be specified.[3] Love to G & J, from H.

Aldbourne, Wilts.; 30 April

Dear Fergie,

It was good news to hear about Curwens and the songs, though I'm sorry you could not charm Hawkes into doing them. I rather feel that Curwens are in a decline. (Though, who knows, your songs may put them right again!) However, better Curwens than not at all, and if they go west they'll be taken over by the O.U.P. or Hawkes, so you've always got that to look forward to. I saw Ken Curwen just before I left and managed to get him to scrap everything of mine that he published. 'Footpath and Stile', 2 songs and 'The Cupboard', and left him, as compensation, the full remaining royalties on a couple of school songs which still sell to the tune of a shilling or two a year. This works out at 18/– I think, after which they too, disappear from his catalogue. They were all really bad works, though I may one day revise 'Footpath and Stile' [he did]. Curwen was very decent about it and I've great hopes of being able to get Stainer & Bell [publishers] to do the same. Shall be glad to have a clean slate. Lucky you, with nothing of that sort to worry you.

Alas, I'm not inspired to write your clarinet pieces in the keys of F, B-flat and E-flat. Would you, on the other hand, like to set me some French exercises? I thought of learning French in order to be able to read Constant Lambert's 'Music Ho!'.

I'm not quite so enthusiastic about the Sibelius violin concerto: on the whole it seems rather a bad work, after three hearings. The 1st movement is the best; the 2nd (as Joy described it) like Parma Violets, and the 3rd pretty poor.

I wish we could have offered you all asylum here instead of letting you go to Margate. But we have but one spare bed and it would not be respectable for Pu, Nunky, Betty and you all to get into it. Nor would it be good for the bed. But I must say that the air here is glorious and I've never felt so well in my life. It will probably only be for a year or two, so if you want to explore the country round

[2] Finzi did not oblige.

[3] H.F. could not throw any light on this, save that it was definitely *not* a reference to Charles Koechlin's 1933 *7 Stars Symphony*.

about – and it's better than Lambourne as a centre – you had better take your chance and invite yourself down.

Why, that's all that I said about the violin & orchestra piece (by H.T.) – that it wasn't quite good enough. Anyhow, the back shelf will probably do the job and it will go on re-writing itself meanwhile. What I felt was that it was only the rough sketch for a work.

Have you seen the Aran film [*Man of Aran*]? We shall be coming up for a couple of days within the next fortnight. What I should like to do is to fit it in with 'Schwanda the Bagpiper' [Weinberger]. (I heard the polka from it and it was really delightful and beautifully done.) Would you be able to fit this in and direct me through the intricacies of Covent Garden? It does not really matter which days we come up, so if I hear you can manage it we'll fit it in with whatever day you've got the tickets for.

I'm trying to score 'The Fall of the Leaf' having rather a difficulty with it. [Scoring completed posthumously by H.F. in 1956.]

Joy sends her special love and includes Nunky too. Ever, G.F.

Aldbourne, Wilts. [; May]

Dear Fergie,

I forgot to say that Joy would not be coming to 'Schwanda' in any case, as hot squashes are not too good for her at the moment. I meant the Gallery and stool business, so (if Davie doesn't object) I'll join you both on the 15th, and you can wake me early and take me off to Covent Garden, much as I don't want to go at that hour. If you decide on the earlier date and let me know in time, it will do equally well, or even better. If you phone me up on the evening before we can fix up the time of meeting.

To be sure, you can sleep in our spare bed, but without the celebrated young Busterbator.[4] Can't have you corrupted. I'll buy back 'Footpath and Stile' from you. It explains why I've sold a copy. I've just found out what is supposed not to be found out – that of the Elgar, Ireland and Holst brass-band works only the last scored his own work. Love to Fergie from Joy and G.F.

Aldbourne, Wilts. [; May or June]

Dear Fergie,

We had John [Herbert Sumsion] staying the night here on his way back to Gloucester and the suggestion came up whether – if Alice [John's wife] hasn't already fixed up for you with the Prices – you'd like to put up here. It's only an hour and a half by car from Gloucester and we could motor in for your show (you would probably have to do the motoring, as Joy will not be going) then stay the night outside Gloucester, say Painswick or somesuch place, come in again for the morning concert to hear the Magnificat (V.W.'s) and back here

---

[4] The Finzis' Pekinese. Shameless, evidently.

94

after lunch. If you like the idea send a note to Alice. If you don't like the idea don't hesitate to say so. Our love, ever, G.

[30 Downshire Hill; May or July]

Dear Fergie,

Here are the 2nd proofs of the partsongs [G.F.'s]. I'm not enclosing MS or 1st proofs, which are both in rather a muddle, but you can have 'em if you want 'em. Don't get irritated over correcting these – I don't think you'll find anything – but think of the qualities of life, stern duties and so on and that will help you through the tedium. In checking 2nd proofs I've only tackled the mistakes that were in the 1st proofs. I suppose that things which were correct in the 1st are not likely to have slipped in the 2nd.

We won't worry to see Nunky, knowing what a hectic time he's in for, but if he feels like a meal here, all of you for that matter, you know how we should love to have him.

Hope you found the R.O.'s flourishing and that Aunt Jane didn't fall in love with Davie in kilts. He's too young for the divorce court. Believe me, very truly, Gerald Finzi.

8 East Heath Road, N.W.3 [no date]

Dear Dave,

Here are the proofs. I think they are all right, but perhaps you would look at them and send them off before the weekend. The envelope is correctly stamped.

Ever, H.

Very many thanks.

30 Downshire Hill, N.W.3; 21 July

Dear Fergie,

I've sent your proofs (Two Ballads, Op.1) off to Mr Rosen.[5] Related to Bosen-/Dorfer?

supposin'
He afterwards goes in
A boat to the frozen
Antarctic and throws in
Himself and his woes, in
Despair, since he knows in
His heart that he chose in
His wife one who grows in
Deceit and just blows in
Men's rooms with her clothes in

[5] A refugee originally on the staff of Universal Edition, Vienna, now with Boosey & Hawkes.

> Her hand, and knows sin
> Like the whore
> Who for tin
> Is so easy to win.
> Aye, supposin', supposin'
> He's related to Bosen-Dorfer'
> Poor Mr Rosen.

Yum, yum, glub, glub.

I've sent off the proofs. As far as I can see, everything's all right, though it would have been easier to check with your MSS as well. The only small points were:

Twa Corbies, 2 after B and 1 after C: in the 1st proof you've made rather a mess at this point! but it looks to me as if you want to have the tail of the top E upwards. However, it's a small point and I've left it as it stands. Likewise the ellipsis at every ev'ry. You say it's from the Oxford Book of Ballads, but the OBB gives every. No matter.

I hope the journey was great fun [drive to Glasgow in Cedric Davie's £5 second-hand car], without any busts anywhere. I phoned up at about 8.30 am but found you had left at about 5.

Thought the 8tet (B.B.C. 19 July 1934) sounded fine, though that bassoon wiggle in the scherzo still annoys me frightfully!!

I'm sending 'Heroic Symphony' to Davie.[6] Joy sends her love, so do I. G.F.

Aunt Lilly [Joy Finzi's aunt] used to know old Mrs Craies [friend of H.S. and H.F.] very well indeed.

Full permission to use my numbering method. I may use your duration idea in future.

14 Deramore Park South, Belfast; 25 July

Dear Dave,

The poem is superb; if only for that it would be worth sending you the proofs [of the 'Two Ballads', Op.1]. But that ain't the only reason, for I am glad to know that they seem all right, and am most grateful to you. The two mistakes you speak of I already know about, and the matter of 'tails up or down' in the Corbies is all right: that is, their proof-reader altered them in the 1st proof, whereas I did not want them altered, hence the mess. The 2nd proof is O.K. The word EV'RY in the Dirge I am much more uneasy about. In the MS it is always written EVERY, but set to two notes. Their engraver, seeing this, altered it to EV'RY, which is, I suppose, all he could do in the circumstances, as all the words are divided into their sung syllables. The fault is really mine for setting EVERY disyllabically; but it was all done so long ago (comparatively) that I decided not to alter it now but just leave it as another blot on my escutcheon. By the way, would you set EVERY trisyllabically? for I'm not sure I would even now.

---

[6] Novel by Nora Kennedy (1933).

Another time it would be more satisfactory to go over the proofs together, after the other had looked at them. This time we could not do that, of course, because there was such a dreadful rush.

Do you know that H.S. sent his 'Pipe Suite' to the publisher without a blooming phrase-mark, and I had to put them all in the day before I left, which was when the proofs arrived! Did I swear?!?

The journey up North was the greatest fun. We left at 5.15 am and reached Glasgow at 8.15 pm, which was excellent, considering the car was a 1924 Morris Cowley. We drove turn about in 50 miles stretches, and ate our eats by the roadside. No disasters or bursts.

So glad you thought the 8tet sounded all right. I was in a listening-room at Broadcasting House, and was somewhat alarmed to hear the havoc which the microphone played with balance and colour. What was particularly distressing was the long horn-bassoon pedal in the last movement, which sounded as though it was played on two different instruments (which it is, of course), instead of one, which is what it sounds like in the flesh. Otherwise I thought it was not too bad on the whole, and oddly enough, that bassoon bit in the Scherzo, which so worries you, still leaves me quite cool.

It is good of you to send 'Heroic Symphony' to Cedric to read; I imagine it will be much appreciated.

I'm afraid this letter must be almost unreadable. I am writing on my knee in the car while waiting for my Father, who is talking at unbelievable length to a valuer about his deceased cousin's effects – or rather, the valuer is valuing the effects. Betweenwhiles they are talking about 'old times' twenty to the dozen. I stood it for 20 minutes then fled to the car, where luckily was found paper and envelopes.

My love to G & J & Christopher. Howard.

Aldbourne, Wilts.; 21 August

Fergie,

Alice [Sumsion] writes that I can put up at Mrs Gwynne Holford's [for the Gloucester Festival] Hartbury House. If I stay there Thursday night too, I could pick you up on the Friday morning, as it's only across the road, about 2 miles away. The only thing is that you may have told the Prices that you're not staying over Thursday night.[7] Would you like to alter this or leave things as arranged – it's all the same to me. Also, if time, I could possibly show you some of the things worth seeing in that lovely part of the country, as we motor back.

My great fear is that Mrs G. Holford keeps a butler. So unnerving. Blessings, G.

---

[7] Phillips and Lisa Price, The Grove, Taynton, Gloucester. Mr Price was a Socialist landowner and MP. Festival performers and visitors often enjoyed their hospitality.

Aldbourne, Wilts.; 25 August

[Dear Fergie]

Mrs Gwynne Holford has a butler, so I've refused — even though Keith Falkner was going to be there too! Alice thinks that Mrs Price will be able to put me up, but she can't find out yet. Anyhow, whether or no, I'll be somewhere near there and will pick you up on Friday morning. Our love, [G]

Aldbourne, Wilts. [; August, undated]

Dear Fergie,

Best of thanks. Hawkes is certainly quicker than the O.U.P.! I had no idea that you were camping in Scotland, but just imagined that you had motored up to Glasgow, stayed for a night or two, and then gone on to your Belfast park. It sounds very pleasant. Any swimming?

About meeting in Gloucester. A great deal depends on where I can garage (or park, if weather permits) the car. Gloucester is a delightful sight at Festival time, but rather like Piccadilly Circus (without the prostitutes of course) at a particularly crowded time. I shall probably stay outside somewhere, and then on the Thursday afternoon motor in as near to the Cross as I dare — about a mile or two away — and then we'll pick up the car after 'Gerontius'. At the best of times I'm not a good hand in traffic. Perhaps it will be best for me to phone you up at the Prices on the Thursday morning.

The B.B.C. are doing the 'Introit' at one of their obscurer concerts on 25 Sept and ask what the hiring fee is. I really haven't answered because I've no idea what to say. You might let me have a p.c. giving advice. Our love, J & G & C.

8 East Heath Road, N.W.3; 13 September

Dear Dave,

I meant to send Joy and you a lovely mock Collins, but some more important things have turned up, so that must wait until another time.

The train carried both the fruit and myself home safely on Tuesday, and I found Aunt Lily in when I called to leave-in her share of the spoils. As you predicted, she wanted me to stay, but as the taxi was ticking away outside, that was, alas, impossible.

A packet of alarming dimensions from Boosey & Hawkes awaited my return. I said to myself, 'A-ha, proofs of the Octet', and was delighted to find that that was what it was when I opened the parcel. But not so delighted, as you can well imagine, when I dug a little further into the heap and found two complete sets of Parts of the 8tet, printed and published without me ever having set eyes on the proofs thereof! I almost had a weak turn. How in the world such a thing can have happened is more than I can fathom, but there it is; and somebody is going to get the hell of a letter from me about it. I have not yet had time to find out how many hundreds of misprints there are, but I fear the very worst. It will be interesting to discover whether it would not be as cheap to re-issue the Parts as to print a sufficiently big Errata. The Lord alone knows. Mercifully to goodness, the score has been very well done and there are surprisingly few mistakes. If I may, I shall send you a copy of the 2nd proofs, that you may find all the things I have left out. I have not the least idea yet what is going to be done about the Parts.

The other thing I wanted to talk about is this. You already know that there has been a family rumpus between Cedric and his Grandfather [with whom he stayed while in London]. Well, as he cannot stay there any more, and as Nunky [H.S.] is only going to be here for five days before sailing again for America, I thought I would ask him if he would like to stay here for the whole of this term. Then he can look around for digs for next term at his leisure. I had thought that Nunky was going to be here for much longer than that, and only found to the contrary on my return here; which is the reason I did not ask you about all this when I was at Aldbourne. As it happens, our downstairs pianos are not 'at home' at present; but I know that Cedric wants, if he can, to get a second-hand piano hire-purchase, so that will be all right as far as it goes. But, unfortunately, until he finds one we are rather between the devil and the deep blue sea, for I do not particularly want to hire one if he is getting another later. And that is where you come in. If you are not there yourself, and if it would not be in any way a bother, would you allow him to use your piano at No.30 to work on, until he has had time to look around himself for the one he hopes to buy? Of course, if this would be a nuisance for Edith, you must say so, or if there may be any other reasons against it which I do not know about. So far as I can see, it would only be for a week or so, but in any case, it would automatically stop if you found it necessary to come up at any time. Please be quite frank about this, Dave, and tell me whether it would or would not be possible. If it were all right, I need not tell you how grateful I would be; but if not, we shall soon find another way out of the difficulty.

I am enclosing the key of the hamper. Besides the spots, I have almost contracted diarrhoea through eating too much fruit. But it is worth it.

My love to G & J, and very many thanks for the lovely few days, from Howard.

[Aldbourne, Wilts.; 15 September]

[Dear Fergie]

As they've only sent me a ticket for the concert (B.B.C. [G.F.'s] 'Introit') 6.15 on the 25th I shall go to that and not bother about the rehearsal. It should be quite safe under Boult. I was wondering whether it would be worth your while asking his secretary for a ticket. Then we could go to the concert together and there might be more interesting things on the programme to make it worth your while. G.

8 East Heath Road, N.W.3; 2 October

Dear Dave,

Here are the 2nd proofs of the 8tet score, which you so kindly promised to look at for me. It is no use sending you an MS score, as some alterations have been made; but perhaps you would run through, and keep your eye open for any mistakes, musical or typographical, which my too accustomed eye may have missed. I think these proofs are fairly accurate, but one can never really tell.

The Parts had to be entirely recopied and reprinted, they were so hopeless.

The V.W. Prom was delightful. The new 'Quodlibet' charming,[8] and the 'Greensleeves Fantasy' a welcome form of such a lovely setting – very slight, but worth it. So far as I could see, there were only two cuts in the 'London Symphony'; otherwise it seemed the same as usual. The Tallis Fantasy was, I thought, the finest thing on the programme.

I did not go the Band Festival (Brass, not Elastic) after all. Davie could not come, and the thought of a solitary pilgrimage to the Crystal Palace was more than even my enthusiasm could stand up against. Love to J, G, & C, from Howard.

Would you mind noting anything there may be to note on a piece of paper, and not on the proofs themselves? And let me have them back as soon as you have finished.

8 East Heath Road, N.W.3; 10 October

Dear Dave,

Thank you very much indeed; it was blessed of you to go through the proofs. Of the two things you note, the missing C-sharp in the 1st Violin part is the only actual misprint – but it is just the sort of thing one would so easily overlook. The bowings you remark on are actually right, though they look inconsistent. This is because all the strings must land on a downbow at the beginning of the bar, and, as they have not been playing exactly the same stuff, must take different bows to get there, though the music of that particular bar is the same in each part.

I'm very glad indeed that you like it so much. Which sounds rather an inadequate way of receiving the nice things you say. But if I said 'Thank you' (and the more I said it the worse it would be), that would imply I imagined you were being polite if not perhaps sincere; and that, I know, is not the case. However, be that as it may, I can at least say that it is the opinion of the few friends one really trusts that means so much to one in these matters; and to have an opinion from you means a lot to me.

Brilliant is certainly the word for the V.W. 'Quodlibet'. It was positively dazzling.

---

[8] *The Running Set* (see letter 14 January, 1934). Evidently a revised version performed at Queen's Hall, 27 September, by the B.B.C. Symphony Orchestra conducted by the composer.

'Anthony & Cleopatra' the other night at the Vic was sadly disappointing. Fairly good production; but most of the scenery quite frightful; an Anthony that spoke as though he had a pound of cotton-wool in his mouth, and most of the others like amateur theatricals. Mary Newcombe as Cleopatra was the vixen (not altogether convincingly) at the expense of being the Queen – though she looked fine. And surely 'Age cannot whither, nor custom stale', etc., should not be delivered with a metaphorical slap on the back? Indeed most of the poetry, apart from some of the very end, got badly swamped.

I shall certainly get your Phil tickets, as there may be rather a cram.

Just going to listen to the Sibelius 4tet. My wireless has had something done to its interior and is incredibly good – just as good (if not better) than yours at No.30. Love to G & J.

Aldbourne, Wilts.; 29 December

Dear Fergie,

After posting the Virginia Woolf [*Orlando*] I read a copy myself, but was a bit disappointed. Of course, it's only a slight thing, but even for a slight thing it didn't say very much. However, it said what it said very beautifully.

Double oddly enough, Aunt Lily sent us two VWs too, 'Orlando' and 'The Voyage Out'. I read the former when it first came out , but in this uniform edition there are no illustrations, so I don't know if anyone reading it for the first time would spot that Orlando is V. Sackville West. No matter. It's worth reading on its own account.

Oh, you will be a good clarinetist when this wedding's over.

The Sumsions haven't been over yet, but I'll tickle 'em up about the umbrella.

I listened-in to V.W.'s pupils' concert last night. Maconchy's 'Comedy Overture' was about the best thing, I thought. Grace Williams' 'Two Psalms' poor stuff.[9] I quite enjoyed R.O.'s 'Concertino'; but 'The Mystical Songs' [V.W.], even at this date, put everything in the shade.

Mistake me not, auld Fergie, about the Elgar Violin Concerto. The significant points in that article are not the alterations in the Violin part, so much as the method of composing: one can read between the lines on p.30 for example, and 2nd paragraph on p.35. That's essentially the method of a person whose work grows, on the principle of cutting the worm in half. I can't conceive of R.O., or Stanford or Bach, for example, working on those lines. Naturally, if a work is satisfactory it doesn't matter a hoot how the end is arrived at; but it's of great technical interest to see the way in which one work is *composed*, with a clear-headed view from nearly the beginning, and another work *grows* with the intellect in comparative abeyance: really a difference between conscious and more-or-less-unconscious cerebration. Brahms' great intellectual qualities were

[9] Elizabeth Maconchy (1907–1994), Grace Williams (1906–1977), respectively English and Welsh.

held together by his emotional qualities; Elgar's great emotional qualities were held together by his intellectual ones. But this is insultingly obvious! If you interrupted Brahms in the middle of a work it would have been at bar 72 (Stanford, bar 172): with Elgar it would be loose sheets, alternatives, patches and so on. That's all I meant. Our love to you. G.F.

I think the 'Passionate Allemande' is simply lovely in 'Hands across the Centuries' [Parry]

1935

Aldbourne, Wilts.; 13 April

Dear Fergie,

I left you soundly sleeping and so could not say goodbye. And I got back to find that Joy had a surprise for me by way of the attic completely ready for me. She had spent the two days in clearing the books and had been at the job from about 7 in the morning! She sends her love and thanks for your care of me – Pu of course included (bless her). I do hope you're not exhausted! Good luck with the new work [H.F.'s Partita, Op.5] and let's see you soon. Thanks for the fine time. G. If [Alan] Sinclair [H.F.'s brother-in-law] is still with you, my greetings.

Caernarvon; 2 May

[Dear Fergie]

John [Herbert Sumsion] and I have been spending a few days in these parts. Back to Beech Knoll on Saturday. Hope the work's flourishing. We climbed (or rather walked) up Snowdon, but alas, found we were not the first. John sends his love, too, G.

Aldbourne, Wilts.; 13 May

Dear Fergie,

We tried to get through a personal call to you last Friday or Saturday evening, just to give you a surprise, see how you were, and hear all the news, but you were out. I expect you've had a stiff time with Nunky's Bach Week.

Here we have no news. I had five days with John [Sumsion] in Wales and have got over the Jubilee celebrations and am now getting down to work. The OUP have definitely taken those 'Children's Songs', but I can't say that it has moved my pulse or raised my temperature! Now, if it had been an Octet it might have been exciting.

You'll have to clamber over chairs and tables to get to your spare bed, but the bed's comfortable when you get there.

We may be up next Monday (or Tuesday). If I stay the night(s) may I put up with you? If you see Cedric Thorpe would you remind him that he still has 'The Heritage of Music'? Give him our love. And love to all at No.8. Ever, G.F.

8 East Heath Road, N.W.3; 16 May

Dear Dave,

Do come on Monday night, and Tuesday too if you can manage it. We shall be delighted to see you.

I am so pleased to hear that the OUP have taken the 'Children's Songs'; you are, I know, rather sniffy about them. But nevertheless, they are charming things and very well done. Also, they are quite likely to sell a good deal.

The Bach Week was pretty frightful, though Nunky played better than he has ever been known to play. The blasted Jubilee played Old Harry with his audiences, and for the first time in history he lost some money over these recitals. The effect of all this excitement and trying to write music [my Partita] at the same time, coupled with the disgusting weather we have been having, have all combined to lay me low with a tired cold in the head. Very tiresome, as I have to do an Empire Broadcast with Solde at 5.30 tomorrow *morning*, and am feeling much more like lying in bed twiddling my thumbs.

In spite of these diversions the new work progresses. It has acquired the title of PARTITA since you saw it, and I am hoping that the 1st movement will be quite finished by the time we meet next week. It has not all been very easy and has taken time, but as it is a longish movement (about 8 or 9 minutes) I suppose this is to be expected.

You might give my love to your lady wife, and ask her where my head [Joy's sculpture. Now in Corpus Christi College, Cambridge] is. If it were in the august precincts of Burlington House I might go and visit it; but if not, I would rather like to have a look at it now that it is finished. Also convey my respects to the Monster [Christopher]. Looking forward to seeing you next week. Ever, H.

P.S. I miss you and J. horribly.

8 East Heath Road, N.W.3; 1 June

Dear Dave,

Will it be all right if I descend on you next Friday by the train leaving Paddington 2.45, arriving at Hungerford 4.10? If I don't hear from you I'll take it (a) that this will suit you; (b) that such a train is still running (for I have only looked it up in a 2-year old ABC; and (c) that my hopes will not be dashed if I expect to find somebody awaiting me at Hungerford station. But seriously, don't trouble to write if all this is O.K.

Another movement of the Partita was finished yesterday, so I shall just be feeling ripe for a few days' delightful laze; but for goodness sake don't let this disturb you in your work, as I'm very good at lazing by myself. The new movement is a slow fellow, and will probably be the third and penultimate one in the final order. I shall inflict it on you next week.

By the way, if you want me to bring Court Dress and Decorations with me you had better let me know.

Please thank Joyce very much for her postcard re gardeners; and give her and yourself my love. Ever, Howard.

P.S. I hope Cedric is keeping his nose clean, and behaving himself in general.

Aldbourne, Wilts. [; early June]

Dear Fergie,

There will be a deputation to receive you at Hungerford station 4.10. My ABC is 1 year old but gives the same times. Good news about the Partita, and about the OM for R.V.W.

Davie is behaving very well and I think he is better for his change. He has walked, climbed trees, lazed, read and played table tennis. Our love, G.

Aldbourne, Wilts. [; before 6 June]

Dear Fergie,

I hope you found C. Thorpe Davie looking fitter and that he gave you the prescribed message. We loved having him, and he was like you in being happiest left to his own devices.

Owing to our having to make a very swift decision over the housing question, Peter Harland (the Blisses architect) and his wife are coming down for 24 hours to talk things over and look over this house. He's a very nice person, so I hope you won't mind. They'll be on your train, so if you seen them you might introduce yourself (he looks rather like Paddy Hadley).[1] Don't imagine you'll be in the way because you won't — so long as you don't take offence (in your usual way) at having a different bed for the first night! Our love, GF.

Aldbourne, Wilts.; 6 June

[Dear Fergie]

The Harlands are not coming till Saturday now. So don't accost the wrong person! Ever, G.F.

Aldbourne, Wilts.; 1 August

Fergie,

Greenish 'On Music' gives Ravvivando (and my pocket Italian dictionary only gives Ravvivare). Am I right in using it in the sense Rit - - - Ravvivando - - al - - a tempo? This seems more suggestive in some cases than in Accel: but I don't want

---

[1] Patrick Hadley (1899–1973), English composer, seriously wounded in World War I. Professor of Music, Cambridge University (1946–1963), best known for the cantatas *The Trees so High* (1932) and *The Hills* (1946).

to use it if it doesn't make sense (you may remember my Italian 'accents'). Ravvivare is the active verb, like Rallentare. So I suppose Ravvivando is right, corresponding to Rallentando. Thus does the primitive mind work. Our love. In this case would one say al - - tempo or al - - a tempo? [G]

14 Deramore Park South, Belfast; 2 August

Dear Dave,

So far as I can remember, it is: Rit   Ravvivando - - al - - tempo. Being far away from my scores I cannot conform this, but if you look at either Kodaly's 'Psalmus Hungaricus' or Delius's 'Sea Drift', or in one of the Sibelius or Bax Symphonies, I have a sort of feeling you'll find it there. It is certainly in one of my fairly modern miniature scores, but exactly which one I cannot for the life of me remember. It is an exceedingly useful term, and one which we might use more often with advantage.

The head [Joy Finzi's sculpture of H.F.'s head] came over here with me, being transported in an ancient brown-paper shopping-bag covered in miles of crepe; no one handled it but myself, so it is safe and sound. Please tell your lady wife that it is *much* admired, and also remind her that a further copy is being clamoured for by Nunky now that this has left Hampstead. Seriously, could she get another one done – in whatever material she thinks best – before the end of September?

I was delighted to see the nice understanding notice of the separate issues of 'A Young Man' [G.F.'s 'A Young Man's Exhortation'] in the Musical Times for August.

It seems likely that the Partita will have a rest for the present; the atmosphere here is not altogether conducive to writing, and in any case I feel shockingly lazy – probably after the hot summer in London. Love to G, J, & C, from H.

P.S.   Ravvivare = infinitive, to revive
Ravvivando = present participle, reviving.

P.P.S.   al tempo = to the time
al a tempo = to the time. (Am I right?)

Abbotsbury; 13 August

[Dear Fergie]

Joy and I are here for 2 or 3 days – a lovely spot, and I have a good cottage address if ever you are walking in this direction. Joy wrote to Nunky about the head, which she'll tackle as soon as she gets back to London in September. Very many thanks for information about Ravvivando. [G]

14 Deramore Park South, Belfast; 26 August

Dear Dave,

If you are a member of the Imperial League of Opera[2] you will have heard already; but in case you are not, the first performance of Delius's 'Koanga' is to take place at Covent Garden on 23 September; two further performances will be on 27 Sept. and 3 Oct, all at 8.30. If you are not a member of the I.L.O., booking (Box Office, Covent Garden Opera) opens on 9 Sept.

This is the only interesting news. Your postcard looked delightful – many thanks for it. I shall be passing through London around 5 Sept, then will be back for good on about the 25th. Switzerland in between, I think. I have not done a stroke of writing since I came over here, apart from an introduction to the 4th movement (unwritten) of the Partita, but I don't very much mind, as I wanted a rest. Love to you and Joyce. Ever, H.

Aldbourne, Wilts.; 30 August

Dear Fergie,

Blessings for letting me know. I really don't know if I'm a member of the Imperial League of Opera. Many years ago I sent the required money and received many assurances, a few issues of 'Milo', a few circulars, but have heard nothing since! So I don't quite know what to do. They've certainly not notified me about 'Koanga'. Before I write, let me know if we can go together. I could manage any of the days, but should prefer 3 Oct. If you've fixed up with anyone else, don't bother.

Arthur's string music [Bliss's 'Music for Strings'] is going to be done at a London Museum Concert on 6 November.

Did you see W.II. Reed's very interesting (albeit over-personal) article on Elgar's 3rd Symphony in 'The Listener' for 28 August? Honestly, I think it bears out everything I thought about Elgar's method of composition – judging from internal evidence.[3]

We're going to the Worcester Festival for the Bax (the better Bax, I think), new Dyson, and 'Sancta Civitas' [R.V.W.] – Wednesday and Thursday. Since the few days at Abbotsbury we've been having rather a grisly time, as we've been trying to ease work for Doris owing to her condition ('I can't explain', as my Mother says) by going away for a few days here and a few days there, but always having to come back in between, to keep an eye on the cottage which is going up for them. However, the temporary cook comes very soon now, and all should be well. Our love, not forgetting the Partita. G.

---

[2] A scheme launched by Beecham whereby subscribers who pledged 10 shillings a year for five years would be provided with first-class opera by the British National Opera Company which, after much excellent work, was in the doldrums (eventually ceasing operations in 1929). Although 44,000 people signed up, Beecham's League failed. *Milo* (see letter, 30 August) was its magazine.

[3] Finzi admired Elgar's music and was pleased to find that they shared the same jig-saw method of composition.

Aldbourne, Wilts.; 23 September

Dear Fergie,

Three minutes on the phone didn't give much time to ask how you are and so on, and I think you were also rather in a hurry – putting on a dress-tie or something like that – and hoped the 3 minutes would be 2.

Firstly, thanks for the pipe pieces [H.F.'s 'Five Pipe Pieces', Cramer 1935]. I didn't even know that publication had been fixed up. I'm so glad; and though they're not exactly up to the 8tet, I'm glad to be able to complete my collected edition of the works of H.F. They'll also be good as examples, if I ever try my hand at the same. I think I can just discern you in the 'Air'.

We've written for seats for the 3rd ('Koanga'). It's likely that I shall be with you from the Monday night, if you'll have me, but I'll write later on, when I'm certain. Then I can tell you all about the Worcester and Malvern Festivals and Boughton's 'The Ever Young'⁴ (Steuart Wilson calls it 'Boughton's never-ending youth') in exchange for Chartres. Incidentally, Chartres is one of the few places abroad to which I have always wanted to go, but doubt if I'll ever get there. I feel so un-at-home out of England.

I suppose you've heard about poor old Howells? His boy, only 9 years old, died after only 3 days' illness – infantile paralysis. Now it's touch and go with Herbert Lambert's boy Peter – the best of children – who has got some sort of streptococci infection, both general and local, and had three operations yesterday. Sorry to pass on gloomy news, on top of the newspapers. Joy will be in London next week, and will go into the question of mediums for your head. Our love, G.

Aldbourne, Wilts.; 30 September

[Dear Fergie]

I'll arrive at Paddington tomorrow at 12.55, but as I want to get [the score of] 'Koanga' I thought I would go to Augeners and lunch out, and then come on to you after lunch. Of course, if you happened to be near Paddington, or Augeners, or the M.M.⁵ we could lunch together, and nothing would be more appreciated, by believe me, Yours very truly [G.F.]

Aldbourne, Wilts. [; between 30 September and 19 October]

Dear Fergie,

Just to repay my phone calls and borrowings. Had a good look at the Chartres book, but wished I could have asked you some questions about it. I imagined that white cathedral interiors were English monopolies – heritages of the reformation.

---

⁴ First performed at Boughton's Summer Festival, Bath 9–14 September – his last attempt to recreate the conditions of his Glastonbury Festivals, 1914–1927.
⁵ The Mainly Musicians Club, Oxford Circus.

What do you think of the idea of our taking one or two Cozy Stoves[6] off you? Joy sends her love and was interested to hear about the new house. Love to Nunky and many thanks. G.

I won't remind you about Keith Falkner.

Aldbourne, Wilts.; 19 October

Dear Fergie,

I thought your birthday was the 24th, but looked up The Life of Nelson and found it was the 21st. I hope you won't pretend that the [Hugo] Wolf comes as a great surprise. I haven't yet sent the 4tet [and the 'Italian Serenade'] though I ordered them both together; but you didn't give me very much time. However, I'll post on as soon as it comes. This selection of the Daryush poems[7] contains the two most beautiful – 'I had rather roam' and 'Loose the horses now' – so there's no need to invest in the series. But I had rather my presents were a bit *fatter*: no wonder that Joy looked at the two booklets in contempt and said 'Is that all you're giving Fergie?'

I wasn't quite clear from Joy's account about the MS paper [special full-score MS paper being printed by Augener for H.F. and G.F.]. Have you had a proof yet? I don't particularly want to see one, but I wonder whether you finally decided on Horns or Cors, etc. As you know, I prefer English, but if you particularly prefer the other, I don't mind a bit.

Do you know where one can get really thick blotting-paper, which blots and doesn't smudge?

Don't forget my query about your Cozy Stoves. I don't want to order new ones now, if 2nd-hand ones will be available later on, and a purchaser for one or two of yours might possibly be a convenience to you.

I still don't know whether those 'Children's Songs' will go through with the O.U.P. Accepted and all. Foss is now trying to mulct me for the permission fee for the words.[8] There's no doubt that he hasn't a leg to stand on, but the effrontery of the O.U.P. is positively Italian or German. I should love you to see the correspondence. Would Hawkes be worth considering if I offend Foss too much and he chucks up the whole thing? Do they deal with children's songs? You're a lucky devil to have an honest publisher behind you.

Christopher's whooping-cough is abating. Our love and what I haven't mentioned yet: many happy returns. G.

---

[6] A coal-fired, all-night stove.
[7] Elizabeth Daryush (1887–1977), daughter of Robert Bridges. She published seven books of verse between 1930 and 1971, including *The Last Man* (1936).
[8] Hubert Foss (1899–1953), head of O.U.P.'s music department.

8 East Heath Road, N.W.3; 20 October

Dear Dave,

How ever did you think of the Wolf?? I assure you, you could have knocked me over with a feather when I opened the envelope and saw what was inside. But seriously, thank you very much indeed for it (or rather, them) and the Daryush poems. I am very glad indeed to have both, more especially as I know neither the poems nor the Str 4tet at all. The Serenade I have, of course, heard several times; but nobody ever seems to play the 4tet.

Now to answer the rest of your letter. I am glad that Christopher's whooping-cough is getting less bad: I have an instinctive fellow-feeling for him, as I'm told I suffered badly from the same complaint. May it soon clear up entirely. You do not, by the way, say anything about Herbert Lambert's boy; one hardly knows whether to hope that he is still alive or that he is dead.

Aunt Lily[9] rang up this morning to ask Nunky and self to come in and see Joy either tomorrow or the night after, so perhaps I shall hear then.

As to Cozy Stoves. I thought we said definitely that you could have two of ours. The one snag is that now we may not be leaving here until March next. Will this be too late to let you have them? I hope not.

Good blotting-paper is the thing with which the walls of Heaven are papered. In the meantime I use Ford's, but there might easily be better.

Before I forget, I saw 'Job' again yesterday, for the first time with full orchestra (even unto the saxophone). It makes the greatest difference, as does the new and less sepulchral lighting that appears to have been instituted since last I was there. I believe it was also the first time they put 'Job' in the middle of the programme; this seemed a mistake until one saw 'Façade', which came at the end, and realized what an even greater mistake it would have been to put its delightful futilities before 'Job'. Why, oh why will they insist on raising the curtain several times after 'Job' is finished? It completely ruins the sublime ending, and brings one down to earth with a bump the more painful because of the height one has been raised to before.

It might be worth considering Hawkes for the 'Children's Songs'. I don't know whether they do that sort of thing, but they may. The O.U.P. (cum Foss) is really bloody.

Let me know when you are coming up, and bless you for your good wishes and present.

Ever, H.

[Aldbourne, Wilts.;] 21 Ocotber

Dear Fergie,

Just home from a glorious walk — five or six hours on the Downs and not a soul seen the whole time. The sort of day in October that closes with a frosty mist and you come home to a fire and an egg for tea. I remember one particular

---

[9] Joy Finzi's aunt, who lived at 24 Keat's Grove, Hampstead.

walk we had (Buckinghamshire, I think) that ended like that. You should be down here now instead of in filthy London.

We find Will Rothenstein enchanting and went over to see him on Saturday.[10] But Joy will tell you. By the way, it was at Cirencester that I posted your packet, in the afternoon to make certain you'd get it on Monday morning, but it seems to have reached you the same evening.

I think March will do for the Cozy Stoves, as we have my little one to go on with. (No, you didn't let me know before. Pu thought it would be all right; but when I asked you, at the same time as sending the 4/– stamps, there was no reply.)

About coming: that depends on Keith Falkner to a great extent; but I should like to be up 6 November (Walton Symphony) and 7 November (Phil: Sibelius No.6, Dvorak No.4, and Schönberg Cello Concerto).[11] Could you have me then for 3 or 4 days, and could Keith go through the songs then? I should also bring up the Oboe Work for you to set your seal upon it, and I would try and get Antoinette Rubbra or someone to run through the bowing. Ever, G.

If you have any messages for me via Joy, write 'em down. She forgets! The picture is for you; the cutting (Great Britain) for Davie when you next write, to let him know that things go on in Budapest! [C.T.D. was studying with Kodaly in Budapest.]

8 East Heath Road, N.W.3; 22 October

Dear Dave,

Thanks for note, with enclosures which I enjoy! The MS paper will be ready at the end of this week, so if Joy has the car in town perhaps she would call for it; this will save damage by post. I did not trouble you with the proof as this would have meant more delay. But I think you will like it and approve.

Keith got back yesterday and says he will be able to look at the songs from next week on; so if you could send me one complete set, I will go over them with him and show him vaguely what they are about. Then he can look at them himself and we can all go through them together when you are up on 6th & 7th, etc. Do come then, and whenever you want. I shall be working, but you won't mind that. Don't buy a ticket for the B.B.C., as I have two already, and you can use one of these. Do you want me to get Phil. tickets? We look forward to seeing Joy tonight. Ever, H.

[Aldbourne, Wilts.]; 23 October

Dear Fergie,

I'll come up with Joy on the 4th and leave the following Friday, if this is really all right for you . I'll be out a good deal, so won't be in your way. Could you get

---

[10] (Sir) William Rothenstein (1872–1946), English artist. Friend to many English composers, including Elgar, Delius and Vaughan Williams. All three sat for him.

[11] A reworking (1933) of the Cembalo Concerto in D by Georg Monn (1717–1750).

me a Phil. ticket? Joy doesn't yet know whether she'll be able to get to either of the concerts.

About the songs. Percy R. Rowe [copyist] still has them — he had to put them on one side for some urgent work — but I'll get him to send along those already finished and post them off to you early next week. They'll be something for Keith to go on with and the remainder will follow a day or two later. If you could go through the Oboe Work on the Monday sometime it would be a great help — that is, if the spirit isn't too strongly upon you — so that I can get the bowing done on Tuesday or Wed.

Joy and Aunt Lily loved seeing Nunky. It was good of him to go, and they were so sorry not to have seen you. I do hope the cold's better and that you can tackle the Romeo et Juliette cigar. Love to Nunky and bon voyage. It's very good news that he has gone to Richards [the Finzi's doctor]. Do make him stick to it. Ever, G.

I suppose it would not be possible to phone Britten and ask him whether he had to pay (or have deducted from royalty sheets) the whole or a proportion of the copyright fees of the de la Mare poems (the O.U.P. published three children's songs of his). This would be a tremendous help if I knew. If he did, I should go ahead with Foss. If not, I should not go ahead with my songs. Or anyone else you know, whose school songs have been published by the O.U.P.

8 East Heath Road, N.W.3; 25 October

[Dear Dave]

Britten gets 50% royalty for the de la Mare songs, and de la Mare gets 50%. He says 'It's the same the whole world over, it's the pore as gets the blayme' and that the wretched composer is made to pay up whether one is dealing with the O.U.P. or Boosey & Hawkes.

MORAL: Use words that are non-copyright. Yrs, H.

8 East Heath Road, N.W.3; 27 October

Dear Dave,

Here is the paper. I hope you approve of it, for it suits me down to the ground. As to price: we have done even better than I thought, as Augener are charging £6.5.0 for the 100 quires plus the specially engraved plate (10/−), whereas I was expecting the latter to be extra. This means that the paper in future will not come out so very much more than their standard ones — 50 quires ordinary double paper: usual price £5, professional £3.15; 100 quires special single paper, £5.15. Carriage on the paper was 1/11, therefore you owe me half of £6.6.11, which is £3.3.5½.

I shall get one Phil ticket for you, as you ask. Let me know as soon as you can whether you want the extra B.B.C. ticket I have for the 6th, or whether you and Joy are going to the Gallery. If you don't want it, I shall give it to somebody else.

I have just been listening to a broadcast (international) called 'Youth Sings over the Frontiers'. It was profoundly interesting, but Britain's contribution made me blush. Best of all were Poland, Norway, Czecho-Slovakia and Hungary (fine arrangements by Kodaly for the latter). Looking forward to seeing you on the 4th. Ever, H.

Aldbourne, Wilts.; 30 October

[Dear Fergie]

Many thanks for the paper which I like very much. I'll bring cheque with me. Lord, what a good one you are at figures! Joy will be coming to the Wednesday concert, so I think we had better go Gallery. I gather that your tickets are not Gallery? A pity: I wish we could have all sat together. Could you get the two tickets when getting my Phil? (If it's possible to get one wherever your other two are, then we should be able to sit together.) G.

Aldbourne, Wilts.; 10 November

[Dear Fergie]

I do hope satisfactory news is coming through [of H.F.'s Father's illness]. I'm going straight to Burlington House on Thursday a.m. and after lunch want to try and get into 'Parnell' at the New Theatre, though I'm afraid there'll be little chance. Failing that, Leicester Square Cinema (Rembrandt) or Academy Cinema (nothing could be worse than the French film to which you sent me).[12] After tea I'll come straight up to Hampstead. I don't expect you'll be feeling like the Phil., but we can fix up there. Our love. G.

Aldbourne, Wilts.; 29 November

[Dear Fergie]

Have you been listening-in to the Fauré songs? I find that there are four small collections, apart from the 3 volumes and 'La Bonne Chanson': 'Mirages', 'Le Jardin Clos', 'L'Horizon Chimèrique' and 'La Chanson d'Eve', and some things worth having in them all. This is in case you want to make your Fauré complete. If Joy is coming up Monday 9th may I put up for the night with you? I should like to hear the Lemare concert. Our love. (Say no if in any way inconvenient.) G.

Have just sent off the Parts [of the Oboe 'Interlude'] to Ivor James. Hurrah.

---

[12] *Parnell* was a biographical drama on the life of Charles Stewart Parnell (1846–1891), Irish MP and champion for Home Rule. Written by Elsie T. Schauffler (1888–1935), it was first staged at the Globe Theatre Studio and transferred to the West End only after a tussle with the Lord Chamberlain's office. *Rembrandt* was an outstanding, if historically inaccurate, Alexander Korda film (1936) starring Charles Laughton.

8 East Heath Road, N.W.3; 16 December

Dear Dave,

I wanted to show you these further poems of Toty de Navarro[13] when you were up, but there was no time. You may keep them if you wish, as I have other copies. 'The Secret Flower' appeals to me very much (except the first line, oddly enough, which associates itself in my mind with a dreadful Negro spiritual!); how does it affect you? 'Buckland Crossroads' I include for the beauty of its last 6 lines; apart from this it might be felt to be too strongly influenced by another poet.

Off to Ireland tomorrow. Keep well. With love to J & C, from H.

I have a suspicion that the punctuation of 'Half Way Round the Sun' is incomplete; but that is his fault, as he scribbled it out for me.

As from Aldbourne, Wilts.; 20 December

Dear Fergie,

I could not resist this cheap reprint ('Art-Forms in Nature'), which you deserve for your Partita! Joy says you're above looking at pictures and that I should send you a *reading* book. Our love and a happy Christmas and best of luck in the new house [34 Willoughby Road, N.W.3]. I'm having the hell of a time scoring those songs. Our love, G.

14 Deramore Park South, Belfast; 26 December

Dear Dave,

When that large and well-wrapped package arrived the other day with your writing on the outside, I said to myself 'Ha-ha! a packet of new songs from Dave'. I don't know why I thought of that, but I did, even though it was a little optimistic to expect you to spring a whole new set on me unbeknownst. However, though it isn't quite so exciting as that, it is a very lovely present. Thank you and J very much indeed for it. And why, pray, does your dear wyf (or wife) imagine that looking at picksures is beneath me? I love looking at them, so there! I will admit that the Introduction is a bit above me; but I have a suspicion that it has acquired its somewhat earnest and highfalutin air in the process of translation, and that we must not lay this at the author's door. In any case, the pictures are the thing, and they are just about as lovely as they can be.

I am sorry the scoring of the three songs is being a nuisance. It so often is when one has not thought of the work orchestrally from the beginning. There are some places in the Partita which, for the same reason, are going to give me the hell of a time. About the last movement: I have not yet any feelings of uneasiness about the middle section, beyond a slight desire to remove one single bar. Contrariwise, I do feel that the very end of the movement and one

[13] José Maria de Navarro (1896–1979), archaeologist, poet, Fellow of Trinity College, Cambridge. His mother (see letter 19 September 1938), the beautiful American actress Mary Anderson, held musical soirées at her house in the Cotswolds (Court Farm, Broadway).

113

other place towards the end may require a little seeing-to. Probably only the addition of three or four bars in all, but just that something which is the difference between what one really wants and what one first puts down. I have been playing it over here on two pianos and am pretty certain now that the last movement is a satisfactory finish to the work; I was a little too close to it before to be able to tell, though I was encouraged by what you felt about it. Anyway, it is going to be played over here on 11 January, so I shall then have an opportunity of judging its complete effect.

As things are at present arranged, I shall be back in Hampstead on Monday, 13 Jan. Until we meet then, all the best possible wishes for your work and Joy's and the happiness of both of you in 1936. Ever, H.

P.S. The fiddle Sonata [No.1] is being broadcast on 1 January, in case you want to hear it.

as from Aldbourne, Wilts.; 31 December

Dear Fergie,

Still at Lye Green, but returning to Aldbourne on the 3rd. Would you mind glancing through these questions — especially the clarinet ones, about which you are bound to know better than I — and give counsel's opinion. Then I can at once send it off to the copyist. The 'Milton Sonnets' are done and copied TG but I'm sure will sound very bad. Rehearsals for that concert on 6 February are on 3 Feb. and 6th. So may I put up with you 3–7 Feb? Say no, if inconvenient. I'm glad it will give me 2 clear days for re-scoring everything! What a relief to know that even V.W. still has his scores vetted! He showed me the Viola Suite — it's coming out, by the way (piano version, not full score), likewise the proofs of 'Riders to the Sea'.

I like Navarro's poems very much — none of them absolutely perfect, but weak exactly where you felt them to be weak, though I don't see the connection with another modern poet in 'Buckland Crossroads', though I agree that the last 6 lines are the outstanding ones.

Very delighted to see that you're starting the New Year with the fiddle Sonata. We shall be listening-in.

Rain, rain, rain for 3 weeks. Our love and a happy new year. Yours, G.

1936

14 Deramore Park South, Belfast; 2 January

Dear Dave,

I thought it easiest to write my suggestions on your sheet in red ink and return it to you complete, so here it is. I hope it is decipherable.

Of all the blasted luck! The only two engagements I have so far this year are on the 5th & 6th of Feb. in Dorset. Isn't it pestilential? There is at least nothing on the 3rd, so I shall be able to hear the rehearsal (if I'm allowed in), which is, I suppose better than nothing. You can, of course, stay at No.8, so far as I know, even though I won't be there from 5th–7th; but I shall be very sorry to miss the concert.

I'm so glad you like the Navarro poems. The modern poet I referred to was he who wrote the following:-

> 'Hallelujah' was the only observation
> That escaped Lt. Col. Mary Jane,
> When she fell from off the platform at the station
> And was cut in little pieces by the train.
> 'Hallelujah, Hallelujah, Mary Jane the train ran through yer;
> Let us gather up the fragments that remain.'

That is to say, A.E. Housman; and the particular poem I was reminded of was that which begins: 'I walked alone and thinking', from 'Last Poems'. By the way, it has just struck me what a very fine poem is:

> 'The Wain upon the northern steep
> Descends and lifts away'

You probably know it already, but it had not struck me before.[1]

The Sonata [Violin Sonata No.1] came through very well last night, the last movement being a particular fine performance. I thought Nunky was a bit over-generous with the pedal on occasions, but the feeling of the whole was grand. How I wish I could re-write that fiddle part now! It is quite idiotically difficult, and could be made so much more effective as well as so much easier. Much love to you and J. I hope Christopher flourishes.

    Ever, H.

                    Aldbourne, Wilts., 22 January

[Dear Fergie]

If I come up for the Constant Lambert[2] on 29th and Phil. on the 30th would you be able to put me up Wed. and Thurs. nights? Say no if in any way inconvenient. I'm not yet quite certain, but should like to if I can. Many thanks for red-ink emendations, gratefully received. Nothing from old Boosey yet. G.

                    8 East Heath Road, N.W.3; 13 February

Dear G & J,

'Horace's' head [horsy female friend of Joy's sister Mags] is magnificent. The plaster casts had put me off it somewhat for a time; but now one sees it in all the

---

[1] No. XVII, 'Astronomy', in *Last Poems* (1922).
[2] *Summer's Last Will and Testament*. 2 January at Queen's Hall. B.B.C. Symphony Orchestra and Philharmonic Choir, conducted by the composer.

strength and sensitiveness of the original clay. The medium – whatever it is – is almost perfect. 'Almost' because the pitting is a slight disadvantage; rather that, however, than have any suspicion of shininess, so be careful how you go with cellulose-finishes. Have a good holiday. H.

P.S. I don't know whether to laugh or cry over the enclosed [a newspaper cutting of Mr and Mrs John Masefield on their return from a tour in America]: '. . . and the dear red curve of her lips.'

Aldbourne, Wilts. [; before 17 February]

Dear Fergie,

Would you (and/or Nunky) try and get along to Aunt Lily's sometime or other. Joy has left the head of 'Horace' there, done in this new metal-spraying medium. She has tried it out on a cast of 'Horace' to see if it would be liked for your head. It's done in nickel, though it really looks far more like a cement and we both think it very successful – especially from afar, though from very near it looks slightly pin-pricked. It may need a cellulose finish, to stop the dirt collecting in the 'pin-pricks', but would not be much affected as regards colour. I think you will like it, even more on your head than on 'Horace'.

The concert went off all right. The Songs [Milton Sonnets] sounded rather silly in that particular concert, with the Darnton and Rawsthorne.[3] The latter a very good work, I thought, with a logic and clarity that made it possible to follow its growth from beginning to end. The Darnton completely sterile and boring beyond words. He was his usual self at the rehearsal, which he tried to direct over Iris [Lemare's] head and got some good snubs. Darnton to Iris (*f*, sharply and teutonically): 'Before you begin will you kindly go through one or two passages'. Iris, to orchestra: 'From the beginning, please.' I saw the kind Daily Telegraph, in spite of that I think the Rawsthorne was the most important thing in the concert. The old ladies liked the songs, and the Walter Leighs,[4] Darntons & Co rather contemptuous of them, I think. For once, I agreed with the bright sparks! The scoring was nearly all O.K. Our love, G.

(Old Boosey wrote that although we were not able to agree about the songs he hoped I would continue to send him work!)

as from Aldbourne, Wilts.; 17 February

Dear Fergie,

Joy's so pleased you liked the nickel metal-spraying. She'll experiment with the cellulose finish on 'Horace's' head before doing anything to yours. One of the objections to the pitting is difficulty of keeping clean, but she thinks that a

---

[3] Rawsthorne's work was the *Overture for Chamber Orchestra*. Darnton (see undated letter November 1933) was not on Finzi's wavelength, nor he on his!

[4] Walter Leigh (1905–1942), English composer, killed in action near Tobruk. Remembered for his Concertino for Harpsichord and Strings (1936) – which may have formed part of this concert?

matt cellulose may do the job. We'll be back again early next week and Joy will be in London the following Monday and she's going to work on that right away.

I wonder if you've been to any concerts, including the Tuesday 5.30s, and have heard anything worthwhile – Maconchy, Joyce Chapman[5] and so on. Would you give a message to Cedric Thorpe [Davie] and give our humble apologies that such an important thing as his surname was omitted. (Incidentally, it was not done on purpose or as a joke, but was a real lapse on my spouse's part!) Tell him, also, that changes of fashion in the upbringing of children have taken place since his day. Master Finzi has a change of underwear (& outerwear) more frequently than once in three months. And give him our love. I shall think of you playing the Partita together.

We have spent a lot of time wondering what Mrs Masefield could have been like in years gone by. The only thing to do is to remember his dedication to her, to shut one's eyes and say 'she has meant everything to him and has been responsible for making him work and must really be a very remarkable woman'. Joy says that at least she has an indomitable look in her eyes, which makes up for all that has gone out of her lips. But it's all very pathetic. Rothenstein says that Masefield is taking his Laureateship terribly seriously.

It's been pretty poor weather here [Cornwall] but very warm and muggy. Still, we've been having a grand time, walking, sketching (Joy, not me), reading – one of the objects of the holiday was to get 'The Seven Pillars' [T.E. Lawrence] digested, as it deserves. Joy is proving a wonderful cook, and even I have made a magnificent sardine-dish; but it repeated so much that I've not given it another chance! I've come to the conclusion that Cornish Serpentine is much maligned. Of course, charabanc-loads of trippers go to The Lizard and buy appalling obelisks and lighthouses as souvenirs. But I've got one or two ash-trays and pill-boxes which strike me as quite lovely.

Being away, I haven't done anything about the O.U.P. or old Boosey, but it has occurred to me that the best plan would be as follows. Wait until the Oboe Work has been done. If Hawkes takes it (and I don't for one minute think that he will, for he has already been bitten over one short oboe work [Britten's 'Fantasy' for Oboe, Violin, Viola and Cello], and Britten has a much bigger name than I have). Then go into the question of old Boosey publishing six songs, as offered, and me doing the remaining four. Naturally, I don't want to do this, but it might be a way out of the difficulty. I should have to aim for a bigger royalty – in proportion to the 1/3rd that I should be forking out – and, published in one volume, there could be no question of old B putting it on the shelf (as he undoubtedly would if it had cost him nothing, and he got nothing out of it) because he would have been responsible for 2/3rds of it. How one would manage over the separate issues I don't quite know. However, all this pre-supposes that Hawkes will do the Oboe Work. If, as I genuinely expect, he won't, well then, I must just carry on with the O.U.P.

---

[5] Pupil of R.V.W. at R.C.M.

Let us know when you move and if we're up in London whether the car can be of any use.

Our love, G.

as from Aldbourne, Wilts.; 20 February

Dear Fergie,

My Secretary being at work, I thought I would make use of her, even though she prefers double spacing to single! I have been elected, Dear Fergie, to Associate Membership of The Performing Right Society Ltd,[6] and am having it put on my visiting cards, and my certificate of Membership framed in red and gold. Seriously, have you any idea whether there is some hanky-panky going on about the P.R.S.? This sudden rush of publishers. This enclosed letter from Associated Copyrights Ltd came shortly after I had applied for membership to the PRS. So I thought I would ask the PRS, how they stood in relation to the B.B.C. clause to which my attention is drawn in the letter. The PRS reply quite airily and quite away from the point, as follows: 'With reference to your letter of 12th February, I have not seen the circular referred to, but have been informed of its general purport. I think I may say that you need not regard the B.B.C.'s ruling as applying to manuscript compositions of serious works. In any case, the point is not now of importance as far as you are concerned, for, by virtue of your Membership, the Society controls the public performing right in your manuscript works, and you will be duly credited with the appropriate share of the fees collected by the Society from the B.B.C.'

Your sense of logic will be tickled by the 'comparative unimportance' of a point which compels AC Ltd to stop collecting royalties for me! Now what is going on behind the scenes? If you hear anything, you might let me know. I'm sure the PRS is a bad way out of an even worse job – their book of rules strikes me as being appalling, and giving them a latitude which, if they chose to use it, could leave everybody stranded. Don't chuck away enclosure, but keep it until we meet sometime.

We go home next week. Weather glorious now. Went over the Cutty Sark yesterday. Our love, Gerald Finzi (Associate Member PRS).

A friend of ours, who lent us this cottage in Cornwall, has a sister (who part owns it) living in Falmouth. We had lunch with her yesterday. She had a friend staying with her – a Miss Barnard – who turned out to be a friend of the ROs. As I was a musician, I suppose she thought it would be nice for me to meet another musician, so she asked a friend of hers to lunch too. He knew the ROs too, as he happened to be Conrad Ormand's brother. This shows, as some are fond of saying, how small the world is. (Conrad Ormand's brother is organist of Truro Cathedral, but an even worse musician, I should imagine, than most of that lot. He was giving an organ recital and starting off with 'Finlandia'.)

---

[6] Performing Right Society. Founded in 1914 to collect royalties due to member-composers and publishers on public performances including broadcasts, of all registered works.

[Unsigned]

8 East Heath Road, N.W.3; 14 March

Dear Dave,

This is going to be a most unsatisfactory letter. First of all, the enclosed postcard from B & H explains itself. I wrote to Hawkes about the concert weeks ago, and could not understand why I had had no reply; this is, of course, the reason. It would be worth letting them have a ticket in any case, so would you like to send along one to Mr E. Rosen? I have a couple of tickets myself, so if you are short I could let you have one of them; but only if you really want it, as I know someone who would probably like to go, though I have not asked them definitely yet.

Secondly, I was just about to write and ask you to stay here while you are up for the concert, when Nunky, who departed for Canada yesterday, broke it to me that he had wished the son of a South African friend [named Storr] of his to stay on us for three weeks – I never having even encountered the said son! As Nunky had parked himself on them while in S. Africa, he said he felt he ought to do something for the son when he was looking for a nesting-place over here. A laudable thought, which would have been still more praiseworthy had our Mr Samuel been in residence, and so able to cope with the visitor himself. Since he isn't, I must step into the breach and do my best. The gentleman arrives on Monday, so you can hold thumbs for me then and think of me facing the unknown unbowed.

We were horrified to read in Tuesday's 'Times' the short obituary notice of Herbert Lambert. Neither of us had any notion that he was even ill, much less dead. You must tell me how it happened when we meet. I am not writing to Mrs Lambert as I scarcely know her, having only been introduced to her once.

Did you listen to Britten's Violin and Piano 'Suite' last night? I waited up for it, but I might as well have been in bed for all the pleasure I got. I remember him showing me the MS when it was still unfinished and in pencil, and I thought then that it was a piffley work though dexterous. Performance did not improve it.

The Easdale[7] two-piano works at the last Patrons' Fund Chamber Concert but one (I was not able to get to the last) were beautifully written for two pianos, but not much good musically. A curiously strong influence of Debussy – not so much in idiom as in general method of putting together and in texture. You know: one static figure is started, then a second is added, and finally a tune is put on top. From the way they played his two works I would not have believed it possible for them to play the Ernest Walker 'Waltz Suite' as foully as they did.[8] The work itself was bad enough; but played as they played it, it was quite

[7] Brian Easdale (1909–1995), English composer best known for his score for the 1948 ballet film *The Red Shoes*.

[8] Ernest Walker (1870–1949), English composer and pianist, best remembered as a writer on music and for the concerts he directed at Balliol College, Oxford.

intolerable. Frankie's [Frank Bridge] G minor String 4tet was the first work of his that I have ever heard and enjoyed. Not great music, or anything like it, but how well done. So far as I can remember, I have not heard any further new music.

The last movement of the Partita has been suffering mutilation in several places. I must have taken about 20 bars out what with one thing and another, and many details have been altered. It is better now, I think. 7 bars have also been removed from the first movement: this is a surprising improvement. I have decided to use the score of the first three movements that I have made as a rough draft only. It is not really satisfactory, and it will be simpler to do the whole thing over again. Have you any feelings as to the size of orchestra? I believe I have started off with too small a one (double WW, with trombones & tuba and usual brass). I should really like to go the whole hog and use triple WW, and perhaps even a 3rd trumpet; but I don't know whether this would be unwise. What do you think? Perhaps it would be all right if I cued-in all the extras; that is, the 'thirds' — though I should most likely want a Cor Anglais in any case. You might let me know what your feelings are, if you have any on the matter.

I hope you, Joy, and fat Christopher are all well. I'll be seeing you soon. Ever, Howard.

Aldbourne, Wilts.; 16 March

Dear Fergie,

Poor Fergie, I should say! However, I hope he [H.F.'s visitor from S. Africa] has turned out an angel. I was a bit dubious, in any case, about saddling myself on you, with this move ahead, and now I see that you're likely to suffer something quite as bad. Will it knock dates on the head? Apart from 5.30 on Tuesday, and Bartok on Wednesday (Joy has got two tickets for this) I'm very anxious to see 'St Helena' on Monday night.[9] Joy has seen it and says it is well worth while. So if you are free do try and manage it.

I haven't heard a word about rehearsals for Tuesday and shan't be a bit surprised to hear that Leon [Goosens] has decided not to do it [G.F.'s 'Interlude' for Oboe and String quartet]. I suppose someone will let me know.

I think Mr E. Rosen's card pretty well damns any chance of B & H taking it. I imagine that only the personal interest of Hawkes would have made it possible. Many thanks, all the same, for having written. I'll send him a ticket. A spare came by the same post as your letter. But I very much fear that it'll have to be the O.U.P. again for the 'Interlude' and therefore for the songs. Whoever it is, I must get the songs in their final order, so I hope you won't mind working it out with me. I should like old H.P. Greene [Harry Plunket Greene, Parry's son-in-law] to have had some say about it — for I think he's wonderful about

---

[9] A play by R.C. Sherriff (1896–1975), in collaboration with the actress Jeanne de Casalis, about Napoleon's last days. Presented first at the Old Vic, but transferred to Daly's Theatre in 1936. Sherriff is best known for his enormously successful First World War play *Journey's End* (1927) which he made into a novel in 1930.

that sort of thing, from the singer's point of view – but we'll have a shot by ourselves, if you won't mind.

Yes, it's a great blow to us about Herbert Lambert's death and we shall miss him very much. I thought he would go out like a wire burning too brightly. The immediate cause was angina, though he was ill for about a fortnight. I think there was a slight cerebral haemorrhage too. I should have written and let you know, but I didn't think you knew him very well. He loved your Octet, by the way, when it was done at Bristol I think. I've never met anyone that didn't love it – always excepting Darnton, of course!

I should certainly feel like going the whole hog with the Partita. What it might lose by missing a few provincial performances, it would gain by getting specialized performances, which really mean much more. May we look at the score next week?

Surely Cedric would like the enclosed when you next write to him. Our love, G.

Aldbourne, Wilts.; 22 March

[Dear Fergie]

Is the V.W. Opera [*The Poisoned Kiss*] at Cambridge April or May 11–16? Do you know to whom to write for tickets?

Alas, nothing in 'Times' or 'Observer' about Tuesday – not that it matters in the least, except that it is a curse as far as publishers are affected. It's all due to the B'mouth Festival.[10] Our love, G.

Aldbourne, Wilts.; 31 March

[Dear Fergie]

The furniture removers are: Arts & General Carriers Ltd, West Row, W.10 (Park 7246).

But surely your playing on the 12th May won't go on until the 16th! Our love, G.

Whether Steinway or Arts & General, I pay for the piano [move], Fergie. [G.]

Aldbourne, Wilts.; 15 April

Dear Fergie,

Yes, it is a very remarkable production. We were most grateful that you sent it. I'm suspicious about sending 1/– to the Preaching and Singing Evangelist, but I should dearly love a copy. Could not Cedric get me one when he gets home? After all, every house was presented with one and they must be lying about Glasgow like refuse after a bank-holiday. I gather that Soul is another

---

[10] The Bournemouth Easter Musical Festival, directed by Sir Dan Godfrey (begun in 1922), attracted wide critical attention on account of its adventurous programmes, including first performances of many new British works. At the 1936 Festival, Stravinsky conducted a concert of his own works on 27 March, and inevitably attracted all the London critics.

word for Semen and that porridge oats is an aphrodisiac and lactifier. Isn't this the thesis? Fergie, Joy reminds me that you have a bowl of porridge oats every morning so are evidently one of the saved.

Thanks for Mr Rosen's name. I could not very well say that it went down well or that Leon Goosens had asked for the dedication, etc., so I've said that Mr Rosen heard it. We'll be listening-in to Cedric's work. It's on Regional, so I shall hear pretty well. Our love to him and to you. G.

Aldbourne, Wilts.; 22 April

Dear Fergie,

To my surprise Mr E. Rosen did go and hear the 'Interlude' (thanks to you) and they've accepted it, though I'm not quite certain about the terms, which seem to imply that I part with the copyright for £5 though I receive 10% royalties and half mechanical rights. I've asked Chenhalls' [Alfred Chenhalls, accountant] advice, as you're in Ireland. In any case, beggars can't be choosers, and I must consider myself very lucky. I have a copy of your Head now. The piano and stove have arrived. What do I owe you for the latter and for the delivery? Our love, G.

Aldbourne, Wilts. [; 1 or 8 May]

Dear Fergie,

Here's the cheque for the stove. I've sent to the Arts & General direct. I don't wonder that you've heard no music recently! I listened-in to the Berg and rather admired a lot of it. Alas, we'll miss you at 'The Poisoned Kiss' at Cambridge (our days are Tuesday and Wednesday) which I hope will put new life into you. It should be a good rag, but I don't think a masterpiece, though there are bound to be one or two passages that'll stick in the head (like the letter scene in 'Sir John in Love'); and it's sure to come off, however poor it seems on paper. Some of the libretto is very amusing, though with occasional bits of school-girl humour, particularly in the dialogue. Perhaps it'll be cut out.

Do you know the piano-duet version of Smetana's 'Ma Vlast'? I've been going through it recently and very surprised to find so much Sibelius in it. As you don't read 'The Times', you must have missed that glorious letter: 'Sir, I am curious to know why the piece of operatic sex-appeal called "Parsifal", written by the pure-minded composer of the Venus scene in "Tannhäuser", the incest scene in "Die Walkure", the sex-surrender scene in "Siegfried", the bigamy scene in "Götterdämerung", and the adultery scene in "Tristan", is presented to us in an opera-house as a solemn and sacred rite, which we are forbidden to applaud – supposing that we wish to applaud any of it. I am, etc. Serge Sampson.' What more can one say, except that Beecham's 'Sit down, you bitch' (I'm told to Lady Cunard, who rustled in bits) *did* come over the wireless. And now that you're in the new house [34 Willoughby Road, N.W.3] at last, best of luck in it, Fergie, and love from us both. G.

34 Willoughby Road, N.W.3; 10 May

Dear Dave,

Very many thanks for the cheque for £4.5.0 for Cozy Stove; also for having sent direct to the Arts & General: I am enclosing their receipt for your safe keeping.

The letter from 'The Times' is a gem: thanks so much for having troubled to copy it out. I shall pass it on to Cedric when next I write to him. By the way, I have just heard from him in Helsingfors [C.T.D. was studying with Yryö Kilpinen in Finland], with which he is apparently enchanted; he writes most enthusiastically of everything there.

The miniature score of the Walton Symphony is out (5/−). No, I don't know 'Ma Vlast', but I should like to; will you lend it to me sometime.

Tell Joy that my 'Head' is coming out in the most alarming LEPROUS patches; her urgent attention is obviously required, and will be gratefully welcomed when next she has a free moment in London.

The house is beginning to get straight. I think you will agree it looks rather nice; I am delighted with my room. Blessings on you both, with love, Howard.

P.S. Please *date* your letters. 'Friday' or 'Wednesday' is a horrid habit, and gives one no idea how long one forgets to reply.

Aldbourne, Wilts.; 17 May

Dear Fergie,

Sorry about my dates! I very seldom know the date, without a paper, Radio Times or engagement-book beside me; and if I'm writing in the garden, it's too much fag to get up and look. One day more or less never seems to matter. But you're quite right.

It's certainly disturbing about the 'head'. Fortunately Joy has other casts and it was only an experiment, though she did hope it was going to be successful. She wonders if it has been in the sun, though of course for a permanent thing neither sun nor shade should be of consequence. She'll be up in London early in June and will be sure to look you up and see about it. Perhaps I'll come too, as there are a few little things I want to go through with you, and I'm afraid you're not thinking of basking in the sun here.

I hope the scoring [of the Partita] is going on well. On second thoughts I think the Clarinet *will* come through the Strings, though plus oboe would be just as good. How happy and free you'll feel when it's all done.

So much to tell you about Cambridge [V.W.'s *The Poisoned Kiss*], but must leave it till we meet. I listened to Vogel's 'Wagada Destroyed' and was much impressed.[11] Or was it the transforming powers of the wireless? Though I got tired of so much singing, it seemed a very sincere and moving work. The

---

[11] Vladimir Vogel (1896–1984), Russian-born Swiss composer. *Wagadu's Untergang durch die Eitelkeit* (1930) employs a choral and solo speech in addition to sung solo and chorus accompanied by five saxophones.

choral-speech in canon sounded amazing. Murrill's[12] cello concerto was also much better than I expected – much Stravinsky, some Walton, but very competent. However, since 'The Lady Macbeth' [*The Lady Macbeth of Mtsensk*, by Shostakovich] which sounded so exciting over the wireless and was evidently complete balderdash in the flesh, I'm inclined to put down any good qualities to the machine. Our love, G.

34 Willoughby Road, N.W.3; 18 May

Dear Dave,

Thank you so much for your letter (and for the date! Sorry to be fussy; but if one keeps letters there is nothing more infuriating than to be confronted with a plain Tuesday or Wednesday when trying to sort them).

In case you have not seen the poem which Housman wrote three years ago for his own funeral, I am transcribing it from the copy of the service which Toty sent to me:

> O thou that from thy mansion
>   Through time and place do roam,
> Dost send abroad thy children,
>   And then dost call them home.
>
> That men and tribes and nations
>   And all thy hand hath made
> May shelter them from sunshine
>   In thy eternal shade:
>
> We now to peace and darkness
>   And earth and thee restore
> Thy creature that thou madest
>   And wilt cast forth no more.   AEH

Is there any chance of you being able to put me up, and put up with me, for Whitsun? I would have to work most of the time, but perhaps you wouldn't mind that. You must, of course, be quite honest about it; but if you could have me, I should like to descend on you late on Thursday 28, and would have to leave on Wednesday 3 June. All I'd need would be – not a loaf of bread and a jug of wine, though I wouldn't mind the latter – a table and a piano. Say quite frankly whether this would be at all awkward.

I did not hear any of the works you mention in your letter. Tom James and I had a most delightful day in Cambridge on Saturday. I enjoyed 'The Poisoned Kiss', but not quite enough to go to the Sadlers Wells performance tonight. The old dear conducted himself at the Saturday matinée. Ever, H.

P.S. Dicky, otherwise Sally Sinclair [H.F.'s sister] had a son on Friday last. Both getting on well. I have forgotten whether you are a friend of Emily

[12] Herbert Murrill (1909–1952), English composer and administrator. Became B.B.C.'s Head of Music in 1950.

Daymond; if not, you can tear up the enclosed notice, as I have already sent something. H.

Aldbourne, Wilts.; 18 May

Dear Fergie,

Why yes, the 28th to 3 June will be excellent. You may overlap a day with my step-grandmother (she'll be leaving on 29 or 30) but she's a dear and a nuisance to nobody, intelligent and never in the way. You can have either my room with a grand or the remoter attic with an old square. I don't know which means most to you – a good instrument or remoteness.

The Housman is lovely. I didn't know it though had read about it. Joy has typed it into 'Last Poems', and I suppose, alas, that it really is the last.

I expect your sister Sal wanted a boy this time, so that's good news. I told you, I think, that Richards says our next will be another boy.

I've met Emily Daymond a couple of times and corresponded once, yet I suppose I really can't be classed as a friend (or 'pupil') though I should like to send something, for she's an admirable whirlwind and 'An English Suite' [Parry] is dedicated to her, and that alone should show her worth.

I see that the Oriana[13] are doing something of mine Tuesday 9 June Acolian Hall 8.15. I suppose it'll be one or more of those Bridges part-songs – other than 'Nightingales'. So if you're free do join us, as Joy will be up in London on 8 June and I'll come up with her. Our love, [G]

Have you had an invitation to Sylvia's wedding [Sylvia Spencer, oboist] on 6 June or shall we send you ours?

Aldbourne, Wilts.; 18 May

[Dear Fergie]

B & H have just sent the proofs of that 'Interlude' [for Oboe & String 4tet]. Would you be comfortably free to check them if I posted at the end of the week? At first glance they seem very good, but I suppose they always send 2nd proofs. The only thing is that you might be away or even busier when those come. It looks so nice in the large that I almost regret the miniature score!

Did you put 'opus number' at the end of the Parts? Our love, G.

34 Willoughby Road, N.W.3; 19 May

Dear Dave,

Do you think the melodic bits on the reverse are scored heavily enough? The 'thwacks' [in the allegro of the 1st movement of the Partita] are intended to be big; and, though the between pieces are very much smaller, they must not

[13] Charles Kennedy Scott's Oriana Madrigal Society, founded in 1904.

sound either footling or too far-distant. All suggestions gratefully received, but I don't much want to use Strings.

Send along the 'Interlude' by all means. It may look nice now, but just wait until you see it as a miniature-score and you will then feel yourself to be among 'the classical masters'. Please return this sheet. Ever, H.

Aldbourne, Wilts. [undated: answer to the above]

Dear Fergie,

Personally I do think it's rather like a sparrow in a bombardment and could do with heavier scoring between the thwacks. But I'd think twice before trying to improve on your scoring. However good or bad, the other side shows what I would have done. Bars 1 & 2 you might prefer to delete passages in brackets – so that clarinets (*mf*) take over from trumpets (*mp*), though I know I should like it 'solid'. If you don't like double-bass pizzicato, have you a double-bassoon (then you'd put it in the top register, which I believe is very poor). Any objections to the 3rd Trumpet playing the C-sharp in the thwacks (D in bar 3)? I can't quite make out whether your units are 5 plus 2 or 4 plus 3. I think the former, as you've accented them; but if the latter it might be advisable for the 2nd trumpet to start the 3rds on the 5th quaver instead of the 6th. The 3rd bar is more difficult, because one doesn't know what follows, but do you mind the lower strings there? Anyhow, there may be something worth picking out of this rigmarole. Blessings. 'Interlude' [for oboe & strings] follows in a day or two. Lord! One day I shall have to check your Partita proofs!! Our love, G.

I'm a bit less certain about my woodwind in the 3rd bar, but I do think the lower octave is advisable, but whether it would not be better on the cor anglais instead of the 2nd clarinet I don't know. If you don't like trumpets, have you thought of oboe, Cor Anglais, A clarinets, bassoon and horns? though I think the other is better.

Is this programme of any interest to you for tomorrow, Thursday?

Aldbourne, Wilts.; 17 June

Dear Fergie,

You'll be glad, sorry or interested, to hear that your 'Head' is just beginning to blacken here – and starting at the nose and neck, too. So it looks as if there's much to be said for Joy's explanation.

The enclosed might be worth sending on to Cedric, if he and you haven't already seen it.

I should like to show you Eric Fenby's 'For music on the eve of Palm Sunday' (or if you feel flush, get it from Winthrop Rogers 5d). It's quite lovely and though written at Grez in 1932 has nothing of Delius about it.

Have you been to the Surrealist Exhibition yet? I hear that Walton went to the private view and bought a kipper on the way. It was surreptitiously hung on to some convenient nail or projection, and for quite a time was admired by the artist's admirers as a point of balance!

'Si non' etc., but I'm told it's true. Our love and to Nunky, G.

30 Downshire Hill, N.W.3; 14 August

Dear Fergie,

Here's my little piece and miserably small it appears now. The 'Rules for Compositors' explains a lot – though it doesn't go so far as Ro-rum. However, I hope to see Keith next week and he, as a singer, may have something to say.

Here's a picture of an old flame of yours, taken when she and Aunt Lily were on holiday, I think. In case you don't recognise her, it's someone called Cissie Craies. Aunt Lily would like it back one day, so stick it at the bottom of that vast suitcase of yours. We only thought it might amuse you.

Tell Randolph [Randolph Hokanson, a young American student of H.S.] that 'Fables in Slang' [by George Ade] is reported from America as being quite out of print. So I hope he'll ginger America up when he gets back.

Don't forget to bring back that 'Head' of yours for a coat of tin. I meant to tell you that Joy and I heard the following conversation at The Ballet – a young man giving a preliminary explanation of the 'Prince Igor Dances' to his female admirers: 'It's about someone who captured someone else and said "Let's have a party", and that's the party'.

I thought Walton stood the test of a one-man show very well, and showed a greater range than I had realized before – with P.P. [Portsmouth Point] at one end, and the Symphony, via the Viola Concerto, at the other. One may like or dislike the cold, glittering detachment about it all, but one can't help feeling that technically – for sheer mastery and management – there has never been anything quite to equal it. If he were not so incalculable I should say that he would burn out between 38 & 42, and that such nervous tension could not last a lifetime [he died in 1983]. But he keeps the last card up his sleeve and Harty's perspirations got no more out of the Symphony than Walton's own cool and composed conducting. The Rolls-Royce of Music! Our love – Joy and the infant flourishing. G.

Glen Hue, Newcastle, Co. Down; 17 August

Dear Dave,

What a delightful surprise packet that brought along the score of the 'Interlude'. Thank you very much indeed for it. Somehow I was not expecting it so soon, so the unexpectedness gave additional spice. I think they have done it very nicely, and, though I am not specially enamoured of the cover, yet it gives me a curiously warm feeling to know that the Octet has a similar one and that they will make a pair. I couldn't wish for better company. On looking through it once more in its printed finality ('only the great masters are done in miniature score'), I am again struck by its loveliness, and by the ease and beauty of the writing for that awkward combination. Certainly you seem to have the knack for writing for String Quartet (never to mention the oboe). I wish I had, for it isn't an easy nut to crack.

The 'old flame' whose photo you sent me, I easily recognised. Indeed, I am not sure that I have not seen the very same photo in one of her own albums, but perhaps that is pure imagination. I am returning it in this envelope, with many thanks to Aunt Lily for having conjured it up for me.

I like the conversation overheard at the Ballet: such an all-embracing description of the 'Prince Igor' dances! What were the other things you saw? 'Les Noces' was down on the preliminary prospectus, but does not seem to have been done from what I have seen of any of the newspaper lists. But perhaps this conversation was overheard at the performance when the Berlioz was done, and of which you have already told me.

Of the Walton Prom I enjoyed the Viola Concerto very much more than anything else. The Scherzo and (particularly) the last movement of the Symphony now appear to me to be a come-down from the rest of the work. That fugal second subject is surely a blot; specially in the return, when you realize you have to have it all over again?? if different in tempo and slightly different in form. But I must say I enjoyed the slow movement more than I have done before. The first movement stays much where it was. You can, however, have the whole of the Symphony if you give me in return the beginning and end of the Viola Concerto: that, I think, is the most beautiful music he has written. One is bound to admire the superlative competence of it all, but, my hat! how one longs for something more than competence for most of the time.

Here Randolph and I bathe, read and bask in what sun there is. I could wish that I were in London working, but apart from that faint itch and the lack of a piano, I am enjoying myself. The other I had a letter from Ceddie, who says that he has finished his opera [*Gammer Gurton's Needle*] score and all, and that he is sending it along to me towards the beginning of September; so perhaps we could arrange a meeting for you to see it, if that would amuse you, when I return to London. It is to go on to R.V.W. between Hereford and Norwich. I have not the least idea what it is like.

No further news, so love to Joy and yourself together with respectful salutations to Nigel and Christopher. Send me the 2nd proofs of the songs when they are ready. Ever, H.

30 Downshire Hill, N.W.3. till the 24th, then Aldbourne, Wilts.; 17 August
Dear Fergie,

Don't let your holiday be spoilt for it − unless it's a golfing holiday − but would you mind just glancing through this? It's a 1st proof [of 'Earth and Air and Rain'], but so good that I really don't know that a 2nd proof is necessary. What mistakes there are, are nearly all the fault of the MS. However, your eagle-eye may spot a thing or two.

I've been looking through your two-piano music − do bring some of it down when you and Randolph come. And I think the Humperdinck eight-hand arrangement might be possible, considering that you and he also play.

Love from Joy and blessings on yourself. Yours, G.

Glen Hue, Newcastle, Co. Down; 20 August

Dear Dave,

Here are the proofs, with one or two extra slips spotted. I have marked a cross on the top right-hand edge of each page that has a mistake on it, and the mistakes themselves are noted in the margin in pencil. You will be able to rub them out quite easily. As to the bit in the bass on p.4, I think I incline to the version as printed: it should not muddle the general rhythm, and is certainly better from the point of view of the bass vocal line.

Yesterday Rann and I gave a startling performance of the 'Interlude' on one piano: I trying to be a String Quartet and he an Oboe. Believe me, the result was surprising! But in spite of this, we were able to produce some idea of it, and he was most unbridled in his enthusiasm. Blessing on you both. I hope I haven't kept the proofs too long. Ever, II.

Aldbourne, Wilts.; 3 September

Dear Fergie,

Have you any sort of idea when you and Randolph will feel like coming? John [Sumsion] gets back on 23 September and is pretty full up for some time ahead, but could come over on the 24th if he knew in advance: and I think he'd like to hear the Partita. I suppose you would not feel like coming a few days before and staying the week? If you felt like going to the Crystal Palace Saturday 26th, I'd probably travel up with you. (Arthur's [Bliss] 'Kenilworth' is the test-piece — a real brass-band story-piece, ending with a march 'Homage to Queen Elizabeth.)

I've been looking at 2-piano music for you and Rann to play — though our pianos are a bit out of tune. You'll have to do the Reger Mozart-Variations: the theme is so lovely. Grieg's 'Ballad & Variations' was so bad that I returned it. The chief interest was that early Delius, and particularly 'Appalachia', owes something to it: in fact, at least a page might have come straight from Delius. Very badly written for two pianos and chiefly antiphonal.

'Riders to the Sea' [R.V.W.] is out, and a miniature score of the Sibelius Violin Concerto. Arthur and Trudy [Bliss] are going to sell Pen Pits!!![14] Our love, G.

Will you and Rann mind sharing a room (two beds!), or else separate rooms with one on a sofa?

[14] In 1934 Bliss purchased 30 acres of woodland near the village of Pen Selwood, Somerset. He commissioned a friend, the architect Peter Harland (1900–1973) to design 'Pen Pits', a striking modernist house — angular and white. Harland later designed Finzi's house at Ashmansworth.

Glen Hue, Newcastle, Co. Down, as from 34 Willoughby Road, N.W.3;
9 September

Dear Dave,

Very many thanks for your letter. As it happens, I have to play in Broadway on Wednesday 23rd, and would not be able to leave until the morning of the 24th. Apparently it would be possible for me to reach Hungerford by the train getting in at 12.31 (or Didcot at 11.50, if that is any better); but it would scarcely be worth while coming then unless we could stay over until the Monday following. If you have definitely decided to go up for the Brass Bands on Saturday 26th, that's that. But if you haven't, what about our coming from 24th–28th? I would sooner not come before then, as I must get in some decent practice and other work before the 23rd.

It is not yet certain whether Randolph is going to Broadway too; if not, he could come straight from London by the same train, as I would pick him up at Reading. Of course we wouldn't mind sleeping in the same room, provided (as you promise) you give us separate beds!

Many thanks for telling me about the Sibelius Violin Concerto. I've ordered a copy in readiness for Thursday's Prom, to which we go. Also a copy of 'Riders to the Sea'. I'm not a bit surprised at Arthur and Trudy selling Pen Pits. I never thought they'd keep it (or stick it) long! Arthur is incapable of staying in the country for longer than a few months at a time, I'm certain.

Must fly. Crossing to London tonight, so please reply to Hampstead. Ever, H.

Aldbourne, Wilts.; 12 September

Dear Fergie,

Your letter was just what I wanted, as I was going to write you and say that after all, before the 24th is hopeless. But John will be here on the 24th (returning to Gloucester in the evening), so if you and Rann can manage that day, and stay on till the 28th or later if you feel like it, it will be splendid. Hungerford 12.31 will get you in for lunch and leave plenty of time for John and the Partita.

I'm not particularly anxious to go up for the Brass Band Festival.[15] I don't quite know where your 12.31 is coming from, but you can always verify the train later on and drop me a card. Our love and all news on the 24th. G.

I find the [2nd] proofs of the songs ['Earth and Air and Rain'] here. If I get them done in time I'll send them on to you.

Aldbourne, Wilts. [; before 19 September]

Dear Fergie,

I hope it's not an inconvenient time for just running through these proofs. The first were full of corrections, but these 2nd seem pretty good. Keith

---

[15] To hear Arthur Bliss's *Kenilworth* suite, composed as a test piece.

[Falkner] found the rits. and accels. in 'Lizbie Brown' rather a hindrance to getting some sort of shape into the song so I knocked out as many as possible, though his suggestions were on the spur of the moment, rather than thought out. However, I don't think it makes much difference one way or the other. The screed at the bottom covers a multitude of sins! Awful to think that Boosey has chosen 'Lizbie Brown' and 'Rollicum Rorum' – the two worst songs in the set – for reprinting separately. I should have thought he'd have had the wit to spot 'Lyonesse' or even 'Proud Songsters'. Our love and looking forward to seeing you. G.

I'm glad to say that he's printing the words.

Aldbourne, Wilts.; 19 September

Dear Fergie,

Very many thanks, both for corrections and suggestions. By the way, 'Meos' (not Meus): see Vulgate Po38 'promisti dies meos'. But alas I didn't know about e-le-gi-sti or e-leg-i-sti. And if not the latter, how about de-dux-i-sti and pos-u-i-sti? Can't you ask Madame Navarro?![16] There appear to be conflicting rules about the division of Latin words. V.W. told me that Curwen's proof-reader changed all the underlaying in his Mass and made it *look* all wrong, but assured him it was right! I've followed Steuart Wilson's advice that 'the *root* should be shown, and the *personal* termination, hence fe-ci-sti, which in the 2nd plural would be fe-ci-mus. That shows its anatomy in each case and is logically defensible.' So if you have any further views about e-leg-i-sti, you might drop me a p.c. It's grand of you to suggest doing them for nothing with Keith. But I can't suggest it to him. He knows the songs and it must come from him rather than from me, as I think you'll agree. He's going to do some of them at an Iris Lemare concert on 11 Jan: I wish with you.

This is my two-piano music: Parry, 'Grosses Duo'; Schumann, '6 Studies' and 'Andante & Variations'; Mozart, 'Double Concerto', and Sonata & Fugue; Bach, Concertos in C ma and C mi; Brahms-Haydn Variations, and Sonata (after the 5tet); V.W. 'Running Set'; Reger Variations & Fugue; Bax, 'Moy Mell'; Bairstow, Variations; W.F. Bach, Sonata; Pasquini, 2 Sonatas. Also arrangements: Franck, Symphonic Variations; Walton, Sinfonia Concertante.

Till Thursday, Hungerford 12.31. Ever, G.

34 Willoughby Road, N.W.3; 28 September [; written on MS paper]

Dear Dave,

How about this? [middle section of last movement of Partita] I think it is better than the other version. If you agree, please write OK on a postcard and send it to me by return. You can tear up this sheet.

---

[16] Toty de Navarro's mother (see letter 16 December 1935).

That was a grand weekend: thank you both very much for it. I only wish it could have been longer. Love to G & J, from H.

Aldbourne, Wilts.; 29 September

Dear Fergie,

I should have said *much* better, but it is difficult to be certain without hearing more of the context – before and after. At the moment it feels as though it badly wants a 4-bar phrase (instead of a 3-bar) before the descending passage in octaves – a sort of 'suspense' bar. I don't know whether you would object to keeping the same harmony in the bar; in any case you'd make a better bar of it than that. And, of course, you may have a special reason for the 3-bar phrase. The sequence part of it is a wonderful improvement. Love, G.

34 Willoughby Road, N.W.3; 30 September

[Dear Dave]

Very many thanks. As it happens, a 3-bar phrase is needed there; you would agree if you saw a longer stretch. The air of Aldbourne appears to be unusually invigorating: I have just solved that 'lead-up' at the return, which you spotted and which had been worrying me for so long. Heaven (and Aldbourne) be praised. Ever, H.

Aldbourne, Wilts.; 6 October

Dear Fergie,

I don't know whether these [lyrics by Madam G. Hubi-Newcombe] were sent to you or to Nunky, and then sneakily re-addressed to me! I can't think that my fame has reached Madame G. Hubi-Newcombe – especially as the postmark was Hampstead, N.W.3. Also, it was addressed to Beech *Knole* – a little weakness of yours.

Anyhow, if you haven't already seen this packet it's time that you did. 'The Tempest King' would suit you down to the ground – so like the 'Two Ballads' in spirit. If by any chance they were sent to me by the be-crested authoress (which I don't believe for one minute) does one write a Thank-you-so-much letter? (Courtesy, I need not say, not admiration.)

We listened-in to Arthur's [Bliss] 'Kenilworth', but I'm afraid it was really done on one of his off-days. It isn't even effective, which is strange for Arthur.

You and Rann have made a great impression on Christopher: at least once a day he mentions you.

Can you go to this R.A.M. concert, or hand it on to someone who can? I should have liked to have heard the Concerto for two pianos. Is that the work you mentioned?

What about Trafalgar Day? Would you like 'Sherston's Progress' [Siegfried Sassoon] or what miniature score? Sorry I can't give you a surprise, but it's no good giving you something you don't want. Our love to you, not forgetting Rann and Pu. G.

If I ever come up to London – for instance, Nov 13 'Dona Nobis Pacem' [R.V.W.] and I hope before, I don't think it will be possible for you to put me up, with Rann and Nunky there. But if I ask beforehand don't feel embarrassed at having to say 'No' time after time. I can always go to 24 Keats Grove if Auntie has no one there.

Aldbourne, Wilts. [; between 6 and 14 October]

Meester Ferguson,

After all, I shall be coming to London on Wednesday 21st and staying the night – possibly two nights. May I come to you or may I not? Let me know soon so that I can get on to Aunt Lily. Even if you can't have me we might go on the razzle together – wine, women and song, or failing all three, a concert and theatre or two. Love from Joy. G.

34 Willoughby Road, N.W.3; 13 October

[Dear Dave]

Hurrah! Yes do come here on the 21st, and stay over until the Friday if you can, so that we may go to a theatre on the 22nd. Do you want me to get you a ticket for the 21st? H.

Aldbourne, Wilts.; 14 October

[Dear Fergie]

Good. I'll turn up sometime on Wed. 21st before tea. If you're going to the 'Sea Symphony' [R.V.W.] I'd be glad of a ticket too. I'll try and remember the walking stick. The Housman doesn't come out until the 26th, but it shall be yours. Joy's grateful for those addresses. She can't do anything till after Christmas, being stuck here. But they're valuable to know of, and if she weren't in bed with a bit of a temp., she'd be writing to you herself. Our love. G.

I hope for a theatre on Thursday.

Aldbourne, Wilts.; 3 November

Dear Fergie,

Here are the songs ['Earth and Air and Rain'] at last. They would probably still be in MS but for you. I hope you approve of the get-up. For Boosey, I think it's quite good, though a visible type on the cover would have been preferable. Also, I'm not at all sure that the O.U.P. method of sewing-together isn't better.

The B.B.C. has sent me a ticket for the 13th [R.V.W. 'Dona Nobis Pacem'] and I hope to come up on the 12th. So keep the Thursday open for a wild carouse – Joy says not too wild, but a theatre if there is anything worth seeing.

133

I must try and remember that blasted walking-stick of yours – the journey from Paddington to Hampstead, with the wretched thing catching on my trousers, is a great trial.

I listened-in to the Mahler, and though I thought the end was very moving, it was all a bit tiring and it seemed a very bad performance. Fenby's book on Delius has been quite worth reading.[17] He's a very pious young man, and Delius's sceptical and violently anti-Christian attitude has undoubtedly upset him. But it helps him to see clearly and not adulate too much and to be able to discuss his 'colossal egotism', 'dreadful selfishness' etc. The most surprising thing to me is that Delius seems to have had no literary taste or judgement. He reads no English poetry, and anything he set was chosen for him by his wife.

Were you a bit disappointed in 'More Poems'[18]? I only found about half a dozen that were really up to the level of the previous two books.

Till Thursday 12th. Joy's love. G.

34 Willoughby Road, N.W.3; 4 November

Dear Dave,

Thank you very much indeed for the copy of 'Earth & Air & Rain'. It is fine to see them out: they may have the great success they deserve. I think they have done a great deal better than usual over the typography. Even what you call the 'invisible type on the front cover' does not worry me much; it is a very pleasant combination of colours, and the wording is perfectly clear. Indeed, my only crab is the 'Contents' on the inside cover, which would, I think, have been better in smaller type. But that is a minor point. The present method of sewing the folios together I like much better than the O.U.P. method; and they have at least had the decency not to crowd all the poems up at the beginning of the volume, where they appear alone, as the O.U.P. did. This was a great blot on the latter edition.

No. I was not disappointed over the Housman poems. To tell the truth, I expected them to be much worse as a whole, and was so delighted to find some at least up to the very top-notch standard that I readily forgive the rest. Except perhaps the dreadful

> From the wash the laundress sends
> My collars home with ravelled ends

which sounds like nothing so much as a very cruel parody of his own better poems. How this was passed for the edition is quite beyond me, unless as an awful warning of what he could do on an 'off day'. Apart from this I do not think there is anything regrettable; but much to be thankful for – certainly more than the grudging half dozen which is all that you allow.

I am looking forward to reading the Fenby book on Delius, which I shall

---

[17] Eric Fenby (1906–1997), composer. Acted as amanuensis to the blind and paralysed Delius who was thus able to dictate several important short works.

[18] A.E. Housman (1859–1936). Posthumous publication.

cadge as a birthday present from Nunky. There will be no junkettings on the 12th, I fear. A misplaced sense of duty calls me to Queens Hall that night to hear Bruckner No.4, which I do not know. It even seems problematic whether I shall get to the R.V.W. on Friday night, since that is the day Nunky is due back from S. Africa and he is hardly likely to feel inclined to go to a concert on his first evening at home. But do come in as soon as you get to Hampstead, and we'll see if I can fix in an afternoon entertainment or something of the sort. Now that the Partita is cleared up I shall not have qualms about going out in the afternoon. Blessings on you both. Ever, Howard.

P.S. It is possible that a little persuasion might persuade me to forego the pleasures of Bruckner.

Aldbourne, Wilts.; 5 November

[Dear Fergie]

Could you let me have a card by return. William Busch[19] writes that Sinclair Logan [bass-baritone] would like to give the first broadcast of 'Earth & Air & Rain' if I've made no other arrangements. I don't think it's necessary for me to ask Keith's 'permission', do you? After all, he's had a year to think about it. And of course, now that they're published I feel that anyone who wants to do them is quite at liberty to do so without reference to me. Don't you agree? Incidentally, I believe Sinclair Logan is a good singer.

Why not Bruckner for me too on Thursday evening? I'm all for wild life. Hurrah for the Partita. G.

34 Willoughby Road, N.W.3; 5 November

[Dear Dave]

Sinclair Logan by all means, and no need to say anything to Keith [Falkner].

Nunky, on the boat, has had a clot of blood near the heart (coronary thrombosis), and it is by no means certain he will reach here alive. Just got a wireless this morning. Ever, H.

Aldbourne, Wilts.; 7 November

Dearest Fergie,

I was making all sorts of plans for next Thursday when your card came. We only hope Nunky isn't suffering, and even if he comes through all right, you'll know how much we'll feel for what you have to go through. I won't expect to see you when in London, but I'll phone up to see if you're there and would like to see me. I don't expect there's anything we can do to help, but you know that a wire or phone call will send me North, South, East or West for you. Joy's love. G.

---

[19] William Busch (1901–1945), English pastoral composer of German parentage. Sinclair Logan, blind bass-baritone.

34 Willoughby Road, N.W.3; 8 November

Dearest Dave,

Thank you for your exceedingly kind letter. I should like to see you on Thursday (no special reason) if it is possible, so do phone. If there is anything you can do, I shall certainly call on you. Ever, H.

Hamtun House, Southampton [where H.F. stayed for six weeks, while H.S. was in a nursing-home]; 18 November

[Dearest Dave]

In case Pu has not asked you already, could you possibly ask Rann to stay for a bit? He is getting frightfully depressed at Willoughby Road, and it is not possible to have him here. Write him direct, if you can. Nunky pretty bad. Ever, H.

Aldbourne, Wilts.; 26 November

Dear Fergie,

Rann tells us the news about Nunky, so I'm not adding myself to your list of correspondents. I hope you're keeping fit through it all – though if anyone can manage 'Paradise Lost' [which H.F. was reading] they must be pretty strong.

We're both hard at work, so I don't see much of Rann, except at meals, or a walk, or after supper when we listen-in (or – dare I breathe it – play an occasional duet). I think he's quite happy, though I'm sure a little shocked at my dislike of half of Mozart and all of Haydn! Today he has developed a stinking cold and is staying in bed. It's not to be wondered at, as we haven't been out of the house for three whole days, so foul and cold and completely misty has the weather been.

I have 50 notices to get rid of, so I might as well palm off one on you. I wish Iris had put 'Earth & Air & Rain', and I wish I knew who is to be the accompanist. And yet I don't care sniggle-snaggle about either. No more songs now for a long time. Three cheers.

Audrey's [nurse-maid] ear trouble being no better, and showing no signs of clearing up, she has had to go. So Joy has both infants to cope with, besides hacking her stone. How I wish Pu were 30 years younger and had never met the damned Ferguson family! Joy is looking out, but we don't expect the right angel to fall from the sky at once.

I thought Leslie Heward's performances were very good.[20] I even enjoyed the Berlioz 'Franc Juges' Overture, and Sibelius No.5 strikes me as being wonderfuller and wonderfuller every time I hear it. Our love and don't bother to acknowledge this. G.

---

[20] Leslie Heward (1897–1943), conductor of the City of Birmingham Symphony Orchestra (1930–1943).

Hamtun House, Southampton; 27 November

Dearest Dave,

The accompanist for Keith at the Lemare concert will be either his wife or myself. If Christabel has worked a lot at them with him, she will play; if not, I will.

I do hope Rann's cold is not going to inflict you all. It is truly blessed of you both to have him to stay; it means a considerable weight off my mind, as you can guess.

Nunky's general condition continues to improve. But one rather serious fly in the ointment is his eyes. Ever since his second attack, or collapse, the day the boat arrived here, his vision has been somewhat impaired: that is to say, while he can see out of both eyes to the left-hand side of centre, he cannot see at all to the right. As this defect appeared to be getting no better with his gradual gain of strength, the doctor had in an eye-specialist. After his examination he said that something had been damaged, not in the eye itself, but at the back of the eye; and though this condition may clear up in part or even wholly, he doesn't think it will. Nunky does not know the last part of this verdict. You can imagine what a blow it was to me, as I had hitherto imagined that the defect was only temporary. Please don't pass this information on, as it might so easily get back to Nunky. I have hinted on my P.C. to Rann that something is wrong in that direction; but I don't think there is anything to be gained by telling him fully at the moment.

Another jolly little surprise is that they are claiming about £500 dilapidations on East Heath Road!

Sorry for emptying all this on top of you: I feel I must get it off onto somebody!

Much love to you both, from Howard.

Aldbourne, Wilts.; 30 November

Dear Fergie,

I don't imagine it's the least use offering to lend you the £500 for those appalling East Heath Road dilapidations. Most probably you already have a great many sources which you can tap. But if you do want it, we have the money on deposit, waiting for the eventual house or site, and I don't imagine that we're likely to need it for 6 or 12 months. I'm only sorry we can't give it to you!

Here is a wonderful review [by the literary critic of] The Observer, which I'd like back when you're next writing to Rann. One might have thought a book on music would not be reviewed by someone who had never heard of Schütz. As if you or I would dare to review a book on poetry if we had not heard of Marlowe or Herbert. But the first paragraph is the best of all. Will he ever live it down? To be sure, next month he'll be reviewing another book on music.

My desk has come. It is similar to yours, but with certain additions and modifications which you will be interested to see. A great joy, and what I've always longed for.

Some of those Nadia Boulanger broadcasts were good. A 'Madrigal' by Fauré was enchanting and I also liked Lili Boulanger's 'Revouneau'.

Rann is all right now and back again at his blessed old piano. Marvellous how anyone can play for 4, 6 or 8 hours a day! It's just as well, as we're all busy and I don't feel like excursions etc. at the moment, though I should like to take him over to Gloucester again. The Sumsions have heard all about Nunky (through Aunt Jane, of course – knowing Aunt Jane, I don't expect you have told her about his eye trouble) – and I'm sure Rann and John would enjoy some music-making. You should have heard my attempts at Borodin No.2. Alas, I'm not much fun for him as a duettist! He really has a remarkable fluency: so much so, that I can't conceive of him being a composer, though I've not seen any of his work and make a point of keeping off it (and mine too), but that's the impression I get: of a mind through which things flow, not out of which they flow. Not only does Christopher adore him, but Joy finds him a delightful person in a house and he wants little to make him content, except to get on with his work. Nor does he mind the occasional fish! Something will have to be done nearer Christmas, when Mags [Joy's sister] comes, and we won't have room; but there's no hurry for that yet. When the time comes perhaps you could do it from your end, as we don't want him to feel he's being sent to and fro like a shuttlecock.

Can you give our love to Nunky? This eye business does sound depressing, though the way his remarkable constitution has got over the attack and collapse, may give some hope. If he gets over this will you send him to Richards. Effie Wharton[21] had an eye saved by him (to the great surprise of Duke-Elder), though I know the two troubles are quite different. Our love to you. G.

No need to bother about replying.

Hamtun House, Southampton; 2 December

[Dear Dave],

Thank you for an extraordinarily kind suggestion. As it happens, I don't think anything like that would be necessary: I intend to call on some of Nunky's own personal funds.

That notice from The Observer is a gem. I feel tempted to write about it. I'll let you have it back.

Tell Rann that Nunky had a good night, and that he is getting on satisfactorily. He sends you all his love, and says he hopes you are bringing up your children in the way you yourself are not going! Love, H.

---

[21] A friend of Joy Finzi's parents. An enthusiast who ran the Tunbridge Wells Music Festival.

Aldbourne, Wilts.; 8 December

Dear Fergie,

In case you haven't yet said anything to Rann, there's no need to now, as he asked me if he hadn't better be getting back; but I told him that, as far as we are concerned, he's absolutely welcome to stay on here until Mags turns up before Christmas. The question coming from him made it quite easy. I wish we could have the two of them, but they would have to share a room or a bed, which would not be respectable!

I'm going up to London Thursday night and hope to hear the Bax works on Friday. I suppose I'll be able to get in by ticket, even though it's a contemporary music concert.

It's really rather wonderful about Nunky. I shall phone Pu up, to get all the news I can. Let me know when something definite is fixed up about the Partita. I'll put it in red ink in my diary. Our love to you and Nunky. G.

Aldbourne, Wilts.; 19 December

Dearest Fergie,

I expect you find Rann plumper than when he left you, for he weighs 11 stone 2 lbs (only 1 lb less than me), though he insists that our scales must be wrong.

I do hope the move to London from Southampton [by ambulance] isn't too much for Nunky and that the excitement of getting home isn't too much for him. I'll look in, if I'm allowed to, when I'm up in London round about the 12th.

By the way, was a Suite of [Thorpe] Davie's, for orchestra, which I listened-in to a few weeks ago, an old work or new? It was really awful and for his own dear sake I do wish you could get him to put it on one side!

I see that someone has written a short and very sensible letter to The Musical Times about that Einstein 'History of Music' and Basil de Selincourt. And what a slating the two Milton Sonnets [by G.F.] get! I don't mind the adverse criticism at all – it's quite impersonal and without animosity – but I do hate the bilge and bunkum about composers trying to 'add' to a poem: that a fine poem is complete in itself, and to set it is only to gild the lily, and so on. It's a sort of cliché which goes on being repeated (rather like the phrase 'but art is above national boundaries'). I rather expected it and expect it still more when 'Intimations' is finished. But alas, composers can't rush into print where their own works are concerned – (though I do sometimes have a sneaking wish that editors would ask for one's opinion). Obviously a poem may be unsatisfactory in itself for setting, but that is a purely musical consideration – that it has no architectural possibilities, no broad points where climaxes should be, and so on. But the first and last thing is that a composer is (presumably) moved by a poem and wishes to identify himself with it and to share it. Whether he is moved by a good or a bad poem is beside the question. John hit the nail on the head the other day when we were going through a dreadful biblical cantata, which Armstrong Gibbs had sent to him – Kapellmeister music of the worst sort, only brought up to date. John said, 'He chose his text, it didn't choose him'. I don't think everyone realizes the difference between choosing a text and being chosen by one. (They should see Pirandello's 'Six Characters in Search of an Author'.) But what, to my mind, settles the whole argument is the fact that people will listen to songs sung in a foreign language, of which they don't understand a single word. Sing the Milton 'Sonnets' to a foreigner and he has to judge them as music. This may be good, bad or indifferent, but it can't change its value according to the country in which it is sung.

But enough of all this. Much more exciting is Sibelius No.4. I borrowed the records from John and have been putting it on every day. It grows and grows and grows. 'Tapiola' diminishes, I find.

This is really supposed to be a Christmas letter! This Housman booklet ['The Name and Nature of Poetry'] is instead of a card. Joy sends her best love and all good wishes for a happy Christmas. 1937 will be Partita year! G.

1937

Aldbourne, Wilts.; 1 January

A happy New Year to you.

Fergie, O Fergie, O Fergie! You can't imagine what deliriums, great thoughts and gastric juices are raised by such a present [half a farmhouse Stilton cheese that had been given to H.F. by Toty de Navarro]. It was very generous, in spite of your disclaimer, for it might have gone elsewhere. And if you hadn't said anything about its origin, I should have thought you got it straight from Fortnums. (Now I can't possibly say the same about your cast-off clothes.)

I see by the programme which you enclosed that the 'Five Tudor Portraits' [R.V.W.] is down for the 27th, so I'll come up for that and combine it with those part-songs on the 29th. I'm coming up on the 11th and will see you at the concert. Would it be convenient if I came round to Willoughby Road the next morning about 10.0? (I don't know what time you like on account of Nunky.) I'm told that the first night of Steuart Wilson's production of 'The Lily Maid' is on the 11th, so I might go along to hear it on the 12th.[1] Some out-of-the-way hole – the Palace – or some such place. If it does come off I should like to see not only Steuart conduct, but also what he considers a really economical and satisfactory opera.

All news when we meet. Love to Nunky. I suppose I'll be allowed to see him? Love from Joy. G.

[1] Wilson, who had participated in Rutland Boughton's Glastonbury Festivals, financed a limited run of *The Lily Maid* (the third music drama of Boughton's five-part Arthurian cycle) at the Winter Garden Theatre, Drury Lane.

34 Willoughby Road, N.W.3; 3 January

LIKEWISE, A happy New Year!

Dearest Dave,

So glad you will enjoy the Stilton. It is quite a good one, but not the very best I have ever tasted, so don't let your expectation soar too high.

About the 12th. You may remember that in a previous letter I said there was something I wanted to ask you about when we next met: a question of to be or not to be. To be less mysterious, there is a set of five short pieces for clarinet and piano [H.F.'s 'Four Short Pieces', Op.6] which I would like your opinion on: they are very slight, but well enough done in their way, I think, and I would like to know whether you think they merit publication and a number all to themselves. My feeling is that they do, but I should like to have your agreement before doing anything about it. As I am particularly anxious (for reasons which I will tell you later) that you should hear them played by the clarinet and piano before seeing them, I have asked Pauline Juler to tootle them through with me on the 12th for your especial benefit. She is quite willing to do this, so it only remains to arrange a time. I had provisionally fixed 2.30 in the afternoon of the 12th at either the Blüthner or Wigmore Studios; but this was before receiving your letter in which you suggest coming round here about 10 in the morning. Therefore, if a meeting in town during the morning would suit you better, please drop me a card and I shall arrange it so, for the Juler can manage either. Town would, I think, be better than here, as the clarinet is a penetrating instrument.

We have been having rather a ghastly time with Nunky the last few days. His nightmares have returned in full, or fuller force than ever. The trouble is [it gradually became apparent that his brain had been affected during the second attack] that he cannot connect up with reality when he awakes, and the nurse has the greatest difficulty in keeping him in bed. If he were to get out of bed he would simply fall down, as he could not possibly stand after all this time; but though his legs may be weak, he is as strong as a horse in other directions, and gives the nurse a fearful time. I seem to be the only person that can calm him down on these occasions, so the night before last I was up three times trying to bring him to earth again. I managed to do so then; but each time he went to sleep it happened all over again, which is neither encouraging nor restful. Last night, on returning home at 10.30 after being out to dinner, I found the most frightful rumpus going on, though all had been well when I rang up to enquire little over an hour before. I was able to quiet him this time too, but not bring him down to earth, for nothing I said would make him realize that he was anything but some Scandinavian person. However, he dropped off to sleep after drinking some tea, and when he awoke again at about 11.30, still in the clouds, we were able to give him some morphia, which settled him before long. The rest of the night was quiet. But this morning again he has been completely hopeless; not violent as when he wakes up from a nightmare, but firmly convinced that he was some Scottish person (complete with accent!) whose children had been or were

141

about to be murdered. This went on until just before lunch, when, quite suddenly, he came down to earth. Since lunch he has, I think, been sleeping; so I shall be very surprised if there isn't some more excitement when he wakes.

LATER. No, he did not sleep and there was no more excitement. Let's hope that this may continue, and that he gets a decent night's rest tonight. I don't see how he could possibly stand up to much more of the sort of thing he was having the night before last, with his heart in its present condition.

Rann, with happy genius for falling on his feet, has just been invited by a friend of ours, a Mrs Johnson [a wealthy private pupil of H.S.] to go with her, her adopted daughter and another friend for a fortnight's holiday in Oberammergau. They leave on Thursday next.

Let me know about the 12th. Much love to you both. Ever H.

Aldbourne, Wilts.; 4 January

Dearest Fergie,

I could really fit-in any time that suits the two of you, though on the whole the morning would be better than the afternoon (in case there's a film worth seeing or shopping to be done). What I'd suggest is coming round to you at 10.0 and talking and musicking for a bit; then leaving at 11.30 for the clarinet pieces. If in any way you would rather I didn't come round to Willoughby Road – with Nunky in that disturbing state – then I could meet you wherever you suggest. Good or bad, I'm delighted to hear about the clarinet pieces.

I shall have the same problem to put before you when that foul Serenade is done – in fact, I rather wanted to ask you a few things about it next week. Lucky Rann, but I hope he doesn't swallow the Nazi bull-shit, as Trudy[2] seems to have done! If things appear all rosy there let him tell his first German acquaintance that he is a Liberal – no need to go as far as a Communist – or that his grandfather was a Jew! Let me have a card so that I can fill in times. Our love, G.

Newspaper cutting enclosed: 'From 1 January no 'non-Aryan' is allowed to play on a GERMAN golf-course'. G.F. adds: is this golf-balls.

34 Willoughby Road, N.W.3; 6 January

[Dear Dave]

Have fixed up with the Juler for 12 noon on Tuesday. Do by all means come round here earlier in the morning – though I may not be very intelligent. At the moment I feel pretty done in. Nunky's condition is definitely serious again: they fear his brain may have been affected. H.

---

[2] Trudy Bliss, the composer's wife.

34 Willoughby Road, N.W.3; 15 January

Dear Dave,

Nunky died perfectly peacefully at 4.20 this morning. He was unconscious the whole time. The funeral is to be tomorrow, and the memorial service [at the Liberal Jewish Synagogue, St John's Wood, N.W.] at 6 o'clock the same afternoon. If all should be well, may I come down to you on Wednesday? I think the immediate things should be cleared up by then.

There appears to be a slight hitch in my part of the Will. Besides getting this house I also get the mortgage (£2,350) attached to it: a regrettable condition. In fact it looks as though it would be better for me in the end to refuse the bequest. Poor Nunky! How upset he would have been at this. I shall in any case take legal advice before doing anything. Ever, Howard.

Aldbourne, Wilts. [; 16 January]

Dearest Fergie,

I heard it over the wireless. Even though it was expected it seemed very strange.

We'll expect you on Wednesday for as many days as you can manage. Just PC the train. Even so, if there is *anything* that can be done before then, I'll come up to London – though I don't imagine there is. Our love, G.

Joy rather wished you'd have a death-mask taken. I fancy it would not be a Nunky we knew, and also I think it has to be done at once. But phone if you want the address.

34 Willoughby Road, N.W.3; 17 January

[Dear Dave]

How about the 2.45 on Wednesday, arriving Hungerford 4.10? Don't bother to reply unless this doesn't suit. Thanks so much, but there is really nothing to do but write letters, and that must be done by myself. Ever, H.

34 Willoughby Road, N.W.3; 31 January

Dear G & J,

Herewith the short notice of Friday's concert which appeared in The Daily Telegraph. I was so glad to hear the three [Bridges] part-songs; they are very lovely. On thinking them over, I think I do like 'I have Loved Flowers' best; but the others are fine too.

Mrs Johnson has offered to keep Rann over here for another year, or even two if I think it necessary. Isn't that splendid of her? Please don't tell him, as I shall only fall back on her offer if the American people should fail, and it is as well he should not know just yet.

What a joy it was to be with you both [at Aldbourne]. I feel wonderfully rested now, and somewhat restored after the last awful months. It was tempting to stay longer, but I think it is as well that I should have come home to get a few things done. You must have had a bad drive back on Friday night. Love, H.

[Aldbourne, Wilts.; 4 February]

Dear Fergie,

1) Isn't this rather infuriating, but I don't see how I can possibly let Boosey have them [Bridges part-songs]. Of course I could let Boosey's have the two, and then do another two for the O.U.P. set later on, but I think it would be rather a muddle to have two Robert Bridges sets, don't you?

It makes one grind one's teeth to have to turn down an offer of this sort when I know the alternative will have to come out of my pockets!

2) Do I write to Boult? I really don't know him at all well as you do. If so, do I write Dear Boult or Dear Sir Adrian?

3) Have you any idea yet if Tuesday 23rd would be any good for some more Gurney work [editing the songs]? I thought of coming up for the Lemare concert on the 22nd.

4) to tall Joy and brainy Fergie, a poem:-

> I may be short, I may be stout,
>   But I am not the sluggard sloth;
> For harken ye, and raise a shout,
>   At Badminton I beat you both.

Love, G. Give Boosey's letter back to Joy, please.

Aldbourne, Wilts.; 15 February

Dearest Fergie,

Joy is at her typewriter, so she is sticking in a note or two for me; thus my apparent importance.

I don't know how your many jobs are getting on, but have you any idea yet whether next Tuesday the 23rd would be any good for a field-day with the Gurney songs? To show you how useful our rough tabulation [of the MS songs] is, I find that 'Star Talk' is published by Stainer & Bell in a 1925 version, infinitely inferior to the ones we went through. This shows that dear Miss Marion M. Scott[3] really ought to have had a little masculine wisdom in the form of an index, to which she can refer to, for the best versions.

Our love to you, and even if you cannot manage next Tuesday for work, I hope at least to get a glimpse of you. Hope all goes well, G.

[In Joy's hand] How goes the studio [in Glenilla Road, which H.F. was hoping to buy], and the two strange animals that inhabit same?

---

[3] Marion M. Scott (1877–1953), English musicologist and violinist. A friend of Ivor Gurney, she preserved the manuscripts of his songs and poems and acted as his dedicated, but dilatory, artistic executor.

Aldbourne, Wilts.; 23 February

[Dear Fergie]

Marion Scott says that we have been through considerably more than half of Gurney's work, so I think Saturday 6th will be enough for finishing the remainder. 11 March is all right for her 10.0–1.0, but try not to book up the rest of the day, in case V.W. can't manage the 12th, in which case I'll suggest after lunch on the 11th. I do hope the throat clears up quickly. Our love, G.

34 Willoughby Road, N.W.3; 25 February

[Dear Dave]

O.K. about Maid Marion. I shall also keep the rest of the 11th free.

The Partita is being postponed until the end of June, as Adrian [Boult] himself could not do the April date. This is much more satisfactory all round. Ever, H.

[Aldbourne, Wilts.; 1 March]

[Dear Fergie]

V.W. can manage the 12th all right [for a play-through at Dorking of the Gurney songs], so the dates are all O.K. Our love, G.

Aldbourne, Wilts. [; 27 March]

Dear Fergie,

We were a bit puzzled by the wire, not knowing whether the shyness was to be unmentioned to Betty [Pu's niece] herself, or to the rest of the household, i.e. Mary. But we had already told Mary, so that she would fully understand (and she's very understanding, provided she's not 'on'). However, away with all fears, for Betty seems less shy than I've ever seen her. We had an uproarious party last night and the seven of us [with Cedric Thorpe Davie & Margaret Brown on their honeymoon] played 'Pit'.[4] I had quite forgotten that yesterday was Good Friday and that the trains I had sent Pu were quite imaginary ones; but I suddenly had to go up to London that day (more hereafter) and so we brought them back by car. I think they'll be very happy playing with the children and sitting out in the sun. The weather is heavenly and has been ever since Ceddie & Bruno[5] arrived last Tuesday. They seem happy at The Bell [a pub] and have been over every day. I showed Ceddie some of the Gurney songs, but he couldn't make much of them. (Also, his reading isn't quite up to yours; so much so that, next to him, I don't feel nearly as contemptible a pianist as you'd make me out to be!) Poor chap, I think he's very depressed about his own future as a composer. It's not disappointment about the opera so much as his

[4] Presumably a card game?
[5] Nickname for Margaret Brown, Thorpe Davis's wife.

145

own feeling that it's not as good as he thought it to be. I'm glad you told him about the Holst opera and the Patron's Fund.

Joy and I had a look at that show of Bissell's [George Bissell, a former miner, who lived with his wife next to G.F.'s gardener's cottage at Ashmansworth] at the Leger Galleries and were very agreeably surprised. All very much the same; bare trees, subdued colour, and not yet completely competent; but something of his own that stuck in our minds. Only one picture sold, poor devil, and only two days to run.

The Ashmansworth place was sold, but we found out that it went to a syndicate which buys houses, does them up and sells them at a profit. They're willing to let us buy it back, provided they make a profit without the doing up! But there are several snags, chief of which is the bit of land that juts into the grounds, belonging to this Mr Justice à Beckett Terrell. He (and his father before him to an even greater extent) is a large landowner there, and though it's the only bit of land on the Church Farm side of the road that he owns, he wrote a snorter to the Agent when asked if he would sell it. So I wrote to him myself and made an appointment with him at his Club. Hence the visit to London. You can imagine how uncomfortable I felt in my best and only suit (slightly agricultural you call it, but really not so bad, considering it was bought ready made 7 or 8 years ago!), interviewing a complete stranger, and a peppery little Judge at that, at The Arts Club! He wouldn't budge, but I quite liked him and think he is to be trusted, even though he won't promise not to build on his wretched acre. So perhaps Church Farm may yet be ours.

Our love, also from Pu and Betty. G.

14 Deramore Park South, Belfast; 29 March

Dearest Dave,

On thinking it over, that wire of mine certainly does take the prize for ambiguity. So sorry. But your interpretation was correct: the shyness was not to be mentioned before Betty herself – that was all. It was quite right of you to tell Mary. I had intended sending you a note, but left it too late so had to resort to the wire.

How very exciting about Church Farm. I do hope it pans out satisfactorily and that whatever snags there may be will be smoothed away.

You will have heard from Pu that the business of the Will has now been decided, and that the result is as we expected – that the Bank overdraft is to be paid Pro Rata by the Life Insurance Policies and by me (from the proceeds of the house). Which means that I shall have whatever the house may sell for less approx. £1000, but plus £450 which the Estate already owes me. As the business has been decided thus, I have asked my solicitor to make a firm offer of £1,150 for the Glenilla Road Studio, sending at the same time a cheque for 10 pc of that sum to show I mean business. Let's hope they accept. If they do, my Father and Mother have nobly offered to bridge the gap between the time I have to pay up and such time as Willoughby Road may be sold; so it will not be necessary

146

to call on your most generous offer of the money you and Joyce have on deposit; if Church Farm comes off, perhaps this is as well! However, though I have not had to call on it, I am none the less most touched by your offer; under other circumstances it would have been invaluable.

I'm sure Pu and Betty have been having a high old time. Give them both my love, if they are still with you. How do you like Ceddie's Bruno? I think she is a splendid person for him. I too felt that he was, as you say, depressed as to his future as a composer. And for some reason which I would find difficult to define, I myself am beginning to agree with what you have always said: that he is not a composer really and truly. Nor do I think that this is due wholly to present circumstances, but to something much deeper than that, which is bound up with his whole character. Why I did not see this before I don't know. Perhaps it was a case of the wish (reflecting his own) being father to the thought.

Listening to 'Job' last night I felt that some of Barbirolli's cuts were a considerable improvement for the concert version, but that some, notably the one he made from page 84 to page 100, were a mistake. This last may have gotten rid of the 'Galliard', which never quite convinces me, but it also got rid of the 12/6 counterpoints from page 100 onwards. Also the scoring sounds too heavy just after page 83. But in spite of this and the funereal pace of the opening and of Elihu's dance, it was an enjoyable performance. Love to you both. Ever, H.

P.S. I was glad to hear from Ceddy that relations between himself and Harold Thomson [a Glasgow friend of C.T.D.'s] were, if not exactly as before, at least amiable in a non-committal sort of way. H.

Aldbourne, Wilts. [; 12 April]

Dearest Fergie,

Steuart Wilson has married the Goodchild! [Mary Goodchild]

You will have heard that Pu and Betty returned on Tuesday, and Ceddy took them as far as Dorking. I think it all went off very well, and Pu began to get a bit more sleep (without a sleeping-draught) and had a good, lazy time. She ought to have stayed a bit longer to have made a proper job of it. Betty was absolutely at home, and whatever nervousness she had showed itself in constipation! She seemed quite unperturbed at the prospect of waiting till she got back to London before doing her duties (with four or five days collection inside her), but I soon saw to it that she had a dose and all was well. I told her that I would report it to you, and that you would see that she took liquid paraffin, or some such stuff, every day. But enough of bowelology.

How splendid about Glenilla Road. I do hope it comes off [it didn't]. Keep us informed, as Joy is very anxious for you to get it. Church Farm is still in the air. Peter Harland [architect] comes down to look at it shortly and that may be some help. Undoubtedly we could get it, but the snags are so many and various that it makes one rub one's chin before deciding. And the building itself is in a dreadful state.

'The Bell' at Ramsbury did Ceddy [on his honeymoon] very well. Of course he missed a number of midday meals, but the meals that he did have seem to have been enormous, and with drinks, garage, etc. it came to about four guineas for the two. Pretty good, that. The two of them became powerful Badminton players. Yes, we liked Bruno and certainly think she's the right person to help Ceddy, though we found her a wee bit heavy, if you know what I mean. Still, that's better than sham sparkle, and no doubt with a bit more knowing the heaviness would disappear. It's good that Ceddy has married someone with whom he need feel no sort of restraints. Also, I think she has got exceedingly sound and sensible ideas. I think what you feel about the 'something bound up with his whole character' which will prevent him being a real composer is that his nature lacks the upper and lower notes of the scale. Think of the average wireless, with a good selectivity and a clear straightforward tone, but with a good deal of top and bottom missing. What worries me is whether one isn't making it harder for him by being encouraging. Personally I feel that the whole idea of being a composer will quietly recede, and its disappearance will be made all the more easy and painless by his having a teaching routine [at the Scottish National Academy, Glasgow].

I've been copying out a few of the Gurney songs; so far there are a few problems about which I'm uncertain, but not so many as I expected. I shall be glad when it's all done, especially if Church Farm comes to anything, when I shall have more than enough to contend with.

By the way, Rachel Rothenstein looked us up with her fiancé, Hans Ward. A very nice chap and brother of Wards Bookshop in Baker Street. (He has a bookshop in Sheffield.) What was surprising was his facial resemblance to [Ivor] Gurney. I showed them my half dozen photos and they were as amazed as I was.

We also listened-in to 'Job', but the cuts infuriated me, whether they were authoritative or not, as I was expecting the whole. I missed most of all the 'sad procession' which always moves me tremendously. (Maybe having seen it on the stage.) I thought the 'Flourish for a Coronation' [R.V.W.] pretty much what we expected it would be; perhaps worse. So like Handel on an off day. Even the Lento disappointed a bit, perhaps because Beecham took it at crotchet = 76 when V.W. marked it crotchet = 100. Of course the control-room took fright, and brought everything down to *mf*. Our love, G.

[In Joy's hand] We loved having Pu and Betty. The latter was more at home and animated than I have ever seen her or hoped her to be. A lovely clear burst of sun made them red-nosed, and restored their energy.

Aldbourne, Wilts.; 17 April

Dearest Fergie,

Welcome home, whenever it is that you get home. I want to come and hear Rubbra's Symphony on 30 April, 9.35 p.m.[6] Would you rather or not that I

[6] Symphony No.2.

stayed the night with you? Could you get me into a rehearsal, if it's in the morning or afternoon of the same day?

Church Farm still hangs on. First up, then down, then up, then down. At the moment it seems more hopeful, but it's worn me out. The dear old Irish soul, who built herself that white house opposite Church Farm turns out to be a friend of your family – at least of Sally and Alan Sinclair [H.F.'s sister and brother-in-law], who stayed with her at Doily Hill, nearby, where she used to live. It's curious, isn't it? Mrs Straker is her name.

How are you? We hope to go to the Aran Isles next month about the 22nd. Our love, G.

34 Willoughby Road, N.W.3; 19 April

Dearest Dave,

Yes, do come and stay here for the night of the 30th. The rehearsal of the Rubbra is to be in the Concert Hall, Broadcasting House, at 10 a.m. on the 30th; can you get there in time? I have a ticket to admit two to the rehearsal, so will expect you along in the Concert Hall as soon as you can get there. If you ask at Inquiries in the entrance Hall at Broadcasting House, I shall have left a message telling them to expect you.

You wouldn't care to go to 'Hugh the Drover' [R.V.W.] at Sadlers Wells on Saturday afternoon, 1st May? I am taking my nice Irish friend Mrs MacIlwaine and Rann, and could probably get a ticket for you too. Drop me a postcard saying Yes or No.

The old hag has turned down my offer of £1,150 for the Studio – blast her! I am now getting several friends to go and look at the place, and to offer her less than I have offered, in the hope that this may give her a more proper idea of the value of the place.

Funnily enough, I remember Dicky and Alan mentioning Mrs Straker. But whose friend she is, or where she comes from, I don't know.

I expect you are feeling as unsettled and exasperated about Church Farm as I am about the Belsize Park place. Let's hope it turns out happily-ever-after for both of us.

What a time you and Joy gave Pu and Betty! I hear more and more about it at every meal-time. They are both looking far better than when I left. I can't tell you how grateful I am for all that you did for them. Ever, H.

P.S. If you send your ticket for the 30th to Rann, you and I could go on mine. This would be simpler (as you will be staying here) than Rann going on mine, as is at present arranged. However, if this does not happen to be convenient for you, fix it up otherwise.

34 Willoughby Road, N.W.3; 22 April

Dearest Dave,

Unfortunately the rehearsal ticket is only for two, and I don't think they would allow anybody in without one. I am so glad Joy is coming in the evening: the three of us and Rann can arrange a tryst somewhere and all go in together. I have been able to get you a ticket for 'Hugh the Drover'; not only that, but next door to our three, so we shall make a party.

If you and Joy do not happen to be coming up to go to Westminster Abbey for the Coronation, would you care to put up and put up with your little friend for a few days? He feels that the festivities here would be almost more than he could endure. However, if you have already said you will take in Mags or anybody else, don't worry, for I can always go and park myself on the James family at Hurley [Warwick James, dentist and friend of Harold & H.F.]. If you can have me, I might even suggest killing the Coronation and Whitsun with the same stone by staying 11th–18th; but if that were possible for you, I should have to bring a little work with me (copying).

When you are here next week I want to talk with you on what you would suggest about MSS, etc., after my death, for I am making an 'in case of accidents' Will. Ever, H.

34 Willoughby Road, N.W.3; 23 April

[Dear Dave]

Things are moving. I think I am going to get the Studio for £1,200 or £1,225, and somebody has made an offer for Willoughby Road. Hope you are progressing equally well. H.

Aldbourne, Wilts.; 23 April

Dearest Fergie,

We've decided not to make use of our invitation to the Coronation. It's such a crush, and under those circumstances we felt that the dear King & Queen wouldn't be offended. Of course I've written them a very nice p.c. So do come here on the 10th or 11th and stay till 18th. Joy goes off on the 18th to leave the infants by the seaside, and we leave for Ireland a day or two later. Till the 30th. Ever, G.

Ganly's Hotel, Kilronan, Galway; 30 May

Dearest Fergie,

In case you imagine that the 6ft Islanders have slaughtered me, I thought I'd let you know that I'm quite safe; in fact, getting on very well and happily here. Of course, it's a great help that Joy is remembered with admiration, and so, perhaps, I get a share of the reflected glory! 'It's a fine woman you have' I'm told, and can hardly disagree. They really are a remarkable lot – especially on

Middle Island, where practically no English is spoken and life is really as primitive (and priest-ridden) as it might be in what the missionaries call 'darkest Africa'. Physically the men are mostly superb (except for teeth, which are deplorable) and some of the women are incredibly lovely. And it's all done on bread, potatoes, tea and occasional fish. There's no longer any opening for fishing and kelp and no living of any sort. In this way, the film gave a pretty good idea of the hardness of life (except for humbug of the whale-hunting), but what no one would realise from the film is the laughter, humour and dancing. It's rather wonderful to go into a cottage and find it quite a normal procedure for a melodian or gramophone to start up, and a young couple to stand up in the middle of the room and dance a jig, reel or hornpipe. And marvellously they dance, too. As usual, the priest is the villain of the piece, and a good many of them are under his thumb, though he hasn't yet succeeded in stamping out this wonderfully innocent pastime, as he's trying hard to do. I say innocent, because their morals are really remarkable. Not a marriage for two years on the Islands, so great is the poverty and the impossibility of expansion, yet there haven't been more than two bastard children in 40 years (one of them was strangled at birth, I gather). One might imagine that they knew too much, but according to Pat Mullen, drunk or sober you could trust a man with a woman 'even if you put them in the same bed'. Another great dance sight is to see the crowd that gathers on Sunday night at dusk (it is still dusk at 11.0), when they dance on the 'slip' next to the quay. The nailed boots, a score of them, on the cement floor, make a wonderful 'swish' which puts the clip and clop of the tarantella in the shade. I can't follow the Reel or the Jig, but they dance with a great precision and rhythm. Probably you've seen it elsewhere. It's a great help knowing Pat [Mullen] and we spend most of our spare time down at his cottage. His outside reputation hasn't spoiled him in the least, and I don't think the Islanders realize that he is in any way outstanding. He still meets the boat and earns a few shillings rowing people round, and lives on tea, bread and potatoes. The clothes he wears haven't changed for a twelvemonth, but in spite of that he succeeds in breaking the hearts of all the handsomer female visitors who reach the Island. He has all the Irish blarney, but it goes no further! A grand figure, rather like a coarse, badly-dressed version of Sir William Fisher. We knew that he had been married about 20 years ago in America to some Irish woman, whose chief virtue seems to have been that she could knock a man down! They soon parted and he returned to Aran with his 2-year-old son and left the wife and two daughters behind. I read that his daughter Barbara [later the housekeeper in the well-known TV programme, 'Dr Finlay's Casebook'] had written a book, 'Life is my Adventure', which Fabers were publishing, and in my imagination saw a hefty six foot Irish-American knock-me-down type. And here she is, for the first time out of America, speaking a lovely soft Irish, without a trace of American, completely unspoilt and at home in Aran, able to dance with the rest of them and without any trace of sophistication. She's now about 23, and just sat down and wrote the book because her father told her that as she would have some time on her hands she had better write down her experiences! And it's really quite a remarkable book and well worth reading. We were with them on publication day and took part in the celebrations, which consisted of going up to the village and buying a pot of strawberry-jam and some chocolate! 'All my own book' she said, when the six copies arrived, and then looked at Pat with a wicked eye and said 'Pat Mullen, father of Barbara Mullen'. Joy and I have quite fallen in love with her and find it hard to realise that this demure, almost insignificant, little person, who bakes the bread and wields the duster (very badly too, like all the Irish I should imagine) has been through the life that she writes about, and above all, has the natural talent to write it down. Joy thinks it far more than talent. I'm glad she's got in with Fabers, though I think Richard de la Mare [a Director at Fabers] will scratch his head when he meets her for the first time, so completely is she not of the literary world. She travels over with us on the 6th. With the idea of getting a job in London, typing or dancing is what she'll try for.

I don't know why I'm writing all this rigmarole when there's so much more I could tell you, but a blank hour, pen and paper made me feel like letting you know how much I am enjoying it all. Joy sends her devotion to our Fergie. G.

Aldbourne, Wilts.; 7 June

Dearest Fergie,

I found these tickets waiting for me. Much as I'd like to hear the Oriana do anything of mine I can't get up tomorrow. I suppose there's not the least hope of your being able to go? Failing that, would you phone up Aunt Lily and tell her that you have the two tickets, only don't tell her that I sent them to you, as she would likely spurn them as 2nd-hand clothes! But I should like to know what they do and how they (or it) sound (or sounds), and above all to have you there.

The O.U.P. have taken those other two Bridges part-songs, I'm grateful to say.

Such a damnable post waiting to be tackled. Love, G.

34 Willoughby Road, N.W.3; 10 June

Dearest Dave,

Unfortunately it was not possible for me to use the Oriana tickets, as I had to play myself on Tuesday evening. But I rang up Aunt Lily, saying a friend had given them to me (not mentioning you), and she was glad to have them. I hope whatever they were doing of yours went well.

I never thanked you or Mary, or whoever it was that sent it, for the most superb box of asparagus. It was much appreciated. What lovely ones they were: they fairly slipped down the gullet.

So glad about the O.U.P. and the two Bridges part-songs. It's about time they did them off their own bat, the silly fools.

I have decided to remove the bubbly Rhapsody [eventually it became No.2 of the 'Three Sketches' for flute and piano, Op.14] from my Five Pieces for Clarinet and Piano; not because I don't like it musically, but because it seems impossible to play without making the most frightful clatter with the keys; when I first heard Paul [Pauline Juler] do it I thought it sounded like that because she didn't know it; but it is just as bad now, so I must regretfully conclude that the clatter is inherent. Thus the set will consist of Four instead of Five pieces.

I have written to Toty [de Navarro] to say that if he can manage 15–19 July, or some such date, I would be delighted to go a-sailing with the party [at Blakeney, Norfolk, where Toty kept his small yacht]. Let's hope it will be possible.

Hoping the family is well. Ever, H.

34 Willoughby Road, N.W.3; 21 June

Dearest Dave,

Am I dreaming, or did I send you a note saying that I would be glad if you came here for the nights you are in London? Your postcard has made me uncertain whether I did or not. Do by all means come Saturday and stay over till Wednesday. That would suit me fine. Or, if you would rather, come Monday and stay on after Wednesday; the former arrangement is really best for me, as I would see more of you – but do whichever is easiest for yourself.

This house has been sold. I have only got £2,100 for it; but I felt it was better to accept this, considering the number of people that have been over the place, than let a purchaser go by. I am now looking seriously for another place. It is more than likely I will not find one in time, and will have to store the furniture, but that cannot be helped. I imagine I'll move from here at the end of July. It all happened rather suddenly, the offer coming from a man who only saw the house last week for the first time. He seems a pleasant person.

I finished correcting the Parts [of the Partita; 1st performance under Boult, B.B.C. 29 June] this weekend. It was a pretty frightful job, as they were far from accurate in detail. Copyists seem quite incapable of writing-in hair-pins, etc., as one places them in the MS.

Not having seen Hawkes since I was at Aldbourne, I have had no opportunity of mentioning the Gurney March to him. He is on holiday at the moment, I believe, but I will talk it over with him the next time I see him. He will not be in town for the Partita, but hopes to listen.

The other night I dreamt that I myself was conducting the last movement; the only trouble being that the sounds issuing from the orchestra were of something altogether different! Love to you both. H.

34 Willoughby Road, N.W.3; 23 June

[Dearest Dave]

Have seen a house (new) not far from the Busch's, which I'd like you to have a look at. Any chance of you seeing it Saturday afternoon? Unfortunately I have to be out that evening. H

34 Willoughby Road, N.W.3; 1 July

Dearest Dave,

Though it is as yet impossible to say anything about their lasting powers, the Memphis[7] records of the Partita are quite astonishingly good as far as quality is concerned. They played them through to me on Wednesday afternoon and I was most surprised by them. Even the climaxes come out quite clearly. I cannot understand why anyone should have found the slow movement complicated, as the wireless reproduction of it is perfectly satisfactory: balance O.K. and all the right things coming out. It is invaluable to have the records, and I strongly advise you to have your next broadcast work done if you are at all doubtful about any parts of it.

I played the records through to Hawkes yesterday (incidentally he took a chip out of one of them with his blasted automatic machine), as he had not been able to listen to the broadcast owing to a yachting accident. It was rather a success. He suggested doing a Full-Score, Miniature Score, and Two-Piano version. I shall believe all that when I receive the contract; in the meantime I shall hope for the best.

Re the subtle changes of tempo which seem to occur all over the place: how about just putting occasional metronome-marks in brackets, without any 'poco accel' or 'poco meno mosso' or the like? This should give the idea of a slightly varying tempo, without leaving open the temptation to exaggerate. One might also have a note at the beginning of the work explaining that most of these changes are gradual, not sudden. What do you think? I cannot tell you what a difference it made having you and Joy here for the rehearsals and the performance. Quite apart from the moral support, it was so good to have you on the spot to refer to about the various points. It was an alarming time, but you helped to make it very much less so; and thank goodness it is now satisfactorily over, and that we can all say 'Tomorrow to fresh fields – ' [Milton], as we twitch our mantles blue! Blessings on you both, and love, H.

Aldbourne, Wilts.; 2 July

Dearest Fergie,

About 14 July. Would it be all right for you to leave St Pancras at 10.3 and arrive at Luton 11.16 ? There is a later and better train, leaving St P. 11.0 and getting to Luton 11.38; but I think the earlier would be better, as we have to get to Hundon [G.F.'s mother's house in Suffolk] for lunch. It's a bit difficult to judge times and distances from here, so we might get to Luton a bit early or a bit late: in the latter case a thriller would keep you patient in the waiting-room! If this is all right, I won't write again and send you a reminder, but will expect to see you at Luton on 14 July about 11.16.

I loved my stay with you and hearing the Partita. It turned out to be everything everyone expected it to be, and Joy is terrified that you get all the

---

[7] A small company, able to make private recordings.

gramophones you know to try the records, so that they're worn out by the time you reach here! It will be interesting to hear what the 3rd movement sounds like. Our love to you. G.

The next evening, Wed, I listened-in to Robin Milford's 'Concerto Grosso'.[8] A great step forward and quite the biggest work of his I've heard. It's good.

34 Willoughby Road, N.W.3; 12 July

Dearest Dave,

Luton at 11.16 a.m. should be all right for me. If you are not on the platform to greet me with open arms (and a birthday smile) I shall hang around in the waiting-room until you turn up. I have not been feeling quite up to the mark the last few days; but I think the rest I had in bed all yesterday should put me right. If not, I'll phone Aldbourne tomorrow, Tuesday night. But I do not think this will be necessary.

You will be pleased to hear that I really and truly have a contract for Full Score, Miniature Score and Two-Piano version of the Partita. I have had a wild week putting final alterations into the score, which went to the engravers on Friday. Possibly this accounts for my feeling of general droopiness, combined with the fact that Cyriax [an osteopath] has been taking kinks out of my spine; no doubt a little sea air will get rid of that Ann B-L [Ann Bowes-Lyon, a poet friend of Toty's] cannot come until the 16th, as she has to stay at home and drive her Papa to the golf links!

'Clear and Gentle Stream' was disobligingly broadcast from Droitwich only; so, as my set refused to function on high waves, I was unable to hear it. I hope it sounded well.

I am only bringing foul old clothes to Blakeney; I trust this is all that will be required. Blessings, H.

Aldbourne, Wilts.; 21 July

Dear Fergie,

We found a letter from Mrs Norton when we got back, from which this is an extract: 'I had your letter and tried three times to get in touch with Christine Gregory. This morning I got her, and she says her price is £2,600 still – the agent had rung her up to know the lowest price also. She says it is not worth her while to sell unless she makes a profit, as there is no other studio like hers in Hampstead and the land next door is the only piece of land for sale in Hampstead and is a very high price to buy – and they are holding on to it for some time yet. She was quite put out that I knew she wanted to sell – silly creature – how can she sell unless people do know.'

That rather looks as if she is adamant, though I don't think she will get what she wants, as the general rule is that the type of person wanting a studio is not

---

[8] Robin Milford (1903–1959), English composer, much encouraged by Finzi. His Concerto Grosso had been premiered at the Royal College of Music on 19 January, 1937.

very often the kind that can afford such a price. It is curious that she mentions the land next door, as I never said anything about it. Do you conclude from this that it belongs to Christine Gregory or some other? It would be worth while asking how much it is, though it sounds as if they want a good deal for it. It seems to me silly that C.G. expects to get a profit when even the agents think it is rather stiff.

We called in to see the Taylors' house after we had left you. It was unexpectedly attractive, and with a really beautiful garden, which they had made out of a field. A lovely evening all the way home, and we got in pretty late. A grand long sleep we've had, and washed the last particle of sand from our bodies in a luxuriant bath!

We have unpacked 'Chartres' [a book on Chartres] and again enjoyed it in the sunshine before breakfast. It is a lovely thing to have. Here is a cheque for £4. So many thanks for having helped us out. Our love and love and love. [in Joy's hand] Joyce & Gerald.

34 Willoughby Road, N.W.3; 22 July

Dear Dave and Joy,

Thank you so much for your letter – and the cheque. I rather feared that might be the way Christine Gregory would feel about the matter. As you say, there cannot be much hope of her getting £2,600 for the studio; still, that is her funeral. I would not think of going above £2,000. Even this figure was felt by my Bank Manager, when I spoke to him about it yesterday, to be too much for such a property in such a place. But I don't know whether he quite realizes the difficulty of finding small houses which contain one large room, and that these usually cost more than houses containing more accommodation.

Though that matter appears to be closed – for the moment at any rate – I have one good piece of news for you. The man who has bought this house wrote to me, making the almost incredible suggestion that, as he does not want to move in here until about February next, I should stay on (rent free) until then. This, as you can imagine, suits me down to the ground, so I have most gratefully accepted his offer. I think the reason for making it must be that he has visions of the house lying empty for six months, and gradually going to rack and ruin through want of being lived in and kept warm, etc. This is certainly a possibility, so we can take it that the arrangement is mutually advantageous. My feelings of relief at not having to put the things into storage, and of having six more months to look around me, are tremendous.

What fun we had in Norfolk. I enjoyed the whole thing enormously, not least the drive up there and the drive down to Cambridge. It was an altogether merry party. My raincoat turned up by post the morning after I got back. So evidently Paddy [the Navarro's maid] found it and realized to whom it belonged before Toty got my postcard.

Nothing more to tell you now. With love, H.

Aldbourne, Wilts.; [between 21 July and 15 August]
Dearest Fergie,
That really is a wonderful piece of news. I'm glad beyond words, and think you'll have much more chance of finding what you want with 6 months in which to look out. Rent free, too! I shall be coming to London in August for a few days 4th–7th, but I suppose you won't be there? And I suppose Pu won't be there. Don't bother to answer unless she will be, and it'll be all right for me to put up. I'm pretty sure she'll be away, so I shall go to Keats Grove [Aunt Lily's house].
The Three Short Elegies [by G.F.] are next Thursday night (National) but you'll be off by then, I'm afraid. Not that they're worth staying in London for! Shall be glad to hear Paddy's [Patrick Hadley] work too. Our love, G.
Norfolk was fine, but you never saw March [a wonderful church]. Did you ever see Chekhov's 'The Three Sisters' with their 'Shall we never get to Moscow?'

Rosapenna Hotel, Co. Donegal; 13 August
Dearest Dave,
This is the most delightful place imaginable. We leave tomorrow, but the stay of a fortnight has been very enjoyable. The country is lovelier than any I have seen in Ireland and, indeed, quite unlike any that I have seen elsewhere. Sea-loughs, inland-loughs, hills and mountains, all mixed up together, so that wherever you move the pattern changes completely; and the colour – on the hills and on the sea – is as changeable and as beautiful. I have had some splendid walks by myself in the hills, and bathed many times in the perfect water – perfect, because one can either bathe from rocks into deep water, or else from a 3-mile-long sandy beach. This last is usually so deserted that one can bathe happily in one's birthdaysuit without fear of scandalizing anybody's modesty.
The food in the hotel is good (Oh! what lobsters), and it is otherwise comfortable. The only objections, as far as I am concerned, being that people dress for dinner of an evening and – worse still – a bloody dance-band plays under my window till 12 every night; but as one can get up late for breakfast, the latter is less bad than it might be. Part of my midnight oil has been spent in going over the 1st proofs of the 2-piano version of the Partita. These are surprisingly good, considering how full it is of dots, dashes and other niggledy markings. When I get the 2nd lot I'll pack them off to you. The 1st proofs of the Score – a more formidable job – are on their way, but have so far failed to appear. Perhaps they have been confiscated by the Customs on suspicion of being a long and complicated message in cypher.
I envy Rann and Toty their visit [to Aldbourne] yesterday, and wish I could have been there too. What fun you must all have had. Blessings on you, my chicks, with love to you both, from H.
P.S. Have read 'In Parenthesis' [by David Jones] and find it *most* impressive, with all the curious inevitability of a dream.

Aldbourne, Wilts.; 15 August

Dearest Fergie,

I was glad to hear from Rann that you enjoyed the holiday much more than you expected to. We had a happy visit from him and Toty, and, with a few phone calls and wires to Mama, they were able to stay till after sup. Toty was in good form and brought his presentation spade with him! We wished you and Ann could have been there too. I really think that Norfolk week meant quite a lot to Toty – I don't know how he puts up with the Court Farm life and its perpetual comings and goings. By the way, you must have (in your innocence) told Aunt Jane [Mrs R.O. Morris] about Norfolk, or it must have got to her somehow, for who else could make such a wonderful story out of it? Anyhow, Alice [Sumsion] was under the impression that we had been to Norfolk on a *yachting cruise* with *Ivor Novello*? V.W. was bubbling over with it and wondering whether Joy had succumbed to his charms! I think the corruption of Navarro into Novello is rather good.

We went up to hear Rubbra's 'Fantasia' at the Proms. He conducted surprisingly well. It's a very efficient work, but the general impression is of greyness, almost dullness.

William Busch's 'Variations' were broadcast and I thought them as splendid as ever. I hope he'll do something to equal them.

You'll be glad to hear that the O.U.P. have agreed to publish the 20 Gurney songs. Foss hopes to have them out at the same time as the 'Music & Letters' articles in January. It's terrible to think that all this might have been done a dozen years ago, if his work had not been left in the hands of that possessive, incompetent, mulish, old maid Marion Scott. You know the inside of it all and how impossible she has been, but that was nothing to the three days Joy and I spent in London doing the final cataloguing. This had been agreed on about a month before. The first thing we found was that she had mislaid part of the list of music. This turned up the next day. Then she had not even managed to get copies of the published work to put with the complete works. She put every obstacle in the way of our phoning-up the publishers; but we managed to get our way, and the copies arrived on the last day. I suggested looking into that large packing-case in her room, which she always assured me had nothing of importance in it. I bundled everything out onto the floor and found about 30 complete songs of G's best period, dozens of notebooks, some with complete songs in, and a few thousand papers of various MSS, including 'lost' Violin Sonata movements and so on. Joy and I worked till about 9.30 that night – the temperature of Maid Marion's room was 90 – and begged that we should be treated like the piano-tuner and left alone, whilst the Scott family dined in state. It is rather incredible when you realize everything was supposed to be ready for the cataloguing, sorted and in order, two months ago. But what can you expect from someone who hasn't 'had time' to copy out those two little Violin & Piano pieces you asked for nine months ago? I'm so polite to this fragile fool that I've not had the heart to remind her that I made the time to copy out 24 of his songs in a month. However, the cataloguing seems to be done. 17 portfolios of coherent work and a chestful of asylum stuff, and it's taken about four years of incessant prodding to make the woman move. Now, she says all the music must go back to her Bank! I'm reminded of the little beetle in 'The Insect Play' guarding his pile. I think Howells and V.W. are quite right in feeling she has an unconscious resentment against anything being done for Gurney, unless it's done by herself, but beyond 'guarding his pile' she is incapable of doing anything. Now there'll be all the bother over again if the poems are ever to see the light. I forget whether I told you that Maid Marion, having promised to make a selection of the poems for de la Mare and his article – she would not hear of Joy and me doing it – said it would be a nice quiet job for her when on holiday – sent him the whole collection, sane, incoherent, unsorted. Poor de la Mare, he wrote to me that he was under the impression that a selection would be coming to him, and that Miss Scott had sent him all the unpublished poems, which would entail a good deal of reading, for which he hasn't the leisure nowadays. However, he's going to do his best. But enough of all this.

Do you know why Kodaly grew that apostle-like beard of his? Apparently he married someone considerably his senior and he grew it out of regard for her feelings to make himself look older. Isn't it touching. Joy sends her love. The Snake [a piece of Joy's carving] is really finished and looks grand. Here's a notice about Ann's book [Ann Bowes Lyon's Poems] from the Times Lit. I'm so glad she's had something pleasant at last. Love to you, G.

Aldbourne, Wilts.; 12 September

Dearest Fergie,

Here are those two-partsongs. I had meant to send you the 2nd proofs, but instead of the 2nd proofs the finished article arrived! A characteristically O.U.P. muddle, but fortunately I don't think there are any mistakes. I meant to tell you about the satisfactory outcome of the meetings in London about Gurney's songs (V.W., Foss, Maid Marion and myself), the pleasant day Joy and I spent with Toty at Court Farm, The Three Choirs Festival and so on, but as I expect you'll be back from Ireland any day now (and may even come down to see us for a day or two?) I'll wait till we meet. John [Sumsion] is with us until Thursday, recuperating after Gloucester. How are you, and are you having a struggle over those proofs? Love, G.

[Aldbourne, Wilts.; 14 September]

Dear Fergie,

Dreadful thoughts about your Partita proofs. Hawkes & Boosey really seem very stupid about some things, and I can give you another example. They've already returned my 'Introit'!

That will be absolutely all right about Davie. You don't mention a date and I suppose you mean from the beginning of term. That's the 24th or 25th. Now

I'm going to be up 24–26, so would he mind missing just those days? Otherwise, it's absolutely all right, either before or after then.

No more for now as I want you to get this first post. Our love, G.

34 Willoughby Road, N.W.3; 16 September

Dearest Dave,

Thank you very much for 'Haste on my joys' and 'My spirit sang all day'. It is a delight to be able to add them to the collection. You must have had a bit of a jar when the printed copies arrived instead of the 2nd proofs; but, so far as I can see after only a hasty glance through, you have nothing in them to mourn over. They are beautiful songs.

It seems like an odd inversion of turning the other cheek, to threaten you with the 2nd proofs of the Partita Full Score – not having had the chance of going over either of your two ditties. But I am at least sparing you the Two-Piano version, though that must be small comfort. As I think I told you, B&H did not send me the 1st proofs of the Score, but got somebody else to 'correct' them. In the 2nd proofs (that is, the first lot I got) I made about 2,000 corrections. Pretty good, don't you think for a copy that had already been corrected? If you could give the 3rd proofs the once over after I have been through them, I should be tremendously grateful. I myself have not yet received them, so it will be some time before they are ready.

The enclosed programme tells when the Clarinet bits are being done [4 Short Pieces for Clarinet & Piano: 1st performance Wigmore Hall 12.10.37. Pauline Juler and H.F.], and the rest of the programme too, which is good, I think. Next week Paul and I go to Broadway for Toty's birthday. I loved the postcard you sent from there; but what I look forward to more than anything is your account of The Lady of Court Farm [Toty's exigent mother, Mary Anderson, American ex-actress famed for her beauty].

If John is still with you, give him my love. I'm sure he must be relieved that Gloucester is over. Blessings on you both. I shall hope to breeze down on you – probably sometime after the 12th October – if you'll put up with me. Love from H.

34 Willoughby Road, N.W.3; 27 September

My poor Dave,

You will shortly receive a gigantic parcel of the proofs of the Partita Score – God help you. Only return 3rd proofs, as I can pack MS etc., when I'm next in Aldbourne. Ever, H.

Aldbourne, Wilts.; 28 September

Dearest Fergie,

Proofs to hand: Receipt enclosed! I'll do my very best. I suppose I can have a week or ten days? Engraving really seems so much quicker than composing or proof-reading.

I had a message that Howard Fry, that singer whoever he is, would like me to go through those songs with him next week. I've written to him as follows: 'I wasn't coming up to London next week, but could probably manage any day (except 6th and 8th) that suited you. There is however an even better idea. I don't know whether you know Howard Ferguson, the composer. He is also a very good accompanist, has done them a lot with Keith Falkner and knows them through and through – almost better than I do myself. I know he would be willing to go through them with you – engagements permitting – and am writing to ask him to do this, if you get in touch with him. His address is 34 Willoughby Road, N.W.3. This would have the added advantage of someone who can play the piano – I hardly play at all.'

I hope you don't mind my having done this – the 'engagements permitting' gives you a good loop-hole if you'd rather not. Of course he may not get in touch with you, but if he does, don't bother if you don't want to do it. He has chosen, the idiot, 'Summer Schemes', 'Lyonesse', 'Lizbie Brown' and 'Roll-icum'. So if you can put in a word for one of the songs that's more interesting – 'The Clock of the Years' or 'Proud Songsters' – I'll be glad. It would certainly make me blush less at the concert, though I can't say it would make me more interested. I at last understand a feeling of boredom and disinterestedness [sic] towards a work once published and performed! Love to you, G.

34 Willoughby Road, N.W.3; 29 September

Dearest Dave,

'I am in receipt of your letter' AND receipt, which I shall keep under lock and key, in case you employ a mock gas-inspector to try and get it out of me unawares.

Of course it's all right about Howard Fry. I shall be delighted to go over the songs with him if he should pick on me (it sounds rather like a new Judgement of Paris – only I hope I will be more decently clad than the ladies usually are). It is a pity he has not chosen one of the big songs out of the set; I suspect the look of them frightened him.

Would Friday 15 October be a suitable date for me to descend on Aldbourne? If not, please say so, as a later weekend would do me equally as well. Also say honestly whether it would or not be a bore if I were to bring over for Sunday lunch the Vickers' son, aged 15, from Marlborough. Joy will remember the Vickers as Hertha's [Kraft] friends; as they were (or rather, Mrs Vickers was) amiable in inviting me for the weekend, having never set eyes on me, I thought it might be a way of doing a kindness in return. The son is nice, incidentally, and fond of music. But do just say the word if it would be more than either of you could stand, as I didn't make the suggestion public.

I spent a delightful couple of days at Broadway. We had much music (the Juler was there too), and Toty showed me the new poem 'By Grief withheld' and the revised version of 'Third Anniversary'. The latter struck me as being completely satisfactory now (I like the localizing of the end of a contrast in the unlocalized 'clock whose hours are months'); while the new one is surely of the very finest.

There is no special hurry over the proofs, so for goodness sake don't kill yourself over them. I'll shortly be sending you the finished print of the Clarinet Pieces; as a relief from proof-correcting you will be able to have a good laugh at the many mistakes I have probably let through. May they also serve as an awful warning!

My love to you both, H.

Aldbourne, Wilts.; 30 September

Dearest Fergie,

Could you make it the weekend after (Friday 22nd)? Joy and I will be away until the 18th or 19th. We hope to get up to the concert on the 12th (though much depends on domestic holidays, etc.); and all being well, we want to have two or three days walk after that, as Joy has had a dull time being nursemaid-in-charge for the last fortnight. So if you can make it the 22nd (or before, if you feel like it) we'd be delighted. Most certainly bring the Vickers' son to lunch on the Sunday, that would be the 24th, and if he happens to know a newcomer, Martin Richmond, he can bring him along too. But, at that age, 15 holds 14 in contempt, so one must be careful what one suggests. Martin is a delightful person for whom Joy has a justifiable passion. She has known him since he was very small, but doesn't like the Father, Prof. Richmond ('the Professor' about whom you may have heard us talk – I met him for the first time the other day and didn't dislike him at all).

Thanks so much for putting up with Howard Fry. I hope he writes or phones you. He should do so on the strength of my letter, though, being a singer, he may not like the mention of Keith Falkner. 'You're a better man than I am, Gunga Din.'

The Partita looks grand in print. I loathe proof-correcting, but it's really worth while with such a work. I'm looking forward to the Clarinet Pieces. If you have a spare B.B.C. list of forthcoming concerts, you might shoot it off at me.

I don't agree about Toty's localized clock in 'Third Anniversary'. It's certainly a very fine poem as it now stands – which it wasn't before – but I feel it could be made even greater with a clock-tower, rather than Christchurch in particular. What happens when Christchurch tumbles down? Re-read 'At a lunar eclipse' and substitute for the last line

Heroes, and doctors practising at Guy's.

162

But then, I'm afraid the 'Heavens and Charing Cross' line has always upset me. How often I wish that Blunden [Edmund] had left out the last verse of his magnificent 'Psalm'; 'O God, in whom my deepest being dwells'. Toty's other poem 'By Grief Withheld' is most beautiful. It's quite extraordinary the way his work goes from strength to strength instead of the other way round, as is usual after the age of 35.

Remind me to show you a letter from Blunden about Gurney, on account of the hand-writing which is quite the loveliest I've ever seen. By the way, talking of Blunden, have you the collected poems? If not, would you like a copy for Trafalgar Day, which I've just realized you'll be spending with us (I hope).

Are you getting me the Verdi 'Requiem' as promised? Our love, G.

I'm glad our Poet Laureate approved the Clarinet Pieces.[9]

                                        34 Willoughby Road, N.W.3; 4 October
Dearest Dave,

Yes, that certainly is an astonishing piece of letter-layout from Howard Fry. It looks like vers-libre. But the main thing is that I have arranged a tryst with him for Wednesday morning, and will do my best to expound the songs clearly to him.

Many thanks for your screed before that. The Vickers' son is delighted (or says he is) at the invitation to Sunday lunch on 24th. It might, perhaps, be more politic to introduce the subject of Martin Richmond later rather than earlier: for, as you say, 15 is apt to look down its nose at 14, and feel insulted at being asked to eat at the same board.

I have not yet written to the Hermetic Marion [Scott]. But I have done something about the Verdi 'Requiem', so am not wholly without virtue. Do I deserve the Blunden Poems? I doubt it, but do not doubt my willingness to accept them if they came my way.

Enclosed is a batch of B.B.C. literature; I hope it is what you want. You will be glad to hear that Adrian [Boult] is doing the Partita for them in Belfast, at a public concert on 19 March. I'm pleased it's being done there, as the parents will get some kick out of it.

Toty suggests all of us going to a Matinée on Wednesday afternoon, the 13th. Could you both manage that? I could not manage the evening, as I am going to the B.B.C. at Queens Hall. Did you say something about the evening of Monday 11th? I don't rightly remember; but in any case I think I had better stay at home the night before the concert, so don't count on me.

I went to hear the 'Colour Symphony' [Bliss] and was slightly disappointed. Am going on Saturday afternoon to see 'Checkmate' [Bliss] again. Love to you both. H.

Enclosed is another brochure which may be of interest to you.

[9] John Masefield (1887–1967) had heard the clarinet pieces at one of Madame Navarro's soirees (see letter 19 September 1936).

Aldbourne, Wilts.; 6 October

Dearest Fergie,

As I thought you would be full up with Rann and Toty I've already arranged to go to Aunt Lily. There's just a hundredth chance that she may have a niece coming for a night or two that week, in which case I would come running along to you with gratitude. In any case I may be worrying you a bit later on, as I'm beginning to feel the need of hearing some music again.

Can one get into those Toscanini studio concerts? Would a false beard and moustache get me in? By the way, I see that Morley College are doing two new works for chorus and orchestra by Tippett and Jeffrey Mark[10] on Sunday 7 November. Are there any other things round that date to make a visit worth while? I'm desperately anxious to see 'Checkmate' and it might be on 5, 6, 8 or 9. I listened-in to the 'Colour Symphony'. It's not completed, if you know what I mean, but some lovely lyrical moments, I thought. When you come (on the 22nd?) could you bring the Partita records with you? I could keep the 2nd proofs down here till then, but the 3rd proofs and MS I thought I'd bring up with me on Sunday night or Monday morn, when we expect to come up. I don't think you'd better rely on Wednesday matinée for us, unless you could leave it open till the day itself, so that we can know what the weather is like. But I know Joy wants to get away as soon as possible on Wednesday for these few days change which she badly needs. As it is, she won't have much of a holiday, as she has to go and fetch the children again on Sunday 17th. Sorry we shall have to be without you on Monday night, whatever we do.

Splendid about Belfast, but only to be expected [performance of the Partita]. After that your parents will be made honorary citizens, and they'll be the parents of H.F. instead of H.F. being the son of Mr & Mrs S.F.!!

Dear Mrs Straker brought along a girl called Doreen Maguire, simply because I think she knows you and your family in Belfast.

Many thanks for the enclosures. Till Sunday or Monday morn. I'll phone up beforehand. Love, G.

34 Willoughby Road, N.W.3; 21 October

[Dearest Dave]

Many thanks for your pretty birthday wishes. I look forward to seeing you both tomorrow, and will arrive by the train leaving Paddington at 2.45.

Love, H.

[10] Jeffrey Mark (1898–1965). A mature student at the RCM immediately after World War I, he became a close friend of Michael Tippett and was the dedicatee of his *Concerto for Double String Orchestra* (1939). He is mentioned several times in Tippett's autobiography, *Those Twentieth-Century Blues* (1991).

Aldbourne, Wilts.; 17 November

Dearest Fergie,

Here is a most extraordinary package for you – rather like one of my step-grandmother's collections which sometimes arrive for Christmas. Firstly, spare copies of 'Checkmate' [Bliss] and 'In Honour of the City' [Dyson] in case you know of anyone who might like them. Rann, Ceddy? Then a song by Walton and some piano pieces by Murrill and Berkeley. These are for your amusement and the waste-paper basket. They almost take one back to our 'Cantilever' days [our parodies of 'Les Six']. I hope Alec Rowley's '5 Lyric Studies' and '5 Lyric Pieces' sound better together than they do alone. Do you also see that Ernest Chapman [worked at Boosey & Hawkes] composes. There you will find a [silly] advertisement of Ralph Chubb's latest.[11] (These I would like back, for the collection of curiosities.) How can one distinguish between a 2nd William Blake and a 2nd Josef Holbrooke? 'An English Poet' is too good to be true. Yet Blake's manifesto must have struck his more materialistic contemporaries as being absolutely ridiculous, and Linnel and Richmond may have felt the same about Blake as we do about Chubb. I'd dearly love to see the books before passing an opinion, as the reproductions mean very little. (He will be a new neighbour – Ashford Hill is near Highclere – so you know what strange people you are thinking of consorting with.) Next you'll find a piece of cardboard and a stamped addressed envelope, and somewhere in the middle of this you'll find that 'Oboe Interlude'! Would you mind just glancing through this? Now that it's all written out it's easier to judge as a whole. The few questions are on a separate sheet inside the score, if you would not mind putting yea-nay against them. I still think it's an unsatisfactory way of doing things [publishing before a whole work is completed], but convenient whilst one is quite unknown. (Later on, one can always take it out of the catalogue again.) If you're not too bewildered, all you need do is put the Chubb adverts, the 'Oboe Interlude' questionnaire and cardboard inside the envelope and post off.

I hope you had a satisfactory drive back with Peter [Harland].[12] Joy has had a rotten attack of asthma, such as we had thought she had left behind her, but we'll find a cure yet. She's in bed, but sends her love. G.

34 Willoughby Road, N.W.3; 20 November

Dearest Dave,

The questionnaire has become somewhat involved, so I am resorting to a separate sheet.

Of recent events in the musical world, you will have heard the Tovey Cello

---

[11] Ralph Chubb (1892–1960), a naive pederast who published, at his own expense, a number of poetic effusions, illustrated by his own Blake-like watercolours and woodcuts, extolling the virtues of idealized boy-love. The 1937 publication was *Water-Cherubs: a Book of Original Drawings and Poetry*, issued in an expensive, and fortunately limited, edition bound in green half-morocco.

[12] Peter Harland, architect. See Letter 3 September 1936.

Concerto by wireless.[13] It was a long hour, relieved by sidelong glances at the copy of my next-door neighbour; and though I fully admit the impossibility of grasping a work of that size in one hearing, I did not feel particularly moved to investigate it further, or to spend either 10/− on a piano score or £1.1.0 on a full score. Perhaps this is unenterprising of me.

The Rachmaninoff Symphony at Thursday's Phil was a tiresome piece of pretentiousness. Passing somebody in the street afterwards I said 'Thank goodness we'll never have to hear that again!' 'How will you guarantee that?' they asked. Quoth I, 'By walking out before it commences.'

Mr Bonavia's [music-critic] Quartet last night was very much better than I expected. He knows how to write for strings, which is more than can be said for many people; but he is not so strong on the constructional side. In that direction his last movement was wholly incompetent and his slow movement partly so. As a whole the first two movements were the most satisfactory. His music shows a sensitive but not outstanding creative talent.

I got the O.U.P. to send me a copy of Rubbra's fiddle Sonata. Solde [Isolde Menges] is giving a Wigmore Hall recital in February, and I thought we might try and go through it this week to see whether she would like to play it. What a pity the last movement is so very bad; the other two have great beauty, but they are really let down by the third. I doubt if, for that reason, she will want to play it. I have also got Maid Marion to promise me a copy of the two Gurney pieces; as she says she has already started to copy them (how many months after she first promised?), there seems to be some possibility of me receiving them before Christmas.

Thanks so much for the spare copies of the Walton and of 'Checkmate'; I'm sure Rann will be only too pleased to add them to his collection. The other enclosures were strange in their various ways. The Walton song is harmlessly pleasing in an entirely nondescript sort of way. The Murrill seems to me beneath contempt, and the Berkeley one stage better than the 'vif et gai' period, but only by the skin of its teeth. If that is the result of Boulanger's teaching, God preserve us from it! Mr Chubb is truly astounding. It is certainly difficult to know whether one can take him seriously − judging by the reproduction, I should say not.

What a shame about Joy's asthma. I am very sorry indeed to hear about it. If, by any chance, she is not feeling all right by next weekend, for goodness sake put the party off. If she is better, as I hope she is by now, I shall look forward to seeing you both on Saturday evening next, when I shall arrive by the 6 o'clock train from Paddington. My love to you both. Ever, H.

[13] Sir Donald Francis Tovey (1875–1940), music scholar, composer, pianist. Better known for his *Essays in Musical Analysis* (1935–1939) than for his many ambitious compositions. The Cello Concerto (1935) was written for Casals.

34 Willoughby Road, N.W.3; 23 November

Dearest Dave,

Saturday 11th till Tuesday 14th will do me just as well, if not better, so I shall put it in my little book.

I gathered from Toty when I last saw him that there was some trouble brewing at Cambridge; no doubt that is what keeps him this weekend, with possibly a call from La Belle Dame [his Mother] into the bargain.

No news about the site [at Ashmansworth, for H.F.'s proposed house, which was not built]. I am going to write to Neate [house agent] today, to see if I can get an answer one way or the other. Blessings on you both. Ever, H.

I hope Joy's asthma is better.

34 Willoughby Road, N.W.3; 24 November

Dearest Dave,

This morning I received the following from Neate:- 'We have been able to ascertain the following from the owner of Lots 5 & 6 on the Ashmansworth Estate: that he is not keen to consider selling off these Lots, and would rather sell a site on the other side of the road. We think however that he would be willing to sell if he had a good offer, and perhaps you would kindly let us know if you would like to suggest a price and see if we could tempt him.' What, then, is the next move? Would it be best for you to find out from Cpt. Jobling whether, if I was able to get the land, I would be allowed to build on it? I could, at the same time, go and see Peter [Harland] (as he said I might) and find from him whether it would be possible to build the house I want for £1,500 inclusive of everything except the land. If the answer to both these questions is satisfactory, would it then be best to get Neate to make the people an offer of £500 for the two Lots plus the wood? If they would not take that, one might go as far as £550 or £600, though I think the latter figure is rather more than I should pay.

Let me know what you think and what I had better do. If it would be more satisfactory for me to be on the spot, I could easily come down Monday or Tuesday next, but Sunday is, I am afraid, now impossible.

So sorry to bother you with this. Blessings on you both, from H.

The white wine from Berry's is a Macon Clessé.

34 Willoughby Road, N.W.3; 4 December

Dearest Dave,

After you left yesterday I had a somewhat harassing afternoon. For why? Well first of all I went to see Chenhalls [accountant]; and, though he gave me a cheque for the principle part of the money so there is nothing to worry about in the direction about which I spoke to you, he also gave me the disquieting news that I may get £300 less from Nunky's bequest than I was expecting. This, as you can imagine, is serious from the point of view of my building. The reason for the doubt is that I advanced Nunky £300 towards the purchase of this house, as you know; and it is a question whether I get the proceeds of the sale of the house subject to this debt (apart from all the others I have been landed for), or whether the debt gets paid out of the general estate. If the latter, I get my £300 back again; if the former of course I do not. Counsel's opinion is being sought upon the point, and I hope I shall know what it is by the time we meet at the end of next week.

The next jollification was a visit to Peter, who broke it to me that a house such as I suggested would cost £2,000. This is admittedly not so appalling as the estimate he produced for you; but on top of Chenhall's news it was scarcely cheering. And even £2,000 would not include central-heating! We talked of this and that, and ways of reducing the cost, and finally he asked me to let him go into it more closely and then to let me know the results of his deliberations. I said, 'Fire ahead'. However, if the £300 does not eventuate, something drastic will have to be done. With this possibility in view, I think it might be worth seriously considering whether I could get one of those Lots (the further one) instead of the two, and just risk somebody else building on the nearer one. Even if they did, I should still have my main and perfect view down the valley to the South. How about your sounding Neate on this point if you happen to be near his office during the coming week?

The part-songs [Bridges] have just come through. I like 'Haste on' very much, and would no doubt like it even more if the tenors and basses began in the same key as the rest (poor Dave! I did feel sorry for you having to listen to it like that); 'I have loved Flowers' I like less than the other two; but 'O Joy' is a real beauty. I should love to hear the whole set complete. Blessings on you both. Ever, H.

Aldbourne, Wilts.; 7 December

Dearest Fergie,

I rather think it's better not to say anything to Neate yet. Just wait till he has got something out of Crundell, and see whether it's a refusal or a bargaining tentacle, you can always then make use of the small site idea. If you suggested it now and got a refusal, there would not be much more that you could do. I've got a few vague ideas that might be workable, but we can talk about them on Saturday; and by that time you may also have heard something on the cheerful side about the £300.

Toty writes that unless any catastrophe occurs he'll arrive here about 1 o'clock on Saturday. What about you and Ann? It occurs to me that if you could arrive by the 12.33 at Hungerford (Paddington 10.45) I might be able to get Toty to turn up at 12.0 and then we'd all meet at Hungerford in his car. Or is the position so difficult that he would rather even the chauffeur didn't know that Ann was of the party!

Curiously enough, I liked 'I have loved Flowers' the best of the three part-songs. But 'Haste on' was a truly terrible show! All love, G.

Aldbourne, Wilts.; 18 December

Dearest Fergie,

Here's the 10/— and many thanks. Noel, Noel, Noel. That's about all I can do for Christmas and forgive more. I can't compete with your Christmas card, whatever it's going to be. What we wish for you in 1938 and what we wish about the house, can't be expressed on a Christmas card. Our love, G.

1938

Aldbourne, Wilts.; 1 January

Dearest Fergie,

You'll have seen about Gurney — in fact, the press has given him in his death more attention in a week than they gave his life in 47 years. I thought the enclosed headlines from The Gloucester Citizen would amuse you, knowing what precious little attention his native city paid to him before. I went to his funeral, a sad little affair at Twigworth, and H.H. [Howells] played 'Sleep' and 'Severn Meadows' on a wheezy little organ, whilst his brother Ronald stood by, looking exactly as though he had won a medal, so pleased, complacent and high-collared! Poor Marion Scott, in tears at the end, but remarkably brave and calm considering how much it must have meant to her. And now for 'The Late Christopher Bean'[1] all over again, for there's no doubt that the 'Music and Letters' articles have already set the ball rolling and people are discovering that they have MSS of him, that they knew him quite well, 'and were always amazed at his genius', that they visited him regularly when he was in the asylum, that they were his best friends, etc. etc. Even H.H.[owells], who was a great friend of his in R.C.M. days, but seldom went to the asylum in the latter years, now implies that he was a regular visitor. (But then H.H. is now talking about 'my College at Oxford'. See what a Mus. Doc. at the age of 45 can bring one to!) But, Lord, I'm glad those articles came out before he died, even though he was practically beyond understanding what and whom they were about. It's been worth all the trouble, irritation and obstruction (which reminds me: have you got the two violin pieces yet?), and something, however much in the background, I'm honestly proud to have got done, since his own 'friends' hadn't the spirit to do it.

And when do you get back? I might possibly get up for the Moeran Symphony. Have you any intention of going?

Any word about the site yet? The cottage [gardener's cottage at Ashmansworth] is getting on finely; but alas, each floor, as one gets to it, proves to be rotten — joists and all — and one might as well be building a new place. I think it'll be ready by March, or April for certain.

---

[1] A play by Sidney Howard. Adapted from the French (1933).

The Tuttens are still here and don't leave till the 5th. Three weeks of them is too much: Joy likes having them, but then, she's an angel. They're no nuisance, but I just can't stand the proximity of people, however delightful in themselves, where the contacts are all false. Great on a holiday, but to have to talk about their books three meals a day, for three weeks, makes me feel *murderous*.

A happy New Year to you. Our love, G.

The new Beecham Sibelius 4 is a good recording, but I think the same performance we heard, or very similar. I hate the way he tackles the end of the last movement, but the work stands anything.

14 Deramore Park South, Belfast; 5 January

Dearest Dave,

Thank you so much for your letter with the Gurney cutting (and the other pretty enclosures); it certainly was a near shave – and a lucky one – getting the Music & Letters number out and the songs completed before he died. I feel tolerably certain that neither feat would have been accomplished but for your insistence and energy. One can only feel relief that he should have ceased to suffer such a death-in-life. The same, I think, with Ravel, whose brain-trouble appears to have been of longer standing than I had supposed.

The cutting I enclosed shows the sort of Glastonbury 'Slippershoe' which I meant when I suggested it to Joy for you. (English as she is spoke.) They look comfortable.

No word yet from Neate, or anybody else, about Ashmansworth. How difficult it seems to be to spend £300 when you want to! It is bad luck that the Cottage turns out to have more wrong with it than you supposed; I expect things always turn out like that, and so upset one's calculations.

I won't be going to hear the Moeran Symphony at the Phil, as I have to return to London a day later than expected. I am calling at Manchester on the way, to play that tiresome and unthankful Concerto of lanky-Andrews[2] at a B.B.C. try-out there. The occasion holds every prospect of being piquant, as I understand F-C is to conduct; add to this that I cordially dislike the work, and you will be able to guess what a jolly morning I am in for.

Why don't you write Pu direct and say you would like to stay for the night of the 13th at No.34 Willoughby Road, N.W.3, if you are going to the Moeran? Stay over the next night too, if you like; but I won't be arriving until just before dinner – about 7 o'clock.

See if you can get Belfast on the wireless on Tuesday next, the 11th [for the Two Piano version of the Partita], from 8.35–9.00.

Yes, I actually got both Violin Pieces out of Maid Marion – the second after much writing, and in an appalling copy (I suspect Miss Ethel Henry B) full of

[2] Herbert Kennedy Andrews (1904–1965), Northern Irish organist, music scholar, composer. Best known for *An Introduction to the Technique of Palestrina* and *The Techniques of Byrd's Polyphony*. See Letter 16 January (p.172) for F.C.

wild misprints. Failing a comparison with the original MS, I have simply had to take the law into my own hands and make what alterations I think must be right. God help one from ever doing anything with Maid Marion.

Blessing on you both for 1938 and love, from H.

Aldbourne, Wilts.; 5 January

[Dear Fergie]

Many thanks for prompt reply. I've followed your advice. Oh, how dejecting about the 7th. Still, engagements is engagements. I may be up before the 3rd — that is, if Keith fixes up anything about those songs with old Boosey. I hope he does. I see that Leon [Goossens], the pride of oboeland, is playing with the Isolde Menges Quartet. (5.30 of all times.) Perhaps he'll say that the 'Interlude' isn't big enough for him. Our love, G.

14 Deramore Park South, Belfast; 11 January

Dearest Dave,

You and Joy will probably have received a somewhat astonishing letter from Mrs Vickers before now. I almost feel responsible for it, and should apologize for having brought it on your heads! [G.F had invited their son Burnell (a schoolboy at Marlborough) to lunch.][3] So that you may know how the matter stands, I am enclosing herewith the letter she sent to me, and my reply to the same. Hers is as nice as it could possibly be (and it must have been the hell of a letter to write), and I suppose she and her late husband have every right to make what hay they please of their son's affairs; but, while assuring her that I — and I felt sure you — would respect her wishes in every way, I could not refrain from asking whether all the fuss was necessary or wise. It does not matter two hoots to me; but it does seem a pity to badger the boy, and to try and force him now in a direction which, if left to his own devices, he would probably take naturally in a year or two. I hope my letter to Mrs Vickers is sufficiently restrained? It took me three days to write, so it should be.

I hope you are going to descend on Willoughby Road for the Phil this week. If you do, try and stay over for the Friday night as well, so that I shall see you.

No news since I last wrote. Please return the two enclosed letters to Hampstead, or bring them with you if you are coming. Love to you both. Ever, H.

[3] Burnell, the son of Geoffrey and Helena Vickers (friends of H.F.), wanted to follow a career in music.

34 Willoughby Road, N.W.3; 16 January

Dearest Dave,

I am so sorry that you were not able to stay over for the Friday night. It would have been fun to see you, for there are so many things (not very important) to talk about. I arrived here shortly before 7.0, feeling somewhat tired after the long day. There had been a young gale blowing in Ireland the day before; so, funking a rough sea crossing before running through Lanky's Concerto in Manchester, I flew to Liverpool, stayed there Thursday night and took the train to Manchester early the next morning. The rehearsal went swimmingly, and I must say F-C took endless trouble.[4] We began shortly after ten o'clock and went on till a quarter to one! The work does not appeal to me any more than I expected it would; but I understand they may do it up here and ask me to play it, so it will at least help to swell the exchequer. It was suggested that at the same broadcast I should conduct the Partita. I shied at this; but on thinking things over may say Yes, as it would be a pleasantly secluded spot in which to practise beating fives and sevens. Also, it would be better to make a fool of myself there, in the privacy of the studio, than anywhere more public at a first attempt.

It is splendid about the B.B.C.'s Gurney programmes; though rather pitiful that they should have to wait until he is dead before doing anything about his work. However, we expect that sort of thing. The two little Fiddle Pieces[5] [by Gurney] sound quite pleasant, but nothing more. I am glad you got Maid Marion to realize that the copy of the Scherzo she sent me is far too inaccurate to go to the printer.

Of course I missed the Moeran. Rann was most unenthusiastic, but I would sooner go by your impressions. Perhaps it will be broadcast sometime and I shall be able to hear it then.

Your reaction to Mrs Vickers' letter reassures me that my surprise is not unjustified. I do not feel any particular resentment that she should have written to me like that, for, as I said before, she has done a very difficult thing as delicately and nicely as she possibly could, and has obviously only been actuated by the conviction that she was doing the best for her son. But I would willingly shake both her and her late husband for being such unimaginative donkeys, and for doing their best to force Burnell still further into the sausage-machine of Publicschooldom. Like Joy, I am much more concerned with the effect all this has on him than with any personal feeling of annoyance. It can do nobody any good, least of all a person of Burnell's age, to be suddenly and for no apparent reason dropped like a hot brick by people who have hitherto been friendly. Knowing this, I wrote (when cancelling the invitation I had made him) that, as he probably knew, it was not always possible to make things pan-out as one wished, and that I was very sorry not to have him. I see no reason why Joy should ignore him in any way if they happen to meet at

---

[4] Hubert Foster-Clarke, Head of Music B.B.C. Manchester. A pupil of Sir Malcolm Sargent.
[5] *The Apple Orchard* and *Scherzo*. Written in 1919 and published by O.U.P. in 1940.

Marlborough; surely the letter of the law is fulfilled if you do not invite him to Aldbourne? Certainly I would look upon it in this way, if the occasion arose. Did you not notice in my letter to Mrs Vickers I said 'I am sure Gerald and Joyce Finzi will respect your wishes as much as I shall', but that I did not specify exactly how much I would respect them?

With love to you both from your simple little friend, H.

P.S. I am posting you a large whack of Stilton cheese tomorrow. I am afraid it is not so good as in other years: it has an odd sort of metallic under-flavour.

I have written to Miss Hill to ask whether or not she wants the clavichord.

34 Willoughby Road, N.W.3; 18 January

Dear Joy,

How very exciting! I wrote my Mother immediately and have just received a wire from her to say that she will arrive here in London on Thursday morning. If we were to go down to Newbury on either Friday (which might be preferable) or Saturday, would you or G. be able to collect us in your car and drive us to the site? Quite apart from the usefulness of your presence, I should love it if you were there. Of course, if this is frightfully inconvenient for you, please say so, as we could easily hire a car in Newbury. There appears to be a good train (1933 vintage) arriving at Newbury at 1.39, which we could have lunch on to save time: would this suit you? If you can manage either day, it might be a good plan to fix on the Friday unless it turns out to be pouring cats and dogs; in this case I would phone you shortly after breakfast.

You will be amused to hear that I received the following note from Mrs Vickers:- 'Dear Mr Fergusson (sic), thank you so much for your letter – it was nice of you to understand. I quite see the point you raise, but it seems to me one is always taking risks of doing the wrong thing when trying to bring up the young, and we can only do what we feel at the time is the best way of helping them! I think quite possibly the next year will make a lot of difference. We will try and fix up a weekend when you come back to London. Yours sincerely' which further goes to show her good feeling, but does not in any way lessen my desire to shake her until her teeth fall out. The Lord preserve children from their parents – usually.

With love to you both, from H.

Aldbourne, Wilts.; January? [undated]

Dearest Fergie,

We chewed our lunch to the accompaniment of Brahms No.2 and the four short clarinet pieces (H.F., B.B.C. 24 Jan. 1938]. I think you both played beautifully, and though I don't think Brahms No.2 is up to Brahms No.1, I was very glad to hear it. Pauline Juler is quite right in wanting you to do a Clarinet Sonata. I think you'd do it to perfection, and then there would be no need to revive Stanford and Bax. The little pieces are at least a signpost.

We're coming up to London Friday morning – I've got to see Howells at the R.C.M. 10.45 – may I stay Friday night, and if necessary Saturday night? However, Joy wants to get back on Saturday evening, and I suppose there's no hope of you and Isolde Menges playing together on Friday afternoon, or sometime Saturday morning or afternoon. I'd go to the Lemare concert on Friday night. Our love, G.

Aldbourne, Wilts. [; 2 February?]

Dearest Fergie,

It it's possible for me to get up to London on the 9th, I should try to kill two birds with one stone and go to the Boosey Concert and Mahler.

1) Would you be able to put me up for the night?

2) Are you going to the Mahler?

3) As I should not know until the day before, I'll have to leave the ticket question until getting to London. Should I be able to get it?

4) Should I survive the Mahler?

I think you can get all these replies onto a p.c. I hope you had good news from Toty the other day.

By the way, that delightful couple – Anthony Scott[6] [composer and organist] and his wife – were over here again yesterday, and he turns out to be Ann's cousin. I should like you to meet them when you're here. Love, G.

[G.F. offered to lend H.F. the gardener's cottage, later to be occupied by William, at the Ashmansworth site.] About William's car. It'll be all right, I think. There are a few Saturdays and Sundays in the year when he goes away (to preach, I think), and he naturally doesn't want to hire a car when he has one of his own. But I said that I thought there would be no difficulty at all if he wanted the car, provided he knew the dates ahead.

34 Willoughby Road, N.W.3; 14 February

Dearest Dave,

Here is 'Tom of Bedlam'.[7] Keep the copy, as I have typed it for you. It is some years since I copied it at the B.M., and I cannot for the life of me remember whether the punctuation comes from the MS or from my own head. If you think of setting it you could make certain of that – and of the general accuracy of the transcript, for it was made in rather a hurry – by paying a visit to the B.M. yourself and comparing the transcript with the original. Apparently there was only one word that baffled me completely: the adjective belonging to 'face' in the first line of p.2. I seem to remember other words that were capable of two interpretations: in such cases I brazenly chose the one I liked best, not being an expert in 17th century handwriting.

---

[6] Anthony Scott (1911–2000), English composer. Finzi's only composition pupil.

[7] Anon. Medieval. It begins: 'The moon's my constant mistress/And the lovely owl my marrow'.

The looseleaf book I use for Toty's poems is the 'Kentbury No.806'. Even his long-lined poems will fit into this sized sheet if you begin well over to the l.h. side.

Thank you both for my nice weekend. I was glad to meet Anthony Scott; remember me to him if he is breakfasting with you. Blessings on you. Ever, H.

Aldbourne, Wilts.; 17 February

Dearest Fergie,

Very many thanks: and what a poem ['Tom of Bedlam']! I'd no idea of all the other verses. Do you know de la Mare's selection in 'Come Hither'. He obviously knows the original (as his notes show), but it is amusing to see that 5 out of 6 anthologies that have since followed 'Come Hither' merely copy out his version, including his own particular emendations.

I could not find much 'arrangement' about the [Beethoven] 'Grosse Fuge'. It seemed a pretty straightforward transcription and sounded magnificent over the wireless. Apart from a few pleasant bars here and there I could find nothing in Schumann's Violin Concerto except deadly dullness. I had hoped for at least some sign of wildness.

Yes, Anthony Scott did turn up for breakfast and we went for an 18-mile walk in a North-East wind and it did me a lot of good. I'm glad you met him and got on with each other.

We had a satisfactory morning with Peter [Harland] and I think things are beginning to get a bit more clear. I went over to Winchester to see the tithe map and found that Ordnance Survey and tithe have no connection at all. So it was complicated, considering that several of the fields have changed in division since 1840, when the tithe map was made. Your own particular site was part of a large area No.65 called 'Great Yard'. At first I thought this rather dull, but Joy is converting me into thinking it's lovely! Howard Ferguson, Esq., Greatyard, Ashmansworth. The copse below was divided into two numbers, 66 Bramleaze Coppice and 67 Toppy Ash Coppice.

Good luck on Sunday. The close season hasn't started yet, so I shall be listening-in. Love, G.

Aldbourne, Wilts.; 23 February

Dearest Fergie,

About the car. Morris Garages charge from 15/– to 20/– a day for hire! So I asked Stradlings at Newbury what they would charge for a long-term hire of an old Austin 7 and they said 10/– a day! This seems quite preposterous, and I can't believe that anybody would be so stupid as to pay £15 a month when they could buy a third-hand car for the same price. But I think, in fairness to William, and taking into consideration the wear and tear of tyres, that £1 is too little and you ought to make it £2 a month. About insurance. Do you want a comprehensive or a third party or a third party plus fire and theft? 1) would cost about £7 odd; 2) £3 odd; 3) £4 odd. William himself would have 3), but the risk of not having a comprehensive means that if you do have a smash and are not in the right, you get nothing back. The difficulty is that William doesn't know if you can get a 3 month or 6 month comprehensive, otherwise we would have suggested a comprehensive for you and a third party (for Pu), plus fire and theft for yourself. (The difference of a pound or two means a lot to him.) I'm told that the policy will have to be taken out by yourself, as it's verboten for a person to hire a car under the owner's insurance. But I'll find out more about this, so don't worry about it. Love and I hope you can grasp this rigmarole. G.

34 Willoughby Road, N.W.3; 27 February

Dearest Dave,

Thank you for your letters. Yes, you can have the other half of my Contemporary Concert ticket for the 4th; they sent me one to admit two, so perhaps my letter beat yours by a short head. £2 per month is all right by me for the car. Not having any ideas on the subject myself, I said I would be willing to pay whatever you thought. I should want a comprehensive insurance. You don't say whether £7 covers a year under that heading. I imagine it would, though. If it is not possible to get a 3 or 6 month policy, I would suggest getting one for a year, and then William could pay me the requisite proportion of a third party plus fire & theft Policy when he takes the car over. Then if he has a smash and is in the wrong, he'll be in luck – for a few months anyway. Don't forget to let me know when and from whom I must take out the Policy.

I have been thinking of you with envy this weekend. But it is as well I didn't arrange to go, as I have been absolutely snowed under with things that had to be done. Did you enjoy 'The Riders of the Sea', and did you have a good time with Toty? Unfortunately I shall miss him when he is in town tomorrow, as I won't have time to meet him. I have not even been able to go and see Ann [who was in a nursing home] this weekend; I rang up the Home today and heard that her tummy has not been very grand the last few days.

Our friend Mrs Vickers came to tea, at my invitation, the other day. We talked hard for over an hour, but I don't think I made the slightest impression on her – at least, I fear not. When I pointed out that these prohibitions might result in Burnell feeling he wasn't wanted, and that this was the sort of thing that he wasn't likely to tell her – in spite of the fact that she thinks he would, she merely said that that was a risk she had to take. It does not seem to occur to her that to do this without saying anything about it to Burnell is in the least reprehensible; though she fully realizes that if he did hear about it the fur would fly. When she said that of course he could not be expected to understand, I replied that I didn't think I would under the circumstances. It is a pity you were not at home this weekend; I should very much like to know what she would say if Joy delivered an ultimatum: either Burnell should be told that his Mother did not want him to visit Aldbourne (unless she was there to hold his hand), or else you would go on asking him. I pointed out that you did not feel the position was a fair one to Burnell, but she appeared to be unable to see that. In spite of all this we parted perfectly amicably. I know that the woman is trying to do the best for the boy, but, good God, isn't she a fool?

No more for now. Let me know when you are coming up to town. I am out on Thursday night, and rehearsing with the Grillers on Friday afternoon. Blessings on you both, H.

Aldbourne, Wilts.; 1 March

Dearest Fergie,

I'll turn up in time for 7.30 supper on Friday evening. If you don't want to sup at home let me know and we'll meet in town. My trains (from Newbury) arrive at either 5.50 or 6.50. 'The Riders of the Sea' was a distinct disappointment and fell comparatively flat.[8] I can't quite make up my mind whether it was due to the work itself – in that it raises some difficult problems and doesn't seem to succeed in solving them – or whether it was due to a thoroughly amateurish performance. The Weber, which was piffle, had an adequate performance and at least kept one interested, and the Mozart, which had a first-rate performance, kept one sparkling the whole time. It was really delightful. So, as one enjoyed the works according to the standard of performance, I shall hope to hear the V.W. well done, and be able to revise my feeling that it's a dud – or a relative failure.

Toty was in a depressed state, and I don't think we were able to do much to get him out of it. I don't know whether it was due to Ann or to the fact that he's not able to work at present. Miss Hoare we liked very much [Dorothy Hoare, whom Toty eventually married]. Ann has had a set-back and we weren't able to see her in London.

About insurance. A temporary insurance is so much more expensive that I think it would be best to take out an annual one; then after 3 or 6 months William can pay you back the proportion, as you suggest. Against that there will be the Licence, which works out at £1.10 or £1.15 a quarter. But I should not pay that now; William can deduct it when he's paying you back the Insurance. I think it would be best if you sent him a cheque, uncrossed, for £7.17.6, just for Insurance alone.

See you Friday night. Love, G.

Aldbourne, Wilts.; 28 June

Dearest Fergie,

Toty can't manage this weekend with Miss Hoare, and has put it off till the weekend after, so I'm afraid you'll miss her this time. Mama of course had the phone by her bedside and only let me get through to Toty because she

---

[8] Vaughan Williams' one-act opera had been performed by the Cambridge University Music Society.

thought I was a General Finzi! I'll try the peerage next time if there's any difficulty.

The Boulanger[9] has come. It looks quite terrific, but I must get you to play it and inscribe it. Many, many thanks for it. I expect we'll see you before next Tuesday, but if not I suppose it'll be all right if we turn up about 9.45 or 10.0?

I thought the Gurney 'Ludlow and Teme' a deplorable choice for the first broadcast concert and am glad I hadn't anything to do with it! Love, G.

There exists 'La vie et l'oeuvre de Lili Boulanger' by Camille Manclair, Revue Musicale, Aug. 1921.

Aldbourne, Wilts.; 3 August

Dearest Fergie,

If a Mrs Robinson (of 'American Harp' fame, though not at all as bad as the story makes her sound) writes to you, it's all my fault. Only she asked me to play the Bax fiddle Sonata with Mary Baker (whoever she may be) at one of these Newbury 'hours with contemporary composers'. I thought I had better not accept and gave Mrs Robinson your address in case you might be amused – for I don't think it would be much more than that! Anyway, you always have the excuse that no other composer in the district has – of engagements at the B.B.C.

I saw William Busch in London, and his Piano Concerto is now finished and properly copied out. He's thinking of hiring a room in Baker Street and playing it to a few friends on two pianos. Again, I gave him your address. I was rather candid about his playing of either part and rather hoped that you and Rann might do it! But, of course, as he says, it would be a lot of work and he declares that I only hear his piano playing at its worst. But I do wish you would play at least one of the parts, to give the work a chance. I'm still not absolutely certain about the last movement, but I find it as impressive as ever. I think Busch is going to write to you, and hope you won't curse me too much.

Joy and I went to the Hindemith ballet – 'Nobilissima Visione' – and found it very moving. I've liked nothing better on the ballet line since 'Job'. There are bad patches in it, and it's not such completely 'realized' music as 'Job'; but for once, Hindemith's music takes on an almost ritualistic feeling. It's a symphonic type of work (if Hindemith's music can ever be called that) rather than a set of short movements, and for once I think he has done a good thing. The choreography and decor were lovely, straight from the Italian Primitives, and now I know that the only sort of dancing that moves me is when something speaks through the dance, rather than when the dance speaks for itself, which is only another word for ritual, I suppose. Anyhow, 'Job', those Hindu dancers from Serakaila, this Hindemith ballet, a morris jig like 'I'll go and enlist for a sailor', or the dance of the Kings of the Isle of Man (as danced by Billy Cain) –

[9] Lili Boulanger (1893–1918), French composer. Sister of Nadia Boulanger (1887–1979). The work was a setting of Psalm 130, *De Profundis*.

anything of this sort makes the flimsy-flamsy-on-the-toes, pas-de-deux, corps-de-ballet stuff just too ridiculous for words. Do see 'Nobilissima Visione' if you have the chance.

Rubbra has been with us for a couple of nights. His 2nd Symphony is certainly very impressive, though I don't know if better than the 1st. Lucky chap, the Universal Edition entered into a contract to publish all his work after the Symphony, but he doesn't know if it still holds good after certain events [the prospect of war]. They'll be doing his Brahms-Handel Variations scoring, and he's letting it go to press before hearing it! Bold man, but then Toscanini looked through the score and found no fault with it. We've rather enjoyed his visit.

Your card has just come. The figure [a Riemenschneider carving] certainly looks marvellous, and I hope you bring some more cards home from Germany. Love from J & G.

Village news: The day after you left all the gooseberries were sneaked in the night. But that's nothing to the Boy Scout's [Cpt. Jobling] experience last year. He lost all his gooseberries and found them exhibited at the flower-show! But that's not a thing he could prove. Of course it's that lad Cooke.

If you're anywhere near Würtemberg, William Busch is there till the 20th: Hotel Sommerberg, Wildbad.

Aldbourne, Wilts.; 8 November

Dearest Fergie,

I was so glad you left when you did, for it all got more and more deplorable. The climax was when little pop-eyed Guy Graham made an eloquent speech about the grandeur of the Cornish coast and then played us a descriptive piece in 4/4-time, which lasted for about 15 minutes (14 of them repetitive), and was quite beyond description. I enjoyed 3, 4 & 5 of Robin's pieces [Robin Milford's '5 Diversions', 1st performance by H.F., Newbury 7.11.38], but 2 was hopeless and 1 not much good. Mary Baker played rather as I expected from your account: not quite up to it technically, and tone rather like Tony's description – gnat-piss – but with real understanding and I enjoyed it. The songs [G.F.'s] must have made you squirm almost as much as they made me! I've seldom heard anything quite like it, and can't feel amused at such affairs as you can. I wish to heaven all that set of songs could be recorded by you and Keith, and then I would get 20 sets of the records, which I would send round to any singer who thought of tackling them!

Could you send me a card saying whether the weekend of 19–21 would suit you for Mrs Behrend? [To see the Stanley Spencer chapel at Burghclere.] She may be writing to you, but if she doesn't, I may write to her. Speaking for myself and Joy, we'd rather go alone with you, than join a party, and I rather fancy that Sunday is her party-day. If you are agreeable, I'd ask her if we could come by ourselves on one of three dates.

Congratulations on the new house [106 Wildwood Road, N.W.11], and an end of all your unsettled-ness. I can't help giving a portion of condolence to ourselves at losing you from Ashmansworth.

Mrs Johnson seems wonderfully brave over her adopted-daughter's illness [a TB operation]. I do hope it goes off without a hitch. Our love, G.

We shall be up on Friday 11th for the Sibelius concert. Peter [Harland] in the morning, and could lunch at the M.M.[10] or nearby if you liked.

        62 St John's Wood Court, N.W.8 [Mrs Johnson's flat]; 9 November
Dearest Dave,

Yes, 'bloody' is the only word I can use for the mauling (I cannot say 'performance') your songs received on Monday (in Newbury). It was outrageous. Milford writes, 'Bennet is a nice sort of a cove; but, dear God Almighty, that such things should be, and should pass as a performance of music.' When Bennet announced that his wife had arisen from a bed of sickness, I heartily wished that she had stayed where she was, so that I could have taken her place.[11] 'Waiting Both' was quite unbelievable. Do you think she knew she was playing double time?

Gnat-piss is good for Mary Baker's tone; but at least she is an excellent musician and got the spirit of the thing.

The weekend of the 18th–21st should be all right for me. But please point out to Mrs B that my plans are rather uncertain at the moment, and that, if the date of the 2nd operation [on Primrose, Mrs Johnson's adopted daughter, who was suffering from TB] were changed, I might have to cancel our meeting. The 1st operation (the worst) went off very well yesterday.

Let's meet at the M.M. at 12.45 (or 12.30 if possible) on Friday. I have to be with Solde at Barnes by 2.30. Blessings, H.

P.S. Don't you hate *coy and arch* singers?

        Aldbourne, Wilts.; 24 November
Dearest Fergie,

I've heard that the B.B.C. Singers are doing all those Bridges part-songs (and the 3 short Elegies) Thursday 29 December 2.30–5.0 p.m. I'm rather glad, even though it is only part-songs. Do you think it would be a good idea to get two recordings – one by the Memphis people and the other by the M.M.S.[12] – as a test (for future occasions) as to which really are the better of the two? I think you always go to Memphis, but have you tried M.M.S.? In any case that would not be a fair test, as you would never have tried out the two on the same performance. What do you think, apart from the question of expense, which may put me completely off? (I suppose it will be about £2.10 for 25 minutes?).

[10] The Mainly Musicians Club, Oxford Circus.
[11] Local 'musicians'.
[12] Evidently a small recording company (see Letter 1 July 1937).

I've not got the M.M.S. address. Have you? Memphis, I know, is Wigmore Street. I don't have to get the B.B.C.'s permission, do I; and do I have to send copies of the part-songs? I'm particularly anxious not to have little things like that cut in half!

I do hope you are none the worse for my visit. Instead of clearing up I got much worse after leaving you, and have been in bed most of the time since! If my head clears up and these excruciating headaches (which are better now) clear up, Joy and I may go up to Ashmansworth and sleep there Saturday night. We can be off early if you are coming for the day on Sunday. Pu knows.

How is Primrose Johnson, and did you find things all right with Mrs Johnson when you got there? [H.F. was staying at Mrs J's flat while 106 Wildwood Rd was being prepared.]

How did the Mahler go off (B.B.C. 23.11.38). I could not face listening-in to anything last night. Love, G.

14 Deramore Park South, Belfast; 21 December

Dearest Dave,

Here is a cheque of £2 for William, closing the payments for hire of the car. Will you ask him to get it changed as soon as possible, and tell him how grateful I am to have been able to use it (the car, I mean).

Ceddy and Bruno were well and sent you both their love. It is as cold as possible (what Aldbourne must be like I shudder to think), and it looks like more snow here.

I shall not be sending Christmas-cards – the change-of-address ones were enough effort – so this must bring you both my love and every good wish for Christmas and the New Year in the new house, when you get there. With love from Howard.

Aldbourne, Wilts.; 7 December

Dearest Fergie,

Many thanks for William's cheque, which I have duly handed on with your remarks. I wonder if you've persuaded Ceddie to put up with his unhappy state in Glasgow? And did you listen-in to that B.B.C. concert? I thought the Britten Piano Concerto the most incredible piffle I had ever heard. The Howells Concerto had a charming Elgarian slow movement, but I forget the rest. The Rubbra Symphony impressed me more with each hearing, particularly the scherzo and slow movement; but I still feel that the 1st movement is unsatisfactory: that enormous opening tune which says precisely nothing, and the monotonous scoring, etc.[13]

Thank God Christmas will soon be over! Still, it was very lovely to have the

---

[13] Howells: Concerto for String Orchestra. Britten: Piano Concerto No.1. Rubbra: Symphony No.2.

traditional Christmas-card weather, even to the robins perched on a snowman! Aldbourne was snowed-up for a day or two, and Ashmansworth completely unapproachable for a week.

When you write or when I see you: the real gem is Galton's method of keeping one's clothes dry in the rain! I wish the book could be republished.

Do you know Dvorak's Quartets in D minor, Op.34 and E-flat major, Op.51? They are both very good works and the slow movement of the former absolutely wonderful. The later Quartet in G major, Op.106, I found rather dull. Love to you from us both, G.

Love to Rann. I'm finding the inkstand very useful. Not so Cecil Beaton's scrapbook!

                                    Aldbourne, Wilts. [; 30 December]
Dearest Fergie,

Here's 'Dies Natalis' [MS for the printer] as far as it goes. Could you let me have it back as soon as possible, if it doesn't interfere with anything you're doing. I want all your suggestions, markings, etc. as if it were going to press – in pencil.

William Busch's Piano Concerto (B.B.C. 6.1.39) sounded much better than I expected (the scoring, I mean) at the first rehearsal. He plays it as badly as ever! Naturally, seated at the piano he can't hear what's going on, so Rubbra and I are going to be his 'ears' at the next rehearsals and point out definite miscalculations and things that don't sound. But I think it should come off pretty well. The part-songs were rehearsed beautifully, but the performance (B.B.C. 29.12.39) wasn't quite so good, except in one or two of them. I've had records done by a firm called 'Billy (?Higgshed) – too good to be true – recommended by Trevor Harvey and they seem very good. Love, G.

[After Harold's death I no longer wished to live in Willoughby Road; but the difficulty was that house prices in London were higher than I could afford. I looked at a small studio-house in Glenilla Road, Hampstead, but the owner would not accept what I could pay for it.

Gerald and Joyce then came to the rescue by most generously offering me the use of the unoccupied gardener's cottage at Ashmansworth, high on the downs south of Newbury, where they were planning to build their home, Church Farm. We could stay there until I found somewhere more permanent, possibly building a small house for myself at Ashmansworth. As I then had no car, I could hire the ancient Austin 7 belonging to the Finzis' gardener, William. So it was in that that Pu, Betty and I drove to Ashmansworth on 1 April 1938.

Another problem was that I had promised to join a 2-car holiday at Oberammergau in Bavaria with Mrs Margaret Johnson (the wealthy former amateur pupil of Harold's), her adopted-daughter Primrose, and Randolph Hokanson, part of the Salzburg Festival being included. With the Nazis rampant in Germany, and Austria recently annexed by Hitler, it scarcely seemed the right moment to visit either country. But had I not gone, it would have disrupted the party, so I went. Curiously enough, my most exciting experience during the trip was not musical, but the chance it gave me to see some of the woodcarvings of the great Bavarian sculptor Tilman Riemenscheider. When I saw his altarpiece at Creglingen in Franken, I determined to come back one day (I did) to see as much of his work as possible.

I spite of alarums and excursions we got back to England unscathed. This was at the time of the Munich Crisis, whose one advantage (as far as I was concerned) was that it sent house prices in London plummeting. As a result, I was able to afford a delightful house-with-studio at 106 Wildwood Road, near the Hampstead Heath Extension; and there I lived happily for over 30 years.]

1939

14 Deramore Park South, Belfast; 4 January

Dearest Dave,

Here is 'Dies Natalis'. I have marked fairly fully Nos. 1, 2 & 5; but 4, the Arioso, defeats me utterly. I can feel a general emotional rise and fall in it, but I cannot for the life of me feel the harmonic 'breathing places' that condition phrasing: it just seems to move on and on without ever sitting down. If you had marked the phrasing I could have put in the dynamics; but as I do not seem to have the wit to disentangle the phrasing for myself, and as I cannot do the dynamics without it, I must leave both to you. The few points I have put in are things I feel definitely; but they are more or less shots in the dark, so don't go by them. I am so sorry to be obtuse about this. As you know, I have never liked the Arioso as much as the rest, and I think the reason must be that I have never been able to follow it clearly. I has seemed like a beautiful but somewhat inchoate piece of emotional illustration. Doubtless I am wrong about this; but that, for present purposes, is beside the point. And I still feel that it belongs to the period when you relied, as I see it, too much on emotional rise and fall as a means of giving shape to a work, and not enough on a synthesis between emotional rise and fall and purely musical shapes, such as you have now so successfully achieved. But though I feel this very strongly, I do not expect you to agree with me.

I enjoyed listening to the two sets of part-songs very much. They came through only moderately well as far as transmission was concerned. In some way they seemed to require more air and space than they got; for though they were not exactly hurried, yet they needed more spaciousness and loving-care of detail. I shall be very interested to hear the records and to know how they wear. Incidentally, I think the number of singers − eight − is typical of the B.B.C.'s genius for compromise. Songs in four parts would sound infinitely better sung by four people or by sixteen: eight is the worst choice possible, for you can always hear the two individual voices wobbling.

I shall be listening to William Busch's Concerto on Friday night, and hope all will go well. Hadn't we better subscribe to buy him a pair of waterproof pants?

The Christmas-card of the children was delightful. I hope they, and you both, are well and no longer snow-bound. Perhaps it's as well we weren't at Ashmansworth during the last few weeks.

I expect to get back to Wildwood Road on Saturday 14th, after which we shall no doubt meet. Blessings on you both, and a more peaceful New Year for all of us than the last. Ever, H.

106 Wildwood Road, N.W.11; 15 January

Dearest Dave,

How alarming about the MS. I am so glad it turned up in the end, and trust you are not thinking dreadful things about my supposed dilatoriness.

Are you coming up for the R.V.W. Sextet[1] at Wigmore Hall on Saturday afternoon? And would you care to stay here? If so, please let me know as soon as you can; also what night to expect you. A postcard will do, as I won't be in tomorrow (Monday) evening to answer a phone call.

I enclose the promised missing bits from 'The Seven Pillars' [copied from Warwick James's copy of the original limited edition]. Love to you both, H.

Aldbourne, Wilts.; 16 January

Dearest Fergie,

Welcome home, and good luck to the new house. We are starting our packing up here in earnest, so everything is really rather pandemoniacal. We expect to start the removal [to Church Farm, Ashmansworth] on 19 February, when Mags comes down with her horse-box. I don't expect we'll be up in town much before March or April, though when I've done that little movement for 'Dies Natalis' I should like to go through it with you. But as far as worrying you about points of scoring, etc., I don't think there's any hurry at all, so you needn't fear a visitation yet awhile!

Now about your markings. These were a great help and most of them I've kept. I quite agree with all you say about No.4, except that I like it, – though I see its weaknesses through your spectacles even more since trying to do the phrasing myself! John was over here and had a few suggestions about it, though I was often stumped by the question 'do you mean this or that?', which means that my musical digestion was not up to the food in the days when I wrote it,

---

[1] Actual title: *Double Trio* (for string sextet). First performed at the Wigmore Hall, 21 January 1939. Revised in 1942 for a National Gallery concert, and then rewritten (1946–1948) as the *Partita for Double String Orchestra* and first performed at the 1948 Promenade Concerts on 29 July.

even though it has been partially re-written. I wouldn't write it now, yet still I like it.

Later, 17th. Your letter just to hand. Alas, there's no hope for the R.V.W. Sextet at Wigmore. It's a great disappointment, as I was very anxious to hear it. Until the removal is over I simply can't go anywhere. Would you be angelic and tell me something about it, and if you think it's a good work. I'm sure to hear it sooner or later. Dear old V.W. He heard Steuart Wilson sing 'The Sigh' and 'A Ditty' over the wireless, and sent me pages about it!

What is the best thing to do about our change-of address cards: Mr & Mrs Gerald Finzi; Joyce and Gerald Finzi, or what? I rather feel that Gerald Finzi would be enough, and then she could be 'Joyce' or 'Mrs' as the case required. But doesn't this seem rather presumptuous for the husband to take it all upon himself? By the way, I'd like your little printer's address.

I bought some second-hand music in Oxford the other day, amongst which was 'Four Aquarellen' by Tor Aulin,[2] Stockholm, Lundquists Kongl. Hof-musikhandl. Quite attractive short pieces for violin and piano, for anyone wanting something like the Dvorak 'Four Romantic Pieces'. A little tamer than those, and more Schumannesque, but I thought they might interest you and Solde, as I know short violin pieces are hard to come by.

We often wonder about Mrs Johnson and how you find her. Our love, G.

I can't fill in the void form for rates of cottage until I know when William is going in, but there'll be something coming back to you.

106 Wildwood Road, N.W.11; 22 January

Dearest Joy and Dave,

Many thanks for your letters of well-wishing for the new house. I'm longing for you to see it, now that it is properly finished, for really it is most attractive in every way. Indeed, I am so happy about it that I can hardly believe it will last. Would that your moving was also safely over, and all of you comfortably settled at Ashmansworth – even if it was snowed-up for a week! Once you have that off your minds you will both be able to get on with your work, which must be quite impossible at the moment.

It was a pity Dave was not able to come up for the R.V.W. Sextet. I was at a two-hour rehearsal of it on Wednesday, and so was able to get into it fairly thoroughly. I like it very much indeed. R.O., who was sitting just in front of me at the concert, said that he didn't get much out of it; but I'm inclined to think that may have lain more with him than with any lack in the work itself. The style of the work is a curious fusion between the F minor Symphony and the early String Quintet. This may sound rather odd; but perhaps what is odder still is that it is a real fusion and not just a mix-up. There are four movements; the first three of which, a Fantasy, Scherzo and Intermezzo, are somewhat grey

---

[2] Tor Aulin (1866–1914), Swedish composer and violinist, directed the Aulin Quartet (1887–1912).

in colour, while the last (a Rondino) is rough and merry – though it too ends quietly with a reference to the opening movement. The work is much more human than the Symphony and much less harsh; but it shows the same preoccupation with subtle across-the-bar rhythms: in fact one feels in the Fantasy and Intermezzo that the bars are used more as a guide to the eye of the player than for any accentual purpose. In the Intermezzo the 2nd violin, viola and cello play pizzicato throughout, while the 1st weaves uneven rhythmed melodies above them. It's a beautiful effect. In the middle of the Scherzo the texture, I think, becomes almost too orchestral; for the rhythmic complications seem to ask for the clear definition which orchestral strings can give but solo strings cannot. Perhaps when the players know the work better, this lack of rhythmic definition might disappear. On the whole, the first three movements seem to me to be on one level of excellence; the fourth stands a little more like 'made' music, though it is thoroughly successful in its place and as a rounding-off of the work. The whole thing last about twenty minutes.

About your change-of-address cards. The printer who did mine was A.H. Hartshorn & Co. Ltd., 313 Euston Road, N.W.1. They charged 11/6 for a hundred; but if you were ordering more than that, the price would be correspondingly cheaper. Personally, I would love both names put on: i.e. Gerald & Joyce Finzi, rather than Mr & Mrs Gerald Finzi. I think it would be dreadful to have Gerald Finzi alone, for then one might expect to receive a second card the week after, giving the new address of Joyce (late) Finzi; the implication being that you no longer lived together!

I am enclosing the charming cutting you sent me from The Listener, as I cannot remember whether you wanted it back or not. It gave us great pleasure in Ireland.

I don't believe I ever thanked you two properly for my eight months at the cottage at Ashmansworth. In spite of this, you will know that it was not from lack of appreciation. I don't think it would have been possible for anyone to give me a more helpful present at that particular moment. It gave me a break from London, which I badly needed, and gave me the chance of seeing whether the country would be workable from my point of view. Even though, in the end, it turned out not to be, I had one of the most delightful summers imaginable, and got thoroughly set up bodily and (I hope) mentally after the difficulties and uncertainties of the last two years. To have done all this for somebody was no small service, and I feel more grateful to you both than I can well say.

Blessings on you both. I won't say I wish I could do your moving for you, for that isn't true. But I do hope that it all goes off easily and with as few hitches as possible, and that you'll be comfortably settled in the new house before you know where you are. Love, Howard.

P.S. My new chariot [a Morris 1,000, a present from two kind aunts in Belfast] has arrived. It is one of the new 1939 Morris Eights, and seems to go very well.

Today we move to Ashmansworth; March 1939

Dearest Fergie,

Many thanks for returning Hansen's [piano dealer] letter. It occurs to me that it might be a good idea to have any piano(s) we decide upon down on a week's trial – I don't imagine that Hansen would object if I paid cartage, and I should certainly be kinder than Elstree [film studios], etc. It would help to decide between say, the Feuerbach and the Broadwood.

Bob de Ropp[3] has got married, Aunt Ad has just written. She is quite sure that domesticity is going to be the right thing for him!

Can you tell me if you had any undue interference with your wireless at Ashmansworth? Alexander has been carrying out tests with mine and thinks the trouble may be due to the power-cables and transfer near us. What, by the way, was the name of your wireless?

Love, G.

Ashmansworth; before 23 March

Dearest Fergie, Pu & Betty,

It was a pleasant surprise to be handed your telegram by William as we entered in state. We're wonderfully glad to be in, though you've no conception of the muddle, because the painter and carpenter are still holding the fort. However, we shall drive them out within the next week, I hope. It's going to be wonderful here, and although the house will have its usual measure of death, burglaries, frozen pipes and broken windows, it's got a very happy feeling about it and I think we'll get lots of work done. We shall see you soon here; the spare room is the best of the lot.

I'd have answered your telegram before, but oh, the pandemonium!

Love, G.

P.S. Fergie, I listened-in to the Bloch Violin Concerto and liked it very much. It's easy to imagine posterity finding a style-of-the-age and giving V.W. and Bloch as examples, whereas you could never find it, say, between Bax and V.W. Bloch's music always (no, not always) strikes me as being extraordinarily English! The slow movement of the Concerto Grosso, the Quartet, the Sacred Service, this work, might almost be written by V.W.'s brother. (Musical brother, not blood!) And if one finds, probably by suggestion, slight oriental turns, what could be more oriental than 'Flos Campi'? Of course biblical is the word, not oriental, but you'll know what I mean.

Hansen hopes to write you in a day or two about the Broadwood. If you think it's worth it, I'll come up to London. Honest man, Hansen. He's sent me the cheque without even seeing the pianos. Love, G.

---

[3] The slightly eccentric relative of Adeline (Aunt Ad), the first Mrs Vaughan Williams.

Ashmansworth; 23 March

Dearest Fergie,

Joy and I talked over the piano question when I got home, and she thought it might be worth while considering those Steinways we saw at Hansens. It would mean that I should not be able to think of a 2nd, smaller piano for a long while; but, as you say, we should have at least one good one to go on with. So I wrote to Hansen and asked him the lowest price he would take for either of them, bearing in mind that the question of case-work didn't worry me much. He phoned up this morning and said the black Steinway (5ft 6″) could not be less than £110. The mahogany one (after it had been finally adjusted – and I'm very anxious for you to give it a try under better conditions) £105. This is also a 5ft 6″ instrument. He also said that another one had just come in, a 5ft 10″, which he could let me have for £100.

Now every £5 does mean something to us at the moment, and if you thought the £100 was as good as the others it might be worth while considering. On the other hand, I don't want to drop a pearl for the want of a penny. As it is, Hansen seems quite agreeable to let me pay partly in instalments. As regards size, we could manage a 5ft 10″. Naturally the smaller the better, in view of the eventual 2nd smaller piano; but my experience of 5ft instruments last Monday has put me off considering them. Incidentally, Hansen says that he has got a 5ft Fahr Zeitz piano, which is considerably better than either a Broadwood or a Rogers, and that's the sort of thing that might do for a 2nd piano later on. I'd like you to try it, if you're in that direction. Dearest Fergie, I hope no more visits to Hansen (until the question of a 2nd piano turns up) and with your approval I'll decide on one of the Steinways; which one ought to be left to your judgement.

A letter from Ceddie. He suggests a visit here around 15–23 June, and hopes you could come too. That would be grand. You would have to sleep in my 'dressing-room', but you would not mind that. Love from us both, G.

106 Wildwood Road, N.W.11; 12 April

Dearest Dave,

So glad you smoked the cigars: they were certainly not worth posting on, and I was just about to write and tell you to use them yourself when your card appeared. I trust you enjoyed them.

I am so glad to hear that the piano has arrived safely and that you and Joy approve. I shall be most interested to hear it and play on it 'in Situ'.

The enclosed cheque for £5 is for the long-promised scale-buoys [water-softeners for the cistern]; or, if that should be too unromantic, it can be put towards any other use in the new house. I only wish it were twenty times as much. But though the spirit is willing, the Bank Account is distinctly weak.

You remember my setting of 'The Flower of Magherally' [No.3 of H.F.'s 'Four Diversions', Op.7], which neither you nor I thought as good as 'The King of Spain's Daughter'? Well, it has produced the following from Norman Hay,

188

the man who deals with the things over there: 'Will you accept my congratulations and very sincere thanks for your beautiful arrangement of 'The Flower of Magherally'? This impresses me very much as a work at once a strikingly apt treatment of the air and an intimate, speaking transmission of *yourself*. In other words, it is an excellent arrangement, and a real individual creation.' He goes on to say that though he likes 'The King of Spain's Daughter', he likes this very much better. What I say is, there ain't no accounting, likewise praises be for different tastes.

Under separate cover I am returning the Dover Wilson 'Hamlet', which I found most interesting. Many thanks for the loan. I hope the holiday is, or has been, a success. The international situation is hardly a help, and I cannot expect you to be able to adopt the blinker-attitude with which I am preserving my equanimity at the moment. I want to get on with my writing, and cannot do so otherwise. For the moment I have left the middle movement of the Sonata [Piano, Sonata, Op.8], and have started on the last, about which I feel more certain.

I am very keen for you and Joy to see some of Nigel's[4] recent paintings. They seem to be quite remarkable. Any chance of your returning by way of London? Love to you both, Howard.

Ashmansworth; 17 April

Dearest Fergie,

We got back on Saturday night after a good few days rest, and although most of the time was spent at Hundon [his Mother's house in Suffolk], it was not so bad as it sounds, for the weather was heavenly and we spent most of the time just lying in the fields, reading and chewing grass. We only had four clear days, but welcome, none the less.

I did smoke one of your cigars but felt so sick after it that I'm keeping the other till you come down! Either I haven't your masculine stomach or the Lord means me to stick to my pipe.

It was extraordinarily good of you to send that £5. We feel a little uncomfortable about accepting it just at the moment, knowing that you are none too well off. The scale-buoys being paid for (and they'd come too expensive for the house, so we're not having them here till more really necessary things are settled), we'll put it towards these devastating furnishing expenses. Probably a rug for the sitting-room or bookroom.

I'm glad Norman Hay liked 'The Flower of Magherally'. I don't dislike the setting, but thought it just anybody's. It's probably most effective, but there's not much of Fergie about it and probably the learned doctor doesn't know what is you and what isn't — at least, not so well as I do.

We've thought a lot about you during these last few really bloody days and

[4] Nigel Barnicot, biologist, physiologist, London University. An exceptional amateur painter.

189

hoped you would be able to keep your detachment – at least, until something really happens – and get on with the Piano Sonata.

I only managed to hear the last movement and half of the middle movement of the Elgar Violin Sonata (Isolde Menges & H.F., B.B.C. 16 April 1939). It sounded a good performance. I've grown to love the work a great deal.

Did you listen-in to Tutenkamen's trumpets? One always imagined Egyptian music to be of the wiggly snake-charming sort, as one hears in Egypt today; but the trumpets made me wonder whether it was of the tonic-dominant variety, major and minor scales.

When you finally settle dates with Ceddie and Bruno do you think a day or two later than the 15th at Ashmansworth could be managed? We may be going to Norfolk from June 1–15, and Joy thinks we ought to have a couple of days or so, to air the beds and get things straight. I suppose it would mean an extra day or so in London for Ceddie, unless he could come to you a couple of days later than originally planned and then all come down to us on the 18th or 19th or thereabouts. I'm not saying anything to Ceddie as I think he might get it into his head that he was being a bother, which is far from the truth. It's going to be great fun, and I only wish we had two pianos. Still there'll be plenty of duets. Have you found out where the glass inkstand came from? Have you discovered any decanters yet, and if so, are they, or is it, plain?

As you're interested in Rounds, you might be interested in Warlock's edition of Ravencroft's 'Pammelia', O.U.P. 'Hamlet' hasn't turned up yet, but I'm in no hurry. I only mention it because you say you're returning it. Our love, G.

Ashmansworth; 12 May

Dearest Fergic,

Would it be all right for you if I came and stayed the night either on the 22nd or 23rd? I'd rather like to hear Graham Carrit's lecture-recital on the 23rd – it must be an intriguing experience to hear oneself talked about! – but much more important is shopping etc., and I want to bring up that 'History of the World' for your bookbinder friend to tackle.

Also, could you let me know the position as regards those two Violin pieces of Gurney's.[5] The V.W.s were here the other day, and he's going to have a talk with The Maid very soon, but wants a few facts to go on. How long have they been 'going to be published', etc. Love, G.

Ann's coming next weekend. The Husseys tell me that Graham Carrit is rather a bore.[6] Now, coming from the Husseys, what do you think of that?

[5] 'The Apple Orchard' and 'Scherzo'.
[6] Dyneley Hussey (1893–1972), a *Times* music critic. Carrit was a contemporary of H.F. at the Royal College and also a music critic.

106 Wildwood Road, N.W.11; 28 May

Dearest Dave,

Of all the blasted nuisances, Solde has asked me whether I can possibly play for her at Rugby on Sunday 18 June. If it were myself I would refuse, but I cannot very well let her down. I think the best thing will be for me to drive over there from Ashmansworth (the concert is a five o'clock one, I think), and return the same evening; it is almost 200 miles there and back, but there seem to be no cross-country train connections.

Did you listen to the Mass [Beethoven, conducted by Toscanini] on Friday evening? I though it was a staggering performance, although occasional tempi seemed quite beyond the bounds of possibility. The chorus and soloists all deserved medals. Ann and I were completely bowled over.

I hope your 'holiday' goes off well, and that it does not prove too exhausting for all the parents! Love, Howard.

Let me know the address of your windmill [where they stayed] on a postcard.

Ashmansworth; 29 May

Dearest Fergie,

Our address from 2nd will be: The Windmill, Over Staithe, near Burnham Market, Norfolk.

Wouldn't it be simpler for you if you all came down here Sunday, you from Rugby after the concert. It seems rather hard and unnecessary for you to travel London to Ashmansworth on the Saturday, and Rugby and back on the Sunday. The whole of the following week is free for us, till 23rd or 24th, when Peter and Lisa may be coming to see the house.[7] Probably the 24th.

I didn't listen to the Mass. With this wretched move on hand I didn't feel able to listen to music; but it's just about finished now.

Thanks for putting up with me last week. I do so look forward to a few quiet days with you in London, perhaps with Joy and a few theatres etc., all done in 'easy time'.

Hope the Sonata is budding somewhere. Love to you, G.

Till 14th: The Old Windmill, Overy Staithe; 10 June

Dearest Fergie,

What am I to do about this [Dies Natalis]? As you know, the whole thing went to Leslie Boosey (I sent it to Chapman, but I suppose on the strength of a vocal line, and the previous songs, he thought it had better go to Boosey) and Boosey obviously approaches it from the Boosey-Ballad standpoint; whereas other members of the firm might have been quite glad to have a Festival work, particularly with a useful small string Intrada. He leaves the gate open, but in a way that most certainly doesn't invite one to enter! Do for Heaven's sake advise,

---

[7] The architect Peter Harland and his wife.

as the matter is rather urgent. I've not tried the O.U.P. yet, and don't want to; and even if I do, I think one knows the result beforehand! Love, G.

I hope Ceddie has brought his kilt!

P.S. I suppose we couldn't expect Elsie Suddaby[8] [who was to sing 'Dies'], if she liked the work, to write a stinker to Boosey? After all, a Suddaby (or a Dame Clara)[9] impresses Boosey far more than a mere composer. I can't believe that 'Dies Natalis' has less possibilities of performance and sale than 'Our Hunting Fathers'.[10] If you thought I ought to see Elsie Suddaby at once, and you could make an appointment with her for me (and you, if you had time), I could come up to London any day at a few hours notice. I have a copy of the work with me. Love, G.

106 Wildwood Road, N.W.11; 12 June

Dearest Dave,

It is really maddening about Boosey and 'Dies Natalis'. You know that I myself thought in the first place that it might be difficult to get the work published; but Boosey's first reactions seemed to suggest that my fears were misplaced. Now it appears they were not . . . though that's no help. Perhaps it would be best for you to come up and see Elsie Suddaby and go through the work with her; then, if she likes it (as I think she will) you can arrange between you what would be the best mode of procedure. I have rung her up and find that she is free on Friday, so will you write her direct and say what time you will be along. Her address is 24 Holly Hill, Hampstead, N.W.3. I will try and come along too, so let me know what time you fix up. Her house is just near Hampstead tube station.

I think if you press the matter Boosey will publish the work, from what he says in his letter, as he obviously feels uncomfortable about turning it down at this stage of the proceedings; and it is always possible that a letter from Elsie Suddaby might help, though she would be better able to say about that than I am, as I don't know how much weight she carries with B&H. As to 'Our Hunting Fathers': I think that is an uncommercial proposition of the most flagrant kind, so for heaven's sake don't compare 'Dies' to it. 'Dies' is at least attractive music, written for string orchestra, whereas the other work is most unattractive and requires xylophones, bedpans and the Lord knows what. I should be inclined to accept the fact that the work *as a whole* is not commercially particularly tempting, but stress the fact that the Intrada (which ought to be published separately) is a commercial proposition; they are always clamouring for fairly straightforward string music, and when they win on the roundabouts they must be prepared to lose a little on the swings.

---

[8] Elsie Suddaby (1898–1980), English soprano. One of the sixteen singers for whom Vaughan Williams wrote his *Serenade to Music* in 1938.

[9] Dame Clara Butt (1872–1936), formidable English contralto. Elgar's *Sea Pictures* were written for her (1899), but her singing tastes also embraced sentimental Ballads.

[10] Benjamin Britten. Orchestral Song Cycle to words by W.H. Auden, first performed at the Norfolk and Norwich Triennial Music Festival, 25 September 1936.

So very sorry that this has happened. Let me know what you fix up, and I'll come to Elsie Suddaby's if I possibly can. Love to you both, Howard.

P.S. Got a wire this morning from Ceddy saying: 'Expect us anytime, car trouble', sent off from Whorlton (wherever that may be) at 9.44; so goodness knows when they'll turn up.

As from Ashmansworth; 13 June

Dearest Fergie,

I'll come up on Friday by the 9.50-something from Newbury, which gets in at Paddington round about 11.0 (being still at The Windmill we have no A.B.C. but we think that's right), and I've told Elsie Suddaby that I'll turn up at 11.30. I do hope you can manage it. It shouldn't take me more than $\frac{1}{2}$ an hour to get to Hampstead tube station.

Yes, I think with pressing Boosey will take it (a humiliating business in itself), but what devastating terms is the pressing likely to enable him to impose? Anyway, we'll see what E.S. has to say. If only she could play the virago to Boosey! Thanks awfully for making the appointment. Love, G

Home on Thursday. Joy has done some painting.

Ashmansworth; 23 June

Dearest Fergie,

As we expected, the O.U.P. have turned it down, so I've written off to Boosey. Thanks so much for all your help when you were here. I'm afraid it wasn't much of a holiday for you, though Ceddie, Bruno and Toty lightened it up a bit.

Ann has sent some lovely poems – particularly the one beginning:

I would build my nest on a high branch . . .

I'm glad I went to the funeral [Aunt Lily's]. Somehow or other it was easier after having seen her. Although I don't know anything about the future and have pretty few hopes, it *was* something of a comfort to know what an empty shell was being buried, though she looked terrific. Joy drew her. Love to you, G.

Ashmansworth; 4 July

Dearest Fergie,

I thought I'd let you see this from Boosey. It's quite damnable, isn't it, having to let such an opportunity go by. I've sent it off to Novello as a last hope, though I'd be very surprised (and possibly disappointed!) if they took it. After that I don't think there's anything to be done, apart from offering to do it myself with Boosey, which I don't feel inclined to do. It would mean he would always expect it. Boosey, by the way, never answered my question about his volte-face, after his original opinion.

One other thing. You remember that letter we got off to Dobell[11] about permission to use the Traherne words in the programme? It was returned. So I looked up their address in the telephone-book and found they had moved to Charing Cross Road. I wrote there at once – about 10 days ago – but have had no reply. Would it be possible to phone them up, speaking as me, as I can't hold up the Three Choirs programme much longer, and if one writes and gets no answer, what can one do? Blessings. Love, G.

106 Wildwood Road, N.W.11; 5 July

Dearest Dave,

It really is too bad about Boosey. I must say he has treated you very badly; for I thought, after what he said in the first place, that with the help of a little firmness he would publish in the end. I feel you are quite right not to share the cost with him; but if Novello were to make the same suggestion, it might be worth considering. Have phoned Dobell, who say O.K. to printing poems in programme: I asked them to confirm by letter direct to you. Love to you both, H.

14 Deramore Park South, Belfast, 2 August

Dearest Dave,

Certainly they were quick over the engraving [Boosey & Hawkes changed their mind about 'Dies Natalis']. I hope you don't mind my having marked all suggestions on the proofs: it is so much easier than writing on a separate sheet. I think the dynamics of the Intrada are O.K. as far as the piano arrangement is concerned. If they require to be different in the score, I don't see why they should not be; that is so often necessary. At the end of the Intrada I believe you want something like SEGUE No.2, as the little note does not explain the situation sufficiently quickly to the eye. Also, the note should be shifted along to the right. Blessings on you, from H.

14 Deramore Park, Belfast; 2 September

Dearest Dave,

Isn't this just bloody? It is too disappointing that 'Dies' should be put off, after all the work and trouble you have had getting it ready for Hereford. And the reason [the war] for it all is just past words – but we need not go into that just at the moment.

About plans: I hope that you, with your slightly blotted health record of former years, may be spared the more violent and dangerous forms of work, and that you will be able to remain at Ashmansworth or somewhere near, and

[11] Bertram Dobell, book publisher, 77 Charing Cross Road. Edited and published *The Poetical Works of Thomas Traherne* (1906).

so have a reasonable chance of surviving intact. I am in a different position, being tiresomely hale and hearty. I therefore propose to remain here in Belfast for three months, during which time I shall try to finish off the loose ends of my work, if that is at all possible; and then I imagine I shall have to go off and do something deemed more generally useful – whatever that may be. So Wildwood Road remains closed for the present (unless prematurely opened by a bomb), and Pu remains somewhere in Ireland, though exactly where I cannot at the moment say; nor do I know where Betty's nursing activities may lead her.

I'll write later on if anything different should happen. In the meantime all my love to you both, and God help us all. Ever, Howard.

14 Deramore Park South, Belfast; 6 October

[Dearest Dave]

Very many thanks for letter with complete set of Bridges part-songs: they look so nice like that.

This morning I finished the slow movement of the Sonata [Piano Sonata]. I *may* be coming to London next week to help Myra Hess with her daily National Gallery Concerts, but I'll let you know definitely later. Ever, H.

62 St John's Wood Court, N.W.8 [Mrs Johnson's flat]; 15 October

[Dearest Dave]

Just to let you know that I've come over, and am staying here for the moment. I hope to open Wildwood Road at the beginning of November – unless it gets blown up in the meantime! Pu is champing to be back.

The National Gallery Concerts are wonderful [they started on 10 Oct. 1939; I arrived in London on 11 Oct. 1939]: it is a joy to be having a hand in them. Love to you both, H.

As from 106 Wildwood Road, N.W.11; 25 October

Dearest Dave,

The cheese dish is a delightful companion. Very many thanks to you and Joy for it. Pu also will be very glad to have it, when she returns at (I think) the end of next week. It was lovely seeing Joy again last week and I only wished you had been there too. Do come up here sometime after we have opened the house. After 6 November, if possible, as I have to traipse all the way to Bristol [for B.B.C. broadcast] that Sunday. Have you ever heard of anything so ridiculous? Remember to write to William Busch and get the key of his house, so that you can go over there and work away as much as you like. I am apt to be away from here at all sorts of odd hours with these National Gallery Concerts, but it is never safe to rely on that. The Sonata continues to progress slowly. I am longing to play you the slow movement. Myra seems quite besotted about it.

It would be an excellent plan to start scoring 'The Fall of the Leaf' [by G.F.]. Why don't you bring it up with you? Then, if you want, we could talk about it. Blessings, in haste, from H.

106 Wildwood Road, N.W.11; 7 November

[Dearest Dave]

Hurrah! Do come on the 13th and stay until the 18th — longer if you like. Lovely to see Joy at the N.G. this midday. Peter Harland stepped into my carriage on the way back from Bristol yesterday. Ever, H.

Ashmansworth; 11 December

Dearest Fergie,

I hear from Ernest Chapman that one Maurice Miles[12] (who used to run the Bath Pump-Room orchestra) is starting one of the innumerable string orchestras and wants to give the first performance of 'Dies Natalis' at the end of January, Wigmore Hall. Chapman says that there is no doubt that he will have a first-class orchestra, but I am rather worried (and so is Chapman) by the size of it, 2, 1, 1, 1. Anyhow, what I have arranged is this, to come up next Thursday for a run-through of his first rehearsal at Boosey & Hawkes studio, 1.30. Probably you are engaged, but if you can possibly manage to turn up, it would be a great help.

I hope the 20th is all clear, and that we shall see the three of you. We can't get an omelette-pan here. I suppose you couldn't phone up Staines [hardware-shop in Soho] and order the same as yours? I am presuming yours has a ground bottom suitable for an Esse stove. We might even let you display your talents whilst you are here!

Also, if you are getting a Wallace tooth brush,[13] don't forget one for me; and Toty's poems when you come. Love and Joy's love.

He [Miles] intended to have John Fullard as soloist, but I'm pressing for Elsie Suddaby — should probably like to stay the night, but can it be left open, even if you can have me?

Ashmansworth; 16 December

Dearest Fergie,

About next Thursday 21st. Could you take the train which arrives at Newbury 1.06? I don't know what time it leaves Paddington. We'll meet you — no, only one of us, on account of car-space — and then decide how many of us

---

[12] Maurice Miles later became conductor of the Belfast Symphony Orchestra (1955–1966) and taught conducting at the Royal Academy of Music.

[13] The 'Wallace' tooth brush had short, black bristles and was recommended by their dentist Warwick James.

can get home by car. I think one of us, Pu, the luggage and children (plus two other children who have to be dropped on the way). The rest can lunch in Newbury and take either the 2.30 bus or the 3.30. The former goes as far as the Three Legged Cross, and I don't know whether Betty would feel like the walk. The latter goes past Doily Bottom. Of course if it's raining we can meet the bus.

Another thing: the black slug [an unsatisfactory cook] had the chance of another job, so we packed her off gratefully. It'll be much happier for all of us at Christmas.

Yet another thing. The artillery won't be coming until January now, so there's no need to fix on the 27th for a return. Just leave it open if you can. Love, G.

106 Wildwood Road, N.W.11; 19 December

[Dearest Dave]

Yes, we'll arrive Newbury 1.06 on Thursday. Betty and I could easily bus and walk, but Pu couldn't as her knee has chosen this minute to play her false. Sorry I was so blear-eyed the other day: I felt done. Our omelette pan hasn't got a ground bottom, so it wouldn't do for you. H.

1940

106 Wildwood Road, N.W.11; 16 January

[Dearest Dave]

The 'Interlude' [G.F.'s for oboe & string quartet] is fixed for Monday next, the 22nd, at the Gallery; sandwiched between Haydn (I think) and Dohnanyi Quartets. The players are Edward Selwyn and the Strattons.

No letter yet from David Martin. I envy you your skating! H.

106 Wildwood Road, N.W.11; 4 February

Dearest Dave,

I had a horrid feeling at the time that Bradford would prove to be the last straw. It did; and the camel is now writing you from his bed, having had to cancel Manchester, Belfast and the two Dublin concerts. However, as Myra says, there is nothing so pleasant as having some nice engagements to look forward to, and then being able to put them off! The doctor is allowing me up tomorrow; in the meantime I'm rather enjoying the first idleness I have experienced for weeks.

There did not seem to be time the other week to tell you how much I enjoyed 'Dies'. It is a most lovely work. The performance, too, seemed fairly adequate; but I can imagine that a greater sense of forward-movement and line would be an improvement. Just occasionally both Suddaby and Miles allowed things to sag, which is fatal where such a subtle line is concerned. It is the greatest pity in the world that the performance was not in Hereford: that, or some such place, would provide the perfect atmosphere, which is painfully lacking in Wigmore Hall.

I still feel 'The Fall of the Leaf' shows signs of its chequered genesis. Nor can I convince myself that this is altogether because I happen to have inside information on the subject. However much one may know of the difficulties that a work has gone through, if that work finally reaches an inevitable shape one immediately and automatically forgets all the tentative steps that have led up to it. This I cannot do with 'The Fall'. Though I feel that so much of the material of it is fine, I cannot feel that the whole of it is either final or inevitable. It is not that this or that point sticks out as being unsatisfactory, but that the thing as a whole lacks the quality, which every complete work of art must have, of *seeming* to be the result of a 'single pouring out of molten metal'. Too often in 'The Fall' I feel that this little bit has had to be screwed on afterwards, or the position of that little bit slightly altered for some reason or other: so that, like Mr Dolmetsch's famous harpsichord, it buckles in the middle when you play on it, instead of staying put like the genuine, cast-frame article. And, in spite of what I say about 'this little bit and that little bit', I do not think that tinkering about with details is going to put the matter right. More than likely I am wrong about this; but I feel at present that what the work needs is re-living and re-thinking from beginning to end. Forgive me if this is a somewhat devastating suggestion. I would not make it if I did not think it might be worth considering. Blessings on you both, with love from Howard.

P.S. Nice notice of 'Dies' in The Times, but I couldn't find anything in The Telegraph.

Ashmansworth; 5 February

Dearest Fergie,

I quite thought that you were in the middle of your grand tour, giving first performances of the Sonata and recuperating in Ireland, and I was waiting for your return to thank you for having come to the rescue at B&H [playing the duet version of 'The Fall of the Leaf'] in spite of feeling rotten. To my surprise, Chapman and Stein were not so damping as I expected. Of course, they didn't say, 'Superb, we'll publish it tomorrow', but wanted me to score it and then come and play it again, when Hawkes gets back from America.

No, I don't think your feeling about 'The Fall' is due to a knowledge of the 'workings'! After all, these first and second versions which I nearly always produce, are only the equivalent of most composers' first sketches. Only my first sketches are a bit less fluid and more formed. I have a feeling that it may be *constitutional* – just as with 'Dies' you thought No.4 (the Arioso) unsatisfactory and felt equally doubtful about it after revision. Both have a wayward quality which offends your reason! All the same (you old devil) you came to approve of the Arioso in its place. Anyhow, I'll score 'The Fall' and hear it (if I can) and then see what I (and you) feel about it [H.F. completed the scoring after G.F.'s death].

I wish you could have got ill here. For we've been having such a lovely and quiet time. The only snag has been the last week's weather, which has created havoc with our trees. The ice formed on everything till the strongest boughs could stand it no longer, and we had a regular St. Bartholomew's Night, hearing limb after limb crashing down. The ice is off now and what's left of the trees is being overhauled. Still, I'm glad you've taken things in time and are having a good rest. You certainly looked rotten.

Yes, I saw The Times notice and Chenny [Alfred Chenhalls] sent me a patronizing one by someone called R.A. Forsyth in The Star ('pleasing music, but not very original'). Otherwise I've missed God's cousin[1] but Miles promises to let me see it. I'm glad you liked it. It was a good enough performance, but I still feel it needs a larger body of strings – particularly more bass and cello. Somehow or other I can't get those repeated notes in The Rapture to come through, and I still don't know whether it's a matter of scoring or of marking-up the violas and cellos – or whether it would be different with a larger body. And I still don't know whether to leave them arco or a two-fingered pizzicato. I'd be glad of your advice, if you noticed the point yourself. Probably you were in too exhausted a state. I've re-written the middle of that song – 'The Market Girl' – as you suggested. It's a great improvement and I always knew it needed it.

Love from Joy and G.

106 Wildwood Road, N.W.11; 8 February

Dearest Dave,

So glad you are not letting my rather drastic remarks deter you. You are probably right in diagnosing them as 'constitutional' – my feeling, I mean; for, now you mention it, I believe it is what you call 'the wayward quality' in both 'The Fall of the Leaf' and the Ariosa of 'Dies' that makes me itchy all over. The latter I can accept perfectly in its place in the middle of a work; but not, curiously enough, when I look at it separately. Then I feel, as I do in 'The Fall', that it is not so much a question of the *quality* of waywardness as the *defect* of lack of direction. However, as you say, this is probably a purely personal matter; and now I've mentioned it we needn't bother any more about it.

I seem to remember hearing the repeated E-flat quavers in The Rapture. Did you think they were hidden? In any case I imagine that they would be perfectly all right with a bigger number of players – which the whole thing screams for. Two cellos, after all, are alarmingly easily swamped. I wouldn't bother about it, if I were you.

Out yesterday for the first time, but still feeling a bit knock-kneed. In haste, H.

---

[1] Edwin Evans (1871–1945), music critic and scholar. Critic on the *Pall Mall Gazette* (1912–23) and the *Daily Mail* (1933–1945).

Ashmansworth; 20 February

Dearest Fergie,

Would it be all right if I came for a night, or possibly two, on the 28th–29th? I'd let you know for certain early in the week. I heard from Toty about the Partita from Brussels on 6 March. Grand news. We shall be able to hear it pretty well, I think.

Rather wonderful about Barbara Mullen, don't you think? I don't know what the play ('Jeannie') is like, but there's no doubt about every single press notice, from the picture-rag to The Times and The New Statesman, being enthusiastic about her. It's going to the West End and with a West End lead, and two film contracts a year: she's better off than we are! It's very good.

Dvorak's Quintet with double-bass is one of the worst things of his I've ever heard. Do you know any Ernest Walker?[2] There's a Violin Sonata, Op.8, published 1898, which has a lovely Larghetto. It's more Brahms than Brahms, but really most beautiful the more one knows it. Alas, the rest of the work is not up to it. One can see how things like that get overlooked: Walker carrying on with a tradition that was already beginning to peter out, whilst his contemporaries like V.W. were on a different path. I imagine that to a young V.W. and Holst, Walker's music would be a deadly bore, and that it needs a new generation to re-value things. Still, for all I know Walker may be a deadly bore and he has just struck lucky in this one movement.

I'm glad Howes [The Times critic] seems to have approved of your playing at the N.G. Concerts! Love, G.

Just a card to let me know about 28–29, and add if you're all right again.

106 Wildwood Road, N.W.11; 9 March

Dearest Dave,

As you don't get the Saturday Telegraph any longer, you may like to see the enclosed. I think it is a good letter, and I only hope it may bear some fruit.

Very good Partita performance from Brussels, though the fading made it a bit difficult to hear in Belfast. In haste, H.

Press-cutting enclosed:

The Artist in Wartime. Claims of Military Service.

To the Editor of The Daily Telegraph.

Sir,

There has been considerable ventilation of opinion on the question of war-work and reservation of artists from normal military service, notably in letters by Mr Bernard Shaw and others, in recent issues of THE DAILY TELEGRAPH in connection with the male dancers of the Vic-Wells Ballet Company.

There is clearly a great body of opinion which believes that artists, whether they be painters, musicians, dancers, actors, writers or composers, are of more value to their country in their trained capacity, often in key positions, than serving generally

[2] See letter 14 March 1936.

with the fighting forces. In the immediate war circumstances they render service of a national character in the maintenance of morale, and their art serves well as a balance to the inhuman tendencies which are the inevitable accompaniments of war. Our art is a measure of our civilisation, and our artists its guardians; it would indeed be a grim irony if, by neglect, we lost the means of its preservation in a struggle for its protection.

The urgency, then, for the preservation of our art, for the protection, even against their will, of its practitioners, and the need in war for all talent to be used to its best advantage, prompts us to suggest that a council should at once be set up to advise The Ministry of Labour to reserve some measure of our talent and devise the best means of its employment in this emergency.

Such a council should be composed of men whose standing in the cultural field will command respect from all sections of the community as a safeguard against thoughtless criticism from the general public or accusations of partisanship from among the professions. The professional bodies will, we know, consent to set up the necessary machinery and provide what data may be needed, if the request is made to them.

Whatever the final decision may be as to what measure of reservation is desirable, there is no time to be lost if irreparable damage to our cultural life is to be avoided.

We are, Sir, yours etc.

Berners, Paul Nash, J B.S. Haldane, Hermon Ould, Myra Hess, Osbert Sitwell, Stanley Marchant, R. Vaughan Williams, Edward Marsh, Hugh Walpole

Art and Entertainment Emergency Council, London, W.1, March 4.

Ashmansworth; 13 March

Dearest Fergie,

Mrs Johnson was such an angel and went along to see a piano which I had heard about – our only chance of getting a 2nd piano. I wonder what you think of Ibachs as a whole?

We listened to the Partita too. The reception [from Brussels] was only fair – screeching females loomed up from nowhere – but one could get an outline of the performance. It seemed a good and sound one, but I thought he missed the sensuous urge in the 2nd movement. Wasn't it a point too slow? Anyhow, he made up for it with the exciting accelerando at the climax.

Many thanks for The Daily Telegraph letter. Nothing of the sort has appeared in The Times. It's absolutely first-rate and I don't think could be bettered in any way. Of course that's the solution, the only solution, if anything comes of it. And I hope you don't think, from what I said, that I put a secondary importance on the artist in such emergencies as these. I feel that our work, if not ourselves, is about the only justification for mankind's existence! And as for being the ultimate representatives of our countries and civilization, well, the point's not worth discussing, for *there never have been others*. So you know that my feelings are the same as yours about the absurdity of Milford 'pioneering', you 'nursing', or me 'fighting'. All I feel is that no self-respecting person (unless he's an out-and-out-pacifist) can claim exemption on account of his own import-ance. His country must make that claim for him, and I think that letter is almost unanswerable on that point.

Nigel's operation [son's tonsils] has been fixed for 13 April, so we shall be up for the Sonata [1st performance at the National Gallery Concerts, 21 April], and I should like to stay for 2 or 3 days if I may.

We had some friends up to tea and they turn out to be great friends of the Vickers – or rather of Geoffrey Vickers, whom they regard as one of the great men of the world! (Did you know, by the way, that he won the V.C. on his 21st birthday?) But they have a horror of Helen Vickers! Love from Joy and G.

Glad you had Tony [Scott] staying with you. I'm getting quite hopeless about his ever getting down to work.

106 Wildwood Road, N.W.11; 28 March

Dearest Dave,

The Sonata is not going to be on 10 April. The date is almost certainly Wednesday 24 April [actually it was on the 23rd], when it will be done at both the midday and the 5 o'clock concerts. The latter, once-a-week to begin with, are starting on that day. Myra is playing the sonata on Wednesday next at the R.A.M. (Review Week), by way of a trial trip for herself; but the official first performance is at the Gallery. Love, Howard.

106 Wildwood Road, N.W.11; 5 April

[Dearest Dave]

Programme. After Busch concert on Tuesday J., G. & H. have a meal somewhere, and go on to look at Nigel's [Barnicot] pictures. Wednesday: Fauré concert at N.G. Thursday: H. and Solde at N.G., playing new Matthews[3] work, after which G. goes to Nigel to be painted, at say 2.45. William Busch comes to dinner at 7 o'clock (if you can manage to get away from Nigel by then). Hertha [Mrs Hertha Kraft, H.F.'s German teacher, who later married Nigel Barnicot] has to have an operation next week, so I thought it best not to invite ourselves to a meal.

Sonata went finely at R.A.M. on Wednesday. Love, Howard.

[3] Denis Matthews (1919–1988), pianist. Pupil of Harold Craxton. Studied composition with William Alwyn at the Royal Academy of Music (1935–1940). Appeared frequently in National Gallery concerts, and in piano duo with H.F.

106 Wildwood Road, N.W.11; 25 April

[Dearest Dave]

Yes, Sunday evening at 7.30 should be all right for me – though I am afraid I cannot put you up for the night, as my sister will be here then. So sorry.

We had a devastatingly moving performance of the Brahms 'Four Serious Songs' at the Gallery today, by one Robert Irwin. I was simply laid out, in spite of the fact that I was turning pages. Ever, Howard.

Ashmansworth; 25 April

[Dearest Fergie]

Alas the worst has happened and [cellist] Peter Beavan (who writes very nicely) has fixed on next Sunday 28th at 7.30 for the Prelude and Fugue [G.F.'s String Trio]. and I suppose that's hopeless for you. Nor can I think of anyone to ask along who might be interested, or whose opinion would be worth having as to whether the work stands by itself. If you're away, I probably shan't stay the night: Joy might motor up and back with me, or I might stay the night locally in St John's Wood. Let me know the worst! If you can come, though I think you said next Sunday was no good.

Beavan's address is 14 Oxford Road, N.W.6. Love, G.

106 Wildwood Road, N.W.11; 6 June

Dearest Dave,

For some unaccountable reason I do not expect bombs for a week or two. But here [prior to going into the R.A.F.] to be on the safe side, is one of the duplicate copies of my Sonata. I would be most grateful if you could keep it for me. Myra has her own copy: and the third (which should be used for engraving if possible) will be either here or at Boosey & Hawkes At the moment I have it.

The 'Three Diversions' [later 'Four'], which are down for a 1st performance at the Proms on Friday, 13 September – a long story which I shall tell you later – will be at Boosey & Hawkes from probably tomorrow so that the Parts may be copied. There is a duplicate score in the possession of: Mrs MacIlwaine, Coondara, Donaghadee, Co. Down: and the N. Ireland B.B.C. have a Score and set of Parts which are their own property. In both Irish copies of 'The Rambling Sailor' (the third of the pieces) there are two small passages which should be altered as shown on the enclosed MS paper. This version gets rid of the 'music-hall' harmonization which gives you the jim-jams! As you know, I want the Sonata to be published. The 'Diversions' might also be done, I think; but I am not so particular about them. The three arrangements I made for clarinet & piano of the Schumann Pedal-Piano pieces can be published if anybody wants them; but I don't mind tuppence one way or the other. Pauline Juler has an MS copy of them, and so have I. Otherwise I cannot recall to mind anything about which there could be any doubt.

Toty is enclosing some revises together with a note. He is keeping up marvellously; but I hope to goodness he won't go flop when he gets back to Broadway.

Blessings on you both, with much love, from Howard.

Ashmanswoth; 7 June

[Dearest Fergie]

The Sonata will be in safe-keeping. Delighted to hear about the 'Three Diversions'. How did you manage it, especially as the B.B.C. (albeit the N. Ireland variety) had a hand in them! When *shall* we meet I wonder. Dear Toty, it's a grand thing that he had you to come to. We like most of the versions he sent very much. Love, G.

Ashmansworth; 16 June

Dearest Fergie,

That's splendid about the Anglo-French Concerts.[4] I had no idea your Sonata was in the series. The Tuesday concert is the one I should most like to hear, together with the Sonata on Wednesday; but it can't be managed, £.s.d. for one thing, and I'm doing L.D.V. [Local Defence Volunteer] work all night on Monday – at least, till 5.30 a.m. – which leaves me incapacitated for Tuesday.

By the way, surely you want a piano duet version done of the Octet, and the score of the 'Two Ballads' done? So many things like this I want to talk to you about, as well as my own affairs. I'm doing some work, and also 'tidying-up' work. Not that one expects the worst, but one must be prepared for it.

Did Nigel [Barnicot] show you those last three pencil drawings? One of them's quite lovely. He left them here for safety's sake. Love from us both, G.

I've got that supplementary volume of Grove and am glad to find you sensibly discussed. I find to my horror that my 'Severn Rhapsody' and Violin Concerto are both included, though I purposely left them out in the form I had to fill in. J.A.W.[5] must have gone to Rubbra's article for his information.

106 Wildwood Road, N.W.11; 11 July

Dearest Dave,

This is to wish you many happier returns of your birthday. 'Le quatorze Juillet' may be under a cloud at the moment, but then so are many things! The only thing my addled brain can think of for a slight birthday present is the Yeats-Dorothy Wellesley letters. Have you got them? If not, I'll send them to

[4] A series sponsored by Boosey & Hawkes at the Wigmore Hall.
[5] Jack Westrup (1904–1975), critic, teacher and scholar. Assistant music critic, *Daily Telegraph* (1934–1940). His academic career culminated as Heather Professor at Oxford University (1947–1971).

you; but if so, please suggest something else as I should like to send you something.

It seems likely that the Griller Quartet[6] and I will soon enter the R.A.F. as a Quintet – after the fashion of Denis Matthews and the others. Up to the time of France's collapse the Ministry of Information was all anxious that the Grillers should fulfil their American engagements as arranged. Since then, however, the complexion of things has altered, and they have been told they cannot leave the country. This one can understand. Myra was terribly upset and worried about them, and decided to approach O'Donnell of the R.A.F. to see whether he could suggest anything. The upshot of it was that they and I should join forces and go and regale all and sundry with light music, etc. On the strength of this I am thinking of obtaining the Complete Works of Albert Ketelbey. We have already filled up the necessary forms and have had our medical examinations. To our intense amusement we have all passed as Grade 1, in spite of the fact that Griller has suffered from duodenal trouble, Colin Hampton was recently on the verge of a breakdown, and Philip Burton and I have more than a nodding acquaintance with 'that distressing and almost universal complaint', piles! However, such things are details. We are now awaiting further instructions. When these come we shall be spirited away for three or four weeks training (Denis went to Bridgnorth in Shropshire), after which we hope to return to these parts once more. It seems quite likely that when we return we will be allowed to sleep at home and go to Uxbridge daily, as at the moment they simply have so many people they don't know what to do with them. This would be a considerable blessing, as it would enable me to continue helping Myra with the Gallery programmes. If I cannot run the car, I might even think of purchasing a motor-bicycle to shorten the time taken over the daily journeys between here and Uxbridge; but it is pointless to try and decide until I find out how things pan out. We'll be a comic-looking crew in R.A.F. uniform and those absurd little hats, won't we?

By great good fortune Hawkes had decided to do my Sonata before this unexpected turn of events came, and they have very decently rushed through the engraving at top speed, so that I can have the thing corrected before I depart. I actually had the 1st proofs just over a fortnight after I sent them the MS! The printing of the work may be held up because of the new paper restrictions: but I do not mind about this so long as the proofs are done. If I may, I will send on the 2nd proofs to you after I have been through them myself; I have gone through the 1st lot very carefully, so there should not be too many mistakes.

How are things with you? Can you read a prismatic compass yet? and have they loosed you with a rifle, or do you still have to run and fetch the nearest policeman 'while keeping the parachutist under observation'? I should love to see you skipping over hedge and ditch in a wild effort to reach Highclere and, at the same time, not to lose sight of the invader.

---

[6] Sidney Griller, Jack O'Brien (violins), Philip Burton (viola), Colin Hampton (cello).

Toty is coming here for Tuesday and Wednesday nights of next week. Let me know if there is any chance of you getting up anytime, in case I have not departed.

After the audiences getting worse and worse (with the news) for several weeks, people have suddenly started to come to the Gallery in crowds again. As someone said, if only there was another allied navy for us to attack, we would soon have the House Full boards out.

A bon-bouche for the end. Hertha and Nigel [Barnicot] were married last September . . . so you see there is nothing left for me to do but say 'Peccavi' to you and Joyce!

Much love to you both, from Howard.

Ashmansworth; 13 July

Dearest Fergie,

It was so good to get your letter, because I guessed 'things' were happening and longed to know what they were. There's so much to talk about that I certainly hope to get up to London or to see you down here. But it's no good unless you are fairly free for a couple of days, because there's this new fiddle piece [G.F.'s 'Elegy' for violin & piano] (good, I think), a couple of new songs, and five revised old ones, besides 'Come away Death' still to be marked, and – above all – everything you've got to tell me from Sir H.J.W. [Henry Wood] and the 'Three Diversions' onwards.

Of course I'll look through the 2nd proofs of the Sonata. I think it's splendid of Hawkes to have got it out so quickly. I suppose you know that both Kalmus and Stein[7] have been interned. It's really appalling, the stupidity of the one-track military mind.

Certainly, I've been loosed with a rifle and a uniform *and* a forage cap! We've had a little rifle-practice, and I suppose I was the only one of the whole lot who (secretly) had his ears stuffed up! It's quite incredible to me – that 99 people out of a 100 appear to be quite insensitive to the crack of a service rifle. I find it dreadful, but I'm not a bad shot and must get used to it. (For nothing in the world would persuade either the Grillers or the Air Force that I am a good enough pianist!)

What is the three or four weeks training? Musical or disciplinary? I suppose I ought to feel glad about this Air Force business and so I am, for music's and your sake, in spite of the ridiculousness of it all. Alas, the only solution – that of exemption committees attached to each profession – now seems further away than ever. (The same method should have been applied to the Aliens question. How could the War Office know that Kalmus was about the most distinguished music publisher on the continent and likely to bring the same distinction to music publishing in England if given a chance?)

---

[7] Alfred Kalmus (1889–1972), Erwin Stein (1885–1958), distinguished Viennese musicians working for Universal Edition. Forced to flee Nazi persecution, they joined the staff of Boosey & Hawkes.

But to revert to you as entertainer to H.M. Forces: this would have meant, what we should all like to see, that you were *right out of it all*, or (if the exemption committee had thought poorly of your musical capabilities) a proper soldier. As it is, I suppose one can only say that it's the best way out of a poor piece of organization. And one can't be too grateful to Myra.

Now tell me, do you think there's any chance of your getting down here soon for a few days? Don't imagine that we're right out of it — being less than 40 miles from Southampton. The nearest points of attack have been an old Colonel's drive at Highclere, the Downs at Coombe, and buildings at Thatcham. We've also had a running fight above Ashmansworth — machine-guns and all — but hidden by low clouds. Yet in spite of this one doesn't get that awful feeling of mass hysteria that large gatherings seem to produce, and Ashmansworth is just about what it was when you were here a couple of years ago.

How interesting about Hertha and Nigel. But even we didn't think they were *married*. (It's curious that he reminds me so very much of R.O., and that Jane is also very much R.O.'s senior.) Is it public and do we congratulate? That's another thing I'm longing to hear about.

Why, I'd be delighted to have the Yeats-Dorothy Wellesley letters: I've wanted to read them badly. That reminds me, not knowing where we shall all be by next Trafalgar Day, I got something for you which I think you may be glad to have: the Whittaker essays.[8] So don't get 'em if you have thought of it: that's why I'm mentioning it, even though it takes the 'surprise' element away.

Give my love to Toty, and I do hope he is managing to do some work. I hope to go on till the last minute. It's rather like the band playing whilst the Titanic sank — except that we're by no means sunk yet. Love from Joy and G.

106 Wildwood Road, N.W.11; 29 July

Dearest Dave,

Just a hurried note to tell you that the Grillers and I expect to 'take the veil' tomorrow morning. It has all been rather sudden in the end, principally because Colin Hampton was being threatened with immediate absorption into the Army, and O'Donnell (the head of the R.A.F. Bands) thought the only thing was to grab us immediately, while the going was good. Because of this haste, it is quite possible that we will not go away for the usual training — or at least not yet; and that we will be sleeping in our own homes after a week or so. In any case, I'll let you know how things plan out. I have not yet cancelled my broadcast with Solde for Sunday 4th, as I am still hoping it will be possible to fit it in. We are doing my own Sonata, so perhaps you would listen if you haven't fallen asleep by 11 o'clock. If you find the programme changed, you'll know I wasn't able to get off.

---

[8] William Gillies Whittaker (1876–1944), composer and scholar. His *Collected Essays* were published by O.U.P, in 1940.

Another broadcast about which I feel particularly pleased, is to be on Wednesday, 7 August, when Defauw[9] (the Belgian) is going to do the Partita for the B.B.C. in a programme with the Brahms-Haydns and one of the Daphnis suites by Ravel. Defauw managed to escape first from Belgium and then from France, and I was overjoyed to see him at the Gallery the other day; he told me that the B.B.C. had invited him to conduct, but did not say a word about the Partita until it was all settled.

Would you be a saint and look through the 2nd proofs of the piano Sonata for me? I have been through the 1st proofs very closely, and think I have found most of the bloomers: but you know what frightful things one can let pass. I am sending you not only the 2nd proofs, but the 1st proofs also and the MS from which they were engraved, as you will find that I have made some alterations in detail since I sent off the MS which is now in your keeping. Indeed, I have made some alterations even in the 1st proofs, so not even this 'engraver's MS' is entirely accurate. You will, I am afraid, have to refer in cases of doubt to both the 'engraver's MS' and the 1st proofs. So sorry to make all these complications and give you such trouble but certain points really required clearing-up.

I am very disappointed not to have been able to get down to Ashmansworth. But it might even be possible later on, during a weekend's leave; or perhaps you could come up here and we might be able to fit in some work during the evenings. We can make some sort of arrangement when I discover how we are placed. The string parts of my 'Diversions' have to be corrected before tonight, so please forgive this hurried note. Much love to you both, from Howard.

P.S. I liked the look of Joy's new bit [of sculpture] very much — as far as one can get any idea of such things from a photograph.

Ashmansworth; 27 July

Dearest Fergie,

The Yeats-Wellesley letters arrived from Bumpus yesterday. I'm delighted to have them and will be even more so when your signature is inside. (I suppose you realize that 'Penns-in-the-Rocks' [Dorothy Wellesley's home in Kent] is at Lye Green, not five minutes away from the Cottage and Bingles.) At a first glance the book seems to have the same sort of value as the Strauss-Hofmannsthal correspondence, though I'm bewildered at his admiration for her work, as also for his other 'discovery', W.J. Turner.

Your ominous silence makes me fear that you've already started your three weeks 'training'. If not, and you can find time, glance through my letter again, as there are several things that want an answer — from cures for piles to Nigel's marriage! And if you have left for Uxbridge there'll be no chance, alas, alas, of seeing you here, not even to play duets with John [Sumsion], who is with us for

[9] Désiré Defauw (1885–1960), Belgian-born American conductor and violinist. Conducted the Brussels Conservatory concerts (1926–1940) and the Chicago Symphony Orchestra (1943–1947).

ten days or so. I expect you know that Alice has taken the three children to America. Poor John, for he has a horror of loneliness and of being without his family.

Tony [Scott] spent his last evening up here and is now in Bedfordshire. He will be an Air Force Mechanic — too old for a pilot or observer, I'm glad to say — and I have a horrible feeling that this will be the end of his music. His difficulties of expression are too great to stand a complete break of this nature, though I hope I'm wrong. He is likely to come through all right, but it will be to a different sort of life. I've told him I'll go on doing exercises by correspondence if he gets the time, so long as I can; but then my own time grows short and I suppose I shall have to register in a couple of months and be actually called-up in about two months after that.

Love from us both and again very many thanks. G. Love to Pu & Betty.

Ashmansworth; 2 August

Dearest Fergie,

Yes, keep in touch with what they're doing to you, and then we may be able to fix up something later. Anyhow, I hope it'll be before 'all the billows go over my head' [quotation from R.V.W.'s 'Shepherds of the Delectable Mountains']. Pretty free, except 16 August for a few days, when the Rubbras are coming. You might let me know rehearsals of 'Three Diversions', in case it's possible to get up to London, though at present I'm only banking on the actual performance. (Have you a Prom. list, by the way, that you could let me have?) We shall try and keep awake next Sunday!! [for H.F.'s broadcast]. Fortunately Sundays and Wednesdays are two of my free nights — Monday, Friday and Saturday evenings are all taken up with the L.D.V., and one other night in the week the whole night. So we shall get a decent performance of the Partita. It's splendid that you've got performances of the two works fairly close together. Added to that, John [Sumsion] is playing your Sonata all day here! He admires it greatly.

I sent a note to Isolde Menges, in case she had a free five minutes at Downe House [host to summer-school near Newbury], but guessed that she wouldn't, as I know what those summer-schools are like.

I'll do the proofs of the Piano Sonata and send them back to you (not to B&H). But I can't do them before Sunday, but then will be able to give up the whole day to them.

Do have your photo taken in uniform, with a palm on one side and the hand resting on a chair. Love, G.

You'll have had my other letter by now, letting you know that the Yeats letters had arrived.

106 Wildwood Road, N.W.11; 6 August

Dearest Dave,

Three of the Grillers and I were duly sworn-in to the R.A.F. last week. But as the papers of Griller himself had not yet come through, they packed us off home again. This is all thoroughly satisfactory, since it means that none of us can be hiked-off into the Army or elsewhere, though in the meantime we can go on leading our ordinary lives. We have no idea when Griller's papers will come through: it might not be for several weeks, or it might be this week as ever is. We hear to our infinite relief that the training which Aircrafthand/Musicians are now given lasts only one week! Also, that it takes place at Uxbridge; so there will be no going up North for three or four weeks for the likes of us, even though Denis and his crew had to do so. What could be better?

Is there any hope of you getting up here for two or three days? I cannot very well go away myself, in case 'my call comes'; but if you could come we could probably get quite a lot of your work done. The first rehearsal of my 'Diversions' is this Friday afternoon, which seems strangely early as the performance is not until 13 September. Friday is, I know, a difficult day for you, so I would not suggest you trying to get up for this 1st rehearsal. Unfortunately the 2nd rehearsal is on the day of the performance, 13 September, which is also a Friday; but if you can manage the performance you can probably fit in the rehearsal too. The latter, by the way, is at 9.30 in the morning. From what you say of your L.D.V.-ing[10] I imagine the beginning of the week would be best for you. Next week would be possible, but the week of the 19th would be even better or me, and I think we might risk my still being available. How about that for you?

You are a saint to go through the Sonata proofs. Yes, please return them to me here and not to B&H. Prom. list which you ask for is enclosed. For your information, miniature scores are now available of Elgar, 'Serenade', Op.20; Sibelius 'En Saga', Op.9, 'Karelia Suite', Op.11 and 'The Bard', Op.64; British & Continental Music Agencies Ltd (that is, Breitkopf's usual agents Feldman) are the publishers and all are printed in England.

If John is still with you, please give him my love; and tell him from me not to play through my Sonata too often, or the household will wish me (and him) at the bottom of the sea. I hope the fiddle Sonata came through all right on Sunday evening. We were pleased and surprised not to have a single air-raid warning while we were in Bristol; it was the first night for about three weeks that they did not have either one or two. It must be rather wearing, don't you think?

I don't think here is any more chat to pass on to you. Much love to you both, and remember to let me know about the week after next. Blessings, Howard.

---

[10] Local Defence Volunteers.

Ashmansworth; 13 August

Dearest Fergie,

Here's the portrait [Peter Scott's drawing of Denis Matthews]. Joy rather liked it as a drawing, not knowing its relation to the original.

If all right for you, I'll be coming up Tuesday 10 September and leaving Saturday 14 September (I won't forget sugar and butter this time! [because of rationing]). Is it possible for you to get two tickets for Prom 10th and 14th for Joy and me, unless you think there'll be no difficulty in getting in.

Rubbra has sent me Britten's 'Les Illuminations'. It's just like soap-bubbles, irridescent and easily exploded.

I do hope there's to be a decent N.G. Concert between the 10th and 14th. Perhaps you and Matthews will be doing another duet affair. I'd be interested to hear him play in the flesh, as I certainly don't believe your and Myra's terrific admiration is based on nothing. Your description of his 'thinking in music' in the way that Nunky did makes me ponder on the difference between thinking in music and thinking of music.

Hertha comes for a couple of nights later in the week, and Nigel for one. Hertha says he doesn't mind where he sleeps, so I conclude that we are supposed to know nothing about the marriage, and should give them separate rooms. Our love, G.

106 Wildwood Road, N.W.11; 18 August

Dearest Dave,

I have a rather heart-breaking piece of news. Toty's marriage [to Dorothy Hoare] is off for the moment – and indeed indefinitely, though the engagement is not actually broken-off. He rang me on Saturday morning, in a dreadful state, to say that Dorothy was beginning to jib at some of the religious difficulties. I could not gather what the exact trouble was, but have an idea that it was the feeling that all personal problems (or, at least, what she and you and I would consider purely personal) should have to be referred to the Church. While one has every sympathy with her over this, it is hard not to wish she had thought of it before now. Having accepted the necessity of any children being brought up in the Catholic faith, one would have thought that the rest would follow automatically; but apparently it has not done so. One must hope that, given time, she will get the problem sorted out to her own satisfaction. My only fear is that behind it all there may be the reason, perhaps subconscious, that she does not want to get married at all. If this were so, and she were finally to refuse him, I am almost afraid to think what the effect on our Toty will be. I will know more about it all when Toty comes here on Tuesday for a night or two. I tried to get him to stay here this weekend, but he had to get back to Broadway to see about the wages being paid or somesuch nonsense. I shall keep him here as long as possible, as I don't think he should be too much alone at the moment. This is merely to let you know what the position is.

If it is not too much trouble, could you post me the MS of my Sonata which you have. I don't think there is any need to register it. My love to you both. Ever, H.

Ashmansworth [; 29 July]

Dearest Fergie,

Many thanks for letting me know. It's really most distressing and one only wishes you could go and have a talk with Dorothy! Quite frankly, as a rationalist, I can quite understand her jibbing at all this (to you and me) Catholic twaddle: but that's quite beside the point, for one has to face the fact that Toty's Catholicism is an integral part of his make-up. All the same, I think the obstacles are of the sort that would probably disappear once they are married — I mean that they are probably mainly theoretical. I hope to heaven it will all clear up. What crimes dogmatic religion are responsible for. Here's the Sonata. Love, G.

106 Wildwood Road, N.W.11; 28 August

Dearest Dave,

The Grillers and I take the veil finally and irrevocably the day after tomorrow. We will, presumably, be at large again by the 10th of September; but in case there is any hitch, here are your tickets for the 10th (R.V.W.) and the 13th (H.F.). The first are Balcony unreserved, and the second Grand Circle reserved. I hope you don't mind the latter, but Beethoven nights are always the most awful jam and I wanted us all to sit together: Pu & Betty, Toty and Denis will be there too, so it looks as though I shall be well supported. I take it that you will stay here from 10th–14th? Our nights are not as undisturbed as they were, but we mustn't complain if that's all that bites us.

Toty comes here again tomorrow [for Myra's first performance of the 'Emperor' Concerto, which she was giving at the Proms. The day H.F. and the Grillers entered the R.A.F., and the night the Blitz began]. I am so glad he is going on to you for the weekend. No sign yet of the clouds breaking, but I do not wholly despair. Blessings on you both, H.

Ashmansworth; 30 August

Dearest Fergie,

Many thanks for tickets. I'll settle up when we meet. All being well, we shall be up on the 10th and stay until the 14th. (Joy will be staying in St John's Wood.) If things should be bad enough to make our visit inadvisable, perhaps you would let me have a line.

You'll be in uniform by then and the audience will be impressed by your splendid part in the National Effort! Alas, I have no chance of displaying my battle-dress, forage cap and three stripes (awarded by virtue of having a telephone).

I hope you won't have any of the horrors that Tony [Scott] has had to suffer, and that you won't have to line up twice a week for V.D. inspection (you file past the doctors, who flip up your shirt as you pass.) But then, Tony is with a set of slum toughs, who don't even know the use of lavatory paper, and on whom no amount of bromide-in-the-tea could act as a sedative.

Ashmansworth is to have a small R.A.F. wireless station. 20 lads have been billeted at two hours notice. Mrs Straker has 2 – you can imagine her despair and resignation – but the joke is that (so far) we have been left unmolested, owing to Gisa [their Czech refugee]. Having an alien in the house makes us, apparently, a very dangerous quantity! (Picture Post is quite right. Germany has one or two English enemies and makes them into Lord Haw-Haws. We have 6,000 of Hitler's greatest enemies over here and we put them into internment-camps.)

I've altered that violin piece [the 'Elegy'] and it's an improvement, I think. Love, G.

Ashmansworth [; between 30 August and 8 September]
Dearest Fergie,

Toty is still with us. He goes up and down like a temperature-chart, according to the post. My own feeling is that it will all come right. There's no reason why it shouldn't.

I hope things aren't too bad at Uxbridge College for Young Gentlemen.[11] If you get this in time (and are likely to be back in time) you might let me know whether you'd like me to bring up some music. I have some interesting stuff on approval which must otherwise go back. Piano and Piano-Duet.

We had a few bombs over Ashmansworth a few nights ago. Damned noise and it woke us all up, but no damage. The children and Joy were away at the time. So you see, like the inhabitants of Wildwood Road, we are almost like Dunkirk veterans. Love, G.

[H.F. entered the R.A.F. with the Griller String Quartet on 30 August 1940, but was able to continue helping Myra Hess with the running of The National Gallery Concerts.]

Ashmansworth; 8 September
Dearest Fergie,

Our plans are still to come up on Tuesday – unless you advise us to the contrary. (We don't really know the state of things in London.) But there may be hitches, and if so, I shall probably not be able to let you know.

11 R.A.F. Uxbridge.

Last night the H.G. had an emergency call and we had to stand-to from 1.0 till 4.0 a.m. I don't quite know that the game was, but apparently something was expected, possibly a sprayed-gas attack, as a new anti-gas stuff was issued. I'm told that the powers-that-be expect zero-hour this week, but it may all be bunkum. However, if I am called out it will knock the London visit on the head, or part of it, and I'll just have to turn up when and if and how I can. But don't let anyone stay up late for me.

Meanwhile, if things get really bad, and you think Pu & Betty ought to get out, we should love to do all we can to make them comfortable here; and if they wouldn't mind camp beds and odd places to sleep, we could easily fix up something for them. They would be emergency conditions, but I know they'd understand. At the moment, Toty tells us, Pu is as cool as a cucumber, but that may only be outward. Love, G.

Ashmansworth; 11 September

Dearest Fergie,

I was dreadfully sorry to hear the news (cancellation of Proms [because of bombing of Queens Hall] over the wireless last night). The only consolation is that when the pieces [The Three Diversions] do eventually get performed it will be before a bigger audience than you would probably get at the moment. I wish I could have seen you all the same, but there's no justification for a visit now that the Proms are postponed.

I wish I could hear your news and know what you really have to do at Uxbridge, and how good or bad you find it all; and I want to play you 'Channel Firing', but that must wait till the bomb-dropping stops. Pu sounded wonderful over the phone.

Our love, G.

Ashmansworth; 1 October

Dearest Fergie,

I'm glad to see that you and Matthews were playing last Monday, and so to know that all's well with you. If you get time, for heaven's sake let us know how things are going with you; what Uxbridge entails; whether you get any time for work (apart from the N.G. Concerts, which are a marvellous achievement); and how Pu & Betty are standing it. I hear nothing from London now, and there seems no point in coming up when getting about is so difficult and music is so scarce. And I suppose leave for you, and a day or two here, is unthinkable for a long while yet. Anyhow, my dressing-room remains free, though it's about the only thing left!

Have you heard about Hon?[12] She has been killed, though he was dug out

---

[12] Honorine Williamson, niece of R.O. Morris. Married the trumpet player Bernard Brown.

safely. He is down with the V.W.s and I think they must all be having an agonizing time; for I think they grew to be very fond of her.

No news from Toty, and I dread to ask him about his affair. We met Balfour Gardiner the other day.[13] He's an enchanting old bear, and has a surprisingly good critical faculty after all these years.

I owe you for those Prom. tickets and I asked Nigel Barnicot to settle up with you (as he is visiting the Professor next weekend) if he saw you. If he hasn't done so I'll send you a cheque.

No work here since finishing 'Channel Firing'. I get called up a good bit in connection with H.G. [Home Guard] duties. The other night we were called out, as parachutes were reported by the H.G. (and also by a searchlight unit independently) descending over Crux Easton Wood. We were out till 3.30 a.m. and again the following morning, yet nothing was found! Still, our little adventures are now nothing next to yours.

Love from us both. [G. and J.]

Ashmansworth; 8 October

Dearest Fergie,

Hertha and Nigel give nothing but good news of you and say that you've never looked better. Lord, but I hope you don't join the Regulars!

Here's a cheque to settle for those Prom. tickets. I fancy Hertha said The Diversions were broadcast [no, they weren't] after the Prom. miscarriage, but I missed them if they were.

Here's 'Father home from the Front' [a photograph]. Do you look as handsome as I do? If you could but see the other arm you would see three stripes. You've already had one premature birthday present by way of Pu's portrait [a wonderful pencil head by Joy], which I gather is a triumph. So here's another (not to be opened until Trafalgar Day). It's better to deliver it this way, now that posts take anything up to a week. I had hoped, on the strength of one or two of Whittaker's articles, that it might be something to put next to, or near, Tovey. But there's a lot of dull stuff about tonic-solfa, and too much about Mr Jones or Mr Smith of Newcastle. However, I shall value my copy for the North Country Folk Music article and, above all, the Purcell article.

Joy and Nigel have been hard at work on the Professor, with what results I don't yet know. But she's been doing a portrait of me, which is, she said, the first time anyone's got a likeness of me. It looks a bit too heroic, I think, but she says it's stubbornness, not heroism! Anyway, it's a lovely drawing, and now she says she wants to do you.

Love to Pu & Betty and don't do anything dangerous in the air. G.

What is your correct designation?

---

[13] Balfour Gardiner (1877–1950), wealthy English composer and patron of English music.

106 Wildwood Road, N.W.11; 20 October

Dearest Dave,

The parcel via Hertha has reached me safely. My curiosity could hold out no longer than this morning, when (it being Sunday and therefore a day of more leisure for me than usual) I had the pleasure of opening it and delving shortly into Whittaker's book. Very many thanks indeed for it. It may not, as you say, be quite on the Tovey level; but it is certainly a delightful and useful present: I very much doubt whether I would have succeeded in screwing up my Scotch soul sufficiently to pay for a copy myself! Now that you have supplied one, I need not make the effort.

Before I go any further, I must ask whether you know that Toty and Dorothy were supposed to be married on Thursday last? He asked me to be Best Man, but (alas and alack) I could not get away as I had concerts in Uxbridge – chamber music forsooth – on both the Wednesday and Thursday. In my absence, Schofield the University Librarian was to officiate. They were not going to announce it until it was all over and they safely away from Cambridge, as they wanted it to take place quietly. Not having heard from them since, I can only hope that it really did take place this time – specially as I sent them a wire to wish them well. I think we can feel as gratified as Toty himself must do. They should be very happy together.

To return to your letter. The cheque for the Prom. tickets is quite unnecessary. I asked Hertha to tell you this, but evidently she forgot. I have sent back the ticket to Queens Hall – at least the ones that I had – and been given the money for them, so that's that. If you would do likewise with your two, that would be another 6/– saved from the wreck. The Diversions were *not* broadcast, though at the time there were endless rumours to the contrary. Henry has announced his intention of giving the first performance of them at a concert in Torquay, of all places, sometime in November. If he does that, let's hope he will also broadcast them at some time so that I myself can hear them.

Before I forget: Myra is broadcasting the Sonata on Sunday next the 27th, at some late hour. You will probably, and very wisely, be in your bed; but I shall brave the consequences and listen supposing that I can hear anything besides gunfire and bombs.

I still find it difficult to understand how we manage to get so much sleep. The noise at times [anti-aircraft guns on the nearby Heath] is quite frightful, but one seems to grow accustomed in some extraordinary way to both that and the possibility of a bomb blowing the house to smithereens. No doubt it all has a subconscious effect on one; to account for one's alarming lack of energy; but, all things considered, it is very surprising to me to find that I am so comparatively little affected by it. Pu is as calm and unruffled as one would expect.

I don't think I like 'Father home from the Front' [G.'s photo in uniform] very much. It looks much more as though Father was just about to return there, with everyone ready to burst into tears. I have no companion piece in regalia to send you, so you'll have to wait until we meet. It is a handsome sight, believe me. My full title, for which you ask, is: AC/2 FERGUSON, H. Aircrafthand/Musician

2nd Class). We always hope that the 2nd Class refers to the aircrafthand rather than the musician: but there's no telling. Incidentally, there is a rumour afloat that we are shortly to be attached officially to the Central Band of the R.A.F., in which case we shall, I believe, drop the Aircrafthand bit, and (I hope) the 2nd Class.

Nigel's portrait of Pu is, I think, about the best thing he has done in that line, with the possible exception of the unfinished one of the Professor. I should love to see Joy's one of you, stubborn, heroic or whatnot. Nigel and Hertha are very depressed, as well they might be, at the thought of moving to Leeds. The only conclusion is that so far it has remained more or less unbombed.

They probably told you that Denis Matthews is staying here [because the Craxtons' house,[14] were he was staying before, was bombed]. He is a pleasant person to have in the house, and as yet neither of us has evinced any desire to slit the throat of the other . . . though that may, of course, come with time. He has the small Bechstein up in the spare-room, so we can work without disturbing one another. An H.E. bomb landed in Grove End Road opposite the Craxtons' house last week, so it was as well that showers of incendiaries had shifted him some weeks ago. Strange to say, the house is still standing, though a chimney-stack fell through the roof, and other bits of devastation occurred. The same bomb blew in Mrs Johnson's spare-room windows, she being away up North at the time.

I now have the car on the road again, which makes life a lot easier. The R.A.F. is the means of producing some extra petrol (a wonderful document beginning, 'It is essential in the National Interest that etc.'); and, by working in conjunction with another Bandite who lives nearby, one has sufficient to drive to and from Uxbridge most days.

We all send our love to you both, and hope that things (refugees, etc.) are not being too devastatingly trying. Blessings and thanks, from Howard.

Ashmansworth; 26 October

Dearest Fergie,

Yes, we know about Toty and Dorothy. Shortly after writing to you we heard from him saying that they were going to be married the next day. A great relief, as his previous letter had left things rather in the air. Well, that's that, and thank Heavens for it.

Alas for the Prom. tickets: I tore them up after I sent you the cheque, and I don't see why you should bear the burden. However, we'll settle that when we meet, otherwise that damned cheque will go to and fro, and my accounts will be out of order!

We'll be listening-in to the Sonata [Piano Sonata] tomorrow. I'm so glad you mentioned it, as we don't go through The Radio Times much nowadays.

---

[14] Harold Craxton (1885–1971), pianist and teacher. Father of Janet Craxton (oboe) and John Craxton (painter).

Programmes are seldom worth it, and reception is bloody — worse still, I fancy, since the R.A.F. wireless station has been working.

Aircrafthand/Musician 2nd Class is glorious. If you ever get here, we shall have to see that you don't run into any of the R.A.F. fellows. They might start talking shop and then where would you be?

Joy and I spent a couple of nights with the Rubbras. It was a relief to get away from our not-too-congenial housemates, and have lots of music. And by the way, apart from our Czech (and she's very nice and unobtrusive), we shall have an *empty house* (D.V.!) from 2–28 December. So if you could get a day or two off during the month, it would be splendid. Matthews too, if he'd care to come. It's certainly amazing that you are able to sleep, but though you all may be feeling comfortable, it's not easy for your friends to feel so. I wish you were all out of it, though I suppose your N.G. work justifies a lot.

Poor Nigel and Hertha: they'll loathe Leeds. I want to show the Behrends his latest pictures, as I know they're in need of cash. Small hopes of any results, though the Behrends were distinctly interested in his work.

There are one or two of Joy's latest portraits that she may get photographed, and if she does I'll include mine. The trouble is that they're all on paper and don't stand up, unless in a frame or mounted. I suppose the one [of Denis] you sent to Kodaks was stiff, on board, or else mounted.

Our love to you all, and now I've got to waste the afternoon being a parachutist, attempting to attack an imaginary post without being caught! G.

106 Wildwood Road, N.W.11; 6 November

[Dearest Dave]

Back again from durance vile. It was, on the whole, much less trying than we feared it would be; nevertheless, it is delightful to be in one's home again — even if one has to leave it at 6.30 each morning. It will be better when I have the car. You are, I take it, coming on Tuesday next? A bomb fell the other night on a house almost opposite to Myra's[15] and blew it to Jericho; but a little thing like that won't deter you will it? Odd to relate, not a single window in Myra's house was broken. Ceddy has been here quite unexpectedly for a week, writing music for an M.O.I. [Ministry of Information] Film. He sent his love, as I do, H.

106 Wildwood Road, N.W.11; 30 November

Dearest Dave,

Here is your copy of my Piano Sonata. I trust that you will be able to play it nice and accurately when next we meet. I think B&H have got it up very pleasantly in spite of the necessary economy over paper, etc. The cover is commendably plain and unornamental.

Things continue much as before, though the last week has been more quiet

---

[15] 36 Wildwood Road, N.W.11.

than usual. I got down to Torquay on Thursday for old Henry's [Henry Wood] first performance of my Diversions. The orchestra[16] is execrable, but the performance was not too bad, all things considered. He seemed to enjoy them, and so did the audience.

It appears that we are to get a week's leave at Christmas. I, alas, must go over to Ireland, and Betty may go too to see her family; if this is so, would you possibly have room for Pu that week? You must, of course, say if it would be impossible or inconvenient, or even if you both feel you couldn't bear to have another person in the house. Please be quite frank. Would that I could come to you instead of making that frightful journey. Much love to you both, Howard.

Ashmansworth; 2 December

Dearest Fergie,

Three cheers for the Piano Sonata, and many thanks. It's well got-up, though one could have wished for thicker paper. Anyhow, it's in print, and that's the main thing. I'm awfully glad to have it at last.

Why, of course Pu can come here and we should love to have her. We are four extra here and shall only be two over Christmas, so you see we can manage it easily. She'll even be in time for our little concert [start of Newbury String Players] on the 28th in the church! A small string orchestra of the best players out of the Newbury Orchestra – Mrs Turner, Mrs Neate, and people like that – doing Boyce Symphony No.4, Bach Violin Concerto in E (Rosie Roth playing), Holst 'St Paul's Suite', and the 'Pastorale' from the Corelli Concerto No.8. Conductor: G.F. I find I'm getting on quite well and becoming much more efficient at it than I ever expected.

I wish I could have heard The Diversions in Torquay. I gather that Henry enjoyed them, the audience enjoyed them, but that you didn't. Next time, I'll conduct.

I hope to send you a photo of Joy's portrait of me, and if you don't like it I hope you'll post it back. If Joy herself wasn't so pleased with it I would not be inflicting it on you. I've seldom known her so pleased.

I know you're busy, but keep us going with an occasional line. We're naturally a bit anxious about you sleeping in London. Alas, we saw a horrid red glow over Southampton last night; shells, tracer-bullet, flare, etc.

Joy wants to come up to London badly to see the [Augustus] John exhibition sometime this week. If I could have been certain of seeing you in the afternoon and then catching the 6.0 train back, I might come too. But I don't know your hours. You wouldn't like to waste a bob on a phone call (Crux Easton 36) on receipt of this, as letters are still much delayed? Our love to you, G.

---

[16] Torquay Municipal Orchestra. Founded by Basil Cameron in 1911, but in decline in the 1940s. Folded in October 1952.

1941

Ashmansworth; 1 January

Dearest Fergie,

A happy new year. This is hardly an expectation, but it's a hope. We had a pleasant Christmas here, all things considered, and I hope you did too.

I'm returning 'The English Map' [by Charles Close, head of the Ordnance Survey]. It's an informative little book. (If you ever see a 2nd hand copy I'd be glad if you would get it from me, as it's out of print.)

I also returning your Pu, in good condition I think. She was undoubtedly very tired when she came, and though she's not the sort of person that can be made to go to bed, she at least had a quiet time, with nothing to worry about. Perhaps the worst thing was having to read to the children, who fell for her at once and who, I suppose, thought it would be as nice for Pu as for themselves to have 'The Three Bears' four times over. How I wish we could keep Pu and send you our evacuees!

Our concert went off quite well. Pu will tell you. The church was crowded – fuller than probably it has ever been for a few centuries, since all the Chapel came too! – and everyone seems to have enjoyed it (even Robin [Milford], whose conscience is upset by having 'pagan' works like Holst's 'St Paul's Suite' performed in a church!). The scene and setting were lovely and the acoustics turned out to be marvellous. Well, I shall never make much of a conductor, but I'm glad the players want to carry on, as it's something to fill the terrible hollow feeling that the absence of music and music-making gives me. Curiously enough, I find conducting a sort of watertight compartment, and it seems to bear no relation to the creative side of one's mind. Perhaps not with a Toscanini, but I can now better understand why conductors, for all their experience, are not necessarily intelligent musicians, and are so often incompetent scorers. Anyhow, it'll all be useful if it ever again comes to conducting my own stuff. And in the meantime, until I'm called-up, there's the pleasure of doing things like Parry's 'English Suite', Elgar's 'Serenade', Holst, Bach, Corelli and much else, in a not-too-bad fashion. Amateur music-making usually gives me the pip, but this is just a bit better. Rosie Roth is rather a trial as a Leader. I'd much rather have someone like Mary Baker, even though she's not so good a fiddler. These foreign would-be virtuosi are quite remarkable in their ignorance and conservatism. She had never played the Bach E major before! – what *must* the Budapest Conservatoire have been like? – and suggested as a *novelty* Tartini's 'Devil's Trill'!! (She supposed it was arranged for string orchestra, with herself as soloist.)

Rubbra stays here Saturday night on his way to Bristol. No doubt he will bring a new Symphony. Sinclair Logan is doing a group out of 'Earth and Air and Rain' [by G.F.] on Monday 1.25 with him. Our love, G.

I feel that Pu is going back to the life of a fallen woman, after being rescued by us and given a room and a bed to herself. [Pu, Betty and I (and any guest) shared a reinforced ground-floor anti-bomb bedroom at Wildwood Road.]

106 Wildwood Road, N.W.11; 2 January

Dearest Dave,

I think this might be more use to you than the Chas. Close book. In any case, keep it as it is rather above my head. You were saints to Pu and she enjoyed her stay with you. Thanks a thousand times. We got in [from Belfast, via Stranraer] at 4 this afternoon instead of 8 this morning; otherwise a comfortable journey. Love to you both, H.

Ashmansworth; 31 January

Dearest Fergie,

Busy as you are, could you get a quick line off to your parents, or Sally, or any suitable person, musician or otherwise, who would like Tony and give him an occasional hour's refuge, if he can get away. We saw a lot of him during his last leave and then he expected to go outside Belfast. Unfortunately his placename address has been censored, but his postal address is 1154071 Scott, A.L. A/C 1, R.A.F./B Flight/502 Squadron/N. Ireland.

I expect you've read that the 39s and 40s go pretty soon.

Love to all of you and a special hug for Pu. G.

Ashmansworth; 5 February

[Dearest Fergie]

What's this about Reading on 6 March? [Duets with Denis Matthews, and H.F.'s Piano Sonata, *not* the Liszt!] And is it afternoon or evening? Mrs Turner asks me if I'm going and tells me you are playing the Liszt Sonata (which I find hard to believe), but I have to tell her that I know nothing about it. Love, G.

106 Wildwood Road, N.W.11; 23 February

Dearest Dave,

It was as delightful as it was unexpected to see Joy at the N.G. on Thursday. The Grillers and I were there (all in a hurry) to take the place of Dino Borgioli,[1] who was unwell. The comic thing was that we had never done any Trios together before, apart from the little G major Mozart; and when Myra asked us to step into the breach two days earlier, it only left us one day in which to work-up another Trio to fill-out our non-existent repertoire. Questions of discretion, as well as the charm of the work itself, made us pitch on the little-known Haydn

[1] Dino Borgioli (1891–1960), Italian tenor, specialized in Mozart and Rossini.

in A major, No.7 [Hob. XV/18]. All things considered, I think we played it astonishingly well – though I says it as shouldn't.

We are playing this same little Haydn, together with the Fauré G minor Quartet at Reading on Thursday next (in the evening, I believe), when I am stepping in to take the place of Jack O'Brien [2nd Violin of the Grillers] who has been in hospital with pleurisy. The Reading concert the week after, on 6 March, is at 1 o'clock. At it, Denis and I are playing a quaint programme consisting of the Beethoven D major Duet Sonata, Op.6; my own little trifle (*not* the Liszt, as rumoured by Mrs Turner); a group of Brahms from Denis; and the Schubert F minor duet Fantasia. Joy says that you both hope to come to this. If so, let us all eat together after the concert. I shall book a table at a nearby hotel, and tell them we shall be along about 2 or 2.15.

I wrote to my nice sister Sally [Sinclair], giving her Tony's number and address, but have not heard whether they've been able to ask him along. It is, of course, possible that he may not be sufficiently near Belfast to get in. But I hope they meet, as I think they would get on well together.

I have been more than a little worried at the thought of your approaching call-up date. Have you any idea whether, because of your age, etc., they are at all likely to leave you in the Home Guard? This, to me, seems possible. But if it were not so, I should very strongly advise you to express a preference for some branch of the R.A.F., perhaps photographic, since you're interested in that sort of thing. It is pointless to sit back and say: since the authorities won't make use of me in my proper function, I'll simply go where they push me. They would, I imagine, push you into the Artillery, or somesuch place, where you would be quite useless. Why not, therefore, make some effort to go somewhere where you'd be less miserable, but also very much more useful? Whether one would succeed in getting into the R.A.F. or its photographic branch is, of course, another matter. But it does seem foolish not to make any effort to do so . . . or to try and get into something that holds out a reasonable chance of being congenial.

No more for the present. I have to rush off and meet the Grillers to play our repertoire at the Czech Institute this afternoon. My love to you both, Howard.

Ashmansworth; 24 February

Dearest Fergie,

Yes, we'll be coming along [to Reading] on Thursday 6 March. So book a table and don't go back to London too early. What a pity you can't slip over from Reading and put in a night here, but the call of the colours is too strong. Fife and drum call you back to Camp.

I'm sorry about Jack O'Brien [he had pleurisy]. It might mean his discharge. What would Quartet do then, 3 in uniform and one out of it! I can see O'Brien putting on a stage-version of the R.A.F. uniform which would pass muster, yet be within the law and keep the Quartet ensemble. Joy thought you played the Trios remarkably well, though she much preferred the Mozart to the Haydn. But, as Mrs Disraeli said, 'You should see my Dizzy in his bath' – and you should hear my orchestra in their happy splashings!! Next performances 5 April Burghclere Church, 30 April Corn Exchange. What an amazing world when the parts for the Bach D minor two-fiddle concerto are out of print.

Toty in his last letter enclosed this 'amazing letter from Harold, a copy of which I enclose. Perhaps you would send it to Howard when you next write. I have not the heart to part with the original'.

The Photographic idea has possibilities. I'm not in the least interested in photography, beyond pressing the trigger and sending a packet to the chemist. It's certainly quieter than Artillery; both being equally waste of time. The whole V.R. [Volunteer Reserve] business is a gigantic fraud and it needs a lot of thinking over. We'll talk about it on the 6th. My Home Guard work and my age don't in any way affect me. It just happens that I've been doing rather useful work in the H.G. owing to my isolated district, comparative intelligence, telephone, car, map work, etc. But these aren't things that fall into War Office categories and therefore, like the philosopher, poet or musician, they just don't exist. Also, I'm only the platoon sergeant. If I were the platoon commander I might possibly be left alone. I think I told you that if I were a mole-catcher I should also be in a reserved occupation! Love from us both and I hope you've been free from incendiaries, etc., and that Pu & Betty are flourishing. From G.

Tony's in a well-known camp outside Belfast and he can get in to the town.

106 Wildwood Road, N.W.11; 22 March

[Dearest Dave]
Rubbra's [Symphony] No.3 came through on the wireless without interruption. I was very disappointed with it – as a work, I mean – at first hearing. All well here. Love, Howard.

Ashmansworth; 22 March

[Dearest Fergie]
I'm glad you were able to listen-in. We went over to Bristol for it – the night of the Blitz, but we wisely slept in Bath – and were very impressed by nearly all of it. I think you'll be after other hearings.

By the way, I was interested to hear Boult say that he conducts all the Bax Symphonies and can't remember one from the other – as with all of us. The rest of the programme piffle – an Armenian piano concerto and some drivel by Roussel, which I don't think was broadcast. Love from us both, G.

Ashmansworth; 16 May

Dearest Fergie,
You are so occupied that there's just a chance you may not have heard of Aunt Jane's [Mrs R.O. Morris] death last week. V.W. wrote that they were

expecting it and that R.O. will probably be staying on at White Gates [V.W.'s house in Dorking].

I do hope the raids in Belfast and London have still left you all unshattered. I have to register on the 30th. Shall I put in for the A.F.S. [Auxiliary Fire Service] to try and protect you all? Nothing seems to have come of the Roskill idea.

15 new songs of Gurney's have turned up. A few good ones among them. They were sent to Felix Goodwin 20 years ago, and have only now been disgorged. Maid Marion's sister has got married to a man she met in the last war, so perhaps Maid Marion will get married to a man she met in the Boer War.

Did you hear the ghastly news about Robin?[2] He was staying with us over the Newbury Festival when we were doing his enchanting early Suite for oboe and strings. In unusually good form for him and he enjoyed the Festival, as we all did. He went home the next day and within 24 hours Barnaby [his small son] was killed by a tradesman's van. You can imagine what it has been like for those two, whose everything went into Barnaby and they hardly had any life outside him.

Love to the household from us both. G.

106 Wildwood Road, N.W.11; 19 May

Dearest Dave,

It was thoughtful of you to write about Aunt Jane. Alas you were too late, for as ill luck would have it I had already put my foot in it, not having seen the notice in the paper (as you rightly suspected) and having chosen that very moment to drop a note to R.O. However, he wrote back an extraordinarily nice letter, and would be the first to understand how badly I felt about it.

Your news about Barnaby Milford is frightful. I cannot imagine what those two unhappy people will do now they have lost him. It sounds like the end of Robin. I think it is better for me not to write at this stage, for it would only rub salt in the wound.

I am very worried about your registration, and wish you would get in touch with Roskill again. [He was hoping to get G.F. a non-combatant job, which was eventually found in the Ministry of War Transport by Sir Gilmour Jenkins, a friend of Ursula V.W.'s] It is such an idiotic waste simply to do nothing about it at all. Please try.

All is well with us here. So far we have escaped anything very close, even in the recent bad raids. My family in Ireland is also all right, Mother and Father having left Belfast [for Newcastle] after the first go.

I could have wept when I saw Queens Hall the other day.[3] It may have been a hideous old place, but we have had such very memorable times there. The only

---

[2] Robin Milford (1903–1959), English composer. His oratorio *A Prophet in the Land* was first performed at the 1931 Gloucester meeting of the Three Choirs Festival.
[3] Queen's Hall was destroyed by incendiary bombs on the night of May 10–11, 1941.

thing to be thankful for is that 'Gerontius' was the last work performed there, for that's not a bad swan-song.

Pu & Betty are both well and send their love. Denis has been sent, temporarily we hope, to the Isle of Sheppey, which is not a spot one would choose; but he can still get up for concerts. All my love to you both – and please, please do get in touch with Roskill again. Ever, Howard.

106 Wildwood Road, N.W.11; 10 June

Dearest Dave,

That would be splendid. Best of all if you could stay the night of Wednesday 18th, then we would have the whole evening together after you finished your meeting. The night of Tuesday 17th would also be possible, but (as you know) I would be away at Uxbridge all Wednesday morning.

Things have been very busy these last few weeks. I was very tired at the end of last week, but a quiet Sunday helped matters a lot. The Sunday before we spent filming at the National Gallery from 9 a.m. to 7.15 p.m., with one interval of half an hour and three sandwiches to act as sustenance! The R.A.F. Orchestra are playing for Myra on Friday at the Gallery. She is doing the heavenly Mozart G major Concerto with them; and O'Donnell[4] said he would like to do my Diversions. They do the latter quite well, in spite of my fears to the contrary. I wish you could come along and hear them – though I couldn't offer you any entertainment afterwards, as we have to do an extra bit of filming from 3 until 6 o'clock. The odd things one does!

I seem to live in a perpetual state of being just behind-hand with my work. Much love to you both, Howard.

[The filming was for the Crown Film Unit's 'Listen to Britain', in which Myra played the Mozart G major Piano Concerto, while H.F. turned the pages.]

Ashmansworth; 11 June

[Dearest Fergie]

Right you are. I'll come along soon after 4.45 on 18 June and stay the night. That'll be grand. I saw about the Diversions [at the National Gallery] and longed to get up for them, but it can't be done.

I wish I knew what this filming means. Are you acting or playing? Anyhow Fergie and filming sound the oddest of combinations! Love G.

Christopher is learning the cello with Effie Richardson! I remember you arranging something for her about 15 years ago. I'll bring up those two Clarinet Pieces [From G.F.'s 'Bagatelles'] in case there's any chance of P. Juler phrasing them.

---

[4] Wing-Commander Peter O'Donnell, conductor of the R.A.F. Orchestra which had been formed at Uxbridge from the R.A.F. Band by drafting in professional musicians who had been called up for military service.

106 Wildwood Road, N.W.11; 19 July

[Dearest Dave]

What a marvellous solution of the housing problem. If you would like to come here while you are settling into Frognal [a room in Prof. Watson's house], let me know. Love to you both, from Howard.

106 Wildwood Road, N.W.11; 13 August

Dearest Dave,

When you phoned last night, Myra was in the middle of reading to me the draft of a speech she has got to make on Thursday; so please forgive me if I was a little distrait.

So sorry it is not possible to fix anything with Paul [Pauline Juler] this week or next. The week of the 25th would be more hopeful for me. Could you possibly put into the MS full markings – in pencil if you like; then we can take these as a starting-point for any suggestions which might occur to us instrumentally. This, I am sure, would be much more satisfactory than leaving the whole of the phrasing, dynamics and whatnot to our caprice. In haste, Howard.

106 Wildwood Road, N.W.11; 20 August

[Dearest Dave]

How about Tuesday evening next for our meeting with Pauline? If she and I come along to Frognal Lane at 7.30 or 8.0 that would give you time to have eaten your dinner, yes or no? In haste as usual, Howard.

14 Frognal Lane, N.W.3 [where Gerald stayed during his work at the Ministry of War Transport]; 22 October

[Dearest Fergie]

Alas, alas, alas. Trafalgar Day utterly slipped my mind, in spite of Foreign Shipping Relations! I hope you had a good tour. Mrs Lambert wrote that she met you in Bath, but that you were pre-occupied – a pre-occupation I can fully understand.

'Let me know when you can manage 1) to finish the 3rd of those Clarinet Pieces with me; 2) to run-through (with Denis Matthews) the two posthumous Symphonies of Dvorak (really his two early Symphonies) of which I have Piano Duet copies. I can manage Thursday or Friday this week or any day next. Usual time. If it's easier for you and Pu I can give you and D.M. a meal here without any difficulty.

I managed to get along to hear the Bloch Quartet and also the V.W. 'Household Music'.[5] Remind me to tell you about the Polish Quartet!! Love, G.

---

[5] 'Three Preludes on Welsh Hymn Tunes', though designed primarily for string quartet,

Ashmansworth; 23 December

Dearest Fergie,

Surprisingly and unexpectedly I've got back [from London] for a couple of nights at Christmas, though I have to return by the devastatingly early train on Boxing Day. However, this isn't a Christmas letter. Like you, I've dropped all pretence at trying to keep up Christmas, birthdays, etc., whilst one has to lead this absurd war-time life. What I'm writing about is the question of your playing with the Newbury strings. I've been asked to help-out with a few Festival concerts round about (on the lines of what we did in Newbury last year) places like Wokingham, Abington, etc. You know the sort of thing: village choirs, a singer, 'Jerusalem' at the end, and of course 'Jesu, Joy of man's desiring' thrown in somewhere. Nowadays, I believe the competitive element is temporarily done away with, and they just try to keep the idea alive by having a Festival Concert without any Festival. Certainly last year at Newbury was rather fun, and the addition of strings livened the whole thing up a great deal.

Would it be agony, or would you enjoy doing the Bach D minor at Wokingham on Wednesday 1 April? They've got the use of Wellington College instead of the Town Hall, so the piano should be all right. Our contribution, apart from accompanying part-songs, etc., would simply be the Bach and one other work. they'd probably want the 'St Paul's Suite' for the other work. I believe they'd pay you the princely sum of £2.2.0!

Of course, it would be a dreadful disappointment if, on account of this, we had to miss getting you down to one of our *real* little concerts later on, when we hoped to have you for the weekend. But you might feel equal to the two. Anyhow, let me know.

I told Mrs Sanderson of Wargrave, who has something to do with the Wokingham Festival, that I'd ask you and she was thrilled.

I had one of V.W.'s characteristic little notes to say that there was a run-through of his new Symphony [No.5] at Trinity College [London], with Foss and Alan Richardson playing, 'to see whether he liked it well enough to go on with it. Your criticism would be valued'!!! There was no one else there, beyond Colles and the two pianists' wives, and needless to say the 'sketch' which he mentioned in his letter proved to be the finished work, scored and all. It's got both heavenly and magnificent stuff in it, but on the whole, I should not say it was quite up to the 'Pastoral' or No.4. It's a much more reasonable work. After all, the excessive contemplation of the 'Pastoral' or the royal fury of No.4 does not make for a reasonable work in either case. This one is better balanced from that aspect, but possibly loses from the defects of its virtues. 4 movements: a Prelude, Romance, Scherzo and Passacaglia. Dedicated, in a rather flowery dedication (which I do hope he'll scrap) to Sibelius. The Scherzo is very much like the Scherzo of No.4, and some of the tunes in the work are taken from an unfinished opera 'The Pilgrim's Progress'. That sounds interesting. I find it

could be played by almost any combination of available instruments. First performed by the Bloch Quartet, 4 October 1941.

difficult to imagine what is left of 'The Pilgrim's Progress' after the Shepherds episode has been taken out. [He added the latter to the end of the opera.]

Heaps of love from us all. G.

1942

106 Wildwood Road, N.W.11; 11 January

Dearest Dave,

Thank you very much or your letter. It was good to find it waiting here for my return, and to know that you have been able to get home at Christmas after all.

About the Bach Concerto: I would quite honestly sooner not do it at Wokingham on 1 April – though the date is almost irresistible. There are two reasons, the lesser being that it is difficult for me to get away on week-nights, and the greater, that while I would be amused to come and play the work one Sunday in the charming obscurity of one of your local churches, I would hesitate to do so anywhere more public, never to mention an occasion that calls itself a Festival Concert. Sorry to be tiresome, but there it is. The Concerto is difficult and would need a lot of work to play really well; and I have not enough time for that – more especially as I begin to feel that I may have been wrong in imagining that I could write nothing more while the war lasted.

We [H.F. and the Griller Quartet at R.A.F. stations] had a very pleasant time in Ireland, though the pianos were of an even lower standard than usual (and that's saying some!). I feel much refreshed after the change. Tomorrow the Orchestra, with me in tow, go off on a ten days' tour of Army Co-Operation Units in the Andover district. It doesn't sound so far away from Ashmansworth, does it? What fun if it were possible for me to run over sometime. Unfortunately I don't know our address yet; but if there's any chance I'll phone up.

For your information, the Grillers are repeating the Bloch Quartet at the Gallery on Friday 23rd. And are giving the 1st performance of Arthur's new Quartet[1] there sometime in March (the 12th I think). I have had a go at the score of the latter, and have heard them play bits of it; both methods of enquiry lead me to the painful conclusion that the work is disappointing and nothing like so good as, say, the Clarinet Quintet. Sad. They are also going to play a new Britten quartet[2] at a Boosey & Hawkes concert, but I have not yet seen that. I hope to be able to get to Wigmore on the 24th to hear the bits of 'Dies'.

Very exciting about the new V.W. Symphony.[3] Any word of a 1st performance? So much for the present. Love, Howard.

---

[1] Arthur Bliss: String Quartet No.1 in B flat.
[2] String Quartet No.1 in D. First performed at the Wigmore Hall, 23 April 1943.
[3] Symphony No.5 in D. First performed at the 1943 Promenade Concerts, 24 June.

14 Frognal Lane, N.W.3; 14 June

Dearest Fergie,

It's very annoying of the R.A.F. to take you away on tour just at a time when Pauline Juler and I had designs on you. She wrote and asked me about the remaining Clarinet Piece [the Bagatelles] and I replied that it was finished, but that I wanted to run it through first with you, before facing her. It has turned out to be rather larger in scale, and more difficult, than the others and I only hope that it's not outside the 'Bagatelle' radius. And there are the usual small points etc., and I would be deeply grateful if you would let me know as soon as you are back and try and fix up something as early as possible. Then I can make a decent copy and Juler can have the lot – that is, if they are worth doing. So will you phone me up without further reminder?

It doesn't matter about the so-called Festival Concerts. I've asked Denis Matthews and he'll do the Bach D minor.

It's grand news that you are thinking of composing – which probably means that you are already half through a string quartet [it was never finished]. Anyhow, it's an excuse that can be allowed, though I'm sorry you won't hear the Women's Institute choirs and their part-songs. We'll keep you to a village Church.

By the way, Matthews and his Mira came to sup and I quite fell for her. I think she's intelligent, delightful and good-looking (without the need for a paint-box). I think they are both dears.

Most grateful for letting me know about the Bloch Quartet. As Joy will be up that day, we're going to have a shot at hearing it. I hope to get to the Boosey & Hawkes concert. No hope, I'm afraid, of getting to a rehearsal. Boult is sure to do it all wrong.

V.W. is putting the Symphony [No.5] on one side for a bit. He's on something else now. Joy and I went down to Dorking for the day during my leave. They're a bit distressed about R.O. [after his wife's death] and they only wish he had a job. Other than his usual catlike routine (plus Times cross-word puzzles) [R.O. regularly composed crossword puzzles for *The Times*] I found R.O. very much his old delightful self again. Love, G.

[14 Frognal Lane, N.W.3; between 23 Dec. 1941 and 18 May 1942]

Dearest Fergie,

Here are the clarinet pieces [G.F.'s Bagatelles]. Prelude: bar 1, pencilled instructions O.K.? Bars 6, 7 & 8, I think the dashes over the crotchets in the piano part are advisable to differentiate between the marcato and the *ben legato* bars which follow. Page 5, bars 4–12: have I got my dynamics right now? I think those *mp* and *mf* accents are the best way. Page 6, bars 9 & 10: what dynamics do you suggest – as pencilled? About the Berceuse: I'm much puzzled about the title. Apparently a Forlane (or Forlana) [the latter was the piece's eventual title] is a 'Venetian peasants dance much beloved of gondoliers' (it sounds like a vice), though it still remains a Berceuse in my mind. I think you're quite right about the title suggesting a much slower tempo than intended. In any case I shall mark it Andante Grazioso. Would that help? Then there's the suggestion of Siciliana. Romance: the bar that worries you (1 before 2) does not worry me. Nor Joy; I tried it out on her.

Forgive mess. Tired. Love, G.

106 Wildwood Road, N.W.11; 22 April

Dearest Dave,

The Shakespeare songs ['Let us Garlands Bring'] have arrived safely. I do love them – particularly 'Come away, death' and 'It was a lover'. I'll try and see Irwin [Robert Irwin, baritone, who was to give the 1st performance] later this week. Howard.

14 Frognal, N.W.3; 18 May

Dearest Fergie,

Here are the 2nd proofs of the Prelude & Fugue [G.F.'s String Trio]. I corrected the 1st pretty thoroughly, and have only checked up those corrections in the 2nd. They will be able to move the systems forward, so as to make a 9-page score instead of an 8. But apparently they don't do that until the very end. (I think, however, I will ask for an advance copy.)

You know how grateful I'll be if you can run through them fairly soon or perhaps check up the Parts with the Score. I think they're all right; but I'm so tired at nights that I can't risk it without you having a look through. The following are the only alterations in notes since the performance [two chords of music shown]. Love G.

For your interest: although they can move the systems forward, they can't widen the individual systems. These vary from under 1 inch in the closely engraved pages to over 1 inch in the more spacious pages. But even though all the pages except p.3 will have four systems, where the 'gauge' is already narrow it will have to so remain.

106 Wildwood Road, N.W.11; 20 May

Dearest Dave,

There was an opportunity to go through the score and parts of the Prelude & Fugue [for String Trio] at Uxbridge today. I found quite a few things worth altering: mostly not very important, but one or two well worth while. Having a suspicion that *Tempo di Preludio* was incorrect, I asked someone who knows Italian who confirmed my doubts: it should, apparently be *Il Tempo del Preludio*. I should alter this.

I like the three alterations – though cannot hear very clearly in my mind the added double-stop in the viola, 1 bar before 8.

Hope the Abingdon concert went well. With love, from H.

Ashmansworth; 24 May

[Dearest Fergie]

Blessings and thanks for the proofs, and for the speed and devastating efficiency with which you have done them. It makes me think I must be even tireder than I thought I was!

Yes, we enjoyed Abingdon a great deal, in fact all four have been a delight, and I only hope Denis [who played the Bach D minor Concerto] has got half as much pleasure as the audience and orchestra did.

Looking forward to Thursday evening. Joy sends love too, G.

106 Wildwood Road, N.W.11; 15 August

Dearest Dave,

Yesterday evening was very pleasant: I enjoyed it a lot, and Joy being there made it perfect. Many thanks for the concert tickets.

Here are the proofs. An H. in the top r.h. corner means that I've been over it; a cross under the H, that some query is noted which you have not already raised.

Monday week is all right for me. I'll come to you, as I'll be off the next morning.

Have a good holiday. With love to you both, ever H.

106 Wildwood Road, N.W.11; 18 September

[Dearest Dave]

Grinke, Forbes, Phillips are broadcasting your Prelude & Fugue [for String Trio] to Latin America on the night of 17–18 October.[4]

Away today until Tuesday evening. In haste, H.

14 Frognal, N.W.3; 12 October

Dearest Fergie,

I do hope the lumbago is better. It was wonderful of you to see the performance through [1st performance of 'Let us Garlands Bring' at the Gallery, 12th Oct. 1942 by Robert Irwin and H.F., for V.W.'s 70th birthday], and show no sign of it in your playing, though you could not conceal that there was something wrong somewhere by your attempts to walk across the platform. Probably most people thought you wanted to go to the lavatory!

Here's £3 to go on with. I didn't want to talk about the bill [lunch at The Garrick] in front of the others, so if it was more, will you let me know please. I didn't quite know what was going on, but I'm immensely obliged to you for settling it all in your own quiet way, and I fancy there are a few more shillings owing which I can't send through the post.

[4] Frederick Grinke (violin), Watson Forbes (viola), James Phillips (cello).

It was a good lunch and I think it was nice to have Denis, Mira and Gabrielle[5] as we're all rather on the old side, and a few very young people usually cheer the old man [V.W.] up.

We went along to the Studio for the concert of tributes. [Works dedicated to V.W., and broadcast on his birthday.] I thought the results: Alan Bush, ghastly; Rubbra, like a bit of his 4th Symphony – I liked it; Hadley, rather fussy and uninteresting; Gordon Jacob, technically the best, and brilliantly done; Constant Lambert, balls; Maconchy, not worth while, but good fun. Hubert Foss appeared to be absolutely sober, though I wasn't so sure about this when I heard him talk about 'Let us Garland sing'. (Or doesn't he know the poem?)

Thanks and thanks again dear Fergie. Joy joins me in love. G.

106 Wildwood Road, N.W.11; 18 October. NB: This is a tiresome note. Dearest Dave,

The broadcast [of the string version of 'Let us Garlands Bring'] is just over – the Mozart massacre following your songs gave one some idea of exactly how bad it must have been, yet it was still possible to get an idea of what the string version is like. With the exception of 'O Mistress Mine', which takes kindly to such treatment, it seems to me that they are all too literally transcribed from the piano version. One longs for a real string layout, instead of the close writing which the limitation of one pair of hands imposes. This type of writing would be all right for part of the time, but there is too much of it. Apart altogether from the monotony of sound – and it is a curiously enervating monotony, for the fiddles play so much in their dullest register – it seems such a waste of the resources and opportunities of a String Orchestra. The low tessitura of the accompaniment in the first three songs is a bit risky even in the piano version when they are sung in order; in the string version it is fatal.

Probably I would have done the very same sort of thing if I had been scoring the songs myself, so it's not much use saying how very sorry I am that I did not read and think of the scores as one complete unit instead of a lot of separate bits. But, having heard the result, I realize how mistaken I would have been. Dave dear, please do not think me very tiresome and do not swear at me too much if I say that I feel you ought to consider very carefully either re-thinking them as a whole for the new medium, or withdrawing the String Version altogether. Honestly I am not sure that the latter would not be the better plan, for they do seem to me to be real piano songs – apart, that is, from 'Fear no more', which would in any case require a fairly large orchestra to do it justice. I say this because I feel very strongly that performance of this version would do no service to the songs or to you yourself.

Irwin, I thought, sang them even more beautifully than he did at the Gallery.

---

[5] Mira, wife of Denis Matthews, and her sister Gabrielle.

But I must confess that I prefer H.F., even with a touch of lumbago, to Clarry Raybould and the boys of the B.B.C.[6]

Let's meet before I go away (for a fortnight) on Sunday next. Ever, H.

14 Frognal Lane, N.W.3; 4 November

Dearest Fergie,

Welcome home. I hope you haven't had too bad a time on tour [with the R.A.F. Orchestra], and the foul weather didn't bring on a return of lumbago. I've had to spend a couple of days in bed with a temp and a bad cold, but am up again and suppose I ought to be glad.

Here's the little Prelude & Fugue [the String Trio], and I hope one day you'll get to like it better than you do! And I hope you'll approve of the analysis [with the printed score]. Alas, I see that I've said 'at four bars after 8' a codetta leads into the 3rd section. Badly expressed, as it's the 3rd section which begins four bars after 8, not the codetta. I wonder whether I ought to send copies to Grinke and David Martin? (I see the Phil. Trio is broadcasting it on the day you get back. I shan't be able to hear that, either, as it's on just when I'm catching my train at 1.45. I'd take a later one but for having to take a rehearsal as soon as I get to Newbury at 3.30).

Don't forget Gerald Cooper and the Purcell Society. Any news when we meet. Love, G.

106 Wildwood Road, N.W.11; 7 November

Dearest Dave,

How delightful to find the Score and Parts of the 'Prelude & Fugue' awaiting my return. Thank you very much for them. I knew the Score was out, as Grinke and Martin each had one while we were away on tour (no need to send them one); but I am very pleased to have my own, private copy! The analysis seems to me excellent – apart from the ambiguous point you mention. Like you, I was in the train today when it was broadcast. Most annoying!! Incidentally, Martin & Co like the work now, if ever they didn't.

It's good to be back from tour, which was a bore – with no water nearer than $\frac{1}{2}$ mile from our billets. But thank goodness we were warmly housed. Bad luck about the cold, though a couple of days in bed is rather a pleasant change! The lumbago has almost disappeared, thank heaven. Love, H.

---

[6] Clarence Raybould (1886–1972), conductor and accompanist. Assistant conductor of the B.B.C. Symphony Orchestra, 1939–1945.

1943

Ashmansworth; 17 January

Dearest Fergie,

I don't know what it [the Piano Sonata] was like in reality, but over the wireless it sounded a splendid performance and I thought Myra got all the bite and tang that you yourself want and get. It's a grand work, and I hope Myra will go on and on and on playing it. And after all, what big-scale work of the last 30 or 40 years have we got to touch it? Though I have a liking for some of the Ireland Sonata, you can have it, and the Dale, and the numerous Bax ramblings – and the lot of them aren't worth a page of yours. However, comparisons are odorous [sic].

I was very surprised to find notices of those Bagatelles [G.F.'s: 1st performance, Pauline Juler and H.F. at N.G. Concerts. 15.1.43] in both The Times and D. Telegraph. Favourable ones, too. Something must indeed be going wrong now that I can no longer write [because of his war-work]! Well, you know how grateful I am for the good send-off you've given them, and though I've made it clear enough that they are only trifles, the performance has been one of the few things to which I've been able to look forward whilst this interminable dreary waste land has to be crossed. My only fear is that I may get bogged down in the middle. At 40 it's a bad thing to give up entirely, and I'm only grateful that you are able to keep up at least one side of your work, even though it's not the one that matters most to you and the country.

What are the Rawsthorne 'Bagatelles' which Denis has recorded. Surely not published? Well, I'll be along on Thursday evening. Tiresome for you, but a straw for me getting that work scored. Joy sends heaps of love. G.

[H.F. was released from the R.A.F. on 17 March 1943, in order to devote all his time to the National Gallery Concerts.]

[Ashmansworth; before 15 June, 1943]

Dearest Fergie,

The X-ray seems to have been satisfactory and only showed old scars. It's all very odd.

We shall look forward to seeing you both [H.F. and Arnold van Wyk][1] next Tuesday, 22nd. Unless we hear to the contrary, we'll presume that you are taking the 12.30 which gets in at 1.15, and catching the Andover bus from The Wharf at 2.30 for Doiley Bottom. Heaps of love. G.

[1] Arnold van Wyk (1916–1983), South African composer. Studied at the Royal Academy of Music and, unofficially, with H.F. His works include two symphonies and an orchestral suite *Primavera*.

106 Wildwood Road, N.W.11; 15 June

Dearest Dave,

Very many thanks for your note. It is a great relief to know that the X-rays are O.K. You say it's all very odd: but honestly I think it would have been much odder if you showed no signs of the pressure you have been working under for the last two years. There is such a thing as over-work. And on top of that, you must add the important, if unpleasant, fact that this work acts as a continual irritant, for you feel the whole time that it is keeping you away from your proper work. If the machine temporarily gives out under a double strain of this kind, is it not to be wondered at? I should be very surprised if it did not.

The 12.30 on Tuesday next would waste half the day, so would it be all the same to you if we caught the 8.55 (arriving Newbury 10.27)? Perhaps you'd let me know on a postcard if this is all right, and if there is a bus that connects with it.

I'll get the film from Kodaks when I go into the Gallery this morning.

Love to all, from Howard.

[Ashmansworth; before 27 June]

Dearest Fergie,

Here is the draft — forgive a few mistakes, but I'm rushing to catch the first post. I do hope that you, Myra, Osbert Sitwell etc., will feel that you can associate yourselves with it. I don't think I have made a clear distinction between creative and executive musicians, but is it necessary? C.E.M.A.[2] is of course some outlet for the latter, but I am chary of specifically sorting out for personal reasons. By the way, I think The New Statesman ought to be included: oddly enough, more questions seem to be asked as a result of letters there than even from letters to The Times.

Heaps of love. It was grand having you. Gerald.

Daniel Neale, Baker Street, have a few odd plimsoll shoes in brown, black and white, like the ones Arnold borrowed from G. Could you tell him this, as he wanted to get a pair. They are only a few coupons. Joy.

106 Wildwood Road, N.W.11; 27 June

Dearest Dave,

I have thought a great deal over the Tippett letter,[3] and have shown your rough draft to Myra and talked it over with her. As you probably gathered, I had odd, half-formed doubts about it from the word go; and Myra, entirely off her own bat and without knowing what I thought, feels equally doubtful

---

[2] Council for the Encouragement of Music and the Arts. Established during the war, it became the Arts Council of Great Britain in 1948.

[3] In support of Tippett who had been sentenced to three months' imprisonment for refusing to compromise his conscientious objection to military service by accepting alternative war work. He was sent to Wormwood Scrubs, but, qualifying for one third remission, was released on 21 August 1943.

about it. Our reasons are slightly different. She feels she does not know nearly enough about the details of this case – and about other cases such as Clifford Curzon, Britten, Pears, etc. – to be in a position to tell the powers that be that they have not conducted it as satisfactorily as they might. I feel that the real point of your letter is contained in paragraph three, which covers the wider issue of employment of creative musicians by the state in wartime. And that Tippett is the worst possible person one could choose to illustrate this point, as his case is so inextricably mixed up with the difficulties of conscientious objection – which is a different matter altogether. Before such a complicated set of circumstances can be tackled, the state must agree that you (from the Ministry of War Transport), Rawsthorne (from the Army), and many others would be better employed in writing music than in trying to do fiddling war-jobs; but we, being composers as well as private individuals who deplore the waste of Tippett's powers, are not the people to set such an agitation afoot, for we are too nearly concerned ourselves. That is how the whole thing strikes me, now that I have had a chance of disentangling it in my own mind; and that is why I felt instinctively that I would not want to sign such a letter.

Is the enclosed map the one you want? If so, you can keep it, as I have a duplicate. The book [Denton Welch's 'Maiden Voyage', 1943] is for quatorze juillet: it is [page missing] [H.F.]

Ashmansworth; 28 June

Dearest Fergie,

I fully understand the difficulty of apparently making out one's own case, and agree that the gist of my draft is in paragraph three; yet there is no other possible way of backing up Tippett without that explanation, since we don't agree with his pacifist views. Naturally I'm sorry that you and Myra don't feel that you can sign it, though I absolutely understand your point. Yet I hate to think of Tippett going to prison without a single word of backing from his fellow-musicians, except one of the oldest generation [V.W.]. However, it's no good arguing about this. I shall be seeing V.W. on Friday and will sound him; probably he loathed being brought into it all!

The map is the very one I was after. Most grateful for it. As for the book: Joy seized it at once and retired to her usual reading-place – with the lid down, she can sit for hours on that hard seat – and thinks it a most interesting work. She is half through it already and appalled by the account of Repton, and thanks heaven every hour that we have decided on a comparatively cranky school like Bedales! The book and author are entirely new to me and I'm most grateful. Back to London and God knows what next Monday. Love, G.

14 Frognal Lane, N.W.3 [; 17th Dec. 1943]

Dearest Fergie,

Here is my little list for your acquaintance who is going to the States. If you think it's worthwhile adding the Concerto volume in the Bach-Gesellschaft and the Oboe-Concerto volume in the Handel-Gesellschaft, would you do so. I've no idea whether the position for things like that is even worse over there than here. There's just a hope for the others.

'Dies' will be at the Maida Vale Studios 21.12.43. The B.B.C. is going to let me know if it is going to be in a reasonably large studio, in which case I'll go. But if it's in a cramped room, then there's no fun and it's better to listen-in at home. Ursula[4] wants to go too. By the way, she tells me that 'Job' [ballet by V.W.] is on the 22nd, so I hope to go with her. We must get Arnold to see it, too.

Isn't it odd, Elizabeth Rivers, who lodges with Myra's sister, is an old friend of ours. So tired.[5] Love, G.

[4] Ursula Wood, later the second wife of Ralph Vaughan Williams. They married on 7 February 1953.
[5] Finzi's work with the Ministry of Transport involved long hours.

The complete Finzi–Ferguson correspondence, which dated from 10 April 1928, comes to an end on 20 October 1944. From then on, save for one or two letters of little narrative significance, only Howard Ferguson's side of the story was to be preserved. The reason, he believed, was simple. He had not discussed the matter of his homosexuality with either Joy or Gerald. There was no need to. His friendship with Finzi had sprung from a meeting of like minds — fed by their devotion to music and literature, and their determination to prove themselves as composers. The matter of sexual inclination did not arise when they first met, and as time went on and their friendship deepened Ferguson saw no point in challenging it with news that was, so far as he was concerned, completely irrelevant. Their affection for each other operated on an entirely different plane.

At some point, however, it seems that Finzi became aware of physical intimacies between Ferguson and one of his friends. Disconcerted, he expressed his misgivings. Ferguson, doubtless feeling embarrassed, took umbrage and, for reasons which in later years he could neither explain nor justify, decided not to keep his friend's letters, even though they continued to write to each other in much the same affectionate terms as before.

Viewed from present-day perspectives, it must seem strange that Finzi remained so long in the dark. But in those days homosexuality was not a subject for discussion — scarcely for acknowledgement. Ferguson did not accord to any popular stereotype, either in looks or behaviour. His private life was discreet, and though more worldly-wise colleagues such as Myra Hess or Denis Matthews might have recognised the obvious, Finzi, adept at constructing his own special image, simply constructed an ideal image for his friend and found it hard to take when the illusion was challenged.

Even so, the friendship survived — each as supportive of the other's career and general welfare as before. Finzi in particular grew steadily in stature as a composer: the Clarinet

Concerto was completed in 1949, the choral setting of Wordsworth's Intimations of Immortality *followed in 1950, a Cello Concerto in 1952. Even the giant struggles with the Piano Concerto finally resolved themselves in 1954 in the shape of a* Grand Fantasia and Toccata. *And all the while came sets of marvellous Hardy songs:* Earth and Air and Rain, Before and After Summer, *and the posthumously published cycles* Till Earth Outwears, *and* I Said to Love.

Ferguson's output also proceeded along its fastidious path: a second Violin Sonata in 1946, a Concerto for Piano and Strings in 1951, a Waltonish Overture for an Occasion *in 1953. In 1956 he completed a large-scale work for chorus and orchestra, a setting of the anonymous late 14th-century poem* Amore Langueo, *following it in 1958 with a choral setting of an Anglo-Saxon poem* The Dream of the Rood. *First performances followed at the Gloucester meetings of the Three Choirs Festival in 1956 and 1959 respectively. Thereafter he fell silent. Never a 'driven' composer, he felt he had said all he had to say, that the time had come to abandon composition, and that in future he would devote himself to editing.*

And it may even be that the events of Finzi's life contributed something to his decision. Towards the end of 1951 Finzi had learned that he was suffering from Hodgkinson's Disease — a form of leukaemia which suppresses the immune system and opens the body to opportunistic infections. One such, chicken pox, he encountered in September 1956 — at Chosen Hill in Gloucestershire, beloved of Ivor Gurney and the spot where, thirty years earlier, Finzi had found the inspiration for his cantata In terra pax *which, together with* Amore Langueo *had formed part of the Three Choirs Festival. The end came quickly. He died on 27 September.*

1944

106 Wildwood Road, N.W.11; 20 April

Dearest Dave,

First, here is a small tin box containing the microfilm of the National Gallery 'List of works performed'. Could you possibly take it with you to Ashmansworth this weekend, and keep it out of harms way? Once the book has been printed [on the 5th anniversary of the N.G. Concerts] it won't be necessary to keep it any longer. I've tried to stick a label onto it, but the damned thing comes off in spite of every effort!

Second, will you turn this over in your mind, and — if it passes a preliminary scrutiny — talk it over with Joy? Nols [Arnold van Wyk] is going to try and get a four-weeks holiday if he can, as he needs to get away from that pestilential B.B.C. for a bit. He has no idea where to go, with an occasionally available piano, some walking and (if possible) a little mild work in a garden or somesuch. I thought I would write and ask whether there was the faintest likelihood of you and Joy being able to cope with him at Ashmansworth. While I have an idea he'd love this more than anything, I also know that such an extra person for that length of time might just be beyond the bounds of practical politics as far as your already knotty household arrangements are concerned – and besides, Joy just mightn't want him for a stay like that. But I thought I'd ask thus 'on the side', a) so that you can think it over fully and talk it over with Joy; and b) so that you can say 'NO' without any embarrassment if it isn't possible. You must be quite honest, please, like a dear. With love to you both, Howard.

P.S. Or would a room be available anywhere in the village? The money-side would, I think, be quite O.K. H.

106 Wildwood Road, N.W.11; 25 April

Dearest Joy,

That's marvellous, and most kind of you both. I'll tell Nols, and push him off to a doctor to get a suitable certificate; then he can make the necessary arrangements direct with you. There is, of course, no need for you to write to him. It's really saintly of you to take him in, when things are already so complicated in the house; the only comfort is that he's an easy person to have around and about. I do hope it won't be just the last straw. All my love, from Howard.

P.S. The perfect substitute for olive oil in salad-dressings or mayonnaise is LIQUID PARAFFIN, believe it or not! I defy anyone to tell the difference, so if you've run out of oil you now know what to do. H.

[Ashmansworth]; 20 October

Dearest Fergie,

A happy birthday, many more and much work. This mysterious bit of paper is a new sort of token. If you place it under your pillow, after soaking it in equal quantities of coltsfoot, peppermint, crushed frogs' livers, and aqua pippenga, it will on 21 October turn into a book. On the other hand, if you don't do this it will also turn into a book. Love, G.

106 Wildwood Road, N.W.11; 21 October

Dearest Dave,

Even if Tony [Scott] never turned up at all [he was the bearer of the 'mysterious piece of paper'], I feel Trafalgar Day would have been worthily celebrated by your masterpiece of a letter. It was one of those flashes of nonsense that hit you in the middle and made you shake like a jelly for hours afterwards. Very pleasing. And, in the meantime, I have (of course) all the excitement of hoping that the coltsfoot, etc., really will work. All my love, H.

106 Wildwood Road, N.W.11; 4 November

Dearest Dave,

I've talked over the housing-question with Pu, but not very helpfully I'm afraid. The difficulty as far as we are concerned is this: during the past two and a half years we've made rather a point of telling Nols that he can come up here whenever he wants, as we felt he needed an anchorage of some sort. He has taken us at our word about this, and generally comes up three or even four nights a week. If he had any other anchorage I would not hesitate to say that we couldn't have him for a couple of months; but he hasn't; and failing something of the sort, I'd always be frightened of a repetition of that occasion when I only just appeared in time to prevent him doing away with himself. As you know, he's not a very firmly balanced person, and to take away this queer sort of support might, I think, be a very risky thing to do. Anyway, it's a risk I don't feel I can take.

It seems frightfully unfriendly to say we can't cope with you in this crisis; but I think you'll understand the reason and appreciate it. I wish it could be otherwise. Ever, H.

Looking forward to Thursday night.

106 Wildwood Road, N.W.11; 12 December

Dearest Dave,

Rotten luck. Hope the 'flu is getting on (or off), and that you will have a nice rest in bed. Joe's [my eldest brother] birthday is no good; but Wednesday 20th would be possible, if you can manage that?

Winifred Roberts [violinist] played yesterday [at the N.G. Concerts] and seems absolutely outstanding. We'll hope to have her often again.

Love to your Secretary and yourself, from H.

1945

106 Wildwood Road, N.W.11; 16 June

Dearest Dave,

Quite all right about 'Grimes' [Britten] on Wednesday next. I'll probably be going again, and the next performance would suit Myra just as well. I enclose ticket, as it will perhaps be easiest to meet in our seats. It appears to begin at 6.45. I don't think there's a hope of getting food up there afterwards, so will you get something beforehand? Can you stay here that night? Ever, H.

106 Wildwood Road, N.W.11; 3 July

Dearest Dave,

Here are a couple of yesterday's programmes. Robby [Robert Irwin's performance of 'Earth & Air & Rain' with Gerald Moore] sang very well, I thought, though he said he was frightfully nervous; however, it didn't show. People enjoyed it very much and made him sing 'O Mistress Mine' at the end – Gerald being a slightly ponderous guitar in the background! They made a complete break after 'Rollicum-Rorum', and came off the platform, which I think is an excellent idea. I also like 'Song of the Yew Tree' – but why not 'In a Churchyard', as you have it, instead of 'The Churchyard'?

I wish I could have played for him, but it wouldn't have been possible to fit in proper rehearsals at this particular moment, with Johnny [John Amis, then Secretary of the Concerts] away on holiday. I go off to Broadway on Friday for 10 days, thank goodness. How wise you are to stay at home for a while. Love to you all, from H.

106 Wildwood Road, N.W.11; 23 July

Dearest Dave,

Thank you so much for the elegant copy of the 'Bagatelles' (yours, not mine!), I'm so glad they're out. As a melancholy reminder that all flesh is as the grass, we are but human, and whatnot, here are three misprints that you might note for the 2nd edition. Why do you suppose we miss these little things in proof? It's quite unaccountable, isn't it?

I'm horrified to realize that the Quatorze Juillet came and went during my ten days holiday without due celebration. As I'm little better than half-wit at the moment, I hope you'll overlook the slip. Can you, also, suggest some music or a book (preferably not the complete works of Hardy!) that might be welcome, and is not yet on the Ashmansworth shelves.

With love to Joy and yourself, never to mention Kiffer[1] and Nigel, from Howard.

P.S. Can you give me the name and address of your Marylebone bookbinder? Love to Nols, if he is still with you.

Ashmansworth; 26 July

Dearest Fergie,

What a brute you are! I felt so sure that the 'Bagatelles' were free of misprints. As far as I can remember I didn't bother you with the proofs, as I felt you were even more exhausted than I was. So you're excused. But on the other hand, did you play from the final proofs once or twice? The missing 'hairpin' is what vexes me.

The book-binder's address is: C. Fox, 72 Marylebone Lane, Wigmore Street,

---

[1] Christopher Finzi's childhood attempts to pronounce his first name was adopted by friends and family.

W.1. Wartime considered they are good and not too slow. (They did, however, letter Liszt as List, but put it right again within 24 hours!)

We had a lovely weekend with Toty and Dorothy. It was a marvellous rest, and did us a lot of good. Nols, too, [after his stay at Ashmansworth] seems a different person after his early to bed and early to rise. He returns to London tomorrow for his Friday broadcast.

Don't worry about le quatorze juillet. Sometime in the future if you find a Bach Schemelli book in the cheap Breitkopf edition ('Geistliche Lieder und Arien aus Schemelli's Gesangbuch') or the 7th or 13th Barcaroles of Fauré to complete my set, or those three missing Concertos of Mozart in the Cotta edition (Nos 11, 12, 21 solo parts). Probably all impossible, so you can feel absolved for 1945.

Love from us both, G.

106 Wildwood Road, N.W.11; 24 October

Dearest Dave,

a) I don't think you could possibly do [Mozart's] K.488 with strings alone. Denis *has* played it that way (with the Slough something-or-other), but I can't imagine it was a howling success. In any case it shouldn't be perpetrated again *and* at a Festival Concert. K.449 is, of course, a different matter. If he can't play it, would Kathleen Long be enough of a 'name' — I know she does the work.

b) I think it would be a mistake to ask Myra. She'd almost feel bound to do it, merely because of you; and yet it would put her in a completely impossible position with regard to all the other similarly placed societies that ask for her. That — not the actual money side of it — is always the difficulty about yes to one and no to another. I'm sure you'll understand this point.

Apart from Kathleen Long, I'm afraid I can't make any helpful suggestions. She's the only person I know who plays K.449; also you can judge better than I can as to who would be a sufficient draw for your people. Love, H.

P.S. Many thanks for birthday wishes. I'm so looking forward to 'The Gorbals' [Arthur Bliss's ballet, 'Miracle in the Gorbals'].

1946

Dearest Dave,

Yes, the night of Wednesday 13th is all right. The only pity is that I shall be at 'Grimes' — but perhaps you are going too? Anyway, I could pick you up in town afterwards, as I will have to drive Tim Scott[1] to Paddington after the show is over, as he has to get back to his R.A.F. dump.

---

[1] A friend of H.F., working at the R.A.F.'s photographic unit at Medmenham.

It's a great tragedy about the Gallery [the closing down of the Concerts on 10 April]. I think, however, much worse is the Trustees' manner of doing it, which you shall hear when we meet.

Alas, I missed Paul's broadcast of the Bagatelles [G.F.'s]. I'm glad it was satisfactory; but I'm puzzled to know why they didn't ask me to play them with her. I shall look into that.

Let me know where to pick you up on Wednesday. Love, Howard.

106 Wildwood Road, N.W.11; 21 March

Dearest Dave,

Many thanks for your letter. I think something should be done about it, but I don't know quite what. Myra is almost demented at the moment, what with one thing and another, and our usual 'point of contact' [Sir Stafford Cripps] is, as you know, away in India. But we'll see.

How very odd about your Haydns. I got a complete set of the 83 Quartets in the little Heckel edition this week too! *Not* for 10/6; still it was worth it. The only difference seems to be that mine is in 6 volumes, and you say yours is in 5. [I later discovered that one of the Quartets was missing from my set.] I've now got all the Heckel scores, except the little volume of Mozart Divertimentos (Sextets) which I'm still looking out for. [I never found one.] Love, Howard

106 Wildwood Road, N.W.11; 30 March

Dearest Dave,

Thanks for letting me know about the eggs. Nols gets home today, I think, so probably I'll hear from him and the eggs at the same time. If not, I'll do something about it before they have a chance to wither away.

Do stay here on the 9th. I don't know quite what to say about 'Sir John'; I'd love to see it again – but I may have a 2 a.m. broadcast the night before (if I can't get it pre-recorded), and the last Gallery Concert is on the 10th, so it's a moot point whether I'll be in a state to take in anything on the 9th. But may we, perhaps, risk it? Unless there's someone who hasn't seen it and would greatly like to go.

Disappointing about the Mahler [a book on Mahler and Bruckner by Hans Redlich]: I had hoped it would be a good book and that it would fill a real gap. Love to both, H.

106 Wildwood Road, N.W.11; 29 August

Dearest Dave,

Those few days at Ashmansworth were a complete life-saver. Bless you for them, and for putting up with my sudden appearance. I feel completely restored.

Mr Rosen received the page of MS in his own fair hands at about 3.45, so it

243

didn't do too badly in its somewhat uncertain conveyance. Pu & Betty emitted polite cries of delight when I brought in the box of fruit. They are absolutely delighted, and as grateful for it as I am.

Much love to Joy when she comes up on Monday, with a spot to yourself, from H.

P.S. I do like that Crashaw setting ['Lo, the full final Sacrifice' by G.F.]: it's most beautiful.

106 Wildwood Road, N.W.11; 12 September

Dearest Dave,

So glad to get the copy of 'The Sacrifice', for which very many thanks indeed. It looks good in print, and I like your Amen! Three tiresome misprints hit me on playing it through (doubtless due to a particularly juicy bit of Gordon Jacob's 50-shilling tailoring, as they're all in a lump).

p.21, bar 5: Organ 1.h., F flat not double-flat

22,   1: Organ r.h., B flat on last beat, to contradict double-flat.

23,   1: Organ r.h., G sharp.

So sorry for these, my sins of omission (or are they commission?)

I'll be holding thumbs for 'Dies' tomorrow, and am delighted that old trout [Sir Ivor Atkins, organist and conductor at Worcester] gave you 20 minutes for it in the Cathedral

Love to Joy, John and Alice and all from H.

106 Wildwood Road, N.W.11; 30 September

Dearest Dave,

For the life of me I can't think of any way of 'administering' such a gift of music other than giving it to one of the schools of music. Personally, if it rested with me, I'd give it to the R.A.M. as they have a *really* well-run library with a first-rate librarian. The Library at the R.C.M. used to be a shambles – though doubtless the efficient George Dyson [the new Director] has cleaned that up as well as the drains. But I know from personal experience that the R.A.M. Library is efficient, helpful and friendly, and is therefore worth helping. Love, H.

Let's meet at the Lyric Theatre (Shaftesbury Avenue) 10 minutes before the performance on Wednesday 9th.

106 Wildwood Road, N.W.11; 16 October

Dearest Dave,

I can't for the life of me remember any comprehensive book or article dealing with Cadenzas – though there must certainly be a treatise called 'Die Entwicklung des Instrumentalcadence von Jomelli bis zum heutigen Tag', by a very learned German. At a guess, I would say that instrumental cadenzas

244

came from the vocal cadenzas that probably first appeared in Italian operas (perhaps of the Neapolitan school?); and that they were originally introduced into instrumental music either by Italian or by non-Italian composers working under Italian influence. The singers had to be given a chance to let-off fireworks, so why shouldn't the poor instrumentalist be allowed to do likewise? I think you're wrong when you say it must have made its entrance between J.S.B. and J.C.B. J.S.B. was essentially North German (apart altogether from temperament) and would have been outside the influence of that particular innovation; whereas J.C.B. was virtually an Italian composer, to whom papa would have been vieux jeux. I have the feeling it arose contemporaneously, with (or even more likely before) J.S.B., but in Italy, since the whole set-up of opera at the time was Italian. Handel surely imported it into his Organ Concertos via his own Italian operas? (It would therefore have nothing in particular to do with the Mannheim School either.) I'm afraid I'm lamentably ignorant of composers of that period in Italy; but you'd find the 'culprit' among them, if you had a chance of poking around sufficiently, I imagine. How about Vivaldi, by the way. Would he be a possibility? Sorry I can't be more helpful.

Love to you both, from Howard.

The first movement [of Violin Sonata No.2, written in reverse order of movements, i.e. 3, 2, 1] has started moving.

106 Wildwood Road, N.W.11; 6 November

Dearest Dave,

The only works I have for strings, 2 oboes and 2 horns, apart from Mozart, are:

Haydn, Symphony 45 in F sharp ('The Farewell')
    "   "   55, in E flat ('The Schoolmaster')
There is also, with 2 trumpets and timps added:

Haydn, Symphony 48, in C (the 'Maria Theresia')

I imagine 'The Farewell' is rather awkward, as quite a lot of it is in F-sharp major, which is an uncomfortable key for strings. 'The Schoolmaster' looks less difficult.

There must be many other Haydn symphonies (early or middle) with this scoring, but I don't happen to possess them. [I now have them all.] Would it be worth while asking Goodwin & Tabb what they have in that line in their hire-library? They could probably also produce some symphonies by J.C. Bach with the same scoring, which would be less tricky than Haydn.

I'm afraid this is all I can suggest. Love to you both, from Howard.

106 Wildwood Road, N.W.11; 2 December

Dearest Dave,

How lovely to see the score of 'Dies'. Thank you so much for it. It looks very good, I think; though the thought of those monster sheets [to be reduced later] with 'Ivy' and 'Pearl' working on them gives me the creeps.[2] Surely, by the way, I & P should have included Traherne somewhere or other? His name has vanished, like as it were into a puff of smoke.

The new fiddle Sonata is practically finished. We'll give you a grand private performance the next time you are in town – if you can stand it. Love to you both, Howard.

Good luck to the play.

106 Wildwood Road, N.W.11; 4 December

Dearest Dave,

Do come for the weekend of the 14th. I'll be out most of the time myself, rehearsing a programme for a Third Programme recital on the 16th; but if you're going to be at the B.B.C. the whole time, that won't matter. Let me know later when to expect you. Love to both from H.

Finished the fiddle Sonata last night.

106 Wildwood Road, N.W.11; 6 December

Dearest Dave,

On Saturday (14th) evening I'll probably be working with Denis; so if you're arriving as late as 8.35, why don't you get a meal at Paddington Hotel or Station, jump on a 27 bus, and pick me up at 47 Bedford Gardens? The car will be there, and it'll save you the walk at t'other end. Bedford Gardens is about ½ way down Church Street, Kensington (along which the bus runs), and the conductor would tell you where to get off. It's easy to find.

Let me know if this is O.K. Otherwise I'll send you a key. Love to you both, from H.

106 Wildwood Road, N.W.11; 25 December

Dearest Dave,

You're a saint to have sent the Burney [piano] duets. Thanks so much. They certainly are dull as music; but they're interesting to me historically, and his charming Preface will be invaluable for this paper I'm writing. It contains such sound sense.

Thanks, too, for the Mozart score. I've sent off a postal-order for 3/8 to Styles, so you'll get the receipt from them in due course. Yfrah and I leave for Paris on 2nd January. Then on to Holland for the 1st performance of the new [violin] Sonata at The Hague on the 10th and Amsterdam on the 12th. I broadcast the Piano Sonata from Hilversum on the 15th, and return here probably on the 17th.

Love to you all, and every good wish for 1947. Ever H.

[2] Nicknames for two employees of Boosey & Hawkes working on stencils for the scores of *Dies natalis*.

1947

Postcard of Vermeer's 'Gezicht Op Delft' Amsterdam; 13 January
[Dearest Dave]
Alas, no sign of the music you want in Paris, Brussels or Amsterdam; in fact there appears to be nothing on sale but HAWKES POCKET SCORES – which may be good for business, but isn't awfully exciting. Love to all, from Howard.

106 Wildwood Road, N.W.11; 2 February
Dearest Dave,
As far as the enclosed Errata are concerned, your guess is as good as mine; that is to say, mine are *only* guesses, for I don't really know one way or t'other.
The miniature-score place – but more out-of-the-way new scores than second-hand ones – is: Miller's music Shop, Sidney Street, Cambridge. It's worth asking them for even the most unlikely things.
Sickening about the 'Dies' recording [power-cuts altered the pitch between movements]. This cold and its consequences is (or are) really frightful. You're lucky to have central heating. Love to you both, from H.

106 Wildwood Road, N.W.11; 31 March
Dearest Dave,
Many thanks for your card. The weekend of 9 May would *probably* be all right; the only thing is that a friend of Raymond's [Raymond Clausen was a South African friend of mine] is going into the R.A.F. about that time, and if it proved to be that very weekend we might have to rally around and help to get him off. But may we risk it and say 'Yes', with the slight possibility of a last-minute alternative? So sorry to be thus indefinite – but I think it should be all right.
I sat at my desk and busily typed all the time I should have listened to 'Dies' and my own Bach Fugue the other afternoon. Quite mental.
Much love to you both, from H.
I'm going to see Nigel [Barnicot] on Thursday.

106 Wildwood Road, N.W.11; 7 April
Dearest Joy and Dave,
Just a line to let you know we reached town in comfortable time, and to thank you for those perfect few days. I was awfully grateful to you for allowing me to bring Ray down, a) because I'm fond of him, b) because I wanted him to know you both, and c) because it was nice for him to see the country for the first

time [he had recently arrived from S. Africa]; apart from these admirable reasons, I feel a different person as a result. The *Bynium Amarra* [a tonic] might almost be emptied down the sink tomorrow. My love and thanks to you all. H.

P.S. If Ray left a yellow tin cigarette box (flat) on the living-room window-sill, could you possibly pop it in an envelope and send it to me. Sorry!

106 Wildwood Road, N.W.11; 11 April

Dearest Dave,

Blessings on you for the cigarette tin, received safely this morning. Ray will be so grateful that it has been saved.

I've spoken to Myra about the letter. She thinks it's very good, and is all for signing it. She doesn't like 'integrated' either (no more did I; but since I couldn't think of a satisfactory alternative, I held my peace!); but she thinks that Hussey's [a music-critic on *The Times*] 'reduced to a lower level' is a suitable substitute; '(particularly the executant)' is certainly better. I would suggest altering the last line to: 'to peacetime service in the armed forces'. [This was a letter to *The Times*, advocating that artists (painters, musicians and writers) should be kept out of the forces.]

If you haven't already written to Uncle Ralph [R.V.W.], it might be worth while telling him that Myra is keen, for it acted like a spur when last I asked him for something of the sort. Myra suggests for the other: Sammons, Tertis and Sargent, with possibly E.M. Forster: the first two mainly in case either says No. Those, with herself and V.W. should be enough, I think. Have you any other ideas? Addresses are enclosed on a separate piece of paper, in case you want them. If you want me to do it, please let me have a copy (or copies) of the revised version, and the address (Hussey's) where the completed affair is to be sent. Love to you all, from Howard.

P.S. Bright idea: what about 'and that its cultural life is being debased'? That's the word I've been looking for, used in the sense of a currency being debased.

106 Wildwood Road, N.W.11; 15 April

Dearest Dave,

Version I [of music] is much the best. C [major] is near enough to F to make the two halves join satisfactorily; whereas both D and A are just too far away for a short piece – this one at least. The pencil alterations are all better, I think. I've added suggested dynamics and phrasing.

How miserable about poor little Moth [a kitten]. It's a grisly story, and I'm glad the Tom has been disposed of. Love, H.

Many thanks for the 7 copies of The Times letter.

106 Wildwood Road, N.W.11; 21 April

[Dearest Dave]

R.V.W.'s signed reply came by Saturday's post. I've got the others off this morning, to Sargent, Lambert, Sammons and Tertis (not, on second thoughts, to Forster, as it seems specifically a musical gathering), and will let you know what the eventual result may be. Love, H.

Ben Frankel's 2nd Quarter min. score is out (Augener).[1]

106 Wildwood Road, N.W.11; 5 May

Dearest Dave,

Many thanks for your letter. It was most kind of you to think of the Hawkins' History[2] at the shop in Winchester; but as my bank balance isn't in a wildly flourishing state at the moment, and there are some expensive little items in the offing (such as the Deutsch 'Schubert'), I think I'll restrain myself.

Concerning the Haydn Symphonies: I don't happen to know the Peters Edition of them. But, judging by their edition of the Piano Sonatas, I have come across an entirely different numbering, for no reason that I can discover – apart from the whim of the publisher – so it seems probable that the Symphonies are in like case. The Mandiczefsky numbering, as given in the Gesammtausgabe, is the only one that attempts to be chronological. Haven't you already got these particular Symphonies in Eulenberg? I would have thought it was likely.

Despairing of any answer from Lambert [Constant], I've sent the letter off to Howes with a note to ask whether he'd feel inclined to pass it on to the Editor with his blessing. Sammons, Tertis and V.W. signed without a murmur, but Sargent wouldn't. His somewhat incoherent and muddleheaded reasons are given on the enclosed letter. If you feel like concocting a reply, we might send it off at the weekend.

That is, if you and Joy can really cope with Ray and me, as you so rashly suggest? He's staying here at the moment, until he gets moved into his new flat, so we'd love to come, if you can have us. Would it be all right if we appeared about supper-time on Friday, as we did last time? By the way, if there are any difficulties about 'Lebensraum' (though I don't suppose there will be, as the boys must have returned to school), we don't quarrel if put in one room together. May I leave it that silence means consent concerning the weekend? Love to you both, from H.

---

[1] Benjamin Frankel (1906–1973), English composer of 8 symphonies and more than 100 film scores.

[2] Sir John Hawkins (1719–1789), English music historian and antiquarian. *A General History of the Science and Practice of Music* was published in 1776.

106 Wildwood Road, N.W.11; 8 July

[Dearest Dave]

Would you like to have the book on 'Mozart's Symphonies' by Saint-Foix for Quatorze Juillet? If not, what? Nols' [Arnold van Wyk] Quartet is being done by the Zorians on the Third Programme on Monday next at (I think) 7–8. They gave the 1st performance last night, but I didn't know in time to tell you. I thought it was superb. Love, H.

Dearest Dave

Good! Though it's not as good a book [St Foix's 'Mozart Symphonies'] as it should be, and the translation's a bit odd, but perhaps it will serve to commemorate The Fall of the Bastille, or whatever it was.

I listened to 'Herring' [Britten's *Albert Herring*] (Hussey's[3] 'Soft roes on toast' was rather nice) and felt it was the sort of work that must be 'seen and not heard'. Certainly I thought it was piddling musically, apart from one or two spots.

Lots of luck for the scoring and writing. As it's a case of 'Oh Gawd', I take it that Blunden has produced the Ode [G.F.'s 'For St Cecilia', words by Blunden], and that you're working against time. A happy birthday amidst it all, and much love, from H.

P.S. I'll be in Belfast (14 Deramore Park South) from 1 August to 1 September.

106 Wildwood Road, N.W.11; 22 September

Dearest Dave,

Many thanks for your card. I've just phoned Geraint [Jones], who says he took the watch to his man one day last week.[4] The verdict was not altogether encouraging. He said that the inscription on the back (to you from your dearly-loved uncle) is engraved so deeply on the rather thin gold that the only way to get rid of it would be to remove the back, melt it down, and make a new one. He would also have to remove the names Mappin & Webb from the front, as this would not (apparently) encourage purchasers. Finally, the chain – which otherwise would have raised the value of the whole thing considerably – is not nearly such good gold as the watch. (Trust your uncle, the old sod.) If the watch-man does all this work, he would still only be able to sell the finished result for about £28.10.0, so he feels he can only offer you £20 for it as it stands.

Will you be a dear and let Geraint know on a card whether you are willing to accept £20 for the watch, or whether you would rather have it back again. His address is: 5 Orchard House, The Orchard, Blackheath, SE3. Geraint says that the man is absolutely trustworthy and reliable. He thinks this is a fair price, and he would accept it if the watch were his.

[3] Dyneley Hussey (1893–1972), *The Times* music critic.
[4] Geraint Jones (b.1917), Welsh organist, harpsichordist, conductor. Also an expert on clocks and watches.

Good luck to Old Cecily ['Ode to St Cecilia']. I'll look forward to hearing about The Three Choirs when next we meet. Love, H.

[Ashmansworth; before October 19]

Dearest Fergie,

Here is a messy draft of the end of St Cecilia. You will see that it adds another two and a half bars or so. But the first thing to consider is the space at bars G & H. One must remember that we have had a cut-off at figure 27, so I don't want to break up the thing too much. On the other hand, a good step back before the final leap gives a splendid finality, as well as vocal tone. The alternatives are, 1) to turn bar G into a 4/4, put a pause over the quaver-rest, and then the chorus comes in on the B as the 4th beat. The objection is that it leaves you at the mercy of the conductor. The other alternative is to make bar H into a 2/4 bar – V.W.'s suggestion, but it seems a bit fussy to me. (He thinks a 5/4 would be a mistake, but seems to have no objection to 3/4 plus 2/4, followed by a 4/4.) This end seems to be most important, and that's why I am being rather a fuss-pot. Then the 'fanfares' in the chorus. 'Blest' is a nasty word to sing and must always be the lower note. One wants the maximum of tone with the maximum of logic in the music. I meant the bass in bar C to be a tone higher than their blast in bar A, but I think B-flat would be better in view of the trombone C, don't you? In bar E I have put the tenors and basses on the 2nd beat, but this leaves the sopranos and altos exposed for a crotchet & a half, and may possibly weaken the effect. It does at least give the tenors and basses a chance of getting their breath. Even so, I don't know whether the stretch from bars E to G isn't too much for them. And what do you think of the last pencilled-in 'if the life' in bar F? Lastly, in bar N I've doubled the time, as you suggested. What do you think of the trombones doing the pencilled-in semiquavers? At that speed they'd be easy enough – all in the 4th position, but it might sound rather messy.

We're coming up for the Symphony [a run-through of V.W.'s 6th Symphony at Maida Vale B.B.C.] so you might like to give it [G.F.'s MS] back to me if you are going to be there.

Joy and I have just been down to Dorking for a couple of nights. She did two portraits of V.W. The one for Trinity College is quite the best portrait I've seen of him for a long time. As he has refused to be drawn ever since that wretched Rothenstein effort 25 years ago, Joy was very lucky to have got the commission, but I must admit she has come through with flying colours, and both he and Mrs V.W. have approved!

Our love, G.

106 Wildwood Road, N.W.11; 19 October

Dearest Dave,

Peccavi! I have a horror of leaving bits of luggage behind (it always reminds me of Pont's[5] 'The British at Home', p.97), so all my apologies to poor Joy.

I have the Full Score of the 12 Organ Concertos of Handel for you from Geraint; but it's too big to post — rather like a bound Bach-Gesellschaft volume — so I'll hang onto it till next we meet. Geraint will let me have the watch anon, so I'll return it at the same time. Much love to you both, AND the cats, from H.

So glad the Mozart scores turned up all right. It's a fine exchange for me, as I've been wanting the 1st ed. of Köchel for some time.

106 Wildwood Road, N.W.11; 23 November

Dearest Dave,

Last night [the 1st performance (at the Albert Hall) of G's 'Ode to St Cecilia'] — that is to say, 'Old Cecily' — was such a very special occasion that it cannot pass without another 'hats off to our G'. The work is a real beauty; not only that, it seems to open out (which is almost more important) such endless possibilities. You yourself may perhaps be too close to notice that anything has happened; but to me it seems much larger in musical scope and intention than anything you have yet written! Your lungs have expanded and your muscles have loosened, and God alone knows what you may do now. Beauty and sensitivity were always there, and to spare; but now you've added real size to them without, moreover, spoiling the one or the other. It's a very great achievement, I do feel so proud that my name should be at the head of it. All my love to you both. Ever H.

Ashmansworth; 24 November

Dearest Fergie,

It was a delight to get your letter but I feel that the thanks should really all be on the other side, not only for all that hospitality and looking after us in London, but also for the marvellous 10 days of support here [for the scoring of St Cecilia]. I *really* don't think I could have got it ready in time if you hadn't been quietly in the background, with your Bridges and Bradley,[6] always on tap for advice. However, I won't dilate on that, as I think you know how grateful I am.

Since I failed you (or you failed me) over cigars, and I'm desperately anxious to celebrate by some means or other, it must now be by a more intellectual and less sensuous means. The enclosed book-token is therefore to be spent on Reese's 'Music of the Middle Ages'.[7] And if you must exchange Toty's book, you can exchange it for something else. I would have sent you the book direct,

[5] Graham Laidler, cartoonist working under the *nom de guerre* 'Pont', gently satirizing aspects of British life.

[6] H.F. was reading *The Correspondence of Henry Bradley and Robert Bridges: 1900–1923*, published 1940.

[7] The actual title of Gustave Reese's important 1940 treatise was *Music in the Middle Ages*.

but such a thing has never been seen in the Newbury shops, and I fear that if I order it you will have already done the intended exchange by the time it comes.

After 16 months the B.B.C. now offer to do 'New Year Music' in a Home Service programme with the Northern Orchestra on 2 January. Will it sound too awful after all these years, I wonder? In any case, the Parts are in the U.S., so I have a good excuse if I don't want it done. But I often find good things in early works which, if not competent, are none the worse for not being the same as later work.

I didn't feel what Howes felt about the fanfares at the beginning of Old Cecily, but if you think there is anything in it, be sure and let me know. Were they crudely scored?

Joy sends her love — no, she says she wants to write as well — and also to Pu and Betty who will be duly toasted in Medlar Jelly. G.

[In Joy's hand] Of course I want to write and add my thanks — equally grateful for everything, most patient of mid-wives. You must know what that timely help meant at such a moment. Not least, all the soothing of our time in London and the giving up of so many of your precious hours. My love and blessings to you and the two villains [Pu & Betty]. Joy.

106 Wildwood Road, N.W.11; 25 November

Dearest Dave,

How very sweet of you to wish to celebrate (even if it's *un*sensuously), but alas the envelope arrived with the flap open and nothing within but your letter. Was the book-token ever put in? It looks as though it may have not been, for the gum is quite fresh.

It's absolute balls about the opening being coarsely scored. If Mr Howes-Hussey[8] had heard the brass rehearsing, he would have understood why it sounded like that. Don't you alter it. After all, a fanfare doesn't want to be played on muted violins.

Love, H.

106 Wildwood Road, N.W.11; 28 November

Dearest Dave,

Blessings on you for the Book-Token, which really arrived this time! I'm celebrating with the Reese 'Music in the Middle Ages', so you can suitably inscribe it when we meet. You will have your watch then, too; for I got it from Geraint yesterday. It will certainly be a lovely and useful book to have, and I am most grateful for it.

Love to you both, from H.

[8] *Times* criticisms were never signed, so the culprit could have been either Frank Howes or Dyneley Hussey.

106 Wildwood Road, N.W.11; 26 December

Dearest Dave,

Please thank Nigel [Finzi] very much for his masterly letter. You can tell him from me that I couldn't have spelt it better myself (can I say more?).

By all means we shall lunch together before Tony's [Scott] 'do' at Maida Vale. Will you either tell me where on a postcard, or else phone as soon as you get to town. I'll probably be working here during the morning.

We can very well put you up on the 31st and 1st, but not, alas, on the 2nd (as you know), for FOUR of Pu's relatives arrive that day. An 8 o'clock train sounds ghastly, so let's hope the 10 o'clock one will do for the rehearsal. I shouldn't have thought there was a hope of you getting out to the Strawsons in time for your broadcast at 10 p.m. Why don't you ask Ursula [Wood] if she can let you hear it? Or, failing that, ask someone at the B.B.C. to let you have a listening-room at Broadcasting House? The latter is perfectly simple I think.

Do thank both Kiffer and Nigel for their magnificent Christmas Cards, for which I was most grateful. They are decorating my mantelpiece at this very minute, and look most elegant.

Much love to you all, from Howard.

1948

106 Wildwood Road, N.W.11; 28 January

Dearest Dave,

The MS-paper [special full-score paper] has arrived — all 1,200 sheets of it. This is rather a blow, as I had hoped they would send you yours direct! As you will see from the enclosed sample, it isn't as good quality as before (I suppose this was hardly to be expected [because of the war]), but at least it doesn't run like blotting-paper.

Will you please send on the enclosed cheque for my share when you are paying Augener's bill (also enclosed). The problem remains: how to convey 600 pages of MS-paper to you, in a parcel four & a half inches thick? Any suggestions. Love, H.

106 Wildwood Road, N.W.11; 30 January

Dearest Dave,

Strike me pink! I never thought of that possibility (lucky I hadn't already packed it off to you, isn't it?). But it suits me well, as the 1,200 sheets will doubtless come in handy, even if I don't live to be 100.

Yes, words of one syllable for Overseas scripts, and as many and obscure polysyllables as possible for the Third. I should leave out Messrs Woodgate and Robinson [the choir trainers] for the Announcer can deal with them, but put in

Parry's dates, etc. Whatever you do the 'hacks' will fit in their wording accordingly, so don't worry too much about that side of it. The only thing that matters is to make it so that it 'speaks' easily (as opposed to 'reads' easily).

I showed Arthur [Bliss] my detailed plan for 'Chauntecleer',[1] and he was enthusiastic about it. He suggested that I should sketch a good deal of it, then show it to de Valois in that very rough form, leaving the real working-out until she and the choreographer had been over it. So I went home and wrote one dance complete, just to see whether I could! Since then I've had quite a few ideas for other bits; but I can't really get going until I've got the very beginning, for I'm a bit hung-up over keys, etc. until I've done that. QAL ['Quia Amore Langueo', Op.18] shows no signs of life yet; but I'm glad you approve. Love, H.

106 Wildwood Road, N.W.11; 6 February

Dearest Dave,

Just off to Wolverhampton, so this must be short and sweet. If your talk is going to last 20 minutes, you must clearly return this contract and tell them that you want 20 Guineas (as you understand the standard rate for Talks is a Guinea per minute). But it would be as well to write to Alec R. [Robertson] at the same time, or phone him, and say if you won't after all want me for illustrations, otherwise we'll find ourselves in The Radio Times before we know where we are. Indeed, it's quite likely we are there already. You might tell him, incidentally, that I don't mind one way or the other about it, so they need have no qualms about cancelling my part in it; but do tell them something definite, as the poor man has booked me already.

Yes, I think 'Hubert Parry: a Revaluation' would be a better title. But it may have already gone to press the other way.

Good about 'New Year Music'. Of course you must go ahead with it. Jack Henderson [of Boosey & Hawkes] told me yesterday that they are bringing out my Violin Sonata [No.2] during 1948. I told him I was so relieved to know it wasn't going to be 1958.

Love, Howard.

106 Wildwood Road, N.W.11; 10 February

Dearest Dave,

I'm afraid my scholastic duties (!) would prevent me coming down to Ashmansworth just before 26th and 27th; and the two preceding weekends are impossible for other reasons. So sorry, as I would have liked it.

But perhaps the enclosed list of Parry's works that I possess will save you bringing one at least of those threatened suitcases.

---

[1] A ballet, based on Chaucer's delightful 'Nun's Priest's Tale' (of Chauntecleer and the fox), written by H.F. to his own scenario, but never performed, and ultimately withdrawn by the composer.

We can easily put you up on the 26th and 27th; and, indeed, on the 18–20, if Latham should fall by the way. Love, H.

106 Wildwood Road, N.W.11; 26 May

Dearest Dave,

Good to see the LLL Songs ['Love's Labour's Lost'] in print. Thanks so much for sending them. They, together with the rest of the music, should be invaluable for stage people; and besides, they are delightful in themselves. (By the way, *To-* who on p.4 is, I imagine, a slip, and might be corrected in later editions.)

None of my reference volumes give the slightest indication of when or why The Golden Sonata [Purcell] is so-called. And the nearest they can get to your Italian composer is 'Braccio', which unfortunately is not quite the same thing [as Bracco]. If you really want to know about Signor Bracco, the B.B.C. Gramophone Library, Rothwell House, New Cavendish Street, W.1, might be able to tell you.

'Mirage' was perfect:[2] I've rarely seen anything quite so blatant. It's gone off to Ceddy, who will also appreciate it.

The Whitsun stay was perfect. Blessings on you both for it. Love, H.

106 Wildwood Road, N.W.11; 13 June

Dearest Dave,

Here is 'Cecily', cleaned, polished and corrected. I've found some obvious mistakes, which I've corrected without further comment (you'll be able to differentiate between my red splodges and your neat marks!). Doubtful points, queries and suggestions are noted on the enclosed sheet of foolscap. (By the way, there's no difference between my red and blue notes: it just depended on which pen happened to be handy!) It looks so good in print, and I'm so proud of the inscription at the head of it. Love, H.

106 Wildwood Road, N.W.11; 17 June

Dearest Dave,

Many thanks for the two cards. I'll look forward to meeting you and Joy at Paddington on Monday next at 5.55. I and the car will be in the place where the taxis congregate.

I've suggested to Tony [Scott] that he comes up to the R.A.M. on Wednesday afternoon at 5 p.m. when Grinke and I would run through his Concerto roughly. Perhaps you could fit it in too?

If you'd like to ask Geraint about Kirkpatrick [Ralph Kirkpatrick, harpsi-

---

[2] Something that had amused Finzi. Cuttings of this kind were always shared with Thorpe Davie.

chordist] you have his address. I happened to see him yesterday, so may not see him again for a week or so. Love, H.

                                        14 Deramore Park South, Belfast; 10 August
Dearest Dave,
   Prinkum-prankum indeed! I'm most awfully glad about the BG volumes [complete sets of the Bach-Gesellschaft volumes, ordered from U.S.A. through Toty de Navarro]. Mine are sitting at a shipping-agent in London, waiting my return; so just think how splendid both will be! About cost: mine were 400 dollars (they put this at £107), plus 30.70 dollars transport from the States to England. I don't yet know what the agent will charge for collection and delivery, but as the case weighs 340 lbs, it may be quite noticeable. Presumably Heffers [the other possible supplier] would get some rake-off on it, so that would have to be allowed for too; then there's the transport between London and Cambridge and between Cambridge and you.
   The price had put me off the Leopold Mozart, but if you say it's worth while I'll get it.
   Amazing that Maid Marion has coughed up the Gurney songs. We could have a weekend, or some few days, at them on my return. Almost any time after the beginning of September, provided Nols's Mrs Baron isn't parked on me, or unless you wouldn't mind if she came too. (We don't share the same room.) She's a pleasant soul and would be enchanted to see the English countryside.
   I've been very busy since arriving here. Besides a broadcast, I've done 75 pages of full-score [of 'Chauntecleer'] in the past fortnight. Unfortunately the two unwritten dances are still unwritten. Otherwise it's going like fun. Another broadcast on the 24th and lots more scoring will keep me going hard for the rest of the month. Much love to you all, from Howard.
   P.S. I wonder did you listen to 'Seraglio' last night? What heavenly nonsense it is.

                                        106 Wildwood Road, N.W.11; 4 September
Dearest Dave,
   Just back the day before yesterday. A most satisfactory Irish stay, during which I got ¾ of 'Chauntecleer' scored − 160 pages of full score in five weeks doesn't seem too bad, does it? Particularly when you add two half-hour broadcasts for make-weight! I'm now working on the two missing dances.
   I had rather assumed that Paul [Pauline Juler] was retiring from the fray (temporarily at any rate) [after her marriage to Bernard Richards]. But much to my surprise she was playing in the broadcast of my Octet on Thursday evening, with the Aeolian Quartet, and playing as beautifully as ever. I tried to ring her up the next morning, to discover what her plans were, but could get no reply, so I just sent her a card to say thank-you. As one can't take up the clarinet for a few weeks and lay it down again (because of the lips) I now assume that she is

taking it up again seriously; in which case I'm sure she would be overjoyed to have a Concerto with strings. However, to turn all obstetric, I have always thought that she was very keen to have children; so if she gets married this month, a simple sum in arithmetic will tell you that she might, perhaps, be somewhat occupied in about a year's time. Would it be possible to leave the matter open for, say, six months, then make the arrangements about a player? I should have thought that that would be plenty of time for booking anybody at that time of year. Then you could get your spies (I'll be in S. Africa, so it will have to be someone else) to keep an eye on Paul's waist-line, so that you can act accordingly.

I should certainly think that Jack Thurston would be better for the job; but I quite see your point about having half-promised it to Paul.

Much love to you all, and best wishes for the Three Choirs. From Howard.

106 Wildwood Road, N.W.11; 2 October

Dearest Dave,

Thank you very much for the copy of 'St Cecilia'. It's good to see her in print – though like you, I feel they might have run to a cover for the poor dear: positively immodest I call it. But the main thing is that it is in print and available for performance, so loud cheers. I feel delighted and proud that my name is at the top. Bless you for putting it there, and for writing such a lovely work.

Much love to all, from Howard.

P.S. Am broadcasting Copland Violin Sonata (which would interest you) Sunday 10th at 6 p.m. 3rd Programme.

106 Wildwood Road, N.W.11; 16 October

Dearest Dave,

Many thanks for your card. Would you care to celebrate Trafalgar Day with the new Lionel Trilling Novel?[3] I've already ordered it, on the strength of that remarkable short story that appeared in Penguin New Writing. So you would be spared all trouble, except, of course, paying the bill!

And talking of trouble could you bear to cast your eyes over these proofs of the Violin Sonata? I've already corrected them; but you'll probably find dozens of mistakes that I've overlooked. If you can do it, I should be most grateful.

Love to all, from H.

I hadn't spotted Kiffer, but now I do so on p.21.

---

[3] Lionel Trilling (1905–1975), American critic. This, *The Middle of the Journey* (1947), was his only novel.

106 Wildwood Road, N.W.11; 31 October

Dearest Dave,

As usual, I'm horrified to find that I should have overlooked twenty mistakes in the proofs of 'Rosebud',[4] and endlessly grateful that you should have discovered them for me before it is too late. Thank you very much indeed for having gone through them so carefully. As I was putting in your corrections I notice quite casually, just to show that we are all (fortunately) human, a beautiful missing clef that both of us had missed! Such is life. Probably there are other little oddments here and there: if so, they'll have to remain. But at least I've been spared 20 heart attacks, thanks to you.

The only query I've done nothing about is about the metronome of the first movement Poco Allegro. I know it is quite illogical to call it a 2/2 and then put crotchet equals 132. My reason is that I don't want it to sound like four beats in a bar; but since it goes into 3/4, and even 5/8, it is rather easier to have a crotchet metronome reference than a minim one.

Of course I'll be delighted to do the proofs of the new 'Dies' parts. But it would have to be before I leave for S. Africa on 16 December, or else after my return at the end of April next. Thank goodness they're going to do them at last.

I have every intention of staying several days when I come on the 10th. Indeed, I had rather thought of staying over until the 15th or 16th, if you will have me? Then we can have a comfortable go at the Gurney songs, without feeling the draught from Time's winged chariot. I may bring some ballet copying with me too.

You'll be pleased to hear that Sadlers Wells show every sign of wanting to do 'Chauntecleer' next season [they didn't]. I had lunch with Guy Warrack on Friday, and found Ursula Moreton [the Director] and John Cranko [a young South African choreographer] in attendance. During lunch they made me tell them what it was all about; then we repaired to the Wells, where I played the whole thing through to them on the most frightful old piano in the Band-room under the stage. I got the impression that they were as enthusiastic and as amused as Lambert [Constant] was bored (and that's saying some!). Then the next day I had a phone call from Warrack to say that all three of them were very keen to do it: this season would be impossible (this suits me down to the ground, because of S. Africa), but they'd like to put it on next season [they didn't], provided they get the O.K. from their finance committee, de Valois, Uncle T and all. So here's hoping. Oddly enough, had they asked me if I had anybody in mind as choreographer, I could only have suggested Cranko as a possibility, so you can guess how pleased I was to find him, as it were, on the doorstep. He's very young, came over from S. Africa a couple of years ago, and did a delightfully amusing little ballet on Debussy's 'Children's Corner'. Yesterday I saw a very short thing of his on [Johann] Strauss's

---

[4] H.F. thought (erroneously) that he would write nothing after his 2nd Violin Sonata. It was to be his 'last word', just as 'Rosebud' was the 'last word' uttered by the eponymous anti-hero of Orson Welles's 1941 film *Citizen Kane*.

'Tritsch-Tratsch Polka', which was absolutely bubbling over with fun; and this confirmed my impression that he was the very person to deal with The Hens, if anybody was going to. I shall try and finish the scoring before I come down on the 10th. Anyway, I'll bring it with me, and inflict the whole thing on your defenceless ears.

Much love to you both, from Howard.

P.S. I don't require 'Calm-Air' until 16 December!

1949

28 Charles Street, Pretoria, S. Africa; 4 January 1949

Dearest Dave and Joy,

First of all, a very happy New Year to you all, and every possible good wish for successful and prosperous work during 1949. Then, thank you a thousand times for sending the photo of Joy's drawing to my Mother and Pu. I had letters from them both this morning, and they are so delighted with it. It was angelic of you to do it. You must let me know what the damage was on my return.

The journey out was fascinating and fantastic. I left Heathrow at 8 a.m. on a Thursday morning, and was met by Nols and Mrs Baron at Johannesburg Airport at 7 p.m. the following evening (Friday). It was quite unbelievable; but not nearly so tiring as I had expected. Nols is looking incredibly well: I've never seen him better. He is really almost black now (with sunburn) and though he doesn't quite enter the H.F. class, he is plumper than one would ever have thought possible. We celebrated with a wonderful meal in Johannesburg – melon, gigantic STEAKS, and strawberries and cream! – then drove the 40 odd miles to Pretoria, where I was most warmly welcomed by the rest of the family. Since then I have been lazing, eating, reading, sleeping and basking in the wonderful sunshine, with only an occasional thought for my luckless friends shivering in frost-bound England.

In about three weeks time I shall be going to Durban for ten days; then down to join Nols again at the Cape for the rest of my stay. During the whole of my time I shall be doing at least ten broadcasts; but as this only involves four separate programmes, I don't think it will be unduly exhausting.

Back, I think, by the Warwick Castle, which leaves Cape Town on 8 April and arrives at Southampton about the 22nd. Nols, alas, will not be coming with me, for he has accepted the post of Senior Lecturer at Cape Town University. I can't make up my mind whether this is a good thing or not: from some points of view it is, for it will bring him £900 a year (with the usual University holidays) and give him something regular to do; but I would have been happier if he could have had another year or so in England before taking it on. However, it may work out all right; and he still seems determined to come back to England at some stage of the proceedings. One thing is that he seems to like being in the

Cape better than any other part of the country, and it certainly seems to agree with him from the health point of view.

The 'Christmas Cantata' [Nols'] was broadcast twice on Christmas Day: once on the 'A' programme (English) and once on the 'B' (Afrikaans). Both were on records. The performance was far from being first class, for the choir was obviously too small, the soloists inadequate (with the exception of Betsy de la Porte), and the orchestra tatty; but one managed to get a reasonable idea of the work — specially the second time round, when one had got used to the standard, or rather lack of it, of the performance. On the whole, I found it less exciting and less individual than the Five Elegies [for String Quartet]: but it is an impressive work, and has many moments of great beauty. The only thing I found definitely unsatisfactory was the final movement, which is a note for note recapitulation of the opening. I think Nols agrees that it will have to be considerably altered: it wants to be shortened and build up to a much bigger climax than it reaches at present; then it will really finish the work, instead of just stopping it. What do you think about The Three Choirs? Would John (or anyone else) be interested in it? It lasts about an hour, or just under, is well written for voices, though not altogether easy. Soloists required: Alto (Mary), Baritone (Evangelist), Tenor (Gabriel), and a rather less important part for a Prophet (Bass), and three Prophetesses (SSA). Orchestra: double woodwind, 4 horns, 3 trumpets, tuba, piano, celesta, harp, percussion and strings. If there were any chance of using it, I would make an English translation [it's in Afrikaans] while I am out here; but I don't want to take time unnecessarily, needless to say!

Enough for the present. Nols particularly asks me to send you all his love; he is planning to write himself, but perhaps a kiss in the hand is worth two in the problematic future! Much love to you all, from Howard.

106 Wildwood Road, N.W.11; 24 April

Dearest Dave,

Back yesterday, to find all well here and this wonderful Spring weather. How glorious everything is looking.

I'd love to come down one weekend to tell you all my traveller's tales. How about 13 May? — unless any complication (unexpected) turns up. Next weekend I'll probably be in Belfast just for a couple of days, if I can get things straightened up by then, so the 30th wouldn't be any good. If Belfast falls through, or I can't get a seat on a plane, I'll let you know, so that you may have the bed here, if you'd care for it.

Much love to you and Joy, and Kiffer, Nigel and Ian, from Howard.

P.S. Jack [O'Brien of the Griller String Quartet] has just flown out to California to join the others.

106 Wildwood Road, N.W.11; 3 Mary
Yes, of course I'd give £5 for the R.O. score, if it's being done. Ask Mervyn
Roberts too (Bryn Aber, Abergele, N. Wales).[1]

106 Wildwood Road, N.W.11; 10 May
[Dearest Dave]
   It appears that Robert [Irwin] can only come on the Sunday. I've asked him
to let you know what train, and so on, so that he can be met.
   That being so, I'll come by the Friday train leaving Paddington 10.45,
arriving Newbury 12.13. Let me know whether you'll be in town for the
shopping, or whether you want me to come up by bus to Doiley Bottom. I can
let you have a gallon of petrol [it was still rationed] if you are in dire distress.
Love to you both, Howard.

106 Wildwood Road, N.W.11; 17 May
Dearest Joy,
   It is really splendid of you to have done that drawing of Pu. I'm so pleased
with it, and so grateful to you, for I feel you've caught her most convincingly –
besides, of course, having produced a very beautiful drawing. Will the enclosed
cheque help towards the damage? £1.8.6. is for the frame, and the rest a very
poor recompense for your trouble. I only wish it could be something nearer
what the drawing is worth, both to me and in itself. Much love, from Howard.

106 Wildwood Road, N.W.11; 27 May
Dearest Dave,
   No, I don't know of any edition of the Mozart 'Adagio & Fugue', K.546, that
has the double-bass part printed – unless it is like that in the Breitkopf
Gesammtausgabe, which I can't call to mind. Koechel says that a facsimile of
the Fugue autograph has been published in something called 'Musica Viva'
(April 1936), whatever that may be. He also remarks that 'Beethoven wrote out
the fugue himself in score. At the end of the autograph (whose? Beethoven's or
Mozart's) one finds the bass part divided into Violoncelli and Contra Basso –
proof that Mozart also had an orchestral performance in mind. [It is thus in
Mozart's autograph, in the British Library.] If you want further information I'm
sure A. Hyatt King of the BM would give it to you. Or you could always get a
photostat of the MS from them: it's only 18 pages long.
   See you on the 3rd at 3.30. Love, Howard.

---

[1] Mervyn Roberts (1906–1990), Welsh composer. Pupil of Gordon Jacob and R.O. Morris at
   the Royal College of Music. O.U.P. was prepared to publish an R.O. Morris score if
   subsidized.

106 Wildwood Road, N.W.11; 17 July

Dearest Dave,

So glad you didn't already have 'Broken Images'.[2] I gather that it is his first book; but it's certainly outstanding, and he seems to be a born writer.

Good for the finale of the Clarinet Concerto. I hope the first movement soon gets closed up too. Interesting about Kenneth Leighton:[3] I'll look forward to seeing and hearing his things.

Sonata No.2 [H.F.'s] is being broadcast (believe it or not) on the Third Programme on Tuesday 26th at 10.40 by Yfrah and self. Then we are going over to Paris to broadcast it again on the 28th. Back on the 29th, and to Belfast on the 5th August, and to Edinburgh on the 1st September for a week at the Festival with Ceddy and Bruno; so it looks as though I won't be here (alas) for The Three Choirs rehearsal. However, perhaps we can introduce Kiffer to the recording machine [purchased in South Africa] at some other time. The only snag is that it wouldn't be easy to record speech unawares. Music, yes; but for speech you have to be only about a foot away from the microphone, which therefore remains somewhat apparent. Love to you both, H.

14 Deramore Park South, Belfast; 23 August

Dearest Dave,

The enclosed [G.F. part songs] were done on the N. Ireland Home Service this evening. They were sung surprisingly well and with real understanding, and I think you would have enjoyed them. (Incidentally, they did the Drummond ones first.)

Sorry you missed the broadcast of my Violin Sonata [No.2]. It went really well – though I say it as shouldn't – and Rostal immediately wrote to say that he's going to put it in his repertoire.

Can you let me have some sort of copy of the new Hardy set ['Before and After Summer'] later on, if, as I think, Robert [Irwin] and I do them at Broadway for Toty's birthday on 23 September?

How goes the Clarinet Concerto? Love to all, Howard.

106 Wildwood Road, N.W.11; 14 October

Dearest Dave,

I don't know who is Dayme's [Dr Emily Daymond] executor; but I'm sure there wouldn't be the least harm in addressing an enquiry about the other volume of [Parry's] 'Instinct and Character' to: The Executor of the late E.D., 17 Carew Road, Eastbourne. You could say she had offered to let you have it;

---

[2] A book, not as yet identified, about plastic surgery and wartime injuries. Not, however, Richard Hillary's *The Last Enemy* (1942).
[3] Kenneth Leighton (1929–1988), English composer. A pupil of Petrassi (after Oxford University), he became Reid Professor of Music at Edinburgh University in 1970.

then, if it turned out she made other arrangements in her Will, they would just tell you so. No harm would be done. May Harrison told me that she [Emily Daymond] had had another stroke, and that she was more or less in a coma towards the end. Anyway, it was all easy and untroubled, and that was what the poor old dear was longing for. I went down to Brighton for the cremation yesterday afternoon. There were only a dozen of us (I knew none of the others) in the hideous little chapel; but the sun shone brightly outside, and I was glad I had gone. Love to you both, from Howard.

106 Wildwood Road, N.W.11; 17 October

Dearest Dave,

It's certainly a magnificent set ['Earth and Air and Rain'], and it was good — for once in a way — to hear it from the outside. But I'm sorry our Robert [Irwin] wasn't in better voice. All the understanding was there, as one would expect; but he was too often just under the note and uncertain in his line. A pity, for he can do it so much better than that. Let's hope he does at the next broadcast! In the meantime, all the congratulations are yours. Love, H.

106 Wildwood Road, N.W.11; 28 December

Dearest Dave,

Right, I'll get the dope for you when the R.A.M. opens again. The Mendelssohn is, I believe, not an R.A.M. scholarship though it is administered by them: that is to say, it enables one to study abroad or anywhere, and this mightn't suit [Kenneth] Leighton from the deferment point of view. Or would it? Anyway, I think it is being competed-for in 1950 (it's two or three-yearly, isn't it?), so that wouldn't do for him. So many of these scholarships are not annual; which probably accounts for Mr Parrott's reply.

I saw Thurston Dart a few weeks before Christmas and spoke to him about 'Pilgrim's Progress'.[4] He completely agreed with our point of view, and promised to get in touch with Hadley about it. This, I gather, has now been done, with satisfactory results. So if nothing goes amiss we should see it, where it ought to be, at Covent Garden. Let's hope so. I was very insistent that no mention of Covent Garden should be made to Uncle Ralph, and I think they realized the importance of this.

Happy new year to you all and much love, from H.

---

[4] Vaughan Williams' opera *The Pilgrim's Progress* was eventually produced (rather badly) at Covent Garden on 26 April, 1951.

1950

106 Wildwood Road, N.W.11; 9 January

Dearest Dave,

What a nice surprise for a Monday morning! It's a great relief to know that Mr Leslie Boosey's 'problem' has finally been solved (at 7/6),[1] and good to see the Stanley out too [G.F.'s edition of one of John Stanley's Concertos]. Many thanks for both: I'm so very glad to have them.

'The Young Man' ['A Young Man's Exhortation' sung by William Herbert and played by Ernest Lush] came through beautifully on Saturday. I thought Lush played really well throughout; and Herbert is a pleasing singer – though I do wish his voice didn't just conk out below E a 3rd above middle C.

Did you hear 'St Nicholas' [Britten] later the same evening? God, what twaddle!

Love to all and again very many thanks, from H.

106 Wildwood Road, N.W.11; 23 January

Dearest Dave,

By the oddest coincidence, Bob Dart said to me quite out of the blue when I saw him on Thursday last how very much he'd like to meet you sometime, as he admires your music. As figured basses are just up his street, couldn't we kill two birds with one stone and arrange a meeting between the two of you? At present he is either in, or on the way back from Paris, having played Continuo in all the Brandenburgs for Boyd Neel. So, if you say the word, I'll drop him a line to Cambridge and find out what he can manage in the way of time and place. Two possibilities suggest themselves. Either you come and meet him in London; or I bring him down to Ashmansworth for the night. Let me know which you would prefer. One advantage about the latter is that Joy would meet him too, and I think she'd be intrigued. But it shall be as you wish and find most convenient. I was going to send him a copy of Stanley No.3 this week anyway, so I'll send along your queries at the same time, then he can turn the whole thing over in his mind.

At a Composers' Guild committee meeting on Friday I saw Guy Warrack, who told me that The Wells have turned down 'Chauntecleer' [my ballet]. Cranko, who was going to do the choreography, doesn't find the story really congenial, 'and animal ballets are so difficult anyway'. It seems to me that both these objections could very well have been produced over a year ago. Guy said that Cranko liked the music and wondered whether I would be interested in

---

[1] Leslie Boosey was more at home with popular ballets, and less at ease when deciding on an appropriate sales price for the kind of songs that Finzi wrote.

doing another ballet with him. I replied, a trifle acidly I'm afraid, that it rather depended on the story! – though, quite honestly, I would like to do a ballet with him sometime or other, between you and the wall. I suppose the next move must be to find out whether the Rambert people would be interested in The Hens. If not, I don't think there is much else to be done. The music depends too much on the story to be really satisfactory for anything else. All very tiresome, isn't it?

Let me know about the Dart meeting on a postcard and I'll make the necessary arrangements. Much love to you both, from Howard.

106 Wildwood Road, N.W.11; 26 January

Dearest Dave,

Bob Dart would love to come to Ashmansworth for the night; but he can't manage either 2nd or 3rd of February. Would either weekend of 18th or 25th February be possible for you and Joy? If you could manage one or the other, I'd suggest that Bob and I come down by an early Sunday afternoon train, and that we pick you up either before, during or after your rehearsal (I have those Banderlog [a café in Newbury] cakes in mind!). Let me know how this strikes you both, and I'll make arrangements accordingly.

Nothing special to forewarn you about; I merely thought Joy would find him interesting. He started off as a mathematician (he's much too clever!), did a mathematical job during the war in the R.A.F., is now a lecturer in music at Cambridge and an excellent harpsichordist and clavichordist. His period is really pre-Bach; but he seems to know the hell of a lot about later stuff too. He's just as fond of food as I am, and is a much better cook! But, so far as I have discovered, he has no quirks about leeks, cold shaving-water, or anything like that. His eyes definitely brightened when I told him your house was both comfortable and warm; but even if it had been as cold as the Pole he would still have wanted to meet you.

I had lunch yesterday with Jack Henderson [of Boosey and Hawkes]. It seems, from something he said, that The Wells may really be going to commission another ballet from me, for 1951. Let's hope he's right.

Let me have a postcard about the weekends. Love to you both, from H.

P.S. Monday 6th was no good either.

106 Wildwood Road, N.W.11; 6 February

Dear[est Dave]

Hurrah! Bob can manage the weekend of 18 March and so can I. So shall we come by the 6 o'clock train, have dinner on it, and hope that you will meet us at Newbury station?

Bob says it would be a bit complicated to write about your queries, and please may he wait and do it by word of mouth when you meet? Love, H.

Fascinating about the Boyce business [a volume of William Boyce edited by G.F. for Musica Britannica].

106 Wildwood Road, N.W.11; 5 June

Dearest Dave,

Herewith the Brigands[2] with one or two notes and queries. 'Nocturne' (New Year Music) is a much better title than the reverse, so do get them to alter it. Also, add timing on p.1, unless it is given elsewhere. Also make them let you see the inside-title with Instrumentation, as with all those alternatives there are sure to be mistakes!

The 'Chauntecleer Suite' is not for any particular performance; but now the thing is done – 116 pages lasting 15 minutes – it is ready if required.

The O of song is enchanting.[3] But alas, being no solver of Crosswords I can't understand a word of it. Love to you both, from H.

P.S. Augener have the plates of our Full-Score paper. Send them a sheet of yours when ordering, otherwise no password necessary.

as from 106 Wildwood Road, N.W.11; 20 August

Dearest Dave,

Back to London tomorrow (after five weeks of almost unremitting rain), so I'll be able to get to the rehearsals for the Three Choirs in London [of G.F.'s 'Intimations of Immortality'] after all. For which I'm very glad. Could you drop me a card to say when they are? Also, what our address in Gloucester will be, and when you plan to get there. I have a Home Service broadcast with Yfrah late on the 30th, but am free after that – so far as I know.

Hope all goes well with you, and that you are safely delivered of the Full Score [of 'Intimations of Immortality']. Is the Vocal Score out yet? Love to all, from Howard.

P.S. Did I celebrate the Quatorze Juillet this year? I was away at Glyndebourne at the time, and can't for the life of me remember whether I did anything about it before leaving. If not, any ideas?

106 Wildwood Road, N.W.11; 10 September

Dearest Dave and Joy,

It was a glorious Festival party and I enjoyed every minute of it. All thanks to you both for being the mainspring thereof. And thanks, too, for allowing Stuart [Stuart Elliot of Cambridge] to bounce in and out as he wished: it made a great difference to someone who might otherwise have been rather on his own.

'Intimations' was a tremendously moving experience. It is a most lovely

---

[2] Not identified. Presumably a book, or even a composition?
[3] Probably an ingenious crossword clue that had amused Finzi.

work, and seems to me far and away the biggest thing you've done; not in size only, of course, but in conception, breadth of vision, and sheer accomplishment. And so much of it has an ecstatic lyric beauty that brings one near to tears, besides and within the larger framework. It's a magnificent achievement and (for me at least) it knocked the other new works into the middle of next week. Many, many congratulations on it.

I meant to ask whether – if I haven't already given you something – you'd like Churchill Vol.3 or the Foss 'V.W.' Do let me know, or make some other suitable suggestion.

Did you see about Ralph Hawkes [his death]? He may have been (I always suspected he was) a little bit of a rogue; but God help the firm – and us – without him.

Again all my thanks to you both for this last week. With love to you both, C and N,[4] from Howard.

___

[4] Christopher and Nigel Finzi.

1951

106 Wildwood Road, N.W.11; 4 January

Dearest Dave,

I don't know what to say about the opening of the Clarinet Concerto (G.F.'s). The only time I heard it in the flesh – at Oxford – the opening in particular struck me as being tremendously exciting and impressive. It would therefore never have occurred to me that anything wanted doing to it. The cellos and basses might certainly make it more exciting; but I don't really feel I know enough of string orchestral writing to say this with any certainty. Why not try them at the next performance and see whether it sounds more to your liking that way?

Finished another movement (the third) of the Piano Concerto the other day. Up to St Andrews next week for a long weekend with Ceddy & Bruno, and a talk to the Music Club on 'Bach's Lute Music and the Keyboard'. Then home to try to get on with the first movement [written last], about which I've had no further ideas.

Much love to all of you, and every possible good wish for 1951. Ever, Howard.

106 Wildwood Road, N.W.11; 30 January

Dearest Dave,

So glad you and Joy were able to listen on Friday last. Many thanks for your card. Oddly enough, I quite enjoyed myself too, for there were more right notes than I had any reason to expect! Also, I was just in the mood.

Menotti? But he isn't here yet, is he? Certainly 'The Consul', which is the name of the opera, hasn't yet come on, for I would have noticed about the 1st performance in the papers. nor is there any sign of it in the theatre advertisements. But I seem to remember reading some time ago that [Laurence] Olivier was bringing it over to the St James, so at least Menotti will be better looked after than last time. I'd love to go with you and J, and will certainly let you know if I hear of any party in the air.

I've already read the Wedgwood ['Social History of England'] and thought it first-rate.

I'd very much like to show you the beginning of the first movement of the [Piano] Concerto, to see whether you think it fits with the rest. Would this weekend be a possibility? If so, I could pick you up at your rehearsal in Newbury on Saturday afternoon, and flit back to town on Sunday evening. But if this is inconvenient, just say so.

Love to you both, from Howard.

106 Wildwood Road, N.W 11; 24 February

Dearest Dave,

I've just been reading scores for The Prevention of Cruelty[1] and came across a short work for Strings (about 5 minutes, I would think) called 'Pieta', by one John Buckland. I know nothing of him; but the card says Age 32, Studied R.C.M. and privately with Alan Rawsthorne; has written incidental music for two dozen B.B.C. programmes, ranging from solo flute to orchestra and singers. Present Occupation: farm labourer (!). A Concerto for Flute & Strings is also mentioned, though I haven't seen this. It looks to me very good, natural string writing — in the way that Tony's is, but without any of the knobs to bark your shins on — and I believe it would be reasonably easy to play, so I thought you might be interested. I'll add his address to the bottom of this letter on Monday morning, in case you'd like to get in touch with him. Love, Howard.

106 Wildwood Road, N.W.11; 14 April

Dearest Dave,

I feel very strongly that Version 2 [of the libretto of 'In Terra Pax'] is the better. It makes a most lovely little work and is perfect as it stands — with the possible addition '. . . on earth peace, goodwill towards men' for pp women's voices at the end. Two things in Version 1 are weak: the repetition of the 4th verse at the end; and the excitement and climax of the 3rd verse, which would kill the Luke extract stone dead. Furthermore, four verses delay Luke too long and turn it from centrepiece (which it should be) into an afterthought.

The title is very difficult. 'Noel' is apt, but suggests Walford Davies or Eric

---

[1] Society for the Promotion of New Music. Founded by Francis Chagrin, it began work in 1943 with Vaughan Williams and Arthur Bliss as its President and Vice President.

Thiman; 'Pax hominibus' possible; 'Fared I forth alone' not very indicative; 'A Frosty Christmas Eve' too wordy. Of your suggestions I prefer 'Pax hominibus'. The only alternative I can think of at the moment is 'Christmas Eve' plain and unadorned.

The Morley is enchanting. Thanks so much for sending it. Whoever is George Rowland of Oxford? I've never heard of him.

It's just possible I'll be going to 'The Pilgrim' [R.V.W.'s *The Pilgrim's Progress* on the 30th instead of the 26th. Love to you all from Howard.

106 Wildwood Road, N.W.11; 1 June

Dearest Dave,

Yes, I have a Full Score of the Piano Concerto [H.F.'s] for you, but have been holding it back until the Cadenza was ready. This should be duplicated by next week, when I'll send the lot off to you. It takes 27 minutes. Did I tell you that Dicky Butt *is* doing both it and Tony Scott's 'Symphonietta' at Cambridge on either 1 or 2 August? The Belfast performance [of the Concerto] on 22 June is being broadcast, but only from Belfast, I think. Alas I couldn't do 22 November, as I shall be in Inverness (!). Why not ask Clive Lythgoe (250 Worple Road, West Wimbledon, S.W.20), who's playing it [the Piano Concerto] in Cambridge? He's good, young and worth encouraging. I could do it with you in October.

About parts: they have already been written on master-sheets. Could you ask Jack H at Boosey & Hawkes to have the right number duplicated for you (I don't know how many you would require), then come to some arrangement about buying them from him, for B&H are only having them for hire under normal circumstances. The duplication of the set for Belfast (8.6.5.4.2) came to £9.11.9, so that will give you some idea of how much they'd be.

Chenhalls [Accountant] never did send me a reminder in April (I should have thought the Income Tax demand was reminder enough!), but I'm sure they'd do so if you asked them.

Yes, do send Stanley [Concerto] No.2 now. I'll try and get the proofs done before I go to Belfast on the 18th.

I haven't seen Mr Redlich's effusion yet.[2] Love to you both, from Howard.

P.S. Sorry you won't be at 'Hamlet'.

106 Wildwood Road, N.W.11; 14 July

Dearest Dave,

Many thanks for card. I would be enormously grateful for 'Musica Antiqua' of October 1909 and April 1913. The rest of your trove I already have. Let me know how much they were. Love, H. Again, Happy Returns.

[2] See letter 5 October 1951.

14 Deramore Park South, Belfast; 1 September

Dearest Dave,

Many thanks for your letter. So sorry to have missed the Three Choirs rehearsals, but I don't get back to London until Monday next, the 3rd. I hope all went well.

Tiresome about Aylesbury. They were trying to fix the 1st London performance for December, which would have made everything O.K.; but I've just heard today from Jackie [of B&H] to say that it will have to be April next. I don't see why this should block a performance outside London, but doubtless he has his reasons. We must ask him when he gets back from his holiday in Italy.

None of the Breitkopf scores of the Mozart Piano Concertos, late or early, show figured-bass notes, or figures in the keyboard part. (I only speak from memory, but I'm pretty sure.) But I don't know that they are to be wholly relied upon. I seem to remember a lot of blaa about it in the Introduction to one of the Eulenburg scores of the late Concertos (perhaps 'The Coronation'?), in which a single bass line is certainly printed in the keyboard part during the tuttis (without figuring, I'm almost certain); but I have a sort of idea that the blaa gets lost or distorted in the translation. I believe there is also something similar in the more recent Peters reprints of some of the Concertos: perhaps the ones edited by Fischer or Soldan? Anyway, it would be worth having a look.

Maddening that they aren't broadcasting 'Intimations' on Tuesday. All possible good wishes for it. Alas I shall be in *Israel* on 6 December. Do you think I ought to be circumcised specially for the occasion?

Love to you both, the boys, Shashy, Stuart, and any other nice people that may be around and about, from Howard.[3]

P.S. I've just written three songs! [of the 'Discovery' cycle, Op.13]. What about those very early Mozart Concertos − arrangements of J.C. Bach, etc., of which you have the scores?

106 Wildwood Road, N.W.11; 14 September

Dearest Dave,

By all means come up here (all of you) on the 20th if you can fit it in. You can only get into the South Bank [Festival of Britain] on a concert-ticket from 7 o'clock onwards; before that you'll have to pay, I think 4/− each extra − which seems rather a waste unless you are going to spend longer than you plan at present. You can certainly eat there cheaply. 'The Thameside Restaurant', which is under Waterloo Bridge and jutting over the river, would be the place. But perhaps a better solution might be to eat somewhere outside at about 6 o'clock, go into the Exhibition at 7.0 on your concert-ticket, and spend the hour

---

[3] 'Sashy' is Richard Shirley Smith (painter and engraver). Stuart is Stuart Elliot, a friend from Cambridge.

between then and the concert looking round the sights. You are also allowed to stray round after the concert; and if it is a fine evening the pretty lights are well worth seeing. If you want to see more of the Exhibition than this implies, it wouldn't be worth coming up to Wildwood Road. So you pays your money (in one case literally) and takes your choice.

I can easily put on the infernal machine – but not without them realizing that something is happening, for you have to speak into the microphone. Playing can be done wholly unawares, but not speaking.

Oddly enough, Bob [Thurston Dart] was here when your letter arrived. He has an article in some stodgy German periodical on the Continuo in Mozart's Piano Concertos, which he is going to send me; then I can tell you what the relevant passages are about. He himself suggests that the reason for the use of continuo in later works, long after the tutti was complete without, may be that the person at the keyboard, who was also the conductor, used the figuring as a check on the correctness of the orchestral playing, since he hadn't a Full Score to follow. This sounds a possible explanation. The chitchat in the Eulenburg Ed of K.537, which I referred to in my letter from Ireland, is as follows: 'At the beginning of each movement is printed a note reading, Technical reasons have made it necessary to omit the Klavier as Thorough-bass Instrument: but see the foreward'. And the incomparable English of the Foreword reads, 'Throughout in the *tutti*, even if they interrupt the soli only for a few bars, it is allotted the part of thorough bass accompaniment which, for technical reasons, could unfortunately not be shown in the score. Throughout Andrés' edition in parts, a single-voiced bass (without figures) is printed in the piano in the tutti.'

Let me know about 20th. Love H.

106 Wildwood Road, N.W.11; 5 October

Dearest Dave,

The magazine Bob sent me, 'Die Musikforschung', is of no interest from the point of view of figured-bass in Mozart Piano Concertos. But he also enclosed an article by your friend Hans F. Redlich on 'Mozart's C minor Piano Concerto', taken from 'Music Review'. I can't tell the date of issue, for the pages have just been cut out. You probably know it already; if not, it would be worth looking at. Even more important, if one could get hold of it, would be the book he mentions: Hans Brunner's 'Die Entwicklung des Klavier Koncertos bis Mozart', 1906; which, he says, deals with the Basso Continuo function of the solo piano in Mozart's Concertos, and links them historically with typical specimens of the earlier 18th cent. But short of the BM, I don't know where you'd find a copy. [I now have one.] Once found, how are you going to read it? Oh dear, ain't life difficult. Love H.

106 Wildwood Road, N.W.11; 3 November

Dearest Dave,

Many thanks for your letter. How brilliant of you to notice that missing natural to the B, in the 2nd movement [of H.F.'s Piano Concerto], 3 bars after 3, r.h. I'm so used to playing it that I would never have thought of it. Please put it into the proofs.

The other query (crotchet or quaver chords in 1st movement, 19 & 23) I feel less certain about. On the whole, I think leave them as they are. I don't mind if the beginning of the Piano semiquavers are a bit masked; but I *would* mind if the weight of the string chords was reduced.

If there are no further queries, perhaps you would send the proofs back to Rosen [at Boosey & Hawkes] direct. But if there are any doubtful points, could you possibly let me have them during this coming week? I'll be in Scotland 12– 22 and would like, if possible, to have it all cleared up before I go. You're a saint to have done them so thoroughly, and I'm most grateful. Very many thanks.

I'm still too near the work [the Piano Concerto] to have any idea whether the 1st movement is out of the top drawer or not. But I feel that it and the rest of the work more or less solves the problem of a satisfactory relationship between soloist and strings, which was one of the main things that bothered me.

Ytrah and I flit off to Israel on, I think, 30 November. We'll be there until about 20 December, and I shall most likely stay for a fortnight in Rome on the way back: thus I should be back in London about 5 or 6 January.

I've got a ticket for the service at St. Sepulchre's on the 22nd [for G.F.'s new Anthem: 'God is gone up'], and will hope to see you there. (But not for the Lunch.)

Love, and again my thanks, from H.

106 Wildwood Road, N.W.11; 25 November

Dearest Dave,

I enjoyed the Anthem enormously at St. Sepulchre's t'other day. But why is it that choirs (however good) and organists always fillet the music they perform by removing every trace of rhythmic bone from it? The journey from Scotland almost got the better of me during the Sermon and the Green anthem[4] (dreary!); otherwise the whole Service was a jolly affair. If we've got to have that sort of thing, let it at least be as full of Popery, copery and jiggery-pokery as possible. Sorry not to see you afterwards; but I had to get back here for lunch.

Off to Israel on 1 December and back here from Rome shortly after 1 January.

Much love to all of you for Christmas, from H.

[4] Perhaps one of the 103 anthems by Maurice Greene (1696–1755)?

1952

106 Wildwood Road, N.W.11; 4 January

Dearest Dave,

Rumour, as so often happens, hath it partly correct. It was the journey *from* Israel that got delayed, not thither. Our plane was hit by lightning on its way from Teheran – that is, *before* we got on it! It came down for repairs in Cyprus, and waited there for five days for a couple of new engines from England. (When plane schedules go wrong they do it in the grand manner.) What time I sat biting my nails in Israel, first for two-and-a-half days at Lydda Airport and then for a further three days in Tel Aviv. By that time I was in such a chronic state of nerves from uncertainty that I decided to cut out Italy altogether and come straight back to England as soon as the plane turned up. (I wanted to be back here by the 1st January anyway.) But it wasn't as easy as all that. The plane finally left Lydda on the morning of the 23rd; but when we reached Rome that afternoon they broke it to us that northern Europe was shrouded in fog and that we'd have to stay there the night. In spite of everything, I wasn't sorry to see Rome for a night at B.O.A.C.'s expense; and it also enabled me to pick up my letters! It's such a wonderful-looking city that I feel I must go back there at the first opportunity; but preferably in Spring or Autumn, and without the prelude of a six-days-thwarted plane journey. Eventually we left Rome at 8 o'clock on the morning of Christmas Eve, and reached Heathrow without further mishap shortly after noon. Pu nearly had a fit when I phoned her.

Israel was enormous fun. For the first ten days the sun shone ceaselessly. When not actually playing, we were able to pick oranges from the trees and watch the people bathing. Then the skies opened. One evening we arrived back from a concert to find our hotel in darkness, the storm having blown away all the electric-light cables. Later, one half of Tel Aviv was cut off from the other by floods. So no wonder the plane services were a bit upset.

Musically, we enjoyed ourselves greatly. Besides the concerts with Yfrah, I did a recording for the Radio of the Piano Concerto and the 2nd Violin Sonata. The Concerto went particularly well, under a young Czech conductor called Zamenek, who was painstaking, enthusiastic and very musical. The first performance [of the Concerto] over here, by the way, is at the Festival Hall on 29 May with Auntie [Myra Hess], the L.P.O. and Adrian [Boult]. Do come if you can, both of you, and lend moral support to your old friend. Two days later, on the 31st, it's being done on the Third Prog.

How useful to get a parcel of food from Nols. His address is 9 Serpentine Road, Oranjezicht, Cape Town, S. Africa. The dear boy sent me a volume of the Oxford History of Music with the inside cut out, and the space neatly filled with cigars!

All well here. A happy New Year to all of you, with love from Howard.

106 Wildwood Road, N.W.11; 21 February

Dearest Dave,

At least it's the 21st, even if not October! The Tovey ['Life' by Mary Grierson] at a quick glance looks fascinating, and I'm so grateful for it. Very many thanks indeed. Thank God it wasn't done by Foss. (Have you heard, by the way, that both he and Herbert Murrill have had the same operation as the King? Not a very good look-out for either of them.) The more I look at his V.W. book the more deplorable it seems.

Lovely to see you both on Monday evening last. It was an interesting and enjoyable concert. But I do wish someone would curb [Kenneth] Leighton's not-so-heavenly length.

Once again, very many thanks for the most welcome book. Love to you both, from H.

106 Wildwood Road, N.W.11; 26 February

Dearest Dave,

Bless my heart! And I didn't even know you were contemplating anything for unaccompanied male voices ['Thou did'st delight my eyes']. It's a lovely song and most welcome. Thanks so much for it. It must be the hell of a medium to write in. But have you ever tried to write for the *Guitar*? That really is a corker. When I was in Israel I met Segovia, who asked if I would write something for him; and as I have nothing big on hand at the moment, I thought it might be fun to try 2 or 3 short pieces. Julian Bream showed me how 'the wheels go round', and now I'm trying to do some homework for him [nothing came of this]. It's rather a lark, though distinctly restricted.

Love to you both, from H.

106 Wildwood Road, N.W.11; 5 March

Dearest Dave and Joy,

I do hope you won't mind my having given your name, address and phone number to Julian Bream, the guitar player. He's an extraordinary child, and I think you might both find him fascinating. He's being hurled into an Army camp near Devizes this week, and is taking with him his ancient Austin 7 whose van-like back is packed with guitars, lutes, vihuelas and whatnot. He hopes to be able to escape occasionally in this and find somewhere to practise. As the noise from these instruments can scarcely be heard from one room to the next, I thought you might possibly be able to put up with him for an odd afternoon, so that he can do a little work. I don't think he'd disturb you in any way – unless his conversation should have the fatal attraction of the sirens' song. But if it should be a bore or inconvenient, just say No. Incidentally, he makes the most heavenly noise on the guitar and is always delighted to show how the wheels go round; so Dave might pick his brains, as I have done already. If, therefore, a very Cockney voice rings you on the phone one day, you'll know who to blame for it. But give it at least a trial, for I think you might find it as entertaining as I do. Love, H.

106 Wildwood Road, N.W.11; 8 March

Dearest Dave,

Alas, the weekend of 16th is no good for me. Would the following one, after your night with Tony and Ruth, be any use? I've got to give a Bach talk to the Phil. Arts Club on Tuesday 25th, 7.30 p.m., but am free till then. Or any time 27–31? Sorry not to hear the Wind Ensemble. That would have been fun. Love, H.

106 Wildwood Road, N.W.11; 20 June

Dearest Dave,

Starting on the principal note wouldn't really help. If you want to avoid the 5th (which I don't myself mind) the only thing would be to do the following [on MS paper]. Perhaps this is in any case the better solution; and it would certainly save you from the reproving fingers of the purists!

Strawberries? They sound wonderful. But the only time I could manage would be the weekend 5 July, on the way back from Glyndebourne, when I'd have a boy-friend (the charming Donald Dunbar) [from South Africa] in tow. Besides, the strawberries might be over by then. What think you? Love to both, from H.

106 Wildwood Road, N.W.11; 21 July

Dearest Dave,

This seems a mean little book to give you for 14 July. But of those you suggested it was the only one the Times Book Club had in stock; so I took it, willy-nilly. (I got the impression you were not particularly keen about the Frank Martin score.) A quick glance suggests that you may like to have it [the book] in spite of its meagre size.

The broadcast came over very well last night. The various movements [G.F.'s Suite from 'Love's Labour's Lost' music] are charming individually; but I'm not so sure they add up into a satisfactory Suite. There seems too little variety emotionally and (particularly) rhythmically in the middle ones. The first is O.K. as an opening – though it sounded rather more bit-y than I had expected from looking at the score – and the last first-rate as an end. But the three soliloquies are too much of a muchness coming together: particularly when followed by the next piece (name forgotten) which, though unmuted, has much the same rhythmic feeling. Even 'Moth' is not so strong a contrast as I would have expected. It seems to me that there is a danger of falling between two stools in trying to make the music serve as both a quarry for stage use and a self-contained Suite for concert performance. If you must print all the music, would it perhaps be possible to add a note to the score suggesting the omission of one (or two) of the soliloquies when the work is played as a concert suite? The two songs are excellent in themselves; but, again, I felt they were completely out of place in a Suite. Scoring sounded wholly satisfactory throughout, as far as one could tell on the radio.

Hope you had fun at Cheltenham. Were Toty and Dorothy there? It is such ages since I have heard from them. Love to you both, from H.

P.S. Sashie [Richard Shirley-Smith] had to have his appendix out quite suddenly on Friday last. He's getting on fine now.

How about the following order for Suite?: 1) Opening; 2) a Soliloquy; 3) Moth; 4) another Soliloquy; 5) movement whose name I've forgotten; 6) finale. With, as appendix, the remaining Soliloquy for stage (or separate) use only.

14 Deramore Park South, Belfast; 22 August

Dearest Dave,

Could you possibly cast your eye over these 'Discovery' [H.F.'s song-cycle] proofs? If so I should be most grateful. I've been over them very carefully, so I don't think there should be many mistakes – but you never know! If you find anything obvious, please just correct it; then send the lot on to our Mr Rosen at 295 Regent Street. Don't bother to return them to me unless absolutely necessary for really doubtful points. I'll be back at Wildwood Road from 31 August: till then, I'm here in Belfast. I hope all is well with all of you. With love from, H.

106 Wildwood Road, N.W.11; 1 September

Dearest Dave,

Blessings for having looked over the proofs [of 'Discovery'] (and to C. [Christopher] for those two missing slurs!); I wouldn't have inflicted them on you had I known you were up to the eyes in a Magnificat.

Just got back from Belfast yesterday. I envy you having heard 'The Highland Fair' [music by Cedric Davie, at the Edinburgh Festival]. Was it fun?

Love to all at St Andrews [where G.F. was outside-examiner] and to yourself, from H.

106 Wildwood Road, N.W.11; 10 September

Dearest Dave,

So glad to get my copy of 'God is gone up' [anthem by G.F.]; very many thanks for it. It's a good piece of its festal kind. By the way, in the 3rd bar from the end (organ part) they've put a sharp to E instead of D. Did I let that through or was it added afterwards? If I did, I'm most awfully sorry. How can one miss these things?

277

What fun you and Ceddy must have had at 'The Highland Fair'. I wish I could have seen it. Love to all, from H.

106 Wildwood Road, N.W.11; 30 September

Dearest Dave,

What a rich parcel! Your 'Romance' [for Strings] and Stanley No.1 all under one cover. Thanks so much for them. It seems to me that 10/— for 13 pages of lithograph Full Score is raving; but I have long since given up trying to understand the 'business' ways of publishers. Doubtless they will be revealed with the unsealing of the seventh seal. However, I do think we might make a protest about only two free copies. That seems to me the sort of cheese-paring gesture that does nobody any good. I'm all for standing out for six copies in one's contract.

So glad C [Christopher Finzi] is enjoying the R.A.M. I haven't seen him there yet; but then, I only go there on Wednesday afternoons, so would easily miss him. Let me know if there is anything I can do for him.

I'm doing the Concerto with John [Russell] in Reading on Thursday week (9th) at a lunchtime concert. Also for the B.B.C. (with Boult and his Boys, alas) on 3rd November. After that, and a performance with you, I retire from the fray as far as playing it is concerned, for I want other people to do it.

Happily you won't be embarrassed by the sight of me writing in the Coronation Overture Competition. The B.B.C. in Belfast have thrown a fly in to see whether I would be interested in doing something for them, so I may write a bright and breezy Overture ['Overture for an Occasion', Op.16] (or another work) in answer to that query. We'll see. At present it's only a suggestion. Can you think of a title? Nothing to do with crowns.

Funny that you should have mentioned the Denton Welch 'Journals'.[1] They are coming out (Hamish Hamilton) on 9 November, and at present I am reading a proof-copy kindly loaned me by the strange Eric Oliver. As you would expect, they are fascinating. Edited, with a slightly disappointing Introduction, by Jocelyn Brooke. Who, as you may remember, was said by Eric Oliver (tripping over my carpet) to 'drink the hell of a lot'. Oliver says that the Third Programme is doing a feature about the Journals on 15 October. Love to you both, from Howard.

106 Wildwood Road, N.W.11; 23 October

Dearest Dave,

Thanks so much for the birthday wishes. The B.B.C. Partita was purely accidental I think; at least, I knew nothing about it beforehand! The performance

---

[1] Denton Welch (1915–1948), writer and artist. Crippled in a motor accident. Publications include *Maiden Voyage* (1943) and *A Voice through a Cloud* (1950). Eric Oliver was his companion, and became heir to his literary estate.

had a certain amount of BRIO, but I do wish people would take some notice of metronome marks: the 2nd movement degenerated into a scramble, and all the other quick parts tended to do likewise. Still, I've heard a lot worse!

As to a suitable gift: I'm longing for a copy of Ronald Searle's 'The Terror of St. Trinian's'. Oddly enough, no one has given me one — presumably on the assumption that everyone else had already done so. It would indeed be welcome.

Love to you both, from H.

106 Wildwood Road, N.W.11; 5 November

Dearest Dave,

Forgive silence. This past week has really been hell, what with the Concerto on Monday, the recital on Sunday, two rehearsals on Saturday, EIGHT hours of recording film music (for Tony Hopkins)[2] on Friday, and one or two other little trifles thrown-in for good measure. I thought I was going to conk out half way through the proceedings.

I missed the noble Lord's comments on Arts & Music in the rush, and now the copy of The Times has gone the way of all flesh. So sorry. Who is he, anyway?

The Searle is fully up to expectations, and has already given great delight to Pu as well as myself. Thank you very much indeed for it. Also for Stanley No.2, which I am delighted to see. I haven't been through it yet; but in the unlikely event of coming across anything peculiar, I'll certainly let you know. At a quick glance it looks very good.

Must rush off and teach my little bastards at the R.A.M., bless their hearts. Love to you both, H.

106 Wildwood Road, N.W.11; 5 December

[Dearest Dave]

Like an ass I've mislaid that misprint in the Bass part of the Piano Concerto that you kindly told me about. Could you possibly jot it down on a postcard for me. So sorry for bother.

Arnold [van Wyk, from South Africa] arrives here on 19 December!! and is staying until about 14 February. Love, H.

106 Wildwood Road, N.W.11; 7 December

[Dearest Dave]

Hubert du Plessis[3] is anxious to have a kitten (male, either dehydrated or not). Can you by any happy chance oblige? He would look after it with the greatest kindness, and probably spoil it outrageously. H.

[2] Antony Hopkins (b. 1921), English composer and broadcaster. Wrote many film scores.
[3] Hubert du Plessis (b. 1922), South African composer. Studied composition at the Royal Academy of Music under Alan Bush and Howard Ferguson.

Have a look at the Schoeck Concerto for Horn & Strings (B&H miniature score); it's rather nice, and quite playable.

Wish I could be at Enbourne [for concert by Newbury String Players]; but I have to rehearse all this afternoon.

106 Wildwood Road, N.W.11; 13 December

Dearest Dave,

Hubert would be enchanted with one of Tina's offspring, and doesn't at all mind waiting the necessary 5 or 6 weeks. (After all, it would never do if it were 'rip't untimely from its mother's womb'.) He says black for preference, but wouldn't say no to a tabby.

'Kerayma' is masterly.[4] Believe it or not, I knew the composer in the R.A.F. He was a jazz boy with higher leanings; but he doesn't seem to have leant quite far enough. I love the gay abandon of the Soprano part of page 3. Love to all, from H.

Ferrier is broadcasting 'Discovery' around Christmas.

[4] Neither composer, nor work identified.

1953

106 Wildwood Road, N.W.11; 31 January

[Dearest Dave]

Sorry I've been able to do nothing about Julian Bream. I've been in bed for the last week with 'flu. Couldn't leave yesterday, as the doctor thought it would be silly; but am hoping to get off tomorrow afternoon.

Hubert has also been in bed with 'flu, but tells me the upstairs people would love to have t'other kitten; so they can hob-nob together on the staircase like mad.

Love, H.

106 Wildwood Road, N.W.11; 12 April

Dearest Dave,

So sorry about the weekend. The last dozen bars of the Overture wouldn't get into place (as so often happens), and I only managed to solve them late on Friday. But that was a day too late for Stockcross, as yesterday had to be spent in copying. I'm very sorry to have missed the concert, seeing John, and being with you all. Next weekend is a possibility for me; but probably you are full, or otherwise, then?

I hardly know the Mozart Divertimentos you speak of, having only heard each one once. D major, K.334, seems a bit on the long side for a not-too-cultivated audience, and I remember thinking that F major, K.247, wasn't the most exciting thing I had ever listened to. Would it be any use thinking of D major, K.205? This may not contain any heaven-storming flights, but it is much more concise (four shortish movements) than t'other two.

I'm afraid I haven't a clue what you should ask the Leeds people [as payment for a commission].[1] No commission I have ever had comes remotely within that category. In like cases of uncertainty I always ask Jackie [Henderson of B&H]. If you don't want to do that, perhaps Ben Frankel would be able to give you a lead. Love to all, Howard.

106 Wildwood Road, N.W.11; 12 May

Dearest Dave,

Very many thanks for the 'Welcome Death' song. Yes, it's certainly a lovely tune, and I'm very glad to have it. By the way, there should be a natural to the B in bar 17 of the voice part; and I rather suspect that bar 26 of the accompaniment should be octave E minims in the r.h., instead of E & F. Otherwise it seems blameless.

About LLL ['Love's Labour's Lost']: Southend and Leigh are next door to one another, so it shouldn't be difficult for me to find Chalkwell Park. I'll come down by car for the performance on Thursday 4th, and bring you back here for the night, then you can set off next morning for Overton. This fits in well with my plans, for I hope to go to the Harrow [School] 'King John' on the 5th or 6th. I'll write to your Mrs Sanger in due course for a 4/– ticket.

I missed the Kenneth Leighton Violin Concerto and (apparently mercifully) 'Irmelin' [Delius].[2] But I went to the dress-rehearsal of 'Henry VIII' [produced by Tyrone Guthrie] at The Old Vic., and thought Ceddy's music excellent; indeed, the whole thing seemed to me good, except for a rather weak Wolsey.

I never thanked you both for that delightful weekend. I enjoyed it so much. Love, Howard.

106 Wildwood Road, N.W.11; 14 May

Dearest Dave,

My miniature score of Mozart K.247 must be the same vintage as yours, for it contains all the misprints you mention (for which, many thanks). On p.17, line 4, bar 5 I find that I have written in pencil, above the stave, a different rhythm; but I can't tell you whether I noted it down after some performance that I heard, or whether it just happened to occur to me one day when I was looking at it. Anyway, I now think that suggestion is WRONG, for it doesn't account for

[1] The commission, presumably from the Leeds Festival, never came to anything.
[2] Delius's 1892 opera received its belated first performance at Oxford, 4 May 1953, under Beecham's direction. A static piece, it was not well received.

the double-dot to the first crotchet. Surely it is much more likely to be exactly the same as a couple of bars later, turn and all? If I can get at a full score within the next few days I'll check it and send you a postcard. In the meantime, if it were my decision, I'd make the two bars identical.

While going through the Augener (Brahms-Chrysander) Couperin recently I noticed some startling mis-readings in Volume 4. Doubtless they come from the original printed edition, where wrong clefs must have been used; but how odd that B & C didn't notice and correct them.

I can't find any more mis-readings of this sort elsewhere in the four volumes, though they are full of obvious, and therefore easily corrected, misprints, such as omitted accidentals, graces, etc. A pity, for otherwise it is much the best available edition. [Perhaps Brahms never saw the proofs of Vol.4?] Love to you both, Howard.

106 Wildwood Road, N.W.11; 20 May

Dearest Dave,

Is there a dress-rehearsal of the 'Magnificat' [G.F.], or anything else like that, that I could go to? Myra is playing at the Festival Hall on the evening of the 29th (if she is fit enough by then), and I'm anxious not to abandon her to her own devices, firstly because she is still a bit wobbly after her operation, and secondly because she has had a particularly harrowing time recently with old friends falling seriously ill or dying. I could manage any other time the same day, if the choir is having a run-through at the Hall, or earlier in the same week. Do let me know on a card if there are any possibilities. So sorry to miss the performance itself; but I know you'll understand the reason. Love to you both, Howard.

106 Wildwood Road, N.W.11; 10 July

Dearest Dave,

As far as I can see, Novello are offering Lady Ponsonby something in return for something else − though they don't put it quite like that.[3] Apparently they now have the right to reduce many of the Parry royalties to 10 per cent, but will not do so on the assumption that Lady Ponsonby will agree, in return, to all mechanical rights being shared equally between herself and Novello. This sounds fair enough, though it's difficult to say for certain without knowing details. Lady Ponsonby is wrong in saying 'if it is the law of copyright why ask if she agrees to their suggestion?' They would be following the law of copyright if they reduced the royalties to 10 per cent. Instead of this, they are offering to leave the royalties at their present level (whatever that may be), with the added suggestion that in future all mechanical rights be shared equally between them. In order to draw-up an agreement on this basis they require her consent.

[3] Lady Dorothea Ponsonby was Parry's daughter and consequently heir to his copyrights.

I'd love to do the Concerto at Aylesbury on Friday 15 October and have put it down in my little book. Love to you both, from Howard.

P.S. Pu is definitely better than she was.

106 Wildwood Road, N.W.11; 13 July

Dearest Dave,

All good wishes for Le Quatorze Juillet. I have no ideas for a suitable present – unless it were the limited edition of 'Gloriana' [Britten] bound in vellum at Ten Guineas[4] – so please make a helpful suggestion.

On Tuesday 21st I expect to be in your neighbourhood, returning from a summer-school of Denise Lassimonne's with a young Frenchman [Marc Herissé] in tow.[5] Would you feel like being descended upon by two visitors that night? If not, or if you are busy, full-up or otherwise engaged, do just say so.

Pu is noticeably better this last fortnight. She can now feed herself, and help to move herself in and out of bed, which is a considerable improvement. Let's hope it continues. Love to you both, from Howard.

106 Wildwood Road, N.W.11; 16 July

[Dearest Dave]

Splendid! I'll look forward to seeing you on Tuesday. Will be leaving Petersfield about 5, so should reach Ashmansworth about 6.30. Will have to leave after breakfast on Wednesday, for R.A.M. at 1.30. Love to you both, H.

106 Wildwood Road, N.W.11; 24 July

Dearest Gerald and Joyce,

Here is the Alain-Fournier ['Le grand Meaulnes', in English 'The Wanderer'] in case you can't get hold of it. I found it magical.

So many thanks for the other evening. I was specially anxious for Marc to see a really attractive English home, so (naturally) Ashmansworth was the obvious place. And how lucky that we chanced on John [Sumsion], fresh and well from Canada. It was altogether delightful. Love to all, from Howard.

106 Wildwood Road, N.W.11; 23 September

Dearest Dave,

Many thanks for your card. I'm most grateful for the correction [in the Piano Concerto] to the double-bass part around 17, and will have it altered in the master-sheets.

---

[4] A sardonic jest.

[5] The pianist Denise Lassimonne held regular Summer Schools at her home in Buriton, near Petersfield, Hampshire.

Variation 4: yes, I think 6-in-a-bar is much safer than 3. First movement: pause after *24*, hold top two notes of Violin II and Viola, and both notes of Violin I octave.

I hope you have already heard from Yfrah. He was not at home when I phoned him after speaking to you, so (as I was going away to Broadway) I could only write him and ask him to let you know about the Bach Concerto [at Aylesbury]. I do hope he can manage it. Love, H.

Ashmansworth; 24 September

Dearest Fergie,

That's marvellous news, and to have you and Yfrah with us [at Aylesbury] will certainly make our concert. The Garth too will be a first performance (I mean since about 1780) and it is a lovely little work.

I want your advice about the order. Do you think the Piano Concerto would make a good finish to the concert? I usually like to end with some short little work like the Bartok 'Romanian Dances' or 'Mock Morris'; that sort of thing. But it struck me that the Piano Concerto might in itself make a splendid ending. The proposed works are: Stanley Concerto No.2; Garth Cello Concerto No.5; Elgar 'Serenade'; Bach Violin Concerto; Dvorak 'Nocturne'; H.F. Concerto.

Heaven knows what sort of Hall the concert will be held in, probably in the Walton Hall; but I like to relate programmes to buildings as well, and had thought of possibly adding the Ricercari [R.O. Morris] at the end, and reversing yours and the fiddle Concerto. An hour and a half music is the maximum. Anyhow, jumble all these together and let me know what you think. Love from us all. G

Another point: the Bach is so often done without Continuo, leaving quite a lot of bare top and bottom, and the Breitkopf parts only have the little Cadenza in the first movement, before the recapitulation, filled in. Shall I not get the keyboard part from Breitkopf? No, I've added this to Yfrah's letter enclosed. G.

106 Wildwood Road, N.W.11; 25 September

[Dearest Dave]

The order you suggest seems excellent (Stanley, Garth,[6] Elgar, Bach, Dvorak, H.F.). Mine should make a good finish, so it seems unnecessary to put anything short after it. Note the spelling YFRAH NEAMAN, not Ifrah. If it is of any help, I could always play Continuo in the Bach Concerto. Let me have particulars of Hall, time of concert and rehearsal when you know them. Love, Howard.

---

[6] John Stanley (1712–1986) and John Garth (c.1722–c.1810). Finzi had edited several of their concertos and generally championed their forgotten contribution to English music.

106 Wildwood Road, N.W.11; 3 October

[Dearest Dave]

Many thanks for times of rehearsal and concert. I'll tell Yfrah and we'll arrive together by car. About dress: doesn't it depend on whether there is anywhere to dress in? If there is, we'd be charmed to do so, if you wish it. Just jot Yes or No on a card.

What fun about your flit to Eire. But whyever there? Have you embraced the Roman faith, or are you going to kiss the Blarney Stone? Love, H.

106 Wildwood Road, N.W.11; 30 October

Dearest Dave,

Very many thanks for your letter. I'm so glad you were able to hear the Overture [Overture for an Occasion, Op.16, B.B.C. 19.10.53] from Co. Leix. No, *not* out of the top drawer! But I'm inclined to think, after that excellent performance and the small alterations I made in the scoring, that it comes from *one* higher drawer than I feared. Which is a comfort.

Eire must have been fun, if a trifle other-worldly. Good that you managed to fit so much into the Dublin bit of it.

I shall be most curious to see the Grand Fantasia in its new version, I wonder what you've done to it? Love to all, from H.

P.S. [on Manuscript-Paper]. Do you think this is the beginning of a String Quartet? [never finished]. I swither between thinking it hopeless and quite possible; so an outside opinion would be a great help. The trouble is that one wants a Quartet to come out of the *TOP* drawer – at least I do! – and at the moment I'm quite incapable of telling whether this does or doesn't. If it stinks, do just say so. Love, H. No need to return this.

106 Wildwood Road, N.W.11; 2 November

Dearest Dave,

Exactly what I wanted to know! Thanks so much. I have a habit of putting middles as beginnings (that's what held me up with the Octet years ago), then wondering why on earth the thing won't get under way.

A Toccata to follow the Fantasia [G.F.'s] sounds an excellent plan. And I don't think the lack of 'Grand' is a great loss in the title: it's surely more for home consumption?

21st October (not 24th, dear boy! Where's your history?):[7] let me ponder a while, then I'll let you know if I have any inspirations. In the meantime, thanks for the suggestion. I've already been sent four copies of Forster's 'The Hill of Devi', so not that, please! Love, H.

---

[7] H.F.'s birthday. Trafalgar Day.

106 Wildwood Road, N.W.11; 2 December

Dearest Dave,

Thank you so much for the four little Wesley Quartets [ed. by G.F.], which I am delighted to have. Certainly Hinrichsen has done you proud, producing miniature scores as well as Parts, and so nicely printed too. They may not be, as you say, altogether my cup of tea; but that in no way lessens their value as pieces for the young and inexperienced – which after all is their main purpose – or the excellence of the editing.

I'm trying to get down to Newbury for Wednesday next, and am hoping to stay the night with Tony and Ruth. Love, H.

106 Wildwood Road, N.W.11; 5 December

[Dearest Dave]

Probably Tony has told you that I will be staying with them on Wednesday next. But I shall go up to town with you on Thursday afternoon and accompany you to the R.C.M. [for G.F.'s Crees Lecture], provided Sir Bullock [Sir Ernest Bullock] sends me the ticket I have asked for. I'm trying to arrange things so that I can come by the train arriving Newbury 6.04. IF not, I'll probably miss just the beginning of the concert, which I trust will not be the Fantasia [G.F.'s]. Ever, H.

106 Wildwood Road, N.W.11; 18 December

[Dearest Dave]

How good to see the Score of the Clarinet Concerto [G.F.'s]. Very many thanks both for it and for the Edith Sitwell. Forgive me for not writing more now; I'm stuck in bed with a slight touch of 'flu. Happy Christmas to all. Love, H.

1954

106 Wildwood Road, N.W.11; 2 January

Dearest Dave,

Alas, I can't do the Oxford thing with John Carol Case, as I've been in bed with jaundice for the last fortnight – and still am – and the doctor seems to think I won't be up to much for the rest of January. I'm so sorry, as otherwise it would have been fun to do the cycles with him. The jaundice is beginning to clear up; but it's famed for its depressing after-effects, and I still feel most appallingly wobbly. I phoned Herma Fiedler [secretary of the Oxford Music Club] last night to say regretfully that it was no go.

As to 'early and late work'. I quite agree that the limitations of the former are often part of its strength; and I can see no harm in using-up self-contained slabs of old stuff, provided they are not mixed up with stuff of a much later vintage. When there *is* such a mixture, difficulties start crowding in. The chief of these in your case, it seems to me, being the amount of time you have to spend tinkering at the old stuff in an attempt (unavailing) to make it fit with the new: time which, to my way of thinking, would be infinitely better employed on something wholly new — even if that were to mean jettisoning some of the old altogether. However, this is a very personal matter, and I don't think argument about it is of much avail: one either sees and agrees, or one disagrees. Having made the point, which has been weighing on me for some time, I shall forever hold my peace about it.

Love and all good wishes for you for 1954, from Howard.

106 Wildwood Road, N.W.11; 20 February

Dearest Dave,

Very many thanks for the completion of the Christina Rossetti songs [by G.F.], which seem to me charming and beautifully adapted to their purpose. I particularly like the Lullaby one. It's good that they should be finally brought together under one publisher.

Quite recovered now from the boring after-effects of jaundice. The two middle movements of the Quartet [H.F.'s abortive string quartet] are finished, so the break doesn't seem to have stopped things entirely. But what a tedious waste of time!

Yfrah enjoyed his concert with you so much. I'm so glad it went off well and that the players liked him. He and I are playing Bach and Brahms on the Home Service at 9.45 p.m. on Tuesday next, in case you aren't doing anything and would like to lend an ear.

Splendid about 8 July [G.F. Concert at the Festival Hall]. I've put it in my little book and shall look forward to swelling the audience. Of course Toty and Dorothy must come. By the way, John [Russell, who was to conduct the concert] asked me a month or so ago whether I thought it would be a good idea for him to play the piano part of the Fantasia & Toccata. I told him I was *very* against it, as he is not primarily a pianist and would confuse the issue if he were to appear at his first big London concert in both capacities. That was one of my reasons. The other is that I honestly don't think he is quite a good enough pianist (from the public-performing point of view) to give the most convincing possible presentation of the work. (This, needless to say, I didn't mention to him.) Do back me up should he ask what you feel; for I think it would be an enormous pity from every point of view. What about someone up-and-coming, like Cyril Preedy? You both like him, he's musical, and he can make a really big noise on the piano, which that work requires. Love to all, from H.

106 Wildwood Road, N.W.11; 13 March

Dearest Dave,

This is just to let you know that I have suggested to an ex-R.A.M. boy, Roy Teed[1] (*not* a pupil of mine!), that he should send you the score of a work of his called 'The Echoing Green', on the chance that you might feel like doing it. It is for Baritone solo and Strings, and consists of three songs plus a string interlude separating songs 2 & 3. I like the look of them and think they should come off; but see what you think. The songs were written for a friend of his, Norman Tattersall (also ex-R.A.M.), who has a nice voice and sings musically. Kiffer may have heard him at the Prevention of Cruelty. I'm sure, if you liked the songs, that he'd be pleased to come and sing them for whatever you can manage to give him. Love to all, Howard.

106 Wildwood Road, N.W.11; 22 March

[Dearest Dave]

The photostat I'm hankering after is of the autograph of the Purcell Sonata in G minor for Violin and Continuo [which I was editing]. It is the only one he wrote for a single violin; and, as I told you, it was said to be in Tokyo. If there were any chance of Blunden [who was in Japan] producing it I would be endlessly grateful. Could you possibly drop him an Airmail? Love to all, from H. No answer needed.

106 Wildwood Road, N.W.11; 22 April

Dearest Dave,

If you have wanted to wring Miss Margaret Glyn's neck as often as I have for not providing a proper index to the Gibbons Keyboard Works, you may be glad of the enclosed, which I have made in odd moments. But you'll have to number the five volumes yourself, counting only the music pages. Love to all from H.

106 Wildwood Road, N.W.11; 12 June

[Dearest Dave]

Love to hear LLL ['Love's Labour's Lost' music] on Friday next at R.C.M. 1.15. Many thanks for letting me know. Love, H.

106 Wildwood Road, N.W.11; 9 July

Dearest Dave,

Congratulations on a memorable evening [G.F. Concert at Festival Hall conducted by John Russell]. I thought John did remarkably well with a big undertaking, and Richard Lewis sang like an angel (even if he doesn't look like

---

[1] English composer (b. 1928).

one) throughout. I have a feeling that you may like St Cecilia less than the rest of the programme; but, as you know, I've always had a particularly warm corner for her, and it was a great delight to hear her and the more familiar works in those surroundings, where everything has clarity and distinction, instead of distantly bombinating in that awful Albert Hall. A pity Blunden couldn't be there: he might have heard some of the words!

I still feel unhappy about the piano work [Fantasia & Toccata].² But I've gone into all the reasons for that — neither rehearsal nor performance altered them as far as I was concerned — so there's no need for a 'redundant recapitulation'! We'll just comfortably agree to differ.

All in all it was a great occasion, and a fitting recognition of a long-sustained and splendid achievement.

Now about the weekend. When I got home about midnight I found that Pu had had a bad turn during the afternoon, and Betty and Mabel (her sister) hadn't been able to get her up stairs. We eventually managed this with some difficulty, and she's had not a bad night; but she's not too bright yet, and I feel it would be better if I did not go away for the next few days. I'm awfully sorry to miss the concert on Sunday and being with you tomorrow evening. Please apologize to Roy and Norman and explain. I know you and they will understand.

Once again congratulations on last night. Love to you all, from Howard.

106 Wildwood Road, N.W.11; 19 July

Dearest Dave,

Mea culpa! Dust, sackcloth and ashes, not to mention the Weeping Wall. The Fall of the Bastille was forgotten, though only temporarily, in the rush of last week. Do let me know some book you might fancy so that I can make-up for lost time, and lost memory. Love to you all, from H.

P.S. Pu still rather under the weather. She's been having congestion.

14 Deramore Park South, Belfast; 31 July

Dearest Dave,

The Bartok 2nd Piano Concerto it shall be: but you won't mind if I leave it till I get back to London towards the end of August?

The Novello-assistant's remark about John Joubert's royalties is, of course, nonsense: the usual publisher's excuse. So far as I remember, he gets the same as you and I do — and no one could call that excessive!

Glad you were able to listen to Yfrah. Myra and I thought it went very well.

Pu was better when I left on Wednesday. I'm hoping for no crises during the next few weeks, as I want to be here with my mother for a bit. All well otherwise.

Love to all, from H.

² H.F. was concerned about the work's shape. It seemed, to him, ineffective.

106 Wildwood Road, N.W.11; 7 September

Dearest Dave,

You know the lovely Byrd piece 'Calen O Custure me' (Fitzwilliam Virginal Book II, p.186), which is really an Irish tune 'Colleen Oge Asthore' and is referred to by Shakespeare in 'Henry 5', IV, iv, 3. Well, while I was in Ireland I found it in the Sam Henry Collection of Folksongs, with the following words attached. Do you know anything about them? They are clearly much older than the usual pseudo-Moore rubbish,[3] and I think very lovely; but they don't sound at all folky to me. What do you think? Love, H.

> Happy 'tis, thou blind, for thee,
> That thou seest not our star;
> Couldst thou see but as we see her
> Thou wouldst be but as we are.
>
> Once I pitied sightless men,
> I was then unscathed by sight;
> Now I envy those who see not,
> They cannot be hurt by light.
>
> Woe who once has seen her please,
> And then sees her not each hour;
> Woe for him her love-mesh binding,
> Whose unwinding passes power.

106 Wildwood Road, N.W.11; 14 September

Dearest Dave,

Thanks so much for 'Welcome Sweet and Sacred Feast' [part-songs by G.F.]. I missed the broadcast unfortunately. A first look suggests that the other two appeal to me rather more — specially 'My Lovely One' — but a hearing might change that. On p.11, last bar, organ part r.h., is the last crotchet G natural or G flat? I would guess the latter, though a natural is perfectly possible.

I hope the Sonata [Bach, Sonata in E minor for Violin and Continuo, edited by H.F.] is filed under B! I would hate to think there was that much F in it. The reason for having left out JS was that (in my mind) 'Bach' stands for him, and I would always give initials to any of the others; that is, when it comes to programme-printing and the saving of space. But I'm quite open to persuasion.

Lovely seeing you on Sunday, and hearing the Christmas piece ['In Terra Pax']. The latter is a beauty. I'll come down to Ashmansworth before India if I possibly can, as I'd love to if it's possible at this end. Love to all, from H.

Finished another of the Irish Songs [5 Irish Folksongs, Op.17] today.

---

[3] Thomas Moore (1779–1852), Irish romantic poet, famous for the verse he wrote to accompany Irish tunes.

106 Wildwood Road, N.W.11; 30 September

Dearest Dave,

There seems to be a slight mix-up here: all this [MS of an opera by one, Parrott][4] arrived for me this morning in an envelope postmarked London W.C.1. Unfortunately the little I've seen of the music wasn't awfully inspiring (I thought): honest, virtuous stodge. But perhaps he is more interesting now.

So good to see you all at the opera [Lennox Berkeley's 'Nelson'] t'other evening. In haste, H.

106 Wildwood Road, N.W.11; 4 October

Dearest Dave,

The revised penultimate paragraph and the rest seems to me admirably clear. The only point I'd like to know more about concerns the bassoons. Could you not say *why* it is clear from the MSS that they were sometimes used?

Just finished a set of five of those Folksongs [5 Irish Folksongs, Op.17] for voice and piano, of which I showed you the first.

I'm still rather uncertain about the Parrott opera [see previous letter] as I'm not wholly convinced one should support things one feels to be second- (or third-) rate. How difficult these things are. Love to all from H.

106 Wildwood Road, N.W.11; 7 October

Dearest Dave,

Very many thanks for the full score of the 'Fantasia'. It may not, as you say, be my best-beloved of your offspring; but it's good to see it in print, and I'm very glad indeed to have a copy.

Richard B's [Richard Rodney Bennett] Quartet went off well on Tuesday. I don't think it's a really satisfactory work: not so good as his 3rd one, though a remarkable effort for someone of his age [he was about 18]. The Macnaghten people played it with great devotion and a tone like damp brown paper. Love to all of you, from H.

P.S. Whatever will Uncle Ralph's Violin Sonata (Home Service, 12 October) be like?

106 Wildwood Road, N.W.11; 10 December

Dearest Dave,

What a delightful pile of welcoming parcels. Thank you so much for one and all. Yes, I now have Stanley 1–5 complete, and will look forward to receiving No.6 next year. Blessings for them. Also for the Leslie Hotson ['The First Night

[4] Ian Parrott (b. 1916), English composer. Professor of Music, University College of Wales, Aberystwyth from 1950, the opera was probably *The Black Ram*, completed in 1953.

of Twelfth Night'], which is fascinating – though I do wish he weren't so cosy and Home-Chat-ish in the way he writes. It is so odd in someone with that degree of scholarship.

Very grateful, too, for the information (even if mainly negative) about the Purcell via Blunden. I'll pass it on to Anthony Lewis [Chairman of the Purcell Society], to whom it may be of use.

India was enormous fun.[5] The only thing against it was that there was not enough time to see all the things we wanted to see. Otherwise it couldn't have been better. Istanbul was rather a frost, as most of the Museums we had gone to see were closed on our only available day! But Athens more than made up for it. It is a magical city, and all the British Council people were so helpful and friendly.

Going to 'Troilus' [Walton] tonight, which will be a pleasant change from hearing myself play. Love to all of you, from H.

106 Wildwood Road, N.W.11; 14 December

Dearest Dave,

No, the Purcell information was not primarily for Tony Lewis: it was for myself. But he had gone to such trouble to try and track-down the MS for me in the States, that I thought it would be a kindly gesture to share even these negative crumbs with him.

I saw 'Troilus' on Friday last and enjoyed it hugely. If only a couple of chunks could be removed from that old bore Calcus[6] near the beginning of Acts 1 & 3, its shape would be perfect. As it stands, things seem to get held-up a bit in those two spots. Peter Pears [as Pandarus] (impersonating Lady Ravensdale) is masterly, and so is [Richard] Lewis [as Troilus]; but it's a pity about [Magda] Lazslo's rather peaky little voice, easy as she is on the eyes.

Nols arrives from S. Africa by air on Sunday.

Could we not have a session up here over the Cello Concerto? Pu has been bad since I got back; and as Mabel returned to Ireland last week, I can't easily leave Betty on her own for the moment. How about Tuesday, before you go to 'Troilus'? Why not come here for lunch? Love, H.

---

[5] H.F. and Yfrah Neaman had undertaken a British Council Tour.
[6] Calkas, Trojan High Priest of Pallas Athene, father of Cressida. Sung by Frederick Dalberg (bass).

1955

106 Wildwood Road, N.W.11; 21 January

[Dearest Dave]

Thanks so much for 'Fantasia' Two-Piano version, which awaited my return from Ireland. So glad to have it. Greatly looking forward to 'In Terra Pax' on 27 February. Love to all, from Howard.

106 Wildwood Road, N.W.11; 5 February

[Dearest Dave]

I know you would want me to tell you that our dear Pu died peacefully this morning. In haste, Howard.

106 Wildwood Road, N.W.11; 9 February

My dears,

Thank you both for your very sweet letter and for the kind and thoughtful enclosure for Betty. It was so good of you to write.

But how frightful about poor Dave's operation [said to be appendicitis, but really the removal of the pancreas]. I am so shocked to hear about it. Thank goodness that it is well over, and that he is getting home again this week. Let this note be a welcome-home as well as anything else, and an ever-so-gentle-and-discreet imploring to take things easily for a bit, Cello Concerto or no: at a pinch they can wait, but burst appendixes won't – if you know what I mean. Bless you both.

With much love from Howard.

106 Wildwood Road, N.W.11; 4 March

Dearest Dave,

Many thanks for your card. I meant to write after the broadcast, but have been in bed with a tiresome flu-y cold. (Better now.) I thought 'In Terra Pax' went very well. Miss Verney [soprano] ought to be put away (painlessly); apart from her, there was nothing to complain of. I still found the Angel's music a little too full of human emotion: otherwise it's a lovely work and a brilliantly successful idea – the Bridges and Bible, I mean. Mudge struck me as being stronger and more individual than Stanley.[1] I liked it. Boyce and Naylor less

---

[1] Richard Mudge (1718–1763) and John Stanley (1713–1786) were two of the neglected English composers whose concerti Finzi championed and edited for modern performance.

exciting; or perhaps I was in a pre-flu-y unreceptive mood? Anyway, it all made a very enjoyable programme. Love to all, H.

106 Wildwood Road, N.W.11; 15 June

Dearest Dave,

So glad to have a chance of reading through the three lectures complete [G.F.'s Crees Lectures][2] – particularly as I missed No.2. It seems to me that it would be a pity to print Selected Pearls from them in 'Tempo', for that, surely, would prejudice the publication of a much larger, almost complete, reprint? Would 'Music & Letters' be the place, in either one longish article or two shorter instalments? I feel sure Blom [editor] would be interested, and I don't think it should involve too much re-writing. Perhaps it would require a little tightening-up here and there, as words for speech are so much more loosely packed than words for reading; and, in No.1, you would need to arrive more quickly at the point half way down p.5, which is the real beginning of your argument. Apart from that, it shouldn't call for a great deal of sweat and toil. And I certainly think it would be worth a modicum of the latter. For our sakes, anyway, since all you have to say is of very real interest and value. Do think it over, or (better still) sound Blom about it, before abandoning bits of it to 'Tempo'.

Had a good time, though slightly curtailed by the strike, with Ceddy & Bruno. I went up by train as far as Edinburgh, where they met me; and returned in state by plane (from Montreal) caught at Prestwick! All very peculiar.

Did I tell you that Nancy Evans and I are doing the 1st performance of the 'Irish Folksongs' on the Home Service at 10.30 p.m. on Friday 24th. We had a run-through today, and she does them beautifully. The Piano Concerto [at the B.B.C.] wasn't too bad, though Geraint[3] isn't as good a conductor of that sort of thing as he is of a chorus.

Q.A.L. [Quia Amore Langueo, Op.18] progresses. The Vocal Score of almost half of it is now finished.

I hope your 3rd movement [of the Cello Concerto] is getting on well. Good luck to it.

Love to all of you, and welcome home to Kiffer, from H.

P.S. B & H have agreed to do Nols' big 'Pastorale & Capriccio' for piano as well as his song-cycle [*Van Liefde en Verlatenheid*].

106 Wildwood Road, N.W.11; 21 July

Dearest Dave,

Tuesday evening [G.F.'s Cello Concerto at the Cheltenham Festival] was a very exciting occasion. I wish I could have stayed behind a little longer after the

[2] Finzi gave three Crees Lectures at the R.C.M. in 1955.
[3] Geraint Jones (b. 1917), Welsh organist, harpsichordist, and conductor.

Cello Concerto, but, as you know, the journey [back to London] lay ahead. What a wonderful performance it was! Bunting [Christopher] played like an angel and Barbirolli moulded the whole thing so incredibly beautifully. I can imagine what pleasure it must have given you.

You asked for anything that struck me. There were only a few points. In the first movement I wondered – and wonder too why I hadn't thought of it before – whether the last pair of orchestral chords (just before the final unison A or E, or whatever it is) should not be followed by the very characteristic rhythm that occurs at the beginning. Without it, the thing feels, in an odd way, incomplete or, at least, so I felt at both rehearsal and performance. Otherwise, both that movement and the last struck me as being very satisfactory from a formal point of view. Quite honestly, I dislike the opening theme of the last movement – perhaps in rather the same way you dislike the second theme in my Piano Concerto last movement! – but that is a question of personal taste and quite immaterial. The only other points are small orchestration ones: that you should add a flute an octave above the oboe when the latter plays a counter-melody above the Cello, as I think that would be better than cutting out the counter-melody altogether; and that you give those two bassoon triplet-bars to a clarinet alone, instead of (as I suggested before) adding a clarinet to the Bassoon. One clarinet would be quite sufficient, as it is so much clearer a sound than a bassoon at that register.

About the slow movement I feel rather the reverse to what I do about the last movement: I think the music is heart-breakingly beautiful, but that formally and emotionally it overbalances the rest of the work. That is to say, as the middle of a big work it is about a third too long. I have an idea that you are very unlikely to do anything about this point, or that you will agree with it, for I get the impression that the movement means something special to you; however, I feel I must mention it, since it struck me so *very* strongly. If it were my baby I would let the return of the opening music after the first climax be the real recapitulation, followed only by that very lovely coda. This would cut out the second climax altogether, which seems to me disproportionate for the material of the movement and the position of the movement in the work as a whole, and it would cut out a largish wad of music which I also felt was redundant. However, it's *not* my baby, and I shall be very surprised if you agree with what I am saying about it!

No more for now. I'm in a hell of a rush, but wanted to get this line off to you without delay (I couldn't write yesterday because of the R.A.M.). Many congratulations on a fine achievement. Much love to all, Howard.

P.S. I'll be in Belfast 28 July–28 August, then Edinburgh for the night of 29, and down here on the evening of 30.

Ashmansworth; 4 August

Dearest Fergie,

The Music Teachers' Association gives an annual concert with a guest composer (whether it's for the benefit of the Teachers or guest composers I can't quite make out!) They sent me specimen programmes of previous occasions

(Howells, Berkeley, etc.) and asked whether they could do me on Saturday, 29 October. I imagine it's rather a music teachers' affair, and the suggested programme is: 1. Clarinet Pieces; 2. group of Songs; 23. 'Interlude' for Oboe & String Quartet; 4. group of Songs; 5. Grand Fantasia & Toccata. How this is to be managed on £25 I can't imagine, but I suppose there could be a fiver for everyone (except the guest). Knowing that you aren't partial to No.5 I'm a bit doubtful about pestering you; but if you happened to be free and willing? It all takes place at the R.A.M. (Duke's Hall, I think). Of course I could get someone to do the solo part – say, John Russell – but he isn't the pianist you are, and would be the first to admit it. If free I'm sure he'd willingly do I or II. For the songs I'm going to try John Carol Case, and some young players for the clarinet and oboe pieces, but the real key to the whole thing is the pianist. Could you let me know and say '29 October is really booked up already', if you don't want to do it.

I went over to Downe House [music summer-school] yesterday and feared the worst when Isolde was announced for the Bach 'Chaconne'. Instead, it turned out to be truly magnificent. It was really great playing. Love from Joy & G.

106 Wildwood Road, N.W.11; 1 September

Dearest Dave,

Just back from Ireland, where Arnold [van Wyk] and I did a month's hard work, and Edinburgh, where we saw a wonderful performance of 'Falstaff' and heard an excellent one of my Octet. (Also saw ex-Joan Duckham, whom I couldn't for the life of me place.)

While we were away Nols made the penetrating and alarming observation that the main theme of one of the later sections of my Q.A.L. comes straight out of your 'Dies' – which indeed it does! Like Uncle Ralph, I have no objection to plagiarism. But it does perhaps seem advisable, where possible, to ask the plagiaree whether *he* objects. Do you? At least the work is dedicated to you, but not, as with 'Hodie' [R.V.W.] for that reason.[4] Love to all of you, from H.

P.S. Off to St Andrews (for a 're-call' [I being outside-examiner]) on Sunday. Back Thursday of next week.

106 Wildwood Road, N.W.11; 4 October

[Dearest Dave]

Vocal Score of 'Amore Langueo' just finished. Perhaps I can show it to you both around the 29th, if you are not in town before then? Love, Howard.

---

[4] Believing that, in composing the choral work *Hodie* (1954), he had inadvertently borrowed a theme from Howells' *Hymnus Paradisi*, Vaughan Williams apologised by dedicating the work to him. Howells, however, claimed that he could never find the passage in question.

106 Wildwood Road, N.W.11; 8 October

Dearest Dave and Joy,

Thanks so much for your sweet note. I felt such a fool having collapsed in the middle of playing 'Amore Langueo' to you the other morning; but when that curtain of throbbing pain descends you simply cannot carry on — it had never happened so suddenly or so violently before. The doctor in the afternoon said it was a sort of nervous exhaustion, coupled with blood pressure that at the moment is slightly higher than it should be; and though he's not the brightest of mortals, I've a feeling that he's right and that things will return to normal, as he says, if I relax completely for a week. This I am doing, and already feel much better and less screwed-up. But you may be absolutely certain that I'll go to Frank [d'Abreu], or someone else really reliable, if there is any recurrence of the trouble.

I'm so glad you approve of everything up to the lethal climax [where I conked out]. I believe the descent from that and the coda are O.K., and I shall greatly look forward to showing them to you later in the month. It was lovely seeing both of you, though I'm sorry the visit should have ended in such a melodramatic way!

Much love, Howard.

106 Wildwood Road, N.W.11; 17 October

Dearest Dave,

Very many thanks for the score of Stanley No.6. Yes, I have them all six now, and splendid it is to know that all your hard work on them can now be of use to others. It may not be my favourite period: but I do enormously admire the way you have done them, the clarity and simplicity with which they are laid-out, and everything about their editing. Many congratulations.

Talking of editing and 'arranging': I happened to see Bob [Dart] just after I last wrote to you. He thinks it's a lost hope to get the Americans to agree — as with the note versus tone controversy.[5] My reply was that the latter does not involve money, whereas the former does: therefore they might conceivably lend an ear. Anyway, it's worth trying. Love and again thanks, from Howard.

106 Wildwood Road, N.W.11; 11 November

Dearest Dave,

About drawing-boards: I think the best and most reasonably priced is the *Imperial size student's type* that Hall Harding produce. Unfortunately the T-square to fit this has (as I told you) the bevel on top instead of underneath, so you can't use it for direct ruling with ink. H.H. would not make one of the right pattern, as they said they had too much regulation work on hand; so I got a

---

[5] The perennial problem of the difference between American and English nomenclature and editing practice.

local carpenter to make one to my own design. The normal T-square is used from the *side* of the board – which is no use for ruling upright barlines; this one is the right size for hanging from the *top* of the board.

A further delicate refinement ('All my own invention'!) is to have a shallow trough cut in the top r.h. corner of the board, into which you can put interchangeable strips of wood, on each of which you stick a strip of paper bearing a scale to show how you can divide one particular size of MS paper into anything from 3 to 8 equal bars. The trough must be sufficiently deep to prevent the T-square fouling the scale-strips.[6] A local carpenter did this too. Love, Howard.

106 Wildwood Road, N.W.11; 18 December

Dearest Dave,

What a delightful surprise – and on a Sunday too! The 'Dublin Virginal MS' [ed. by John Wood (Wellesley College, 1954)] looks a fascinating affair, and scholarly into the bargain. Thank you so much for getting me a copy. I'm particularly pleased to have it, as it helps to fill that tiresome pre-Fitzwilliam Virginal Book gap.

Oddly enough, I've just come back from Dublin, where Yfrah and I were playing. Nols left for S. Africa, with a day in Athens on the way, the day before my return, so the house seems solitary. But three-quarters of the scoring of Q.A.L. remains to be done, and that should keep my mind occupied. All being well, I plan to have it finished by the end of March at latest. Then off to Italy for a long-deferred holiday, to look at pictures and be generally lazy for two or three weeks. Feeling a lot better now; but I think a real holiday would be a good thing.

Love and Christmas greetings to all of you; and once again my thanks for that most thoughtful, useful and fascinating present. Ever, Howard.

106 Wildwood Road, N.W.11; 23 December

Dearest Dave,

A little un-Christmas present [H.F.'s arrangement of Continuo of Bach's Sonata in E minor, BWV 1023] which arrived here today. I'm not sure that I'm particularly enamoured of it, but you must have a copy to keep the collection up to date. Love, H.

---

[6] H.F. employed numerous ingenious devices for making easier the production of manuscripts.

1956

106 Wildwood Road, N.W.11; 14 January

[Dearest Dave]

Many thanks. So long as it reached you, and I don't have to buy two more copies! As to your earlier letter and John's: just think of all the lovely Christmas presents that may not have reached me! So glad [William] Boyce is getting on. It must be the hell of a job. I've finished more than half the scoring of Q.A.L.: see 'Midsummer Night's Dream', III, i, 141: 'Mine eare is much enamoured of thy note'. Love, H.

106 Wildwood Road, N.W.11; 20 January

Dearest Dave,

Could you cast your eye over this, and tell me whether you think the voice would come through? I could score it more lightly if necessary – for instance, after 51 leave out Flute 2 and Bassoon, and so on throughout. I would prefer it as it is, which is the way I'd do it if I had no voice to think of; but I feel rather at a loss to know just through what a voice will or will not carry.

Sorry to bother you with this in the midst of Boyce. Love, H.

106 Wildwood Road, N.W.11; 24 January

Dearest Dave,

Very many thanks. That's exactly what I wanted to know. So long as it is all right in the main, I can easily lighten that one bar before figure 53; the voice there, incidentally, is meant to gradually appear through the surrounding murk, so it wouldn't matter if it were covered to begin with. Yes, I remember reading (in Strauss's preface to 'Capriccio', of all places) that independent high flutes were apt to hide voices and words. But I think I'll cross fingers and hope for the best, as far as the beginning of this section is concerned, as I've always had the flute-colour in mind and would be sorry to change it for strings, unless bitter experience proves it to be absolutely necessary. Anyway, it's a great comfort to know that you think it should be O.K.

Alice [Sumsion] very kindly wrote the other day to ask whether I wanted anything done about accommodation [for the Gloucester Festival]. I replied that I would like best of all to be with all of you at the Headmaster's house, if this were possible. Otherwise, to sleep elsewhere and, again if possible, feed with you. But I left it in her hands, only remarking that I would prefer *not* to share a room with a perfect stranger!

But of course include Joy's portrait of me. It may not be my favourite of all her pictures, but it would be nice to have it there.

Spending most of my time just now at the scoring. With luck it should be finished in about five weeks time, which will be a weight off my mind.

Just after Christmas I saw 'Troilus' again, greatly enjoyed it at a third hearing. 'Magic Flute' the other night was oddly curate's-egg-like. Piper's sets disappointing on the whole, though the idea of them was right. The permanent set was supported by spindly quasi-Egyptian pillars which looked as though the desert sand-storms had eroded them to an altogether unsafe degree; and on these, for some occult reason, were curious graffiti which one can only assume were put there by one of Sarastro's more repressed priests. These and some other Piperesque oddities were distracting; but at least they allowed the work to be played without those ghastly and interminable pauses between scenes, which usually break it up to such an impossible degree. Elsie Morrison was a lovely Pamina. Incidentally, Alexander Young was the Monostatos, and John [Sumsion] was quite right in doubting whether his voice would be big enough for the Cathedral. A pity, because he is so very musical and sensitive.

Love to all, and once again many, many thanks for going over the bit of scoring and returning it so quickly. From H.

106 Wildwood Road, N.W.11; 21 February

[Dearest Dave]

I'm sure you're right. You couldn't possibly have 'the fallow ploughland . . . lie'. He [Hardy] must have failed to notice it when he changed the original plural 'ridges'. Since you can't use 'lies' because of the rhyme, I suppose the only thing to do is to fall back on the original middle verse.[1] What an odd business! Howard.

106 Wildwood Road, N.W.11; 27 April

My dears,

Back from Italy a couple of days ago after a gloriously satisfactory holiday.

These [two copies of Q.A.L.] come with much love. The superscription was always *meant* to come on a symphony; but I don't feel like writing symphonies just yet, so perhaps a choral work will do instead. See you soon-ish. Love, H.

106 Wildwood Road, N.W.11; 14 May

Dearest Dave,

I used two sizes of transparent M.S. paper for the Full Score of 'Amore Langueo': Symfax 755 (30 staves) and Symphax 24/Orch (24 stave).[2] (The latter, by the way, has better spacing than their earlier 24-stave paper.) It wasn't

---

[1] 'At the Middle-Field Gate in February', *Moments of Vision* (1917). No.2 in the posthumously published Finzi collection of Hardy settings *I Said to Love*.

[2] Semi-transparent papers used in copying music. It acted as a negative for photocopying purposes.

possible to keep to one lay-out throughout, as even the 30 staves wouldn't accommodate the soloist, chorus (divided) and full orchestra. I got over that particular difficulty by omitting the harp in tuttis – where it isn't heard anyway! The method of working was to make a rough pencil score, with inked barlines, on our special Augener paper, which always seems to have room for everything. Then each page of the Symphax was planned from this, using only the particular number of staves necessary in each case. This may seem slightly more complicated than drawing the same lay-out on every page (which I couldn't do anyway), but I much prefer the look of it; and it means you don't always have to use the smallest sized staves, which I find rather tiring on the eyes. You can see the finished article when it returns from being duplicated, or bound, or whatever process it happens to be bogged down in at the moment.

I'd love to come down one weekend. Whitsun would be no good, for I have to get back to town on Monday evening and would hate to spend another hour trying to get through Maidenhead in the car. And I'll be in Scotland with Ceddy & Bruno, just opposite the Isle of Skye, for the following one. The first week of June will be rather cluttered with rehearsals for three broadcasts (1st performance of Hubert du Plessis' Duet-Sonata on 5 June, after 3 years of pestering the B.B.C., and 15 letters from me to them!). But the weekend of 9 June might be possible; or, better still, for I'll be clear of all broadcasts by then, the weekend of 15 June. Let me know whether this last would be possible for you; and, if so, I'll put it in my little book.

I listened to the broadcast of [R.V.W.'s Symphony] No.8 from Manchester with Ceddy, who happened to be here that evening. He only liked the Scherzo. I greatly enjoyed 1st movement and Scherzo, but found the other two most disappointing: the slow movement habit-music and the finale distressingly commonplace. However, perhaps one will feel differently this evening at the Festival Hall.

I'm sending this to Hanover Terrace [R.V.W.'s house] in case you want to get some Symphax while you're in town. Love to all of you, from Howard.

106 Wildwood Road, N.W.11; 4 July

[Dearest Dave]

I expect to be passing fairly near you on Friday 13 on my way to Trowbridge. Would you be in at lunchtime if I made the necessary short detour? And, if so, would you feel like feeding the hungry traveller? Love, H.

14 Deramore Park South, Belfast; 10 August

Dearest Dave,

I've just been looking through the score of Gluck's 'Orpheus', and it occurred to me, have you ever thought of doing the enchanting little 'Ballet of the Blessed Spirits' in Act II? It only requires 2 flutes besides the strings (it could be done with 1 flute at a pinch), and lasts about 9 minutes. The second piece is one of the loveliest tunes ever written. If you don't know it, you'll find it as an example in Berlioz's 'Orchestration'.

Can you tell me what clothes are necessary for Gloucester? I'm sure I couldn't get into my Morning Suit, so would an ordinary dark Lounge-Suit do for the daytime? And are Evening Clothes of any sort (tails or dinner-jacket) needed? I will *not* be going, need I add, to the Ball on Friday evening!

Hope all are well with you. I'll be here until the morning of 23 August. Love, H.

106 Wildwood Road, N.W.11; 20 September

My poor Dave,

How awful about the Shingles. I'm told they are hell. All my sympathy and hopes for a quick recovery. You don't say where they are; but I understand they are usually about the waist. Anyway, let's hope not in the mouth, where Myra's friend the unfortunate Sazzie Gunn[3] has recently had it (or them?). I can't imagine how you could be bothered fiddling about with bits of M.S. and razor blades with that maddening itch plaguing you. Personally I would have thrown the whole thing out of the window. However, since you haven't done that, but want the Oboe I parts that have disappeared on you, I am enclosing the latter on a bit of M.S.

Do take care of yourself. Love, H.

P.S. Auntie [Myra] sends her heartfelt sympathy: she says they are the very devil.

FINIS

---

[3] Secretary to Myra Hess.

Postscript

On 6 September 1956 Gerald Finzi conducted the first performance of the full orchestra version of In Terra Pax *at the Gloucester meeting of the Three Choirs Festival. It as a work that had been conceived some thirty years earlier during a Christmas Eve visit to Chosen Hill (a favourite spot for Ivor Gurney and Herbert Howells), when he heard the midnight bells ring out across the Gloucestershire countryside. He recaptured the magic of that moment when, in 1951, he first began to consider a setting of Robert Bridges' words:*

> *A frosty Christmas Eve*
> > *When the stars were shining*
> *Fared I forth alone*
> > *Where westward falls the hill*

After the festival he decided to take Ursula and Ralph Vaughan Williams to see Chosen Hill for themselves. The sexton's cottage he had visited so many years before was still there and they were invited in by the occupants, unaware of the dangers that the chickenpox their children were recovering from might have for someone who, like Finzi, had suffered from Hodgkin's Disease. By 14 September he was in great pain, and by 21st September it was clear that he too had contracted chickenpox. He was taken to the Radcliffe Infirmary in Oxford. His condition, however, worsened and it was there, during the evening of Thursday 27 September, that he died.

But that was not the end of the story. In some respects it was only the beginning, for the formation of a Finzi Trust in 1969 created an intense interest in his life and work. Recordings of his music attracted the attention of the musical world and ensured that his published works were readily available. Regular meetings of the Friends of the Trust took place at Ashmansworth and at the Three Choirs Festivals, so that he quickly achieved a cult status almost unique among English composers. All this was carried out under the watchful eye of Joy Finzi, who died on 14 June 1991.

Ferguson's story, however, had many more years to run. On laying down his composer's pen he turned his attention to meticulously researched, practical editions of important keyboard music. These would eventually include the complete keyboard works of William Tisdale (late sixteenth century), William Croft (1678–1727) and Henry Purcell; Schubert's 'Complete Works for Solo Piano'; the shorter piano works of Schumann and Brahms; volumes devoted to Scarlatti and Mendelssohn, and a remarkable six-volume anthology of keyboard music of the seventeenth, eighteenth, and nineteenth centuries, issued in 1963–1969 by the Oxford University Press under the title Style and Interpretation. *These and similar publications confirmed his reputation as an outstanding musicologist — a reputation that had already been endorsed in 1959 by an Honorary Doctorate from Queen's University, Belfast, and Honorary Membership of Corpus Christi College, Cambridge, in 1973.*

Postscript

And it was to Cambridge that he moved in 1973 after a fire the previous year had rendered 106 Wildwood Road, though still habitable, rather less desirable. There he settled happily in a small but very convenient house in Barton Road, and it was there that he died in his sleep on 1st November 1999. He had just celebrated his ninety-first birthday.

It was typical of Ferguson that, just as he had handed his manuscripts into the Bodleian Library's safekeeping and seen his music definitively recorded on CD, he also found time to organize the letters he and Finzi had exchanged. Michael Hurd, a friend of many years, was recruited to 'edit' the collection for publication (mainly a matter of providing explanatory footnotes and a linking narrative, as Howard had already inserted explanations in square brackets) and on 20 October 1999 was able to take the complete manuscript to Cambridge, in time for Ferguson's birthday and an approving scrutiny of the final task he had set himself.

General Index

Amis, John 241
Andrews, A.K. 170, 172
Armstrong, Dr Thomas 76
Ashton, Algernon 257
Atkins, Ivor 244

Barbirolli, Sir John 147, 295
Baker, Mary 178–80, 220
Barnicot, Nigel 202, 204, 206, 207, 215, 217, 247
Bartok, Bela 21, 51, 52, 284, 289
Bax, Sir Arnold 73, 74, 78, 83, 105, 106, 178
Beecham, Sir Thomas 106, 122, 148, 170, 281
Beerbohm, Sir Max 81
Belcher, George 77
Bell, Adrian 71
Bell, Clive 28, 31, 33
Benjamin, Arthur 34, 44
Bennett, Richard Rodney 291
Berg, Alban 20
Berkeley, Sir Lennox 165, 166, 291
Bissell, George 146
Black, Margaret ('Mags') 115, 138, 184
Blake, William 9, 12, 13, 24, 40, 55, 57, 165
Bliss, Sir Arthur 26, 40, 43, 56, 58, 59, 60, 63, 73, 80, 82, 83, 104, 106, 129, 130, 132, 142, 163, 164, 228, 242
Bloch, Ernest 6, 7, 8, 9, 12, 21, 28, 54, 187, 226, 228
Blunden, Edmund 163, 250, 288, 292
Bonavia, Ferruccio 166
Boosey, Leslie 136, 191, 192, 193, 140, 265
Boulanger, Lili and Nadia 138, 178
Boult, Sir Adrian 50, 63, 77, 99, 144, 153, 163, 223
Bream, Julian 275–6, 280
Bridge, Frank 60, 120
Britten, Benjamin 78, 111, 117, 119, 181, 192, 211, 228, 236, 240, 250, 265
Bryan, Gordan 16
Buckland, John 269
Bunting, Christopher 294
Busch, William 135, 153, 158, 178, 182, 184, 195, 202
Bush, Alan 232, 279

Butt, Dame Clara 192
Butt, Richard 270

Carol Case, John 286, 296
Carrit, Graham 190
Chubb, Ralph 165, 166
Clarke, Rebecca 70
Clausen, Raymond 247–8, 249
Coates, John 88
Copland, Aaron 8
Coward, Noel 58
Craxton, Harold 217
Cranko, John 286, 296
Cuningham, May ('Pu') 3, 4, 16, 23–4, 30–1, 32, 40, 49, 102, 136, 147, 157, 181, 195, 197, 214, 219, 220–1, 223, 240, 253, 260, 262, 274, 278, 279, 289, 292, 293

Dale, Benjamin 234
Dart, Thurston (Bob) 264, 265, 266, 272, 297
Darnton, Christian 89, 115, 120, 121
Davie, Cedric Thorpe 80, 84, 88, 92, 96, 99, 100, 103, 104, 110, 117, 121, 122, 123, 128, 145, 147, 148, 192, 193, 218, 256, 268, 281, 294, 301
Daymond, Emily 14, 21, 37, 125, 263, 264
Dayrush, Elizabeth 108, 109
Debussy, Claude 58
Defau, Désiré 208
Delius, Frederick 22, 51, 52, 54, 58, 80, 103, 106, 126, 129, 134, 281
Dieren, Bernard van 20
Dolmetsch Arnold and Carl 12
Dukes, Ashley 57, 58
Dunbar, Donald 275
Dyson, Sir George 106, 165, 244

Easdale, Brian 119
Eaton, Sybil 9, 15, 16, 18, 20
Elgar, Sir Edward 27, 62, 77–8, 102, 190, 220, 284
Elliot, Stuart 271
Evans, Edwin 199
Evans, Nancy 294

305

Music Index

Part One: The Music of Howard Ferguson and Gerald Finzi

HOWARD FERGUSON

Chamber and Instrumental
Five Irish Folk Tunes 16, 38, 290, 291, 294
Five Pipe Pieces 107
Four Short Pieces (Clarinet and Piano)
141, 160, 162, 163
Octet 16, 83, 84, 87, 89–90, 91, 92, 98–9,
100, 127, 204, 257
Piano Sonata in F minor 189, 195, 198,
203, 204, 205, 206, 208, 209, 212, 216,
218, 219, 234, 246
Sonata for Violin and Piano (No 1) 4, 16,
70, 72, 75, 76, 79, 114, 115
Sonata for Violin and Piano (No 2) 238,
246, 259, 263
Choral
Amore Langueo 238, 255, 294, 296, 297,
298, 299, 300
Dream of the rood, The 238
Solo Vocal
Discovery 271, 277, 280
Five Irish Folksongs 16, 38, 39, 290, 291,
294
Three Medieval Carols 81, 91, 92

Two Ballads: *Lyke-wake Dirge. Twa*
Corbies 16, 43, 47, 49, 50, 55, 73, 81, 91,
96, 132, 204
Orchestral
Concerto for Piano and String Orchestra
238, 268, 269, 270, 273, 283, 284
Four Diversions on an Ulster Air 188–9,
203, 204, 206, 208, 210, 215, 216, 219,
225
Overture for an Occasion 238, 280, 285
Partita 102, 103, 104, 105, 106, 113, 117,
120, 121, 123, 125, 126, 131, 135, 139,
153, 154, 155, 160, 162, 164, 172, 200,
201, 208, 209
Short Symphony 57, 79, 64, 68
Dramatic
Chauntecleer 255, 257, 259, 265–7
Discarded Compositions
Mass 7, 42, 43
Phantasy 9
Sonatina 31, 32
String Quartet 229, 285, 287
Piano Variations 44

GERALD FINZI

Chamber and Instrumental
Elegy 206, 213
Interlude for Oboe and Strings 85, 86,
87, 112, 117, 120, 126, 127, 128, 129,
165, 197, 296
Five Bagatelles for Clarinet and Piano 93,
229–30, 234, 241, 242, 296
Prelude and Fugue 203, 230, 231
Song Collections and Cycles
Before and After Summer 263
Dies natalis 183, 191, 192, 194, 196, 197,
198–9, 228, 237, 245–6, 247, 259
Earth and Air and Rain 128, 130, 133, 134,
220, 238, 241, 264

Footpath and Stile 4, 93
Let Us Garlands Bring 18, 230, 231, 232
Till Earth Outwears 238
Two Milton Sonnets 114, 115, 139, 140
Individual Songs
Clock of the Years, The 161
Come away, Death 206
Comet at Yell'ham, The 10
Channel Firing 214, 215
Joy, To 72
Lizbie Brown 131, 161
Lyonesse 131, 161
Market Girl, The 199
Proud Songsters 161

309

Part Two: Contemporary works that elicited an interesting reaction